Women’s Emancipation in Africa – Reality or Illusion?

AFRICAN THEOLOGICAL STUDIES

Etudes Théologiques Africaines

Edited by Gerhard Droesser and Chibueze Udeani

FACHKLASSIFIKATION
CHRISTLICHE SOZIALETHIK

VOLUME 13

Zu Qualitätssicherung und Peer Review der vorliegenden Publikation

Die Qualität der in dieser Reihe erscheinenden Arbeiten wird vor der Publikation durch einen Herausgeber der Reihe geprüft.

Notes on the quality assurance and peer review of this publication

Prior to publication, the quality of the work published in this series is reviewed by one of the editors of the series.

Paul Mutume

Women's Emancipation in Africa – Reality or Illusion?

A Case Study of Mbarara, Western Uganda

PETER LANG
EDITION

Bibliographic Information published by the Deutsche Nationalbibliothek
The Deutsche Nationalbibliothek lists this publication in the Deutsche Nationalbibliografie; detailed bibliographic data is available in the internet at http://dnb.d-nb.de.

Zugl.: Würzburg, Univ., Diss., 2017

Library of Congress Cataloging-in-Publication Data
Names: Mutume, Paul, author.
Title: Women's emancipation in Africa--reality or illusion? : a case study of Mbarara, western Uganda / Paul Mutume.
Other titles: African theological studies ; v. 13.
Description: New York : Peter Lang GmbH, 2017. | Series: African theological studies ; vol. 13
Identifiers: LCCN 2017017324 | ISBN 9783631723029
Subjects: LCSH: Women—Uganda—Mbarara—Social conditions. | Women's rights—Uganda. | Women—Legal status, laws, etc.—Uganda.
Classification: LCC HQ1797.Z9 M87 2017 | DDC 305.42096761—dc23
LC record available at https://lccn.loc.gov/2017017324

D 20
ISSN 2196-0615
ISBN 978-3-631-72302-9 (Print)
E-ISBN 978-3-631-72303-6 (E-PDF)
E-ISBN 978-3-631-72304-3 (EPUB)
E-ISBN 978-3-631-72305-0 (MOBI
DOI 10.3726/b11294

Peter Lang Edition is an Imprint of Peter Lang GmbH.

Peter Lang – Frankfurt am Main · Bern · Bruxelles · New York · Oxford · Warszawa · Wien

This publication has been peer reviewed.

www.peterlang.com

Table of Contents

Acknowledgement

I wish to express my deepest appreciation to all those who supported and accompanied me in the completion of this study. The success of my doctoral thesis was made possible by many people. I do not have the space to name them all but a few whose prominence and excellency in the realization of this work cannot remain unmentioned.

My utmost gratitude to the Almighty God whose gift of life and abundant blessings cannot be taken for granted. I am also grateful to the Archbishop of Mbarara, Most Rev. Paul Bakyenga, for his permission to complete my studies in Germany. I cannot forget Rt. Rev. Francis Aquirinus Kibira, the Bishop of Kasese Diocese, with whom all this began. My special thanks to my moderator Prof. Dr. Dr. Gerhard Droesser, whose fatherly and friendly approach cannot be forgotten. His in-depth but constructive criticism facilitated the successful completion of this work. I remain indebted to his professional guidance, valuable support and useful recommendations in this study. To my co-moderators, Dr. Frederic Fungula and Prof. Dr. Udeani Chibueze, I express my thanks.

I would also like to extend my thanks to the Diocese of Würzburg, Germany for the financial and spiritual support during my studies. For their generous support, I am grateful to Pfr. Stefan Redelberger and the parish members of Maria Hilf-St. Anton, who welcomed me to Germany and introduced me to its culture, to Mr. Manfred Emmerling and to the parish community of Oberpleichfeld. Pfr. Bernd Bielasik *vielen Dank*, Pfarrvikar Duc Ninh Nguyen, Pfr. Helmut Rügamer, Rev. Fr. Charles Tumusime Rucumu, Pfr. Hans Fischer and Ms. Birgit Jäger thank you very much. I cannot forget the tremendous support from the family of Christian Sandra Miriam Achenrainer, Ms. Lydia Bakecura and those who read through my work and contributed, especially Ms. Kate Dixon, Ms. Ronnah Tumusime and the family of Eddie Rosette Mutetsi Kamugisha; I am very grateful. I am indebted to my strict but very caring German language teacher Ms. Gisela Kugler for her help, and to all my subsequent lecturers and professors who saw me through my study.

Last but not least, I wish to acknowledge the support, care, love, cordiality and sacrifices, prayers and patience of my parents, Henry and Sophia Kabigumira, my sisters and brothers, cousins, my uncle Ignatius Mpurubuki and his wife, other relatives and friends, the Banyatereza sisters of Fortportal Diocese, the priests and religioius men and men of Mbarara archdiocese and everyone who supported me in the completion of my study.

Many would not like to be mentioned and I am very grateful to those whose names do not appear here but who contributed. May God reward you abundantly.

Vorwort

Anliegen des Verfassers ist, die aktuelle Lage der Frauenbewegung in Uganda aus ihrer geschichtlichen Entwicklung zu verstehen, sie kritisch nach ihren objektiven Fortschritten, aber auch nach ihren Defiziten zu beurteilen, sodann ihre zukünftigen Entfaltungschancen zu erwägen.

In seiner Arbeit nimmt er entschieden Partei für die Emanzipation der Frau auf allen gesellschaftlichen Ebenen. Vor der Auseinandersetzung mit den traditionellen wie auch modernen ideologischen Einstellungen, die die Chancen weiblicher Selbstverwirklichung zugunsten der männlichen missachten, scheut er nicht zurück. Damit leistet er in Konkretion christlicher Sozialethik einen sinnvollen Beitrag zu einem tiefgreifenden kulturellen Paradigmenwechsel, der sich – wie zu hoffen ist – in einer umfassenden Lerngeschichte, in der sich die weibliche und ebenso die männliche soziale Identität verändern wird. Dass dieses Unternehmen glückt: die Idee der Emanzipation gesellschaftlich verankert wird, verlangt, dass alle gesellschaftlichen Akteure – Individuen und Institutionen – sie in einer konzertierten Aktion zu ihrer Sache machen. Freiheitschancen müssen in der politischen, rechtlichen, ökonomischen, familialen Dimension, aber eben auch in dem durch Bildung geförderten und stabilisierten Bewusstsein der Individuen, als selbstverständliche Gegebenheiten die alltägliche Praxis bestimmen.

Der Autor hat ein für die Modernisierung afrikanischer Gesellschaften brennendes Thema aufgegriffen. Er nähert sich ihm gleichsam naiv, ohne falsche Voreingenommenheiten. In der Darstellung beweist er Selbständigkeit, soziologische Auffassungskraft und theologisch-ethische Leidenschaft. Dass Vieles verbessert werden kann, ist klar. Das ändert aber nichts am Wert des Konzepts. Die Lektüre ist spannend und regt zum Weiterdenken an. Paul Mutume hat das Potential, seine Studien zu erweitern und zu präzisieren.

Prof. Dr. Dr. Gerhard Droesser

Abstract

This thesis explores the reality of gender equality in Uganda while also investigating the factors that influence this reality. The aim of the study is, therefore, to analyze gender equality or inequality in Uganda and the efforts that have been employed to improve it. The central guiding research question is: To what extent have women been emancipated and what are the successes and challenges of this emancipation? Secondly, the thesis further explores women's emancipation in the major sectors of life and the way forward for future improvement. For these purposes, a well-thought-out study and analysis of literature, oral and statistical data has been done. Evaluation of internationally recognized indicators has been employed to determine the extent of the success of this project. The research has recommended empowerment – both subjective and objective – as a means to the full liberation of women, and consequently the outcome will be gender equality that is beneficial to all Ugandans. Finally, the analysis and research findings show a rather positive progress of gender equality in Uganda.

Chapter One: General Introduction

1.1 A Short Historical Background of Emancipation

Generally, and globally, a lot has been said and written about the liberation struggle of women, especially in the last century. Most of these writings have been essential in the noble struggle for the liberation of women. Despite these writings, a lot remains to be done to enable women to occupy their rightful position in society. Women's contributions to the economic, religious-cultural and socio-political advancement of their countries, international conferences and the universal declaration of human rights, have to be recognized and appreciated. Unfortunately, women have often got only what they have struggled for and not what they deserve.

As such, the emancipation of women remains a matter of concern after a century, especially in Africa. The struggle for women's freedom in a strategically central position in the lives of their families, communities, societies and countries does not seem to be yielding much. Women have always struggled for financial independence, recognition and respect, though with little success. There is a need to address this problem concisely and precisely. The subjection of women to economic manipulation, sexual exploitation, and political marginalization remain the thorn in the flesh of women's liberation today, even in developed countries.

The struggle for the liberation of women is not new or alien to the African people. Throughout African history, women have always fought for their freedom. This fact, though, has always yielded either nothing or no significant effect and was often short-lived. What is clear is: any fruitful and genuine liberation demands sacrifice and, more often than not, martyrdom.

In the last years, the trend and speed of women's emancipation in Uganda has gained momentum and significant progress has been made. The year 1986 remains historic for women because it formally ushered in the liberation struggle, at least in the minds of many Ugandans[1]. Undoubtedly, since 1986, the emancipation of women has taken a central stage on Uganda's

1 The National Resistance Army (NRA) later renamed National Resistance Movement (NRM) seized power and control from the then government and

political, social, economic as well as religious scene. For the first time, it was receiving more public attention than it had during any other epoch in the history of Uganda.

However, the emancipation of women in Uganda had a long history that often remained obscure. The '1986 turning point' did not come as a surprise. It was long overdue. There are factors responsible for this. These can be categorized under remote and immediate factors.

1.1.1 Remote Factors

The remote factors include the political instability, economic stagnation, global trends like women's rights, feminists, emancipationists, the 1980s Nairobi and Beijing conferences and the influence of international media[2]. All these played a very significant role in the struggle for the rights of women. They also awakened the longing for the respect for human freedom. The remote factors are both negative and positive.

The dictatorial regimes and subsequent liberation of Uganda prepared a fertile ground for the awareness of human rights and their abuses. A big part of Uganda's history is dark. Following the authoritarian regimes of the 1970s and early 1980s, which were destructive for nearly every sector of Ugandan society, women and children were those who suffered most during and after. Anarchy and disorder characterized these dark years, and respect for human rights was no longer an issue. The most important thing was survival, and the majority of Ugandans never minded the issues of human rights.

The militaristic regimes were busy plundering Uganda's wealth and quenching their thirst for power as ordinary Ugandans suffered. The abuse of human rights was the order of the day during these aggressive regimes. Cases of extrajudicial killing, sexual harassment and rape of women and

at the centre of its vision for the transformation of Ugandan society was the emancipation and empowerment of women.

2 The Nairobi und Beijing conferences were two of the four world conferences on women organized by the United Nations. These conferences took place in Mexico City, Mexico in 1975, Copenhagen, Denmark in 1980, Nairobi, Kenya in 1985 and Beijing, China in 1995. The 1995 Fourth World Conference on Women in Beijing marked a significant turning point for the global agenda for gender equality. See more at: http://www.unwomen.org/en/how-we-work/intergovernmental-support/world-conferences-on-women.

girls increased significantly as soldiers and security personnel were allowed and encouraged to terrorize the public, often systematically using rape for such ends.[3] It was not only soldiers who did these heinous and terrible crimes but also other men who were in power, or who at least thought they were. They merely looked on, doing nothing to stop these crimes. Unfortunately, this indifference was from top to bottom, from the highest administrative structure to the lowest.

Simultaneously, the lack of the rule of law and enforcement meant that criminals were never held accountable. In this case, rapists were not punished. Justice was never served. Women suffered most because of their already patriarchal and segregational societal structures and these traumatic experiences, and the criminals often walked scot-free. Also, due to the prevalence of such physical violence, women still faced immense structural disadvantages that were accentuated by the repressive and dictatorial atmosphere of Amin's and Obote's regimes.[4] This kind of suffering provoked the need for change.

Sadly, the few women who were already in powerful positions or were counted among the fortunate ones did not help their fellow women.[5] The research did not find significant evidence of women helping women to be free of this misery. They never saw a need to pave the way for the emancipation of the rest of women, the majority of the suffering women. Miria Matembe, one of the most prominent women activists in Uganda, agrees with this point. She writes in her autobiography that the most powerful women during this terrible period were mostly the "wives of big men either in government or religious bodies."[6] She argues further that these women,

---

3 Matembe, M., *Gender, Politics and Constitution Making in Uganda*, Fountain Publishers, Kampala, 2000, p. 75.

4 Amnesty International, Uganda: The Human Rights Record 1986–1989, Amnesty International Publications, New York: 1989, p. 8.

5 One should not put all women under one umbrella. It is true that the majority of women in western Uganda never enjoyed their rightful place in Kinyankole society but there were a few who were privileged. These were women who were in most cases married to politicians and church leaders in the Anglican church. They had a bigger influence in most cases on the decisions of their husbands or families.

6 Matembe M., *Gender, Politics, and Constitution Making in Uganda, op.cit.*, p. 65.

with their conservative views and lack of formal power, refused to acknowledge women's suffering and oppression and never took action to address it.

Meanwhile during this regrettable and repressive period in Uganda, the international women's movement was gaining ground on a world stage and exerting its influence on global policy makers. The United Nations declared 1975 to 1985 as the 'Decade for Women' and required its members to establish government organizations to address women's issues. In Uganda, President Idi Amin Dada "took an initiative and established a National Council of Women in 1978, which he and later Obote used to regulate, control and repress non-governmental women's organizations".[7] Both governments used these women organizations for their own benefit.

These turbulent years left Uganda socially, economically and politically in tatters and almost every sector of life in Uganda was disorganized. As Matembe further writes, "[b]oth the Amin and the Obote II regimes distrusted organizational life of any kind and refused to sanction the development of the women's movement in Uganda."[8] It is important to deduce that as a result of this disorganization and anarchy, Uganda as a country was left out of the trends of development. Worse still, it was left out of the critical debates taking place in international fora concerning human rights in general but also women's rights in particular. As a result, Uganda was cut off from many of the concrete gains made by the international community. The guerrilla war led by the Lt. Gen. Museveni and his army toppled an oppressive government and ended the turbulent years and began a new chapter in the lives of all Ugandans.

To sum it up, Uganda's political instability, global trends like women's rights, feminists, emancipationists, the 1980s Nairobi and Beijing conferences and the influence of international media played a big role in the liberation of women. The "protracted people's war" army, commonly known as a bush war army, that liberated Uganda seems to have been grateful to women for their contribution to the war.[9] Women had not only fought alongside

7 Tamale S., *When Hens Begin to Crow*, Westview Press, Oxford, 1999, p. 15.

8 Matembe, M., *Gender, Politics, and Constitution Making in Uganda, op.cit.*, p. 69.

9 Yoweri Museveni. *Selected Articles from the Uganda Resistance War*. NRM Publications, Nairobi, 1985, p. 11.

their male comrades but had also brought another view of the capability of a woman to liberate. The hitherto misconception that women were a weak sex began to dwindle. That is to say, women took up arms not only to free their fellow countrymen and women, but also their status in society.

1.1.2 Immediate Factors

The immediate factors included the shift in the political and social atmosphere. Until the mid-1980s, the general view of women in Uganda remained very traditional and limited women to the domestic space. After the Museveni government took over, Uganda started to progress though a journey of recovery that favored an environment of democracy, the democratization of many social sectors and respect for human rights. Unalienable and fundamental human rights such as the right to life and freedom of association and expression gave hope to a country that was on the verge of failing. Women and men started identifying and respecting each other's humanity.

This political climate gave rise to the formation of women's groups. These further awakened a need for more freedom of speech and association to demand their rightful position and dignity in society. This disposition gave an opening to the struggle. It yielded the composition and singing of the anthem of Women in Uganda, an anthem which was an indicator of the steps to freedom. One notices the role music plays not only in liberation struggles but also in wars, in demonstrations and assemblies. The anthem of women in Uganda, one of its kind in Africa, cannot be overlooked. It somehow united women and became like a war song or freedom song.

The chorus of the anthem opened a new chapter but also set a challenge for all women:

> Mothers, Daughters
> All women everywhere
> Stand up and embrace
> Your roles today[10]

This short but meaningful chorus was and remains a kind of re-discovery. In this anthem, the women recognize themselves as mothers and daughters.

---

10 Mbowa R., Uganda Women Anthem, Cf. https://www.worldpulse.com/fr/node/mbowa accessed on 23rd November 2012 at 11:04.

These two words are still powerful terminologies in many African languages and cultures. The invocation is not only for Ugandan women but also for all women everywhere. The strength of unity is therefore here intoned. They invite each other to unite for a common cause: embracing their roles as mothers but also as helpers, workers, warriors, farmers, champions, queens and as family and society builders.

They must stand up, something that evokes strength, preparation to attack and challenge, to move or even to guard against an impending or existing opponent. Such a combination was never before imagined: a mother who defends. It was always the role of the father or a man. They stand to defend and embrace their roles and not in the future but today: No more waiting! The choice of words of the composer Prof. Mbowa (now the late) is not to be underestimated. She did not come up with new terminologies and an impressive language as would be expected from a professor, but used simple formulations with such a very powerful message. She writes further:

> We are proud mothers of our nation
> The backbone without which it can never stand
> We wake up, wake up
> We wake up at the crack of dawn
> And feed the nation with our brains
> With love and joy, we care for our baby[11]

This first stanza articulates what these women are or are expected to be. They are proud mothers and the backbone of the nation without which the nation can never stand. They rediscover their identity. This assertion remains a compelling message for all women in the struggle. Also, the call to wake up, a kind of military provocation, is repeated three times. According to many Ugandan tribes and cultural beliefs, three times or the number three denotes emphasis and the seriousness of the matter. After standing up, women should care for the nation because the nation is their baby, meaning they no longer need to fear, for this is the role they are naturally created for.

More to that, in a non-reading culture, singing is always the best medium. The women's anthem was easy to spread even to the women at the grass roots level. Oral transmission of the anthem through singing was and is much easier than written communication in a Ugandan setting. Women

11 Ibid.

were able to teach each other orally but many women also learned it by heart and rehearsed it over and over again. That meant that the anthem was becoming part and parcel of their lives. The role of activists such as Prof. Mbowa and Dr. Miria Matembe and the message they put across increased that yearning for emancipation.

This struggle for the emancipation of women in Uganda has not been easy and has been met with some very serious resistance. Much of the resistance seems to come from men and from a misunderstanding of the whole concept of emancipation. Many did not understand what the women wanted, many feared losing their position in society and yet many identified it as a foreign thing and looked at it as alien and imperialistic.

Despite this resistance, the struggle has had many significant achievements and considerable progress has been made. There is now a considerable number of women in parliament, ministries, the judiciary, and there are women leading government bodies and corporations such as the Uganda Revenue Authority, the National Roads Authority, Kampala City Council Authority, the Uganda National Oil Company, the solicitor general, and the secretary of the Bank of Uganda.

However, this tireless effort has led to excitement for many, hatred for some and indifference for others. Thus, emancipation remains a challenge because it has not been all-sector-embracing.

The fact remains that emancipation has been and remains a global and noble issue that deserves global concern and embrace.[12] It will continue despite immense challenges from within and without.

The future of women in Uganda remains optimistically bright. One of the solutions to Africa's problems would be women's involvement in leadership and other spheres of society. This effort is, of course, not to be deterred. That is a reality men have to live with.

In her book "Frauen auf dem Sprung", Jutta Allmendinger writes *"Die Zukunft ist weiblich, pfeift es von Dächern so laut..."*[13] Allmendinger means that the the future is feminine, it is whistling from the roofs.

---

12 Abid, A.H., *Ugandan Women in development: African development Series 1*, Foundation for African Development, Kampala, 1990, p. 1.

13 Allmendinger J., *Frauen auf dem Sprung,* Pantheon Verlag, München, 2009, p. 11.

Although it would not be directly affirmed that the future is feminine as she puts it, it is agreeable that women remain undeterred from their quest and struggle for liberation. The status of a woman in 1900 in Uganda can never be seen again with the same spectacles as those of 2000. The sad spectacles of 1900, which looked at a woman as an object or as a second class human creature, have been broken.

1.1.3 Age of Emancipation

The combination of the remote and immediate factors together with the changing society led to the steady successes of the struggle for women's liberation. The women who were mainly seen first and foremost as home-makers and mothers extended their social space. The domestic space that characterized their domain gave way to a more open space. This did not mean that they lost their internal space; they only extended it. Where they were not perceived as public actors, they were now in this realm. Women joined a political as well as a social space.

The drafting process of the 1995 Constitution of Uganda included the consideration of women. During the process of drafting the constitution, the legislators tackled the primary concern of women: their long history of institutional, systematic oppression and discrimination especially during pre-colonial, colonial as well as post-independence eras. Major concerns especially in the areas of family, health, and education were also discussed.

Issues of discriminating against a girl-child in favor of a boy-child regarding education were raised. It was clear that most parents preferred boys' education to girls'. When the family failed to raise sufficient school funds for their children, girls would be discontinued in favor of boys. Girls who got pregnant were denied another opportunity to go back to school while the boys responsible continued to study. This issue and the right to education for girls as a fundamental human right were critically analyzed and tackled by the legislators.

On the family or societal level, it was observed that there existed laws that discriminated against women in several aspects: marriage, separation and divorce, property ownership, inheritance and custody of children. It was found by these open-minded legislators that women owned no property. At the time of marriage whatever a woman owned belonged to her parents, and after marriage belonged to her husband and after the death of the husband, it belonged to the relatives of her husband. Women were therefore denied the right to own property. Daughters were excluded from inheriting property from their deceased parents and were never allowed to be heirs to their fathers, even when there was no son in the family. This would even prompt an "emergency inheritance" in which the nephew or the brother of the deceased would be allowed to inherit.

Further injustice was observed in some cultural practices that discriminated against women. These were not only discriminative but also inconsistent with modernity and development. These cultural practices included marrying off or forcing young girls into marriage, the payment of bride price, the traditions of widow inheritance and prohibiting women and children from eating certain nutritious foods.

Against the background of the above issues, which were debated, scrutinized and evaluated, the legislators were faced head-on with the customary law that had an upper hand at the time. All the same these important issues were tackled. Some serious deliberations and conclusions were reached and these have advanced the cause of women emancipation.

The fruits of the deliberations of legislators were coherent and consistent with the fact that Uganda was a signatory to various international legal documents, including the Convention on the Elimination of All Forms of Discrimination against Women (1979). Against this background, Uganda's future image on the international stage seemed to depend on these deliberations.

These discourses and debates culminated in a gender balanced constitution, the inclusion of women in many sectors of society and a historic appointment of the first ever woman to the presidency in Africa. The women's movement gained more support than ever before because the regime and many political leaders were ready to integrate women and listen to their concerns related to oppression and discrimination. That is why this time has been seen as the age of emancipation of women in Uganda. Many successes will be covered in other chapters.

1.2 Aim and Objectives

1.2.1 Aim

After these years, my project is revisiting this reality of emancipation. It revisits its success story and failures. It evaluates the effectiveness of this constitution, seen as gender-compliant, and the effect of liberation movements of women in Ugandan society. Western Uganda is my point of reference. This re-visitation goes through the history of this struggle, deals with the liberation trend and its impact on society up to today.

It looks closely at the freedom that an individual woman could have achieved but also at the failures that could have been encountered. The project views the women's liberation in Uganda in the bigger spectrum of the global stage. It uses the spectacles of global understanding to evaluate the liberation struggle of women in Uganda.

That is to say, the project orients itself mainly to the Ugandan society and applies the global and ethical standards. Nevertheless, the responsibility to liberate women is a global issue that has not yet been thoroughly addressed. As the General Secretary of the United Nations on the International Women's Day on 8th March 2011 noted, even after a century, the struggle to liberate women continues: He notes:

> One hundred years ago, when the world first commemorated International Women's Day, gender equality, and women's empowerment were largely radical ideas. On this centenary, we celebrate the significant progress that has been achieved through determined advocacy, practical action and enlightened policy making. Yet, in too many countries and societies, women remain second-class citizens.[14]

The reference to too many countries does not limit itself to African countries but to countries worldwide. Although it is true that a lot has been achieved in many areas, a wide gap remains between the genders. The Secretary further says:

> Although the gender gap in education is closing, there are wide differences within and across countries, and far too many girls are still denied schooling, leave prematurely or complete school with few skills and fewer opportunities. Women and girls also continue to endure unacceptable discrimination and violence, often

14 Ban Ki-moon, Secretary General's Message on the International Women's Day, 8th March 2011.

> at the hand of intimate partners or relatives. In the home and at school, in the workplace and in the community, being female too often means being vulnerable. And in many conflict zones, sexual violence is deliberately and systematically used to intimidate women and whole communities.[15]

With this in mind, the project ventures to examine, analyze and contribute to this trend of women's emancipation. A firm foundation is a prime requirement, though, and the project is thus an invitation to all freedom fighters to work together to build it. Fighting for freedom is not for women alone but also for the whole humanity.

1.2.2 Objectives

1.2.2.1 Main Objective

The project aims at contributing to the bank of knowledge but also impacting on humanity's quest in the search for its freedom and fulfillment. The achievement of humankind is in its true freedom. This project is not only an academic work but also a medium through which the emancipation of women in Uganda could fully be achieved. This study is meant to reconcile the traditional thinking on women's place with the contemporary thought.

1.2.2.2 Specific Objectives

The specific objectives are fourfold. First, this project aims at discovering the trend of emancipation from the historical background to the current status of women's empowerment in Uganda. Secondly, the project re-discovers the concrete reasons for this liberation and reviews its actions and aspirations.

Thirdly, the project addresses the tension between the concept of women's emancipation and the African societal structure. Fourthly, the project proposes and suggests possible solutions and the way forward for meaningful liberation.

In all, the project offers the right disposition of human thought towards liberation. That is to say, it gives the right attitude with less risk of bringing conflict and tension between emancipation and the proper social, economic,

---

15 Ibid.

political and religious structure. In short, the emancipation of women is a project worth undertaking to reach a point of talking about gender equality.

1.3 Definition of the Project

The word 'emancipation' traces its etymology from the Latin language. The Latin word *emancipatus* together with its linguistic usages refers to the act of being set free from slavery, servitude or deliverance from bondage or controlling influence, prejudice or error.[16]

The translation of emancipation would be *okuzaahuura* in the Kinyankole language, which literally means liberating the near dying or reclaiming someone from slavery or setting free from death[17]. It could also mean liberation from a wrong ideology. There are many words related to setting free, but this is direct to human beings. The project covers the area of Kinyankole speakers.

In this project, the primary emphasis will be laid on the trend, impact and the best way forward for the emancipation of women. It thus tackles the setting free of women from the deprivation of some of their rights from time immemorial to date. In fact, this project critically examines not only the role of women in their struggle but also men's. This work is a double-edged project. Not only should women receive liberation, but also men, from the wrong, long-held ideas, otherwise it will be a waste of time and resources.

In this project, liberation and freedom, deliverance and setting free are synonymously used with emancipation. In this sense, these words mean the same and do not differ in any way from each other regarding the intention of the project.

Mostly, this project looks at emancipation as the re-shaping of the mindset and society's structures, and discarding that which hitherto has stressed the oppression and devaluation of a woman explicitly or implicitly. It also

---

16 Webster, N., *New International Dictionary,* second edition, G&C Merriam Co., Springfield, 1939, 590. Cf. also emancipation from http://www.thefreedictionary.com/emancipation (n.d.) *American Heritage® Dictionary of the English Language, Fifth Edition.* (2011) accessed on 23rd April 2015 at 11:34.

17 Mushanga M, et al., *Kashoboorozi y'Orunyankole,* MK Publishers, Kampala, 2006.

challenges women and men of the present age to think newly and optimistically about women's dignified place that nature and God accorded them.

This project of emancipation is in line with the critique of culture and society on its journey to either discard or emulate the designs of men which have or have not been detrimental to their status quo. However, it is not a *coup d état* of all existing institutions. Neither is it turning women into men or vice versa. It is re-drawing of the boundaries that constitute the lives of humanity which in turn embraces both feminism and masculinity.

All this will be tackled by this project, tracing the emancipation and re-drawing the boundaries. It keeps in mind through such an illusion of changing what belongs to nature and is essential to humanity. It does not change reality but looks at that which has been designed by men intended to oppress women. Emancipation is and remains in line with God's plans.

1.3.1 Other Terms and Terminologies

In this project, many terms and terminologies will be employed but the most technical and recurring ones are defined below. Their usage and importance remain a focus in this work.

1.3.1.1 Gender and Sex

Gender simply refers to the state of being male or female. In the Kinyankole language (Kinyankole is one of the main tribes in Uganda, particularly among the Banyankole people found in the south-west region of Uganda) gender would be referred to as *obuhangwa bw'omuntu*[18]. For our purposes, gender will mean the roles women and men play in a culturally, socially, economically and historically defined context. Gender as a term is widely used in various linguistic structures, but in the social context it has been used in different debates, discussion, agreements, and controversies. In spite of this diversity in its usage, gender is neutral to this project and will be more frequently employed than the word sex.

Also, gender indicates that male and female roles in a given societal set-up are shaped not only by biological nature but by social structure. It

18 Ibid.

further shows that the roles of male and female will not be identical in every culture. So is the case among African tribes.

The term sex is often used interchangeably with gender. In this project, it will still be loosely used as often used in normal usage, not the technical usage. But the difference between gender and sex is there. According to the World Health Organization (WHO), sex refers to the biological and physiological characteristics that define men and women.[19]

While it is essential to accept the differences in sex and the roles gender plays, it is also important to appreciate the need for equality. There is also a possibility of different but equal roles. This fact is critical to human development and the well-being of each community.

1.3.1.2 Gender Equality

The project presupposes that gender equality is about individuals having equal opportunities. Although gender equality poses many challenges, it is possible. Women and girls remain limited in social, economic and political opportunities. In almost every corner of the world, women and girls remain a less advantaged group. They still have lower status, fewer opportunities, and lower income, little or no decision making, have less control over essential resources, and less power than men and boys in their communities.

Therefore, gender equality is the absence of discrimination on the basis of a person's sex in having opportunities and the allocation of resources or benefits or in access to services at a given time. Gender equality presupposes equal opportunities and respect for one another's rights and freedoms. In this case, the word gender equity is appropriate.

1.3.1.3 Gender Equity

This term accrues from the above notion of gender equality. It is the provision of fairness, consideration and justice in the distribution of benefits and responsibilities between women and men. The term appreciates that men and women are created differently and that they have different needs, abilities and power. It recognizes further that these differences should be

---

19 http://www.health-genderviolence.org/training-programme-for-health-care-providers/facts, gender-and-gender-equality/retrieved on 12th May 2012 at 13:00.

clearly put into consideration and addressed in a manner that rectifies the unfairness and imbalances between the sexes.

1.3.1.4 Feminism

One of the terms that is very controversial especially in the field of social academics is the word 'feminism'. The people who profess this theory are called feminists. During the research, many women disassociated themselves from the usage of this term. It will also be applied in this work but in its right context. Feminism is understood as the belief that men and women, boys and girls should have equal rights and opportunities. It could be further defined as an organized activity in support of women's rights and interests about equality of the sexes.[20]

Feminism sounds like gender equality, but feminists believe that society's gender inequality requires a strong measure to overcome it. It is a kind of a reactionary measure to curb the marginalization of women that has been seen throughout the ages. Feminism could otherwise be positively understood as a space where women discuss their issues and experiences, understand them and look for the solutions.

Feminism is, therefore, a concept that is pragmatic and tries to enforce the cause of gender equality and later gender equity. With feminism, the issue of women's inequality is vital, and it attempts to analyze and act systemically on the power structures that privilege men over women in a given society. Thus, it lights a fire that should continue burning.

1.3.1.5 Humanism

The term humanism is not specifically in the area of women emancipation. As a concept, it arose during the Enlightenment in the 18th century. It referred to a movement that promoted reason, ethics, and justice and rejected religious beliefs or dogmas and the idea of supernatural and divine powers.

Today, many women's movements use this background to foster the cause of women's emancipation. There is a considerable active and vibrant humanist movement these days that draws its legacy from that time. They

20 http://www.merriam-webster.com/dictionary/feminism retrieved on 30th June 2015 at 07:01.

combine a commitment to human rights with a secular and rational worldview. However, this does not necessarily focus on gender-equality related issues. Their intention is to have justice for all humans.

1.4 Location and Study Area

The project covers the south-western part of Uganda with emphasis on the greater Mbarara region. This part of the country is preferred because most of the activism to emancipate women in Uganda began there. Most women activists hail from western Uganda as will be covered later. This field covers the geopolitical areas (known as districts) of Mbarara, Bushenyi, Buhweju, Mitooma, Rubirizi, Sheema, Kiruhura, Ibanda, Ntungamo and Isingiro.

This stretch of the area is traditionally called Ankole. The project prefers greater Mbarara because all these districts share the same history and culture but also the same struggle for the liberation of women. The majority of inhabitants are women and children as is the case country wide as shown in the national population census of 2014[21].

Greater Mbarara is traditionally populated by two ethnic groups; Bairu and Bahima. But due to intermarriages, immigration and other reasons the population is now interethnic. Among other groups, the population of different ethnic groups includes: Bakiga, Baganda, Bakoki, Bafumbira, Banyarwanda, Nubians and other migrants who have been integrated.

1.5 Layout of the Project: Scope, Methodology and Division of the Project

The layout of the project is as follows: scope, methodology and division. The scope, methodology and the compartmentalizing of the project help to understand the background and the limits of the matter. It increases the understandability of the case study of the project.

21 http://www.ubos.org/2014-census/census-2014-final-results/, accessed on 22nd December 2014 at 19:30.

1.5.1 Scope

The project covers most of the significant women's groups in the districts of western Uganda. These focus groups were mainly in the rural, urban and in some cases the sub-urban areas. These groups were of interest because they could be conveniently called women's liberation movements. The present study also works with women who are not in such groups – individual women from all walks of life. The project involves some men too. Men play a fundamental role in any fruitful emancipation. That is to say, this is a transitional comparison between the traditional Nyankole societies with the contemporary Nyankole society.

Furthermore, much emphasis is put on the integral liberation of the woman, not only in a particular area of life but also in other important aspects. But the project considers those issues that need considerable attention and have in one way or another resulted in or contributed to the emancipation of women. The study therefore views women from political, cultural, economic, social and psychological perspectives.

More to that, the project covers common or rural women or homemakers, spinsters, widows, divorced and single mothers, mistresses, business women, social workers, married and unmarried women, members of parliaments or politicians and religious women such as nuns and sisters[22]. In short, the project deals with women from all walks of lives.

Optimistically, given time and space, together with logistical help and the willingness of the women and men of goodwill, this project aims at the best. It will contribute to the benefit of the women and all humanity. It intends to be simple but exhaustive.

---

22 According to the common understanding, nuns are religious women in the Catholic Church who live in restricted houses called monasteries and mainly live a contemplative life, and the sisters live in convents and live active lives and they also do social work. Canon law notes that nuns live in monasteries and must observe what is called papal enclosure. The norms or guidelines governing the cloisters are established by the Vatican itself. Sisters, unlike nuns, live in convents and work out in the world but their separation from the world is not as strict as that of nuns. Cf. canon 667.3.

1.5.2 Methodology

The project focuses on and treats the emancipation of women as an urgent and important venture for all people, and this demands a very informed and efficient methodology. Therefore, the approach of this project is mostly historical, comparative, analytical and evaluative. It is historical based on the facts which are evaluated and compared to the reality on the ground and are then critically analyzed. For the project to be efficient and effective enough, we give practical und useful suggestions at the end of the project.

Thus, the methodology of the project is mainly qualitative and quantitative research. This research is primarily through reading the available literature, interviews, and meeting with different women's groups and individuals. The study is supplemented with sociological, psychological and anthropological books, articles in newspapers, magazines, encyclopedias, papal encyclicals and other relevant documents. Precisely put, the project is made up of interviews and library information.

Further still, most of the information obtained owes its originality from childhood experiences, without which the concreteness would have been lost. The gist of the study revolves around real life.

1.5.3 Division of the Project

The project has six chapters. Chapter one gives highlights and the background of the project; chapter two introduces the status of women among the Banyankole and the contemporary trend of emancipation in Ugandan society. Chapter three covers the justification for the genuine emancipation of women from different points of view. Chapter four gives the reality or the impact of freedom; chapter five deals with women's power and empowerment, and evaluations, and finally chapter six gives recommendations, suggestions, and the general conclusion.

The structure of the whole project aims at giving the impression of urgency and importance to women's liberation. This liberation is here meant not only for women but also for all humanity.

Chapter Two: The Status of Women among the Banyankole

2.1 A Short Historical Background of the Banyankole

Precisely, the Banyankole are a people; Ankole or Nkole designates a place, and Runyankole is a language. Banyankole are Bantu by ethnicity. They are among the half-dozen major ethnic groups in Uganda. Like other Bantu groups, the origins of the Banyankole remain unclear, but many historians assume they could have originated from the Congo region.[23]

Ankole was one of the four most important kingdoms of the Great Lakes region that were prestigious and well populated. The kingdoms of the Great Lake region referred to the kingdoms that were established around Lake Victoria and other lakes in central and southern Uganda. The date when the Ankole Kingdom was first established remains unknown, but historians have speculated that it might have started as early as during the fourteenth or fifteenth century. The Banyankole were the earliest group to occupy Uganda between 1000 and 1500 AD.[24] It was ruled by a monarch (*Omugabe* = king) who had political and cultural powers. Ankole only became a focus of study and research in the 1920s and 1930s, as reported by some anthropologists such as K. Oberg and historians such as F. Morris.[25] The monarchy still exists but only has cultural powers.

Originally, Ankole as an area was known as *Kaaro-Karungi*, meaning beautiful scenery and indeed some books still refer to it as such. Many cultural activists prefer this term because of its originality. The word *Nkole* is said to have been adopted during the 17th century following the devastating invasion of *Kaaro-Karungi* by Chawaali, the then King of Bunyoro-Kitara. He was also known as *Omukama*, meaning a king. In the year 1901, the word Ankole was conveniently adopted by British colonial masters to describe the bigger kingdom that was created by adding the former independent

---

23 Nzita, Richard Mbaga-Niwampa, *Peoples and Cultures of Uganda*, Fountain Publishers, Kampala, 1998, p. 43.

24 Ibid.

25 The Making of Ankole, "Uganda Journal", vol. 20, 1(1957), 1–15.

kingdoms of Igara, Sheema, Buhweju, Busongora and parts of Mpororo to the original Nkole. It was then incorporated into the British Protectorate of Uganda through the signing of the Ankole Agreement.

Therefore, the Ankole region, also sometimes referred to as Nkole, was situated in today's south-western Uganda, sharing a common border with Rwanda, Tanzania and Congo. To the east of the Ankole district was Lake Victoria, and to the west were Mount Ruwenzori "and some lakes, including Lake Albert and Lake Tanganyika. The land is over 4,000 feet (1,220 meters) above sea level and it is hilly with rolling plains covered with fine grass."[26] Recently, it has been narrowed down and come to be known as greater Mbarara. This area includes the districts of Mbarara, Bushenyi, Buhweju, Mitooma, Rubirizi, Sheema, Kiruhura, Ibanda, Ntungamo and Isingiro. All these have been carved out of Ankole, also known as Greater Mbarara.[27] These districts are inhabited by the Banyankole. It is important to note that people from the Rukungiri, Rujumbura and Rubabo districts share the same cultural background as the Banyankole.

The Banyankole consist of two major sub-ethnic groups: the *Bahima*, who are cattle keepers also known as pastoralists, and the *Bairu*, who are agriculturists. The *Bairu* were and remain numerically larger, and the *Bahima* are politically and socially dominant. In fact, the generally accepted view is that the current president of Uganda, Yoweri Museveni, is a *Muhima* by tribe. This, however, has remained an issue of debate. Due to intermarriages and the acquisition of formal education, this social stratum has been significantly affected.

Some scholars believe that Ankole was formerly occupied by Bantu-speaking agricultural Bairu. Later, Ankole provided a passage for Hamitic peoples, possibly the Bahima, migrating from Ethiopia southward.[28] These pastoralists conquered the Bairu and proclaimed themselves the rulers of the land. According to some scholars and historians, the more numerous

---

26 *Banyankole (Ankole) People*: Uganda'S … (n.d.) from http://kwekudee-tripdownmemorylane.blogspot.com/2013/07/banyankole.html accessed on 1st December 2015 at 12:34.

27 Ibid.

28 Pearson, Amber L. Muchunguzi, Charles, *The International Journal of African Historical Studies*; 1st Jan 2011.

Bairu were serfs and the Bahima were the dominant ruling class. For the most part, the two ethnic groups coexisted peacefully.[29]

In the early history of Ankole, most of the nomadic pastoralists had no settled dwellings; they kept on the move. Even their leader, the king, had only a small dwelling with a stockade forming an enclosure for his cows at night. This compound was known as *ekikaari ky'omugabe*.[30] Cows were and are the source of prestige, power and wealth for the Banyankole, even in modern times. There was no courthouse, and the king's council met outdoors. There were in most cases distinct trees earmarked for that.

Although Bantu share common origins and linguistic structures, cultural beliefs and customs, there is a distinctive difference between Banyankole from other Bantu tribes in Uganda. They are a hardworking society and their yearning for freedom has always been part of their historical background. The struggle for independence from within and without has always marked the Banyankole as a people.

Against this background, very little is known about the status of a man or woman in the Kinyankole society before the 15th Century. Even thereafter, very little is known. What is clear to us is that the situation of a woman was most likely not like that of man. Therefore, the project here will focus only on the status of women in specifically identified times or eras.

2.2 The Status of Women

The status of women is vital to this project. To talk about the situation of women is to talk about their roles and rights in society. The status of women in society is an indicator of their rights and freedom in a particular time and place. Therefore, the status of women will be seen in the three epochs of Uganda's history. However, only critical areas will be tackled because the project cannot deal with the details of each and every point.

This project will limit itself to the status of women in later different epochs. The earlier epochs lack information and oral sources seem to be biased and sometimes conflicting. This remains an area for future research.

29 Ibid.

30 *Ekikaari* means simply an enclosure or a palace. This was made from reeds and stems of the trees. It was meant to be a fortified palace to ensure the security and privacy of the king and his wives (queens).

The project divides this time into three different periods: the pre-colonial, colonial and post-colonial.

2.2.1 The Pre-Colonial Period: 15th Century to 19th Century

Uganda was not known as one country for many centuries. No single country called Uganda existed in pre-colonial times. Different societies or groups occupied this land, and later others joined them from different directions but they were never one people. Their political set-ups and structures were different, varying in size and mentalities. With this in mind, we can now situate the status of these societies, but dwell mostly on our project.

The period in question covers the period from the 15th century until just before the colonization of Uganda. More than forty different groupings resided in an area with different socio-cultural and political structures and the colonial masters clumped them together and named this Uganda by "the stroke if the imperialist pen"[31] at the turn of the century. This was in the city of Berlin in Germany in 1884 at a conference responsible for the scramble for and partition of Africa[32]. Generally speaking, two types of political systems prevailed in the plurality of Uganda's social structure prior to the advent of British rule: the centrally governed kingdom states of Buganda, Ankole, Toro and Bunyoro and the "non-state" segmentary societies, which followed an age-sect clan system, such as Acholi, Lugbara, the Langi[33]. These seemed to have been the normally organized societies.

Every person or community is unique, as was the case with these societies. The understanding of politics or economics was very diverse. In fact, to an alien observer in that era, the politics of Uganda appeared to be the exclusive realm of men. This was partly because of the male dominance that prevailed in largely patriarchal societies.[34] However, this was not always the case. For example, the intimate inner workings of Banyankole society allowed women to participate in politics on a formal or informal basis. The

31 Tamale, S., *When Hens Begin to Crow* op.cit., p. 4.
32 Cf. https://en.wikipedia.org/wiki/Berlin_Conference accessed on 23rd July 2015 at 04:09.
33 Tamale, S., *When Hens Begin to Crow* op.cit., p. 12.
34 Ibid., p. 13.

reason for the misconception about women's political participation at this time can be attributed to two important factors.

Firstly, in Ankole the interconnectedness of the private and public spheres was never clearly understood. This was alien to societies where there is always a sharp difference between the public and private spheres. In pre-colonial Uganda and Ankole, women had never been confined to the private or domestic sphere. Rather, as Winnie Byanyima states, "multiple responsibilities between and across spheres shaped their political history or juridical spheres heavily depending on personal relationships that women could (and often did) influence."[35]

Secondly, misconceptions about women's political participation in this period stem from the male-authored androcentric texts. Partly because of their male dominated societies and education, mainstream historians tend to assume that women never played a role in the politics of their communities.[36] As a consequence, the role of women in pre-colonial times is mostly obscured or simply ignored.

Banyankole women did not directly participate in political discussions, but their opinions were valued and often sought before decisions were taken. Thus women wielded social and political influence through indirect methods; physical absence did not equal political passivity.[37] Among the Banyankole, women had an enormous influence on the king, who had supreme power, thus making decisions. In most cases, women's decisions overrode those of the chiefs. They were never passive on the matter concerning the administration of the kingdom. In fact, the queen mother or the king's sister would veto the king's decision.

2.2.1.1 The Usage of "Omugabekazi" *(Female King)*

The wife of the king was not known as a queen, as it is generally translated, but as a female-king. This word is of paramount importance to this research in re-locating the place of a woman in the Banyankole social formation before the colonial times. *Omugabekazi* is a feminine form of a king. The

35 Ibid., p. 14.

36 Lloyd Fallers, ed., *The King's men: Leadership and status in Buganda on the Eve of Independence*. Oxford University Press, London, 1964, p. 5.

37 Tamale, S., *When Hens Begin to Crow* op.cit., p. 4–5.

king is *Omugabe*. It is almost like the German usage of *König* to refer to a king and *Königin* to refer to a queen. The sister of the king is named *omwigairire* – the one who blocks or closes, meaning closing or reducing the power of men. Both women had veto power, the *omugabekazi* and *omwigariire* can already be deduced from the very titles they had.

Here one has to know the role a language plays in the relationships of people. This usage has continued even up to present day. Unfortunately, many anthropologists have done little to delve into this linguistic gymnastic.

Needless to say, *Omugabe* and the *Omugabekazi* were equal in status. Of course, not in jurisdictional status. The second dominant personalities were princes (*obaigyinya – omwigyinya* in the singular) and princesses (*abaigarire – omwigarire* in singular). Positions that were almost equal but on different levels existed in the pre-colonial times in the courts of the kings. However, the woman king and the sister of the king seem to have had a great influence on the king. The woman-king or sometimes the king's sister would veto the chief's decisions even when they were not on the council. Therefore, the status of women was better placed in the palace than in ordinary families.

Furthermore, the perception of women in precolonial times as "objects of wealth" originated from writings or ethnographies of early anthropologists, historians and missionaries who fossilized African societies through a bifocal lens of sexism and Eurocentrism.[38] This was mainly in reference to women captured during war commonly called *Abazaana* (the players). Moreover, the capture of women among the Banyankole was never meant for enslavement.

There were other reasons why women were also among prisoners of war. John Tosh suggests that women and girls were particularly targeted as war captives because "it allowed the ideal of polygyny to be more widely attained."[39] Consequently, the capturing of women and girls in warfare was linked to the socio-political and economic growth of precolonial African societies. This was true also for the Ankole society. Polygyny practiced by

38 Roscoe John. *The Baganda: An Account of Their Native Customs and Beliefs*, Macmillan, London, 1911, p. 209.

39 Tosh, John. *Clan Leaders and Colonial Chiefs in Lango: The Political History of an East African Stateless Society*, 1800–1939, Clarendon Press, Oxford, 1978, p. 86.

kings, immediate chiefs and the elite class was instrumental in the development of Ankole's political expansion and state formation.

More to that, the capturing of women and girls on the front lines was not only seen as security for the captured territories to remain royal because of the respect for women but it was also meant for integration. The killing or torturing of a woman was abominable and a sign of cowardice, and was always condemned by the Banyankole. Integration was always the destiny of the captured women and girls. One would probably call it acquiring citizenship by integration or naturalization in our modern times. The children of the captured girls and women were seen as part of the kingdom.

Although there were gender biases in refence to war, conquest and overall social development as observed by some historians, the fact remains that women were crucial to the kingdom's welfare. One cannot avoid mentioning of Nyabaingi of Kigezi, and the political roles played by the queen mothers and the kings' classificatory sisters in the heritage of Ankole kingdom. These, however, have often been omitted from the standard accounts of precolonial history. One important aspect of the Nyankole political set-up regarding the power of women was their influence on the king.

During precolonial times Banyankole women were not as marginalized as they are today but their status was by no means equal to that of men. Being a patriarchal society, Banyankole men dominated positions of political, social, and economic power. Kingship relations linked the two sexes within the nexus of a wider domain of structural conditions that included communities, peoples and the association rooted in their working lives.

Gender differences that stemmed from these relationships were and still are fed by belief systems rooted in inequalities of power and social behavior. The development of a sexual division of labor in Uganda, as in many African societies, preceded the colonial period. However, this is paramount: the dynamics of such sexual division of work at this time were somewhat different from what they became with the introduction of colonial capitalism.[40] Ugandan society did not denigrate women's work as it does today.

Although many look at capitalism as some ideology that paved the way for the openness of society, it worsened the situation of a woman in colonial

40 Tamale, S., *When Hens Begin to Crow* op.cit., p. 4, 7.

Uganda. Colonial capitalism was the beginning of the real oppression of women among the Banyankole but also all Ugandan societies. Taking the advantage of the already shaky status of women in their patriarchal societies, colonizers created a new way of oppression against women.

Before the systematic capitalistic wave, gender relations had a form that was more complementary than hierarchical.[41] Among the Banyankole, men built houses, made drums, carved wood, hunted, herded and milked, fished and fought. Carrying the sick to the medicine-man was also a duty of the men. Women cultivated, processed and marketed crops, collected firewood or cow dung (fuel) and water. They cared mainly for children, the sick and the elderly, made pottery, baskets and mats, cooked, cleaned and washed. There was no negative evaluation attached to these different roles. Driberg states that: "a woman carrying out her duty was held in just as high esteem as a man carrying out his and the nature of the occupation was of no moment."[42]

Religion was another arena in which Banyankole women could gain power, although in many societies it was only male priests who were able to lead most ceremonies. However, many women were noted for their capability to serve as spirit mediums, which frequently resulted in greater and more significant responsibilities for women as a group. For many years after the *Chwezi* dynasty in Ankole, women were employed as priestesses who led a ceremony known as *kubandwa*[43]. These made them revered and respected. The rite of passage, which represented a "marriage" (*okuhongyerwa*

---

41 Plume, Denise, Ed., *Women of Tropical Africa*, University of California Press, Berkeley, 1963, p. 15.

42 Driberg, J, "*The Status of Women among the Nilotics and Nilo Hamitics*." Africa, Vol. 5, no. 4, (1932), 5 no. 4: 409.

43 *Okubandwa* means in the service of the deity or leading others in worshipping a god. Although the Banyankole believed in a higher God called *Ruhanga*, the creator of everything, their idea of *Ruhanga* at a lower level was expressed in the cult of *Emandwa*. These were kind of intermediary gods particular to different families and clans and they were easily approachable in the event of need. Each family or a clan had a shrine where the family gods were supposed to dwell. Whenever beer was brewed or a goat was slaughtered, a gourd full of beer and some small bits of meat were put in the shrine to the *Mandwa*. In the event of sickness or misfortune, the family members would perform rituals called *okubandwa* as a way of supplicating the gods to avert sickness or misfortune. On the clan level, there were priests and priestesses.

emandwa[44]) between young girls and specific deities, served as a principal method for transferring traditions from generation to generation. These were to remain unmarried virgins for this specific role.

The position women could be further studied in the strata of the society. The precolonial Nyankole society was a pastoral as well as an agricultural society divided into satellite households. Although the Banyankole lived in communities and extended families, each constituted a separate unit with agricultural produce controlled by the wife.[45] Bahima women were also responsible for milk products and men for animals. Each seemed independent in his or her role.

Another important aspect in the pre-colonial societies was the payment of bridewealth. Marriages were customary and potentially polygamous and recognized the payment of bridewealth and constituted a contract between the families of the bride and the groom. Bridewealth had an important social significance. It consisted of marriage gifts such as livestock, goats, sheep or some particular symbol of wealth given by the bridegroom to the bride's family before, at or after marriage. They were symbolic of the continuity of the clan or family. It was, therefore, a means of cementing the relationship between all families concerned and of providing stability to the marriage. Driberg epitomizes the pre-colonial idea behind bridewealth thus:

> ...it is one side of legal contract, providing for the filiation of the children and their lawful inheritance: it supplies a religious and ritual sanction, invoking the benevolent regard and interest of the ancestors, from whom the cattle were inherited: it stands as a security for the good treatment of the wife in her new home and serves as a social and political link between the clans of the contracting parties.[46]

Traditional marriage was therefore not a commercial transaction, and the parties involved were largely free partners within the context of societies that emphasized communitarian ideals in contrast to individual autonomy.[47] Indeed, among the Banyankole the term used to describe bridewealth is

---

44 *Okuhongerwa amandwa* was a Banyankole practice of consecrating virgins to a god.

45 Curley, Richard, *Elders, Shades and Women: Ceremonial Change in Lango*, Uganda. Berkeley: University of California Press, 1973, p. 23.

46 Driberg, J, "The Status of Women among the Nilotics and Nilo Hamitics, op.cit., p. 413.

47 Tamale, S., *When Hens Begin to Crow* op.cit., p. 18.

okujuga,[48] a marriage gift transaction distinct from that used for the payment of goods. This process was also sanctioned by the attachment to the deity in most cases. A woman was free to walk out of an abusive marriage and return to her parents and relatives (and often did).

One has to note that within the framework of Nyankole family or clan arrangements, men and women jointly made decisions that governed the norms and ethos of their cultural, political and juridical lives. However, with colonialism several social arrangements and processes were put off balance, setting a dangerous precedence. This in turn set in motion a set of potent factors that decidedly upset the balance of labor, sharpening the superordinate or subordinate relationship between men and women in Ankole and Uganda as a whole.

2.2.2 The Colonial Period

After the famous Berlin Conference on the scramble and partition of Africa in 1884, Uganda landed in the hands of the British. In 1894, Uganda became a British protectorate after a series of so-called "agreements" or "treaties" between the then African chiefs or kings and the colonial British. The colonialists used an extremely elaborate system of indirect rule to govern the protectorate. Chiefs and kings retained their positions and operated in their already established political frameworks but were answerable to Uganda's overall governor, who in turn was initially assisted by an executive and later legislative council (LEGCO)[49]. Their seat was in Buganda and the colonial rulers used it to extend their rule to other parts of the country.

Having secured their political hub, the colonial masters introduced capitalism. This system seems to have been the turning point of the social stratification of societies in Uganda. Ankole was no exception. With the trend of capitalism in Uganda, women's relationship to men was significantly influenced by capital.[50] The right that men already had to their wives' labor was strengthened, and they gained a firmer grip on women's productive and reproductive work. Women's subordination was further secured through their

48 *Okujuga* literally means the mooing of cows, meaning a new voice in a home.
49 Morris, H., and Read J., *Uganda: The Development of its Laws and Constitution*, Stevens and Sons, London, 1966, p. 18.
50 Tamale, S., *When Hens Begin to Crow* op.cit., p. 19.

exclusion from wage employment; the power that comes with a pocketbook at the end of each month was bound to restructure gender relations in the Ugandan household. Roberts provided a succinct summary of the reasons why capitalism increased the subordination of women in the non-capitalist sectors "...the intensification of female labor in peasant economies released male labor for the production of cash crops...their (women's) productive work was intensified to ensure the subsistence basis of labor reserve areas while their reproductive labor provided the maintenance and reproduction of labor power at no cost to the capitalist wage."[51]

Another unfortunate feature of the colonial economic policy was the marginalization of women farmers. While women in rural areas often took responsibility for farming, colonial policies buttressed highly autocratic patriarchal relations of ownership, inheritance and law.[52] The introduction of cash crops such as tobacco, coffee and tea in Ankole by the British engaged men at work. Men had no choice but to engage in the production of these primary products to meet their tax obligation to the colonial government.[53] Thus, men cultivated cash crops while women continued to grow food crops as well as cash crops on the subsistence level.

Under these conditions, Ugandan women became the primary producers, constituting 60 percent of the labor force in the agricultural sector and accounting for 80 percent of food production.[54] The fact that women were and are not paid for their productive and reproductive labor meant that they would provide the chief subsidy to capitalist production. Such exploitation of women's labor markedly lowered their status below that of men. This was a transplant by the British of their own ethnocentric version of male-dominated politics and completely ignored women's political roles. As noted by Smock

> ...colonial policies had rather important influence on sex role definitions or opportunities for women. Christian missionaries and colonial administrators brought with them Victorian conceptions concerning the place of women in society.

51 Roberts, Pepe. "*Feminism in Africa: Feminism and Africa.*" *Review of African Political Economy*, 1984, p. 176.

52 Tamale, S., *When Hens Begin to Crow* op.cit., p. 19.

53 Jamal, V. 1978. "*Taxation and Inequality in Uganda, 1900–1964.*" *Journal of Economic History* 38, no. 2.

54 Econ. Commission for Africa, 1975.

> Generally, they did not appreciate the significant contributions frequently made by the women and their sense of independence.[55]

British systems, structures and policies focused on delineating a clear distinction guided by a chauvinistic ideology that perceived men or males as public actors and women or females as private performers. Colonialists worked hand in hand with the African patriarchs to develop customary inflexible laws, which evolved into new structures and forms of domination. As a result, women found themselves squeezed between colonial oppression on one hand and domestic oppression on the other.

Further, colonial policy on education was among the most potent factors adversely affecting the relative position of women in Africa.[56] As in Victorian Europe, educational opportunities were disproportionately provided to males. Missionary education for women, such as that offered at prestigious all-girls schools like Maryhill, Bweranyangi, Kyeizooba or countrywide Gayaza High, Namagunga senior and Buloba college, was primarily geared toward providing educated men with good wives and homemakers.[57] This, of course, contradicts the earlier proposition that claims that these schools were meant to liberate women. One cannot deny the fact that these girls' schools contributed immensely to the growth of the country and that these women were often more privileged than their fellow women. However, the intention of the founders of these schools should not be ignored. The women trained in these institutions were evaluated based on their homemaker and domestic skills.

More than ever an educated woman was seen as a potential consumer who would motivate her husband's productivity.

> [S]he must be educated to want a better home, better furnishings, better food, better water supplies, etc. and if she wants them she will want them for her children.

55 Smock, Audrey. "*Ghana: From Autonomy to Subordination.*" In Janet Giele and Audrey Smock, eds., *Women: Roles and Status in Eight Countries*, John Wiley, New York, 1977, p. 181.

56 Graham, C.K. *The History of Education in Ghana from the Earliest Times to the Declaration of Independence*, London: F. Cass, 1971.

57 Tamale, S., *When Hens Begin to Crow* op.cit., p. 29.

> In short the sustained effort from the male will only come when the woman is educated to the stage when her wants are never satisfied.[58]

Not only did such training deny women of intellectual skills needed to participate in the western system of politics imposed by the British, but it also introduced new gender roles that radically altered gender ideology. The impact that these modifications had on household structures in Uganda was significant. Women were relegated to a redefined, subordinated domesticity.

Positively to note is the fact that even though missionary education for girls domesticated them, and the education was relatively inferior to that for boys, it nevertheless offered them the opportunity to become exposed to and more amenable to activism. This education was a springboard of the struggle against bad policies.

They became part of the Ugandan nationalists whose pressure and demands coupled with those of multilateral imperialism in the post-war period made it increasingly difficult and unprofitable for Britain to cling to its colonial empire. On the other hand, while women were being relegated to a redefined social participation, power and class differences erupted among women themselves.

Meanwhile on the political scene, the political activists were gaining a grip on the pressure on the colonial masters. The three political parties that were formed and participated in different activities leading to Uganda's independence ignored the active participation of women deliberately. The reason was very clear. All the three political parties: DP (born in 1956), UPC (Uganda People's Congress, founded in 1958) and KY (Kabaka Yekka-Kabaka) were all backed by strong conservative, patriarchal institutions. These were mainly formed from the colonial "trained" elite young men turned rebellious and were mostly selfish and opportunistic – and mostly interested in the personal acquisition of power as noted by historian Karugire.[59] As a result, Uganda was then diseased with divisions which led to inequalities.

Despite these inequalities, the struggle to achieve independence was clear to the men and women of Uganda. Uganda attained formal independence

---

58 Staudt, Kathleen. *The State and Gender in Colonial Africa.*" In Sue Charlton, Jana Everett, and Kathleen Staudt, eds., Women, the State and Development. Albany: State University of New York Press, 1989, p. 78.

59 Karugire, S., *A Political History of Uganda*, Heinemann, Nairobi, 1980, p. 168.

on October 9, 1962, with English as its official language and a unicameral national assembly modelled on the House of Commons replacing the colonial Legco. Milton Obote, the UPC leader who had won national elections in April 1962, ascended to the position of executive prime minister. Sir Edward Mutesa II, the Kabaka of Buganda, was elected by the parliament as ceremonial president and head of state in 1963. Women were granted full suffrage at independence, but it meant little in reality.

In the period leading up to independence in 1962, men had a monopoly on all important positions within the colonial bureaucracy. The group who inherited the colonial state at independence consisted almost entirely of men. Uganda's first independent parliament consisted of eighty-eight men and only two women.[60] The country's first constitution contained no references to gender equality or any specific provisions to ensure women's rights.[61] This was of course very unfortunate and very unjust.

It is important to note that women had not only been sidelined in all negotiations leading up to independence, but colonialism had systematically alienated them from the redefined political structures. These curtailed women from further progressing to achieve their due status in society and these structures grew stronger. They were maintained by the nationalist parties, within which women played only marginal or insignificant roles in decision-making processes and in the designation of political policies. Uganda at this stage only missed out on the opportunity to include women in the political process but also their good input. Undoubtedly, this was a reproduction of the colonial indirect rule, of empowering one group at the expense of the other.

Colonial administrators reproduced the sexism of their own societies by identifying men with authority and thus disregarding the voices of women. As a result, the codification of customary law reflected the political and economic interests of men, which often benefited from the restriction of women's mobility and political participation. As Sylvia Tamale notes, "[w]omen's relationship to men was greatly influenced by women's and men's relationship

60 Matembe Miria. *Gender, Politics, and Constitution Making in Uganda*. op.cit., p. 43.

61 Uganda, *The Uganda (Constitution) Order in Council*, H.M.S.O., London, 1962.

to capital."[62] The colonial state, colonial trading companies and the missionaries encouraged the cultivation of cash crops such as coffee, tea, sugar and tobacco because they needed an unpaid labor source to subsidize the cheap production of these crops.

Pre-colonial "patriarchy intersected with the sexist practices of colonial officials to define women's work as (unpaid) domestic chores while men monopolized the control of cash crops. Colonial officials and African men conspired to create customary laws that limited women's mobility and prevented their access to the benefits of the market economy. With this commercialization"[63], the customary law defined men as the owners of land, leaving their female relatives without a legal claim to their own homes.

2.2.3 The Post-Independence Era

The project has categorized two periods in the post-independence era. This is not a scientific or political categorization but purely a research convenience. It has solely depended on the ordinary categorization from the people who were interviewed and approached in the research field. Secondly, the categorization coincides with major events in Uganda including the political turmoil. Thirdly, the progress in terms of human rights and especially in relation to those of women was put into consideration.

Therefore, the post-independence era was categorized under two phases in this study. The first phase of independence from 1962 to 1986, when women were promised that their cause would be tackled. The second phase stretches from 1986 to 2014. In the first phase, some areas concerning the status of women are highlighted, and in the second phase the emphasis is on what changed. What remained wanting is also implied.

2.2.3.1 From 1962 to 1986

Independence meant in all reality nothing to the status of women. By the time the colonial flag (the Union Jack) was lowered for good, the fate of the public or private divide in Uganda had been indelibly sealed. Social and political structures were in place; law, religion, and the educational system ensured

62 Tamale, S., *When Hens Begin to Crow* op.cit., p. 8.
63 Ibid., p. 4.

that this ideology remained embedded not only in the socio-political strata but also in the consciousness of independent Ugandans. It was very clear that women were excluded from formal politics.

The codification of the hitherto suppressive customs made women's situation even worse than before. In the precolonial time, structures were there to suppress women but they were never written down. In the colonial time, the oppression of women seemed to have been legalized. Colonization went side by side with the evangelization of Africa.

Colonization seemed to have sealed the fate of the future of not only Ugandans but Africa in general. This cut across the whole spectrum of society. The social structures and mentalities were redirected to those of the wishes of the colonial masters. Regarding gender, the colonial masters seemed to have carried with them their sexist mentality and biases towards women to Africa[64].

As a result, on the concrete level, every woman found herself more unfortunate in the new independent Uganda than never before[65]. Men became winners and instruments, or at best good custodians of the new injustice not only against women but against each other, a constellation that later ushered Uganda into civil wars.

This mentality culminated in the suppression of woman's social, political, educational, cultural, religious as well as economic status, and, in fact, determined her fateful position. Indeed, her position would automatically lead to the deprivation of her full rights as a woman and consequently as a human being in Nyankole society.

The pre-colonial and post-colonial epochs did not directly favor the change of women's status. However, they prepared a fertile ground for women to struggle for their own rights. Women learnt from the experience that their liberation was not going to come easily. There was an urge to put

---

64 This refers to the sexist mentality that already existed in Europe. Although, this was a time when there were so many women's movements in Europe, one wonders why they didn't bring with them the already good mentality that was being introduced in their countries back home.

65 There is no literature to confirm that women were better off in the pre-colonial times.

an end to the many years of suffering. They realized that their status quo was far from getting better. This was catalyst for many women in their struggle.

2.2.3.1.1 Socio-Cultural Status

Culturally, the significant role played by a woman was always that of motherhood. With the commercialization of bridewealth, this was more intoned. This apparently earned her an unsurpassable and non-compromisable status, but in reality it confined her more to the home – the private life – and channeled her to downward movement. As a result, children were also seen through the spectacles of their sex. Thus, the quality of the status mainly depended on the sex of one's children. Sex differences became a significant issue because children were seen as a source of income, as reliabilities and assets. For example, a girl was preferred as first born to provide cows or to become a source of bridewealth for her brother. Boys were seen as people who would later work for the government to obtain wages or bring wealth to the family. A woman who produced boys enjoyed a higher status than one who produced girls.

Unfortunately, in both cases, the children belonged to the father, the man. The man, irrespective of class, tribe or social status, held a superior status over a woman. He was seen as a source of everything since he was the one who controlled the finances. In fact, a Munyankole woman regarded it a virtue against this background to remain *omukazi* (a woman), meaning that they always accepted an inferior status *vis-à-vis* a man. Hence, a feeling bequeathed from generation to generation and from mother to daughter of all ages, was that being female means a position less than a man's.

This was commonly aggravated by the social customs that were codified, culturally accepted and cherished as right and sugar coated, all the while containing a peppery content designed for oppressing women. This is to say, some customs looked excellent on the periphery while they were dangerous in themselves. For example, protectionism, lack of choice of marriage partner, acting as domestic animals on sale during marriage through bridewealth.

In most places in Ankole the staple food is millet or bananas. Banana was easy to prepare but millet needed more preparation. Also, acting as a milling machine, a woman would mill millet almost daily as a sign or proof that she was strong, and this would continue up to when the first girl matures (that is around eight years of age).[66] Or if they were only boys, relief would come when her sons married. In this case, the daughters in laws would take over from her. A childless wife was destined to shoulder this milling burden, together with other burdens, up to her grave.

2.2.3.1.2 *Physical Violence*

Physical violence, in the form of beating or physical intimidation for domestic reasons, was neither a surprise nor a crime. This did not change at independence. Beating, slapping or other bodily injuries were used to ensure women's inferior status and to ensure that they remain timid and submissive.

Time for marriage was the repository of this. The culture accepted and propagated induced fears, amidst which a whisper from elderly women *obushwere bugumire* (marriage is difficult) or *omukazi ashwerwa* (a woman endures in marriage) was uttered. Physical violence was always implied in most of the customs and rites. The culture and the colonial officials seemed to have justified physical violence and placed the burdens of the home on the woman.

The good pre-colonial practice of bridewealth, whereby the groom's family (man's family) transferred livestock – especially cows or other items – to the bride's family (woman's family), was commercialized and later transformed into brideprice. This led to the commoditization of women in marital relationships and made it difficult for them to leave abusive husbands.[67] Marriage was made into a kind of eternal contract, whether it was abusive or not. The woman was always torn between two homes: "my home" (where she was born and to where she would turn to at the time of temporary separation) and "my home" meaning the marital home (where she would remain as long as the husband wanted it). All this was sealed by the payment of bridewealth.

Still, monotonous and fatiguing tasks reigned in the world of a woman. These tasks included cultivating crops, normally with a child tied on her back (if she had one), cooking for extended families, sweeping, washing men's feet when required to do so. Meanwhile, men would do a little work

---

66 The Making of Ankole, "*Uganda Journal*", 20, 1(1957), p. 1–15.

67 In his 1953 novel *Lak Tar* (translated as *White Teeth*) Okot p'Bitek examined the implications of brideprice from a male perspective in northern Uganda, but only peripherally acknowledged its restrictive effects on women.

of maintaining coffee plantations or repairing the house or pruning banana plants and in the evenings they would join in drinking sprees for relaxation. Or they would look for work in government farms far from home and would return after a couple of months.

The physical violence accruing from fatiguing tasks would only reduce at the event of producing girls. Hence, as early as nine years of age a girl-child would also be condemned to the oppression of a woman. She would also fall prey to society's discriminatory and inhumane jaws. In this sense, oppression would be bequeathed from the mother to the girl child.

Finally, physical violence had no specific seasons. One woman revealed to me during interviews that she was beaten on her wedding day. She was married in 1972.[68] Whether in season or out of season, pregnant or not pregnant, women were expected to serve her master, the man. In fact, physical violence was the source of women's common complications at birth and high infant mortality rates. Hence, women were getting progressively weaker, and children sicker. Their lives were wrecked beyond belief.[69] This was a common situation of many women in many families.

2.2.3.1.3 Social Violence

In the social scene a woman, like a child, was not supposed to gather or sit in the company of men. This was, however, a common practice in some societies in the precolonial times. The opposite was true of men, as women had nothing to say but gossip. Whenever men gathered, they had important issues to discuss. In churches, missionaries maintained the seats of women separate from the men's. Women often sat with children.

Furthermore, barrenness was the woman's fate and fault even in the precolonial times. This frequently occasioned polygamous marriage, adding insult to an injury for it was more often than not accompanied by jealousy, witchcraft and threats. For a barren woman, the situation was worse. That is why after the death of a childless woman, many rituals were performed around her body for fear that the mistreatment and loneliness subjected to

68 Interview with Bernadette Rukuna, 69, housewife, Rubindi, 23rd September 2013.

69 Graeme Irvine "*A New Day for Women.*" In Together: A Journal of World Vision International, New York, October-December 1992, p. 2.

her could bring revenge through her ghost. This unfair treatment was never dealt with in the colonial time.

Divorce was a purely male prerogative and right. Reasons for divorce were mainly barrenness, adultery, misbehavior or dissatisfaction from the man for any domestic reason. The colonial times had brought with it laws guiding divorce and made it easier. It was not easy for a man to divorce his wife in the precolonial times; a separation was the best solution and polygamy would follow.

Furthermore, following the death of the husband a woman was inherited as any other possession without any objection. Re-marriage was forced whether desired or not; otherwise she could be expelled or returned to her father's home. The immediate and possible husbands were the brothers of the deceased or, in some unfortunate cases, the father of the deceased (her father-in-law) if her husband died young.

To the unmarried women, commonly known as spinsters, the situation was appalling. Many offensive names were given to them as a token of hate. A spinster was not only a burden to society and her parents but also to herself. Many reasons were presumed, and unaccountable numbers of witchdoctors, soothsayers, divines, and deities could be consulted. This often resulted in her sexual abuse.

Like in any other African tribe, Banyankole women were considered and not numbered. But the number was taken for granted as one would take a herd of cattle. Children and women seemed to be in the same category that always needed strict direction from men.

The relationship between girls and boys was not allowed for fear of pregnancy. The penalty for pregnancy on the girl's side was death while the boy's transgression created merely enmity between the two clans or the families concerned. In most cases, the boy was not rebuked at home, and inside the house some fathers would encourage or hail their sons: *ori omushaija* (you are a man). This was also a pre-colonial practice.

Penalties on the women's side for transgressions such as extra-marital sexual relations prompted severe punishments or even death. An interview with women in Mbarara who hailed from Ntungamo district revealed that the punishment of such women among the Bakiga would even be as bad as stoning. Men would escape unharmed, or it would even be considered a sign of bravery.

To sum up, much of the rural woman's world among the Banyankole was characterized by torture, humiliation, violence, anguish, sexual harassment with brief interludes of a good time or seasons. The latter occurred during the time of harvesting millet, cooking for traditional parties or after delivering a baby boy or in giving away their daughters in marriage and so on. Even then, they still had to work and sometimes do heavy work. Hence, the woman's world was tainted with uncertainty, cruelty and fear[70]

2.2.3.1.4 Economic status

In order to understand this short section, the project has employed the word economic status. It is loosely used[71]. This is in relation to the economy of the country. In the previous sections women's contributions were only limited to the family. But that does not mean that women did not contribute to the economy of the country.

Economically, women had little to say and little to own besides the fact that they contributed a lot to the economy. As already discussed in previous sections, in the capitalization of the economy in Ankole, women were the losers. They were producers but not owners. Even at the time of a divorce, a woman in most cases was sent away with only clothes, and if she was lucky or if the husband was lenient enough, with a badly-behaved baby-girl.

The husband was the head of the family; the wife and children were subordinates. The post-independence Uganda did very little to save the situation. The post-independence Uganda had other "pressing and transitional" problems which occupied it at that time. Therefore, the issue of gender was not immediately addressed.

2.2.3.1.5 Religious status

The position of women in the religious life of the Nyankole society was one of a custodian, though this seemed to be the field they most participated in. The introduction of the new religion (Christianity) and the abolition of religious practices as devils and superstitious denied women the little power they had enjoyed before the Christianization.

---

70 Kathy Coffey, *Hidden Women of the Gospels*, the Crossroad Publishing Co., New York, 1996, p. 14.

71 Economy is here a big word when one must define the status of women.

Although they were portraying themselves as saviors of women's situation, the missionaries did not do much to help the women out of their misery. In fact, some missionaries knowingly or unknowingly execrated the situation especially of women who were already in a polygamous marriage.

Secondly, biblical texts, particularly in the book of Genesis and later in subsequent writings, seemed to have produced the legitimating of the behavior of African men. The story of the first sin of humans and especially about the woman as the real cause was a welcome solution to the complex puzzle that had occupied the Banyankole for years.[72] A woman, Eve, being the source of human suffering made a new mentality and women were on the losing side compared to men, who wanted to oppress them. Women were seen as a potential cause of sin and death.

In a society where every death has a cause, the majority of the witches turned out to be females. Understandably, this made the situation worse for women who were priestesses of traditional religions as they were immediately seen as witches. It is thus not surprising that in the early 1980s many women were driven out of their homes and had their houses burnt because they were suspected as witches or charmers.[73]

Women lost even the little power they already had as priestesses or custodians of religious objects. As a result, they took an even more passive role in the religious sphere as mere obeying subjects, but were also considered as the source of evil in their world. Many who were already priestesses were condemned as witches, a thing that even made their situation dangerous.

With the forced introduction of monogamy, many women were either sent back home or were abandoned, which made their lives difficult. Here, the missionaries never offered a solution for the women who were already living in polygamous marriages. Many ended up in a more difficult situation.

The colonial masters made constitutions excluding women or including them just as an afterthought. In most places where they already held a position that made them recognized in society, for example as religious, were just tolerated. Where they were already chiefs, it was hard to maintain them. With the suppression of kingdoms, many women who were either queens or sub queens, positions that could influence the decisions of the kings, were lost.

72 Cf. Gen.3, 1–24.

73 An interview with Mwiruki, 67, peasant, Mbarara, 29th May 2015.

However, because of this position and the responsibility they held, most significant women in palaces later became heroines and feared spirits or deities, for example, *Nyabuzaana, Nyabaasa, Kibubura* and *Kijuma*. A renowned girls' secondary school in Mbarara District was later named after Kibubura.

2.2.3.1.6 Psychological Effects

Meanwhile, the status of a woman in Kinyankole society right from the birth was already predetermined and destined psychologically.[74] The societal structures favored the status of a man more than the status of a woman. Not only were women affected by these structures but they were also infected by the trivialities and prejudice of all that they entailed. This was enhanced and characterized also by mythical, result-oriented and abusive language towards a woman, so much so that mentioning a woman automatically denoted an inferior person, a second-class person or even a good for nothing citizen.

In some cases, the word woman or *omukazi* meant fear or cowardice in the society. The re-definition of the terms that already existed among the Banyankole together with the legalization of the customary law paved the way for a psychological backlash on women.

2.2.3.1.7 Concluding Remarks

All in all, a woman's life in almost all spheres was unnoticed and unfortunate. However, many women had adapted to the situation and became immune to these oppressive societal structures. Most of them came to believe that it was the "normal life" a woman was supposed to live.

This, however, could pose a very challenging situation. When one has no adequate understanding of his or herself, it is not easy to liberate him or her. This is true not only in the case of women but also for all human beings regardless of gender or social situation.

74 Njinya Njinya, Leuben. *African Mind: a journal of Religious and Philosophy in Africa,* Vol. 1, No. 1, Ggaba Publications, Nairobi, 1989.

2.2.3.2 *From 1986 to 2014*

In this research, this period has been found to be of great importance. It has been perhaps the best time ever for women in Uganda. Many women from western Uganda agree that this was a period of liberation. No single period in Uganda has enjoyed relative peace as this one. Thus, the project has termed it the time of emancipation. In the following section, more about this will be given and analyzed.

New experiences were met not only in the civil society but also in the religious realm. Since the 1980s, the Church has relatively reduced the animosity that existed between Catholics and the Protestants, and a new chapter has been opened. This chance was thanks to the system of governance that was all inclusive and never gave space to divisive politics.

In this sense, the term "time for emancipation" has been chosen because of its importance. It is this time that will be historically narrated and critically examined to find its achievement in the area of women's freedom and equal rights for all citizens of Uganda.

2.2.3.2.1 *Time for Emancipation*

On the eve of the third millennium, significant changes and developments in anthropology, technology, economics as well as socio-political studies have realized the need to halt women's suffering. The fifteen years of repressive regimes of Presidents Amin and Obote came to an end when the National Resistance Army (NRA), under the tactical leadership of Yoweri Museveni, took control of the country at the beginning of 1986. This war was acclaimed a "protracted people's war", as already said above.

The NRA became a people's movement and adopted the name National Resistance Movement (NRM).

This NRM stated and promised a commitment to the improvement of the status of women and especially in the area of economic and social positions. Prominent women who fought and were in its military and political wings backed and paved a way for this achievement. As a result, Museveni appointed Dr. Specioza Wandira Kazibwe as the first female vice-president in Uganda as well as in Africa in 1996. Through a concerted effort and an affirmative action initiative, thirty-four seats out of 270 in the newly created National Resistance Council (NRC) were reserved exclusively for women.

"Affirmative action" means positive steps taken to increase the representation of women and minorities in areas of employment, education, and culture from which they have been historically excluded.[75] The NRM's victory cleared a space in which to debate women's rights and created an atmosphere conducive to addressing women's disadvantaged position in Ugandan society. As Matembe notes, the greatest accomplishment of the NRM was its ability to create a "more favorable climate for women."[76]

Despite the progressive efforts of the NRM government, women's activists faced an uphill struggle against an androcentric political culture and systemic male social privilege. For example, from an early age, Miria Matembe (hereafter referred to as Matembe) as a female activist recognized the significance of the law as a mechanism for both protecting and restricting women's rights.[77] Because law codifies a person's rights and can be used to rectify unfair situations, Matembe decided to study law against the wishes of her father[78] and directed much of her energy to ensuring that the law itself was made fair and equitable. As a lawyer during Amin's rule, she saw how the legal system systematically favored those already in power or with money.[79] As a member of the Constitutional Commission and Constituent Assembly, and later as a minister in different ministries, she sought to ensure women's rights, particularly those concerning land, which had been denied under the previous constitution and the legal system inherited from the colonial state[80].

Matembe's and other women's efforts to promote women's rights encountered opposition from conservative forces who disapproved of her challenge to the dominant patriarchal social order. Matembe did not conceal her opposition to "our archaic socio-cultural system," which was in her view structurally oppressive to women.[81] In the mid-1990s, women provided 80 percent of agricultural labor and 90 percent of domestic labor in

75 http://plato.stanford.edu/entries/affirmative-action/ accessed on 23rd July 2013 at 04:09.
76 Matembe, *op.cit.*, p. 64.
77 Ibid., p. 7.
78 Ibid.
79 Ibid., p. 19–20.
80 Ibid.
81 Ibid., p. 164.

Uganda, but less than ten percent of women actually owned land.[82] Despite its origins in colonial policies designed to exploit women's unpaid labor, this division of labor has been accepted by many conservatives as a natural reflection of indigenous tradition. Matembe vehemently attacks the double standard used by these people, who often promote "many things from the Western world [...] as progressive, [... but designate] new (progressive) ideas about gender relations as 'foreign' and 'not suitable' for Africans."[83]

Undoubtedly, this period saw a fundamental change. In 1986, women's councils were elected, seminars held and associations inaugurated. Consequently, women joined politics. In February 1989, more than thirty women were elected to the Ugandan parliament, and in every local community a woman representative was elected[84]. In 1995, the new constitution was promulgated, and every district was supposed to have a woman constituency representative, without forgetting women who defeated male contestants in their constituencies such as Winnie Byanyima for Mbarara Municipality.

There were also parliamentary elections in 1996, and women representing all the districts in Uganda were elected to parliament and district councils. What was really outstanding was the appointment of a woman as the vice president of Uganda, Dr. Specioza W. Kazibwe, and some women as cabinet ministers. This included: Rebecca Kadaga, Janet Mukwaya and Miria Matembe.

a) The Christian Touch in Emancipation

At the beginning of 1980, the Church in Africa committed itself to enculturation and even more importantly, to the re-visitation of biblical hermeneutics and new theological ideas on God's plans in the new evangelization. Theologians reflected more on the human person than on merely the catholic institution. That means the institution started to be viewed as something to serve people and not vice versa.

---

82 Mugyenyi, Mary R. "*Towards the Empowerment of Women: A Critique of NRM Policies and Programmes*" in Hansen (ed). *Developing Uganda*, Ohio University Press, Oxford: 1998. p. 133.

83 Matembe, M., *op.cit.*, p. 209.

84 Kakwenzire J, "*Concessions given to Uganda Women*," in the New Vision, Kampala, 16th March 1989, P. 6.

Humanity was seen as key player in the new evangelization rather than the structures. It was pointed out that God created male and female in His divine image, which means equality in dignity. Both were made co-creators and they were meant to master or subdue the creation. Man was not meant to subdue woman.

Already when the catholic missionaries came preaching the gospel, they somehow spread a seed of liberation for women. They abolished some of the customs, taboos and rites that enslaved women. They did not explicitly intend emancipation but they simply spread Jesus' good news of setting the captives free (Lk.4.8).

Both international and indigenous congregations of religious sisters or nuns had a strong touch in liberating women. They appreciated and recognized their value and dignity through recruiting, educating and forming them. In fact, women who joined these congregations had always commanded and still command respect in Kinyankole society.

The most outstanding beginning of implicit emancipation by the Church was the assurance of a woman's stability in the family if a man remained a committed believer. The wedding ring, wedding certificate and the prayer containing the divine command "what God has united, human beings must not divide" (Mt.19.6b) played a role in the stability of a woman in a family. It was a blow to polygamy, though few men still deviated from that command. This somehow guaranteed a woman some permanence too. But the Church also offered an alternative, and recognized women who were living in polygamous marriages or divorce calling them the *banyanshonga*[85], a term denoting that although she has a something to solve, she is a Christian.

Inspired by the new horizons, the second Vatican Council (1962–1965), which is sometimes called a "pastoral council", opened. African theologians also started reflecting on liberation. The council maintained free association and participation in the Church, thus reducing the clericalism and triumphalism of men.

However, the Christian touch has left much to be desired. The Christian touch on emancipation was neither direct nor was it decisive. It solely paved

85 *Banyanshonga*, a term used to describe the people on the way to solving a problem or repenting.

the way for the dynamic movement that has gone henceforth. Much more will be discussed in chapter three.

b) Abolition of segregative customs, rites and taboos

The superstitious and seemingly pagan rites, taboos and customs that intended to instill fear in women have been discarded either by governments or religions, especially Christianity. Some other rites or customs have disappeared gradually and naturally. These included burial rituals, rites of twins, funeral rites, purification rites after child-birth, marriage customs, to mention but a few. The Church worked hand in hand with the states in some cases to apprehend such cases.

Examples of funeral rites included days of mourning where a woman was not expected to show any joy or smile on her face, and she was to shed tears. Days for mourning the dead depended on sex – if a woman died there were to be two or three days of rest and for a man there were four or more. If a childless woman died, she was buried with a sucker of a banana plant and her body was never taken out of the house through the main door, for it was believed she was a curse and a shame to the whole family. With Christian religion and modernization, this practice has phased out

Most of these exclusive customs and rites have been disapproved and demystified by modern learning. Others have been seen as dangerous to women's health, for example, dietary restrictions where most delicious dishes such as chicken, mutton or fatty meat were not for women but for men. Finally, the abolition of segregative customs, taboos and rites was gradual. However, some of those elements still exist.

2.2.3.3 The General Status Quo Today

After the 1986 event of ushering in the emancipation of women, women's situation seemed to have greatly improved. However, the situation for the majority of Banyankole women remained haphazard. The situation became emptiness and confusion. Women have been told to leave the land of slavery; some have responded while some have not responded. Even those who have left have not yet reached the promised land. Many women among the Banyankole seem to be wandering in the desert and they do not seem to try to reach the promised land. They have left their "Egypt" and they are heading for their “Canaan”, the land where there will be celebrations of the rights once suppressed, dignity once suffocated and freedom once abused.

The situation, though improving, is tending backward. Pressure comes from men who still dream of the ‘golden past’ and struggle, as their last chance, to destabilize and frustrate the efforts of liberation. Some men, or even some women, go around de-campaigning emancipation.

In all, the social status as one generally observes now is not the best. Though women have been recognized, they are not fully accepted. They have not been given their full share of their rights and dignity. There is much to be done to improve the social status of women in Uganda, but particularly of rural women.

2.3 Critique of the Status Quo of Women

Undoubtedly, much has been done to emancipate women worldwide. However, women in developing countries such as Uganda still find it difficult to enjoy their full rights. Some women are on the level of mediocrity and others are on the level of insignificance. To many women, women’s liberation has remained an illusion, only a reality for the very few.

To the fortunate minority, the women’s liberation movement is a blessing because they have benefited from it. These consist of educated women, those married to politicians, politicians, business women and some women in urban areas. They appreciate their being women, but they are fighting for their dignity as human beings. Yet to some women, their emancipation is becoming more of a curse. Emancipation for most rural women has come to mean singing and dancing for their representatives, boasting it aloud to their husbands and sometimes taking them (the husbands) to courts of law.

To some women, it is embraced with the real sense of liberation. It was embraced with a sense of relief. To the last few women (die-hards), they long for the “golden time” of slavery where they “enjoyed” the inferior status.

In today’s newspapers, cases of defilement, rape, seduction, abduction, and sexual harassment against women are hardly absent[86]. Many people believe that the world is unfair, but critically and closely examined this

86 Kiura, Jane M., *Women’s Dignity,* Paulines Publications Africa, Nairobi, 1995, p. 12.

tendency indicates the kind of attitude men (who do or support such violent acts) have towards women and explains their taking them as sexual objects.

This clearly shows that emancipation has a long way to go for both men and women. The liberation endeavor has to cultivate an awareness of the dignity and sacredness of human life of both sexes. More to that, the Church, though preaching the equality of both sexes, has not fully emancipated women. For example, up to this moment the hierarchy of the magisterium still consists of only men. No concrete and convincing theological reasons have been given for this, yet there are more convincing reasons to support and justify women's emancipation as will be treated in the next chapter.

In some areas, the emancipation of women has not been served on a silver plate but achieved through martyrdom. For example, in Rubindi sub-county there are cases of conflict noted down such as separation, divorce in some families, escaping of husbands from their families and taking refuge in prostitute's homes and so on[87]. Also, it is unfortunate to note that in some instances emancipation has been abused, for example, some women have abused this freedom as an excuse to deviate from their moral lives. Hence, we find many sex workers, single mothers in towns and slums or trading centers, some selling their nude photographs and so forth. This certainly further devalues the dignity of the woman.

Finally, emancipation is not yet complete, and genuine emancipation should aim at liberating both the soul and body of women and men. The emancipation of women is complete when men are also emancipated. It is a change of attitude and mentality on both sides. On the one hand, it depends on how women conceive themselves and on the other hand how men perceive women in relation to themselves. It is thus a two-way street. Without this, true emancipation remains a dream.

87 Tibyampasha C, 61, Chairperson Local Council, Rubindi Sub county, 24th September 2012.

Chapter Three: Justification for Genuine Emancipation

3.1 Introduction

In many countries, the emancipation of women is no longer a topical issue. It has evolved to the level of gender equality. Also in Uganda the trend has been focused on development issues rather than on this important area of human rights. Many women's activists, too, seem to have achieved what they wanted or fought for. It is true, something has been achieved but it is too little to be called the liberation of women. Some legislators and many human rights activists also seem to be satisfied with the share that has been given to women.

On the other hand, many conservatives in Uganda look at women's emancipation as a waste of time and money, a non-issue in today's world politics and economic development. The inherited status quo of women's position in society from antiquity still appeals to many countries and most notably to African countries. The reason behind the mentality of keeping women in the background holds, among other things, that women are the weaker sex or a man's property, and they can neither walk side by side nor be on equal footing with a man.

However, the new challenge of our age is redefining the position of a woman. The question is whether we have closed the pages on the past and carefully opened the new for the betterment of all humanity. Or whether we have covered the dark pages and moved on only to give women a raw deal. What is very clear is the fact that women's liberation will bring about the betterment of humanity. As Michaela Karl puts it, *"[d]er Kampf, den Frauen seit Jahrhunderten für ihre Rechte führen, hat die Welt verändert und verändert sie täglich ein klein wenig mehr."*[88]

The assertion of Karl is very true and the fruits of women's struggle can been seen everywhere. This is not only true in Uganda but also worldwide. The fight that women stage for their rights has changed the world and

88 Michaela Karl, *Die Geschichte der Frauenbewegung*, Reclam, Stuttgart, 2011, p. 9.

continually changes it slowly for the better. This struggle is innate and natural to them even from the creation's perspective.

Therefore, modern thinking and a careful re-visitation of biblical and theological studies are indispensable aids to the justification of emancipation. This is the time of scrutiny and reason rather than emotions. Hence, the full women's liberation is not only urgent but crucial for the development of humanity.

Women's emancipation is a divine imperative. The concept of liberation or freedom is central in the understanding of the word of God. Also from a human point of view, the time for liberating humanity is ripe. The word of God awakes the sense of women being aware of what they are, as Grubitzsch and Lagpacan put it; *"wir werden frei geboren wie der Mann, und die Hälfte des Menschengeschlechts darf nicht ungerechterweise der anderen unterworfen sein."*[89]

This innate right must be respected and protected by all the human constitutions. Article 21 of the Constitution of the Republic of Uganda also provides that all persons are equal before the law and shall enjoy equal protection.[90] This is, of course, the very first article of the Universal Declaration of Human rights "all human beings are born free and equal in dignity and rights. They are endowed with reason and conscience and should act towards one another in a spirit of brotherhood."[91]

Although the formulation of the above article is subject to criticism because of its gender insensitivity by the use of the word "brotherhood", which is gender exclusive, the content is significant in the call for the respect and freedom of every human being. With such important documents in place, awareness of them paves the way for the protection of human rights in its totality.

The awakening of respect for the rights of all the living things has dawned. Thus, it is a not uncommon to hear words such as human rights or animal rights in our modern times. In seeking genuine women's liberation,

---

89 Grubitzsch Helga/Lagpacan, Coretta: *Freiheit für Frauen-Freiheit für das Volk*, Frankfurt, 1980, p. 62.

90 Uganda. *The Constitution of the Republic of Uganda, Kampala*, 1995.

91 The Universal Declaration of Human Rights http://www.un.org/en/documents/ accessed on 5th October 2014 at 23:04.

this section will consider what justifies it. Without any doubt, respect for human rights and especially those of women and children can never be overseen. The justification of this cause will be treated under two categories: religious and secular.

3.2 Religious Justification

Strictly speaking, scripture, tradition, and legitimate theological teachings are the very foundations of the Catholic faith. The three aspects anchor the revealed religion of Christianity. It is in these that the answers to fundamental questions in life can be found.

Little has been dedicated to the liberation of women. No encyclical or bull has been devoted to the cause of women and their plight in the modern world. Except a few remarks or letters from popes or bishops to the Christian communities, no binding document has been issued. However, from the Christian religious point of view, it is very clear that there is urgency and justification for gender equality in the world today. The Catholic church and indeed many churches remain burdened with the patriarchal and chauvinistic set-ups that have been in place for ages.

In this section, the project re-establishes the scriptural as well as the theological justification for the status and the central position of women in creation as a whole. It further evokes God's plan, which was designed for complementarity in his co-creation program of man and woman. The following section deals with a precise and understandable scriptural background to justify the emancipation of women and gender equality as a whole.

3.2.1 Scriptural Foundations

Scripture remains a handbook of life for believers and theologians. It is in the Scripture that we find answers to the questions of life. The fundamental question that often cuts through scripture is the liberation of humanity. That is a reason it is called salvation history. Faith holds that salvation begins with and ends with God. It further holds that great things happen when God mixes with humanity. God's intervention is deeply felt and recognized in any situation of oppression or suffering of his people and especially when they cry out. In biblical theology, "to cry out" denotes a judgment or an appeal for help or a claim of one's rights that is being denied or stepped on[92] (Cf. Exo.2.23, Gen.4:10).

The cry of women is evident in their daily lives. It is evident in our society and communities in Uganda. This cry reaches out to the creator, who responds through his word and messengers. It is of paramount importance that the signs of the time are also read and interpreted. God reminds the oppressor and the oppressed that the answers can be obtained from the re-visitation of individual conscience, scripture, and theological reflections.

Furthermore, one of the standard tenets of many religions is the assurance of freedom, either at present or the time to come or at least a longing to achieve it. In religious justification, there is a need to join women in their just anger to heal their wounded hearts and unburden their heavy minds. Theologically speaking, this can be done by digging deep in the "well-kept secrets that are tucked between the words and pages of the scripture."[93]

3.2.1.1 Introduction to Scriptural Reflections

The place of women vis-a-vis men in the scripture has been either taken for granted or as one of the subordination. However, when scriptures are subjected to reason informed by faith and since feminine hermeneutics has come on the scene, then the issue of women's place has been revisited. A further re-visitation of biblical texts regarding the Author's (God's) intention of the role and place of women is called for.

In a critical analysis, the scriptures have all the answers to justify the liberation of humanity. The Old Testament served as the preparatory phase in the history of salvation, and the New Testament became the fulfillment. The whole of the scripture is the word of God, which is always dynamic and efficacious, saving and protecting the weak.

But at one time or the other, it was the same word that was manipulated to serve as an instrument that human beings used against each other, to oppress and suppress each other. In this case, injustices against women were in many cases scripturally defended. Unfortunately, this still goes in many communities of believers and sometimes in the Church.

---

92 Both quotations are based on the New Jerusalem Bible Version.
93 Coffey K., *op.cit.*, p. 1.

3.2.1.2 Old Testament

The book of Genesis seems to be the source of all subordination of women in scriptures. The "rib story" (Gen.2.22–23), together with the fall of humanity (Gen 3), became the anchors for the condemnation of women. Genesis, therefore, became a hinge on which many biblical writers developed their exclusive and discriminatory theories. They seem to use this first book of the Bible to further or even deepen the belief that a woman was and remains a creature unequal to a man.

However, at the deeper level of reflection, God never intended inequality in dignity. Genesis 1:27 clearly states "God created ... in the same image of God ... male and female he created them." In dignity and before him, man and woman were intended to be equal.

The author of Genesis insists on equality and dignity; God created both for the fullness of humanity. Male and female are directly created by God. It is not a man who created a woman. God saw that the divine image was fully reached in the presence of the two. Both are in the image and the likeness of God.

Having created them, he blessed them and gave them responsibility. He wanted them to be sexually different for a purpose. That is why he blessed them and said to them "be fruitful, multiply, fill the earth and subdue it" (Gen.1:28). Both are destined to rule the earth and not to rule or dominate each other.

Therefore, according to the creation of humankind, God never intended inequality. The woman is not inferior but different from the man. God meant companionship and mutual complementarity in fulfillment of His purpose.

The rest of the Pentateuch presents women who contributed much to the deliverance of Israel and humanity as a whole. For examples, Moses' mother (Ex.2:1–6); Hebrew's mid-wives, Shiprah and Puah who defied Pharaoh's order to kill Hebrew male infants (Ex.1:15); Pharaoh's daughter who saved baby Moses (Ex.2:5ff), and so on. These were women through whom God accomplished the work of liberating the Israelites from slavery.

Other women in Genesis and Exodus include Sarah (Gen.21:7), Hagar (Gen.21:17–19), Rebekah (Gen.24:15), Leah and Rachael (Gen.29:15–30), whose importance in God's salvific plan cannot be underestimated. Also, women like Miriam surface as prophetesses who led the Israelites in thanksgiving and praises to Yahweh over his victory (Gen.15–20).

Also, the other Old Testament books portray the great contribution of women in the plan of salvation. Despite the despised position they held, women still dared to contribute something, each one in her capacity and ability. Rehab was a prostitute, and she enabled the Israelites to take Jericho (Josh.2.8). Deborah was a judge of Israel who rendered both legal decisions and carried out military campaigns (Judg.4–5).

More still, one cannot skip the mention of women like Ruth (Ruth 1:1ff), Naomi (Ruth 3:1) and the prophetess Hilda (2Kigs 22:14.20) who lived between 640 and 609 BC. In most cases, the Bible attests to women exercising leadership in families but also in nuclear families, for example Abigail (1Sam.25). Also in their natural roles, some women became great personages to emulate.

Even if Esther (Esther 1:1ff) and Judith (Jud.8:1–9, 9:1ff) are not historical personages, they are portrayed as heroines in the Bible. The Queen of Sheba is described as a courageous woman who visited King Solomon (1kgs. 10:1ff). Queen Sheba is significant to African women because she came from Ethiopia.

Some prophets also fought for women's rights, especially the underprivileged, the widows and the poor. Many prophets and especially the prophet Amos sharply condemned those who oppressed widows and orphans (Amo.5:7–12). Other prophets include Micah (Mic 3:1ff), Isaiah (Is 40:1ff) and Hosea. Hosea even uses the imagery of the woman Gomer to put across his message of God's love. (Hos.1:3–8).

In all, it is not divinely instituted to consider women as second-class citizens. The scriptures disqualify the mentality that God destined women to subordination and that God created them as a weaker sex that need the strong arm of a man. Rather, women's subordination and oppression are men's creation.

3.2.1.3 New Testament

Women stand out in every gospel and the rest of the New Testament books. The core of the New Testament is Jesus' ministry of liberating humanity. He himself said that he came so that humanity may "have life and life in abundance" (Jn.10:10). All his actions and teachings focused on this aspect of salvation. Women too, enjoy this merit. However, Jesus' preaching in word and deed on the equality of women in discipleship has been lost, submerged and re-interpreted by the dominant patriarchal view of succeeding generations. It is high time that Jesus' attitude towards women is revisited.

Luke's gospel is vital in analyzing Jesus' attitude towards women. Luke too, himself a physician, seems to treat humanity as humanity, and his writing is special because of its particular interest in women. Luke's audience appears to have had a considerable number of women, either as converts or catechumens for the initial instruction. But of great significance are the women who were often in the company of Jesus, which was something new at that time. We read in his gospel:

> Now it happened that after this he made his way through towns and villages preaching and proclaiming the good news of the kingdom of God. With him the Twelve as well certain women ... Mary surname the Magdalene ... Joanna, the wife of Herod's steward Chuza, Susanna, and many others who provided for them out of their own resources. *(Cf. Luke 8:1–5)*[94]

Important to note here, women were never named in ancient texts unless they enjoyed social prominence or did spectacular things. From Luke, one observes that Jesus welcomed female disciples into his entourage to be with him and be schooled in the Word and ways of God, along with the male disciples. This kind of behavior was, of course, unusual since Jewish men did not usually speak in public to women or girls outside their kinship circle, much less travel or walk around the countryside with them. Jesus broke this old tradition.

Indeed, he also sent many of his followers to the villages to proclaim the word of God, heal the sick and carry out his mission of salvation. When he sent seventy-two in pairs, scripture mentions nothing about gender. But it could be deduced that since he had a mixture of male and female people in his congregation, it follows logically that he sent them irrespective of their gender.

Luke's gospel involves women as well as men (Cf. Lk 7:2–10, 11–12). Thus, his language, the parables and analogies he used, are much influenced by this audience. For example, the usages of salt, virgins, baking, yeast and

94 https://futurechurch.org/women-in-church-leadership/women-in-church-leadership/ accessed on 23rd May 2014 at 00:12.

weeping women of Jerusalem indicate Jesus' concern and interest in women. The same can be noticed in the Acts of the Apostles.

Mary, the mother of Jesus Christ, serves as the model for the New Testament women's liberation. She shoulders the new era of emancipation. She surrenders to God for total freedom. She uses weapons of humility and love, apparently weak yet the strongest. She wins favor from God because of her inner beauty, humility, and obedience.

Hence, her "soul proclaims the Lord ... for God has pulled down the princes from their thrones and raised the lowly" (Lk 1:52). One cannot directly deduce that Mary referred to herself but the author wanted to emphasize the liberating nature of the new era, the overturning of the old structures in favor of the new ones. The lowly denote here the less privileged in society and women in this case were the majority. But on the other hand, Luke brings Mary, a woman, to the forefront of the salvation of humankind. The salvation came from a woman, something that was unfathomable in the patriarchal society of the Jews.

It was already prophesied in the Old Testament by the prophet Isaiah (Is 7:14) that a young woman shall conceive a child, and the child would become the savior and liberator of the afflicted. The mention of a woman bringing forth salvation to the Israelites was something not to be underestimated. Luke takes up not only the woman who gives birth to the liberation of Israel but the child born becomes a revolutionary.

Jesus becomes a revolutionary in his Jewish culture and inevitably Jesus is an emancipator par excellence just as his father was, is and will be. Just as God liberated the Israelites from Egyptian slavery and never concealed his love and care for the oppressed, so did Jesus, who was anointed to preach the good news. He launched his "Manifesto" as read according to Luke.

> The spirit of the Lord has been given to me for he anointed me. He has sent me to bring the Good news to the poor, to proclaim liberty to captives and to the blind New sight, to set the downtrodden free, to proclaim the Lord's year of favor *(Lk.4:18–19)*

Jesus never concealed his feelings towards women; he invited them to be among his disciples and welcomed them as his friends such as Martha and

Mary[95]. Sometimes he would set them free from the cruel jaws of their oppressors but also with caution (Jn.8). Contrary to the social setting, Jesus remains the Liberator, revealer yet the revealed.

Kathy Coffey holds that Jesus' friendships and even his contacts with women broke the taboos of a patriarchal society. This encouraged them to continue as freed, redeemed and resurrected people today and tomorrow.[96] Coffey believed that the redeeming act of Jesus was the turning point of the Israelites' patriarchal society.

Also, Jesus had great support from many women. Women had in turn reciprocated his favor to them. They were with him in season and out of season; in joys and in pains. They remained loyal up to the time of his death on the cross even though his male followers fled. After his resurrection, they were the first witnesses and were even sent to inform the male disciples. According to the gospel of John, Mary Magdalene was the first to get the new from the angel and later disseminated it to the rest of the apostles and they believed her, despite the then popular belief that one woman was capable of truth[97].

In the Acts of the Apostles, women contributed tremendously to the preaching of the gospel. The first converts were mainly women, and most women converted their husbands. Examples include: Priscilla (Acts 18:2), Phoebe (Rom.16.1), Lydia and Mary (Rom.16.6).

The Pauline epistles are vital in the liberation of women. Apparently, at the first brush, St. Paul seems distanced from women's struggle for freedom. Though "Paul is a gifted visionary, theologian, teacher and organizer, he was not a reformer in the modern sense."[98]

St. Paul, in respect for the Jewish social, traditional set-up, seemed to regard women as inferior to men (I Cor.14.34–35). According to him, women should keep silent in churches and should not be not permitted to speak as the law demanded. They are to ask their husbands if they have any questions, for it is shocking for a woman to speak in a church or at a social gathering.

---

95 Turpin, J., *Women in Church History*, St. Anthony Messenger Press, Ohio, 1990, p. 1.

96 Coffey, K., *op.cit.*, p. 14.

97 According to the Jewish tradition, for any evidence to be credible it needed more than one woman.

98 Sabiiti R., *The Situation of Women in Fortportal Diocese*: A pastoral approach to the Dignity and Liberation, M.A. Dissertation, Nairobi, July 1994, p. 69.

But, Paul neither segregated nor enslaved women for such "transgression". Paul does this in reaction to women who abused the authority and freedom accorded to them in Jesus Christ. Some women had overstepped the boundaries of their newly acquired roles. They were already liberated, but they had overstretched and hence Paul had to intervene. He did this out of pastoral necessity, one has to understand that in its context.

In contrast to the criticism and blame that is put on Paul as being anti women's liberation, he shows a high favor for all followers of Christ. He says "There are no more distinctions between Jew and Greek, slave and free, male and female, but all of you are in Christ Jesus" (Gal 3:28). If Paul was indeed anti-women, this would be a very big contradiction.

Besides Pauline's Epistles, the New Testament continues to portray a variety of outstanding women. Often, women are doing liberated things such as prophesying: Anna (Lk 2:36–38); or ministering as a deaconess: Phoebe (Rom 16:1). There are many more examples of women in the ministry and administration of Pauline communities.

All in all, the New Testament gives hope to the salvation of all. It further shows that patriarchal society structures were not ordained or elected by God and, therefore, can be altered. The liberation emphasized by the gospel that all are one in Christ still needs to be put into practice despite its social ramifications. The whole theme of the New Testament without any doubt justifies the emancipation of women.

3.2.2 Short Theological Foundation

Apart from the Bible, there have been efforts by theologians to understand the place of women in the Church. Following many challenges by female Catholic activists and the changes in the civil society, Catholic theologians have also begun to reflect on this issue.

The question of gender equality remains a challenge to the Church. But the question of liberating women from the injustices of society or oppression should be the principal duty of the catholic church. As such, the project has analyzed some of the theological reflections.

3.2.2.1 *Introduction to Theological Reflections*

The Church revelation is threefold. As already seen, the Bible together with tradition and the teaching of the Church make the revelation complete. Therefore, the teaching of the Church and the tradition of the Church is of primary importance as the revelation through the Word of God. The teaching of the Church is technically called the magisterium.

'Magisterium' is a Latin word that means the teaching authority or office of the Church, accomplished by the Holy Father and the bishops teaching in union with him.[99] In short, it is the teaching authority of the Church.

3.2.2.2 *The Magisterium and Women*

In addition to the biblical women, there are other historical women who already served as leaders in the Church, who were in the teaching office of the Church. The ministry of deaconess was exercised in the first centuries. As already mentioned, Phoebe was a leader of the church at Cenchrae and probably carried Paul's letter to the Romans (Romans 16:2), but other women continued this role.

There were other prominent women who were also deaconesses, this too is well documented. St. Macrina was the leader of the women's monastic community at Annisa and was renowned among the laity and clergy alike as a teacher of the Word and defender of Christian doctrine. St. Olympias was a fourth-century deaconess and a friend and patron of St. John Chrysostom. As Bishop of Constantinople, John put her in charge of all the deacons assigned to the great basilica of *Hagia Sophia*. Dionysia was a fourth-century wife and mother who overcame several crises and was an ordained deaconess of the cathedral at Melitene, Armenia. St. Radegund was a sixth-century queen and deaconess who founded a monastery at Poitiers where she served as the spiritual guide.[100]

With time, the position of women as leaders phased out, and the leadership of the Church became mostly a men's preserve. Women were no longer

---

99 *What Is the Magisterium*? As defined by Thomas Storck and retrieved from http://www.ignatiusinsight.com/features2007/tstorck_magisterium on 7th May 2014 at 12:06.

100 https://futurechurch.org/women-in-church-leadership/women-deacons accessed on 23rd November 2015 at 13:04.

allowed to be deacons and to lead churches. This did not leave them out of the Church and their commitment to it. Women have remained loyal to their churches up to modern times.

Today, women continue to be active in the Church, and even the proportion of women to men is often higher in the Church's activities, suggesting their commitment and love for the Church. In Mbarara Diocese in western Uganda, the established percentage of active women in the Church goes as high as 67 percent.[101] But the challenge remains with the Church's teaching about the same dignity and gender equality.

The new catechism of the Catholic Church leaves no room for doubt and emphasizes: "Man and woman have the same dignity and are of equal value." This is not merely a truth to be acknowledged or politicized but a statement that needs constant, continuous and active promotion. Pope John XXIII, in regard to the equality of sexes, also spoke with approval about women becoming increasingly confident of their natural dignity, and of their "demanding both in domestic and in public life the rights and duties which belong to them as human persons" (Pacem in Terris).[102]

One of the documents of the Second Vatican Council, 'Gaudium et Spes no. 12', insisted on the need for greater recognition of equality of all, and for the eradication of every kind of discrimination, including that based on sex as "contrary to God's intent".[103]

Equality for all is the emphasis and removal of all forms of discrimination, and serves as a testimony to the commitment of the Vatican fathers. This is not limited to mere rights but also to other areas of life, for example the differences in life-styles.

In many places, especially in developing countries, poverty falls disproportionately on the shoulders of women, the notion of the Church's "preferential option for the poor" and underprivileged is also significant, as it argues for greater concern for the physical and spiritual welfare of those trapped in poverty. The Church has to make an option for the poor to make the needs of the poor a particular focus of its love and attention; and

---

101 Mbarara Archdiocese, The Chancellery, Mbarara, 2013, Art. 2.

102 *The Catechism of the Catholic Church*: Revised Edition, Paulines Publications Africa, Nairobi, 2002, no. 2334.

103 Flannery Austin, Vatican Council Vol. 2: Gaudium et Spes, 1976, no. 12.

equally to allow the perspective of the poor to shape the Church's own thinking and practice.[104]

From the very beginning, the magisterium of the Catholic Church seems to have always taken women for granted. The place of women was never taken very seriously. It was Pope Pius XII who gave women's position some consideration. His successors have since developed the teachings of the Church about of this topic.

Pope Pius XII emphasized that man and woman have a dignity in which they are absolutely equal and mostly equal to the focus of the supreme, which is eternal life.[105] On the World Day for Peace on 1 January 1995, the late Pope John Paul II (recently canonized) taught that women have the right to insist that their dignity be respected and they should work for the promotion of the dignity of all persons, men as well as women.[106] Pope Benedict XVI also contributed to this cause. He wrote:

> The Church has the duty to contribute to the recognition and liberation of women, ... Giving women opportunities to make their voice heard and to express their talents through initiatives which reinforce their worth, their self-esteem and their uniqueness would enable them to occupy a place in society equal to that of men ... Bishops should encourage and promote the formation of women so that they may assume their proper share of responsibility and participation in the community life of society and ... of the Church[107]

In modern times, the issue of women's ordination has caused alarm. In fact, friction has been felt. The current position of the Church seems negative to many women. However, there are no convincing scriptural and theological reasons. The only reason given is the appointment of male apostles by Jesus, from which the apostolic succession hails over the centuries.

In defense, the magisterium argues that it has no freedom of changing the tradition whereby the ordained priesthood has been reserved for men,

---

104 www.cafod.org.uk/.../PromotingGenderEq, accessed on 20th May 2015 at 21:08.

105 *New Catholic Encyclopedia*, Vol. 15, p. 998.

106 John Paul II, *Message of His Holiness,* World Day of Peace 1 January 1995.

107 Post Synodal apostolic exhortation Africae Munus of his holiness Pope Benedict XVI, to the Bishops, Clergy, Consecrated persons and the lay faithful on the Church in Africa in service to reconciliation, justice and peace, 2011, part 1, chapter 2.2.

because it believes the practice was handed down by Jesus Christ, and it continued in the apostolic age.[108] So the magisterium shuns the responsibility.

The Church hierarchy views this matter as sensitive. The matter involves key theological issues, such as the nature of the Church, the nature of priesthood, sacramental symbolism, the authority of the Church in its sacramental life, and more importantly the issue of the significance of the differing male and female imagery of God, the significance of human sexuality in God's creation and his purpose for us.[109] So many women see this denial as an injustice but the church fathers say they have no authority to ordain women, and that justice does not mean equal treatment. Not all differentiation constitutes inequality.[110]

When one turns to Banyankole women, women's ordination is a non-issue. The religious sisters or nuns or female catechists are just a good representation in the higher ecclesiastical service and they are comfortable with that. This was clear during research.

From a statistical point of view, this research found out that 86 percent of the women interviewed were totally against women's ordination to the priesthood.[111] However, they recommended the admittance of women to other ministries in the Church. They highly encouraged the recruitment of women as catechists and nuns. That is the reason why the issue of women's ordination was never given special attention in this project.

Finally, while there has been a head-on collision, the magisterium has begun to see the need for women's liberation and their full involvement in evangelization. Sooner or later, women's rights will be recognized and respected. The very fact that women have been dedicated to the Church's teaching justifies their liberation.

3.3 Secular Justification

Outside the Church and its views, there are other reasons justifying women's liberation and later their empowerment in the secular realm. One can

---

108 Flannery Austin, *Vatican Council Vol. 2*: Inter Insigniores, Declaration on the Question of Admission of women to the ministerial priesthood, 1976, no. 4.

109 Flannery, *Vatican Council Ii Vol. 2*, op.cit., no. 6.

110 Ibid., no. 6&7.

111 Mbarara Archdiocese, *The Chancellery*, Mbarara, 2013, Art. 7.

say the secular argument for women's emancipation is very diverse due to different points of view. This has to be limited to an individual setting and also to a particular context. Despite being a contextual issue, one has to be clear that women deserve their rights as human beings. The secular justification has been categorized under the following.

3.3.1 Social Reasons

It is indeed society's history, tradition and customs that have subjected women to oppression and suffering for many centuries. It is the same society that should and must redress the situation. In Nyankole antiquity, one cannot trace a time when a woman's position was in its proper place.

Socially, women are worth liberating from the discriminatory social customs, taboos, totems and mentalities that imbue social evils that enhance the degradation of a woman's dignity. The worst of these are the customs surrounding marriage. These marriage customs we presented earlier deprive a Munyankole woman of the right of decision-making in the family. As a result, many children are produced, finances are misused and other resources are mishandled or misallocated. Decision making should be an issue of both man and woman for the betterment of the home. Planning for the family needs mutual understanding between husband and wife, for behind a successful husband is always a successful wife, so is the belief.

Also, the social bondages need to be loosened so that women may be free. One may think that society today has been sensitized, but the reality on the ground remains unbelievable. In this project, one notices that most rural women are still in the cruel chains of subordination. Society still infringes on the rights of a woman. Many people still believe a woman is destined to suffer. Hence, the liberation of women is easier said than done.

In addition to that, since the future generations are fathered and mothered by families, special care must be taken today in order to not transmit the wrong mentality. The long-held and mistaken attitudes that crowned the man as the absolute authority in the family is both dangerous and misleading. The emancipation of women is justified as it liberates future generations from today's mistakes.

A woman needs to be relieved of the burden of the family that she carries enduringly. Up to now, a peasant woman in Mbarara has quite a boring and tiring routine that takes up much of her energy and time. As a result of this heavy burden, she has little or no time to rest, which is very detrimental to her health. The awareness seminars and workshops have in most cases remained in principle, not in practice. The workability of these programs in many cases continues to be a failure due to sabotage from some men.

In conclusion, not all social structures, taboos, and totems are gender insensitive and sexually discriminatory. Some of them are, in fact, good and useful to society. Sociologically, a woman needs to be delivered from all wrong male-dominated attitudes that oppress and suppress her.

3.3.2 Economic Reasons

Uganda relies mainly on agriculture for its economy. Women and girls considerably contribute 56.6 percent of the agricultural labor.[112] Today the world is a playground of economics and women should not be left out of this important field of our time. Money is the most appealing language today. Women should not only be helped to understand this language but also to be full participants.

Women are important drivers of economic growth in developing countries, especially in Uganda. Their contribution to the emerging market possibilities in Uganda cannot be ignored. It is therefore of paramount importance to recognize their unique and significant roles in agriculture and other small businesses coupled with their responsibilities as a family, household, and community members often provide the basis for multiple gains. This helps to boost not only the economic growth of the country but also the society. In the end, this closes the gender inequality gap, reduces global poverty, and increases food security.

Forthrightly, a woman should be set free from the economic situation where, despite being the one of the producers, she is mainly a dependent. Women must think their way out of the confinement of the man-made structures of the patriarchy.[113]

---

112 Amanda, Ellis, Ed: *Gender and Economic Growth in Uganda: unleashing the power of women*, Washington DC, World Bank, 2006, p. 28.

113 O'Connor F, B., CSC, *Like Bread, Their Voices Rise*: Global Women Challenge the Church, Ave Maria Press, Notre Dame, 1993, p. 3.

Economic independence opens the door to political power, social development as well as the educational opportunities that in turn serve as gates of enlightenment. Enlightenment is the indispensable channel through which women's liberation will be reached.

Women should be liberated from men's selfishness that hitherto has made them controllers and owners of women's economic ventures. This results in economic backwardness on the side of the women, which is characterized by dependence on men for almost everything, poverty, disease, ignorance, primitive methods of farming, low incomes, low standards of living, high death rates, etc.

Dependence on men has not only tied women to the home but has bound them in chains of mental slavery. Most women in Uganda depend on men for almost every basic need. This attitude of husband protectionism is not only dangerous to women's freedom but detrimental to their psychological growth. While it is true that a wife needs protection from her husband, it is also true that over-protectionism always carries with it conditions that reduce women to the level of children.

In today's Nyankole nuclear families, almost all women are full-time attendants of the home. Women should be economically liberated for the smooth running of these homes. Their economic liberation is justified for the benefit of their children and the welfare of the whole family.

Moreover, development-oriented seminars, workshops, and adult education foster woman's ability to manage the home or any responsibility in society. These required payments and issues of income and expenditure planning need an educated and liberated mind.

Most importantly, it is through economic empowerment that the united war against poverty, disease and ignorance will be fought and won. The woman is the most unfortunate victim of these three threats. Notably, women constitute the majority of the poor population in Mbarara and the rest of the world.

In all, African development will depend on the concern of each and every person, irrespective of sex. States and countries of Africa have to unite to fight poverty and respect the rights of every individual in order to overcome the challenges of its time. Unity is strength. "Together we stand, disunited we fall," so is the saying.[114]

3.3.3 Political Reasons

Experience has shown that women can be good leaders, and some women even excel. This fact accrues especially from their God-given gift of integrating motherly care with leadership; their intuitive power helps them to understand and influence people. In Mbarara, most female leaders are doing very well. In the political arena, some of these women even defeated their male contestants in the parliamentary elections of 1998, 2006 and 2013. Through campaigns and consequent rallies, women have irreversibly portrayed the capability to lead. Thus, freeing women from political bondage is both a right and profitable venture.

Unfortunately, out of the 386 members of the Parliament of Uganda, only 135 are female, which represents 34.97 percent.[115] Although this can be seen as a significant improvement compared to previous parliaments, the gap between female and male representation in Uganda remains big. The Ugandan parliament continues to be key to policy-making, legislation and an arm that influences the development of the country. The few numbers in parliament and consequently in other areas of leadership pose a major stumbling block for women to participate in their liberation.

When politically liberated, women will be able to exercise their electoral right entirely, hence influencing policy-making that is in favor of their liberation. Women's freedom, then, does away with the deprivation of a legislative right.

More to that, women have developmental insights and ideas as deduced from the minutes of their meetings and the projects they carry out on the ground. During research, some of these minutes were accessed. They have also lived experiences; therefore, they know what their real wants and needs are at the right time. This self-awareness is indispensable for the development of any society.

114 A common English saying when stressing the importance of unity.
115 http://www.ec.or.ug/, accessed on 29th April 2014 at 18:55.

Uganda has had an unstable political climate since independence 1962. Many enlightened people believe that women's involvement can bring about fundamental change. Already, an outstanding female figure Hon Rebecca Kadaga, the speaker of parliament, is top of the list, shouldering the impeachment of corrupt ministers and officials and fighting corruption in Uganda. Women's liberation is, therefore, justified for the benefit of the nation.

As already shown above, the Ugandan constitution of 1995 considers all Ugandans equal before the law. It respects human rights and forcefully brings forth the equal dignity of women and men. Article 33, clause two states; "the state shall protect women and their rights taking into account their unique status and natural maternal functions in society".[116] Hence, it justifies the liberation of a woman.

Finally, most women have been deprived of their legal status for a long time. Woman have been playing a mediating role between the father and children, family and society but never recognized. Politically liberated women shall contribute to the growth and development of the whole human family while themselves celebrating the joys and pains of humanity.

3.3.4 Humanitarian Reasons

This term 'humanitarian' is concerned with or directed towards improving the lives of people and reducing suffering. It calls for recognizing the other being as having the right to live and the state of being human. Being human means having or showing sympathy, kindness and understanding to each other as people. Women are people as men are, and there is no justified reason for one human being to suffer at the hands of another. Everyone has the right to live peacefully and in communion with others.

Women's liberation is indeed justified on the humanitarian ground. It is a re-awakening of what it means to be human. It is an awareness that humanity has a spiritual center that elevates men and women above everything else on earth and disqualifies any attempt to dominate each other.[117]

---

116 Uganda: *Constitution of the Republic of Uganda*, Kampala, 1995.

117 James A.J, *Classical Philosophical Questions*, 4th Ed., Charles E. Mern Publications Co., Ohio, 1982, p. 537.

In reality, man and woman are the same in their diversity. The stress should be on the essential sameness of male and female although there are biological and physical or natural differences. Falling into unnecessary overemphasis of natural differences is trivial. One admits there are psychosomatic differences but not a major biological dissimilarity.[118] The emphasis is on common humanity.

More to that, the 1948 universal declaration of human rights stresses the equality of sexes, hence a need to respect each other.[119] Notably, male domination and sexual subordination are not necessarily conditions of human societies but a cultural product. This is a time to change for the better.

Finally, being human is living and co-existing with other humans so that the human family attains happiness, growth, and development. Women's emancipation always aims and strengthens this. This has nothing to do religious dogmas but with humanity as humanity.

3.3.5 Demographic Reasons

In terms of numbers, women are a majority in Uganda. Uganda has a population of over 34.4 million people.[120] Though current censuses seem to be inaccurate, the percentage of females is higher than males. Therefore, this implies that enslaving the majority of the society incapacitates the development of the country. Thus, society is deprived of the gifts, insights and accomplishments of more than half of its members.

Naturally, women are generation bearers. Within the African setting, they produce the generation and nurture it. One can say, show me the women and I will tell you the type of the society you have. Demographically, they are significant. If liberated, women are capable of bringing about high-quality generations.

Women play a prominent role in the upbringing of children, and the younger generation is the basis of the society. This too will enable women to curb the current trend of moral degeneration among the youth but also

---

118 Ibid., p. 537–38.

119 http://www.un.org/en/documents/: *The Universal Declaration of Human Rights* accessed on 23rd July 2014 at 23:09.

120 *The New Vision*, Uganda's leading Paper, vol. 7th October 2011, p. 1.

among adults in the community. This, of course, requires co-operation between men and women.

3.4 Implications and a Personal Critique

Women's liberation is more than an appeal. Freedom from social, economic, political, cultural, religious as well as psychological chains is necessary and urgent. It is the great challenge of the present age. Liberation is addressed to every member of the human family to retreat and surrender, if needed, all the instruments that hitherto have played a vast role in the oppression of women. But above all, a genuine and full liberation is required.

More to that, everything has its own time. Change is a fact of life. There has been a time of oppressing and enslaving the women, now is the time to liberate them. However, this is not to be overstretched lest we risk another extreme situation where men also cry out for liberation.

Today, we still have dedicated women like those of the gospels that make up the body of Christ, the church. Women continue to be the majority of the helpers of Christ's messengers, such as priests and catechists, in the transmission of His gospel. This implies that women should emulate their "foremothers" despite the ups and downs encountered.

Though women's contribution has often been underestimated from the salvation history, the time is now ripe to re-write it in the theological theses or books of our time. The real grief has been exposed, which implies that an urgent act for "liberation implies bravado and also the notion that laws can be legitimately challenged ... also liberation implies that pain that cannot be shared is pain that cannot be healed".[121] Hence, it is not a surprise that some liberated men join this noble cause.

Despite all difficulties and wrong situations, it is worth noting that some women have emerged winners, especially in the Church. There are many female saints such as Catherine of Sienna, Joan of Arc and Theresa of Liseaux. In modern times, there are also many great women such as Mother Teresa of Calcutta. Women today should dare too, to bring about their liberation.

---

121 John F. Cragham, Esther: "A Fully Liberated Woman", in *The Bible Today*, Vol. 24, No. 1, January 1986, p. 7–8.

In conclusion, women's struggle implies a sincere claim of rights and dignity. There is no justified reason why women should be denied their rightful place. The project of women's liberation is a demonstration and a march until full and genuine emancipation is attained not only by women but by the whole human race.

Chapter Four: The Reality and Impact of Women's Emancipation So Far

4.0 Introduction

Uganda has made some big achievements towards the emancipation of women and their empowerment. Indeed, as the 2007 Ugandan gender policy points out, key positive milestones and gaps can be highlighted in the sectors of governance, health, economy and social formation. Women's emancipation program has been hailed as a success in many African countries and in international entities.

The project identifies these achievements singly and analyzes them critically. It also identifies the challenges that have been faced and the means that have been engaged to tackle them. In short, the reality on the ground has been evaluated using balanced and unbiased spectacles. Nevertheless, the emphasis or the main focus was mainly on the achievements rather than on the failures.

However, these achievements remain under scrutiny. Both qualitative and quantitative achievements have been evaluated. What the project discusses in this chapter is what it has found in the real lives of women and men, and the reality of this big venture in the sector of human rights.

4.1 The Research Question

The central question of the project examined in this chapter is: To what extent has women's liberation become a reality? What effects does it have on the life of an ordinary woman? How has it been a reality rather than an illusion?

Participatory action research (PAR) was employed to answer the central question. Twenty-five participatory focus groups and thirty-nine interviews with women aged between fifteen and forty-five were conducted with three women's groups across the western region of Uganda. These focus groups consisted of different categories of women, namely wives, mothers, widows, single women, female leaders, religious women and girls. The education levels of these women, their positions in society and their age were also put into consideration. It is assumed in this project that these women contributed to this project according to their different capacities.

Additionally, seven interviews were conducted with experts in the field of gender and women's empowerment specifically within the Ugandan context and additional data was obtained through the study of literature and observations. All these showed the reality of a woman's life in her daily life. The literary sources and oral interviews aimed at tracing women's status in Uganda.

Therefore, in this chapter the project aims at finding out the impact of women's liberation and the advancement of gender equality mainstreaming, and the empowerment of women in the entire Ugandan society by citing the example of western Uganda. The project presupposed that a lot has been done, and there has been a gender sensitive and responsive development in Uganda. But in reality, it has been found that there has been little progress and the desired impact on women's rights and needs has not been achieved. To prove this some indicators were employed. These helped in the research findings.

4.2 Indicators

An indicator is a single figure that summarizes a large amount of information while providing an indication of change over time, often the amount of progress toward a specific goal. Unlike mere descriptive statistics, indicators involve and employ comparisons to a norm or baseline in their interpretation.[122] Thus, it is crucial for this project to employ measurable indicators to determine the extent of gender equality. These measurable indicators should also be contextual and feasible.

Also, indicators can be quantitative or qualitative, a distinction based on information type, use, and interpretation.[123] All the indicators are essential

---

122 Moser A., *Gender and Indicators: Overview Report*. London, England: UNDP. http://www.bridge.ids.ac.uk/reports/IndicatorsORfinal.pdf.Morse, Stephen, and Ernest Tollner. 2007. "Development Indicators and Indices." Accessed on 7th June 2014 at 20:00.

123 Beck, T., *Using Gender-Sensitive Indicators: A Reference Manual for Governments and Other Stakeholders*. London, England: Commonwealth Secretariat. CIDA (Canadian International Development Agency). 1997–1999.

when analyzing a problem, but the project limited itself to the relevant indicators that are contextual to the Ugandan setting. The society of the Banyankole can comfortably represent the whole of western Uganda.

Four direct indicators of gender equality and the women's empowerment program were therefore employed and analyzed in this chapter. These are: governance imbued in a legal and political framework; social formation and participation dealing with education; economic distribution and health, i.e. welfare. This project identified and evaluated these gender-sensitive but also compliant indicators.

Moreover, these indicators were real concerns for many Ugandans during the most turbulent and darkest years in their country's history. That is why these concerns were identified during the process of drafting the 1995 Ugandan constitution. The then legislators argued that the gender equality was real and was defined in these four areas. Therefore, this project's concern was already a concern of a gender-sensitive drafting constitution process. However, these indicators were not only seen in reference to women as women but as citizens of Uganda. This draft constitution naturally meant both men and women, although women here were to be put in special consideration because they were the less advantaged in society.

Further, it is important to note that the indicators or pointers influence one another. They are not mutually exclusive. They are not independent from each other; they are only different sometimes in contextual understanding. This project examines the role each indicator plays in impacting women.

Governance or the political and legal framework will be considered first because it affects decision-making in society. Without decision-making mandate or good decision-making, the country cannot develop. The other indicators, namely social formation or education, economic distribution, health and family have been dealt with analytically because these are areas where women are affected most. The results showed how influential the political, cultural, social and religious structures have favored men more than women in this region. This, too, shows how they have inhibited the ability for both men and women to take actions towards empowerment.

4.2.1 Governance – The Existing Political and Legal Reality

The first indicator is governance. In recent years, Uganda has had a legal and political transformation. A lot has been done across the political spectrum but also across the legal framework to improve women's situation. Uganda has made some significant achievements towards equality and the empowerment of women. Indeed, as the gender policy of 2007 points out, key milestones and gaps can be highlighted in different sectors of society.[124]

This research examines how efficient and proactive this transformation has been for the betterment of women. Almost all women who responded during interviews pointed out that political involvement was key to their emancipation. Many members of parliament were proud to do so and gave this as real emancipation. "We are now at the real source of making, our voice is heard ... we are part of the decision-making process," said a female MP in Mbarara.[125]

Decision making was always the catchphrase in the words of many women who were interviewed. "We are able to steer our country in the right direction," said the Local Council three (LIII) female chairperson during interviews.[126] Although many women did not contribute directly to decision-making or policy-making, they do believe that they have a voice. They believed that they were well represented by their members of parliament or councilors, but especially by female representatives who understand their "problems better than anybody else"[127].

They also believed that this was a good representation of people who supported the emancipation of women and other underprivileged groups. This was hailed by many human rights activists. The fact that the new climate also allowed constitutional reforms and affirmative action became a springboard for women to be part of governance. This was seen as a political breakthrough by many women. In the following, we examine this achievement.

---

124 Ministry of Gender, *Labour and Social Development, The National Action Plan on Women*, Kampala, Uganda, 1999.

125 Emma Boona, 54, Woman Member of Parliament, Kampala, 2nd June 2014.

126 L111 women chairperson Kyabugimbe, 61, interviewed on 13th June 2014.

127 John Byabagambi, Medical doctor, 48, Community officer, Mbarara, Interviewed on 14th June 2014.

4.2.1.1 Political Breakthrough

On the National level, a lot has been achieved. There has been a female vice president in Uganda (the first across the entirety of Africa), who took office in 1994. There has been a constitutional mandate that states that one-third of political representatives must be women.[128] Although many see these achievements as having little effect, the project views these steps as significant. There is a view that the political steps have had little effect on the day-to-day lives of women in the western region, as a female lawyer pointed out during an interview with a group of experts.[129] This will be dealt with in the subsequent chapters.

Undoubtedly, women in Uganda today have the same rights to vote and stand for election as men. Citing the example of the 2011 elections, there were 23 female ministers in the President's 75-member cabinet. The big positions in the government such as the speaker of the National Assembly and the Inspector of Government (commonly known as IGG), who headed the leading government anti-corruption investigative body, were women. There were 135 women in the 386-member National Assembly. The law of Uganda required elections for seats reserved for special interest groups: 112 for women, five for organized labor, five for persons with disabilities and five for youth.

On the regional level, more women than ever before are in political and leadership positions. In the western part of Uganda, which comprises nine districts, a quantifiable effect is seen. For the first time, the number of female members of parliament, councilors, and women in positions of leadership has grown.

Not only that, female politicians have come to the political center stage, the most prominent of whom is engineer Winnie Byanyima, who holds now an international office. Engineer Winnie Byanyima doubled as a member of parliament representing Mbarara Municipality from 1994 until 2004.[130] She was the first ever woman to defeat a male candidate in the history of Mbarara district. She later served as the director of the gender team in the

128 Tripp, A. M., The politics of autonomy and cooptation in Africa: The case for the Ugandan women's movement. *The Journal of Modern African Studies, 39*, 2001, p. 101–28.

129 Busingye, B, 51, female, lawyer, Kampala, interviewed on 4th June 2014.

130 Winnie, op.cit., p. 17.

Bureau for Development Policy at the United Nations Development Programme (UNDP) from 2006, and in May 2013 she was appointed Executive Director of Oxfam International.[131] Another example is Hon. Miria Matembe who is a renowned lawyer and women's activist. She represented women for many years and was a minister of ethics and integrity. For many women, these two and many other women holding positions of influence are personalities that encourage them in their own emancipation.

However, in some key areas women lacked representation. For example, within the ministry of local government (MoLG),[132] there were only 42 women compared to 103 men, who were in most cases their bosses. Looking further at the specific MoLG units, the local government district inspection department demonstrates the highest gender imbalance, with men represented six times more than women. Conversely, both the directorate of local government and the policy analysis unit are not fully gender-balanced. This has nothing to do with qualifications; 59.4 percent of all the people attaining a diploma and graduate level of qualification are women. This means women make up only a small fraction of those achieving a middle management salary of 20 percent.[133]

Secondly, almost throughout all interviews, it was noticed that the zeal of emancipation seems to be dying out. Some women feel they got a raw deal, and that only a few women in Uganda have benefited from this struggle. The beneficiaries of this transformation seem to be women who are an elite class.[134] Rural women especially in remote areas continue to live a life of utter poverty and oppression from their husbands or other men and there is worse abuse than before. This was due to the rights that were accorded them and the lack of structure or follow up to at least enforce them.

---

131 http://www.oxfamblogs.org/eastafrica/=5641 accessed on 30th June 2013 at 10:06.

132 Ministry of Local government (MoLG) statistics at http://www.wikigender.org/index.php/Gender_Statistics_in_Uganda, accessed on 30th June 2013 at 10:13.

133 Ibid.

134 Kyarikunda R, 43, Housewife, Interview at Mushanga on 1st June 2014.

4.2.1.2 *The Legal Framework*

In terms of legislation, a lot has been done to tackle injustices against women and girls in Uganda. Uganda's past three constitutions in 1962, 1966 and 1967 all carried bills of human rights and fundamental freedoms. The bills focused on civil and political rights and fundamental freedoms like the right to life, personal liberty, individual property and other fundamental freedoms like freedom of movement, expression association and assembly. However, the constitutions did not capture the equality of gender in enjoying civil, political, social and economic and cultural rights. The most disadvantaged were women. Women constitute the largest single social group, comprising 51 percent of Uganda's population according to the 2002 census.[135]

Uganda's Constitution of 1995 provided equality between men and women and affirmative action where such equality did not exist. Prior to this constitution, there were hardly any policies that focused on the advancement of gender and the empowerment of women. Although there were legislations in line with gender, none of these laws was gender compliant and yet no government at the time made attempts to mend them. Good examples include the Divorce Act of 1904, the Succession Act of 1906 and the Marriage Act of 1970.

The 1995 Constitution was then itself a breakthrough. It was and is in line with Uganda's commitments under the Convention on the Elimination of All Forms of Discrimination against Women, which Uganda ratified in 1985 without any reservations, as well as with other international obligations on gender equality.[136] From the gender perspective, the Constitution of the Republic of Uganda is hailed as being one of the most gender-sensitive constitutions in Africa.[137] Below are the reasons for this.

a) The 1995 Constitution of Uganda

Uganda's Constitution of 1995 provides equality treatment in all spheres of life under the law and respect between men and women. Various articles

---

135 Uganda Bureau of Statistics, Uganda Demographic Health Survey, 2011.

136 Uganda: *Constitution of the Republic of Uganda*, Kampala, 1995.

137 Mushemeza E. Dickens, "Contribution of Women in Influencing Legislation and Policy Formulation and Implementation in Uganda (1995–2005)", a paper presented at Bishop Stuart University, September 2010.

and sections of Uganda's constitution ban sex discrimination, guarantee gender equality, and mandate affirmative action in favor of women and girls who have been marginalized because of their gender.

The following sections of this constitution are worth mentioning. Uganda's constitution affirms that "... a person shall not be discriminated against on the ground of sex...."[138].

Article 31 clause 1 entitles women and men to equal rights during and after marriage. Equal rights in marriage clearly articulates the need for a couple's respect for one another and their children. Marriage as an institution is key to the emancipation of women in Uganda.

The constitution further mandates that the state to take affirmative action in favor of groups marginalized on the basis of gender ... for the purpose of redressing imbalances that exist against them.[139]

Moreover, the constitution provides that women shall be accorded full and equal dignity of the person with men. And the state shall provide the facilities and opportunities necessary to enhance the welfare of women to enable them to realize their full potential and advancement.

As part of the duty of the state to protect and give security to its citizens, the legal framework of Uganda continues to reassure women of their safety. It says that the state shall protect women and their rights, taking into account their unique status and natural maternal functions in society. And importantly, the women shall have the right to equal treatment with men ... rights shall include equal opportunities in political, economic and social activities.[140]

To address the issue of imbalance the legal framework had foreseen and it was stated: Women shall have the right to affirmative action for the purpose of redressing the imbalances created by history, tradition, and custom.[141] As a result of affirmative action, the Ugandan parliament is already composed of 35.2 percent women and at the local level government, women constitute 30 percent of the positions. In the whole of Uganda, membership in

138 Uganda: *Constitution of the Republic of Uganda*, Kampala, 1995, Article 21 clause 2.
139 Ibid., Article 32, clause 1 p. 32.
140 Ibid., Article 32(1) p. 23.
141 Ibid., Article 32(1) p. 32.

parliament and governance in other sectors stands at 76 percent for men and 24 percent for women.[142]

However, a lot remains to be done. Concluding from the above statistics, leadership is still the preserve of men. This happens automatically because women are not socialized to play political roles, have limited and not highly valued skills. An example can be seen in developmental structures where the male to female ratio of chairpersons of governing district land boards stands at 96 percent to four percent, respectively.[143]

Another significant gender sensitive outcome of the deliberation of the 1995 constitution was that the prohibition of laws, cultures, customs or traditions that are against the dignity, welfare or interest of women or undermine their status is included in this constitution.[144]

Most importantly, it was vital that women were not only liberated but also recognized. Thus, the National Objectives and Directive Principles of State Policy affirmed that "The State shall recognize the significant role that women play in society."[145] Recognition is key to liberation and ignites the fire of the struggle further.

More to that, due to significant changes and constitutional reforms, women are represented at every political level in Uganda, from local government, where one in every three councilors is a woman, to the national parliament, also in western Uganda.

Apart from being eligible and able to compete equally with men to represent all the constituencies in parliament, a special seat (woman district member of parliament) has been reserved for women to represent each of the districts of Uganda. This affirmative action has increased the number of women in politics and in positions of decision-making.

The legal framework and the political setting have been a fertile ground for gender equality and empowerment in Uganda. The political will of some male politicians and leaders has also contributed to this transformation. It remains to be seen if this has had an effect on the day-to-day life of the majority of women. Many interviewees and experts believe that little has been achieved.

142 Mushemeza, op.cit., p. 131.
143 Ibid., 132.
144 Uganda Constitution, Art. 33.
145 National Objectives and Directive Principles of State Policy No. XV.

b) Policies and Bills

As a result of the gender-sensitive constitution of 1995, a political framework was established and in 1997 a national gender policy was published. This was crucial for gender mainstreaming and targeting measures that narrow the gender gap as critical for gender mainstreaming. To implement the political framework and to monitor the legal framework, an institutional framework for gender issues was also established. This is now called the Ministry of Gender, Labor, and Social Development.

The ministry has done some recognizable work on gender. For example, it prepared the national gender policy that was then approved by the cabinet in 1997. The overall goal of the gender policy is to mainstream gender concerns in the national development process to improve the social, legal, civic, political, economic, and cultural conditions of people in Uganda, particularly women.[146] It recognizes gender relations as a development concept, identifying and understanding the social roles and relations of women and men from all walks of life and how these impact on development.

The National Action Plan (1999/2000–2003/2004) identified four critical areas of concern for the government of Uganda. These were: poverty, income generation and economic empowerment; reproductive health and rights; legal framework and decision-making; and the girl child and education. These concerns are no different from the areas that are being treated as indicators in this chapter.

The 2007 gender policy points out that the Ministry of Gender, Labor, and Social Development has the overall responsibility for the issues of gender. It is charged with spearheading, coordinating and supervising gender-responsive development, and in particular ensuring improvement in the status of women.[147] It ensures that all the policies and bills that are in line with gender equality are implemented.

This national machinery is part of the government, and it provides policy guidelines on gender and gives technical support in gender mainstreaming to the stakeholders. It is also involved in the development of gender policies in other sectors, acting both as a catalyst and a facilitator or expert on gender

---

146 Mushemeza, op.cit., p. 179.

147 Ministry of Gender, Labor and Social Development, *The National Action Plan on Women*, 2007, Kampala: Uganda.

issues. The target groups include ministers, permanent secretaries, senior officials, members of district development planning committees.

As a policy, however, it needs implementation and good political and social will. Otherwise, it remains a good policy in the shelves without affecting people's livelihoods, especially women's. It should be translated into the lives of all citizens of Uganda. Thus, it should be understood even at the lowest level of Ugandan society. Unfortunately, a good cross-section of the Ugandan population remains largely ignorant of this policy.

4.2.1.3 Local Levels

Uganda is divided into administrative units called districts, "counties"[148] and sub counties. The sub-counties and districts have well outlined planning guides and systems. The planning guidelines emphasize a bottom-up approach to the soliciting of planning ideas and their prioritization. Gender inclusion in the local government planning and budgeting systems and processes happens through ensuring that the needs of all women and girls are included or incorporated into the village, parish, sub-county, and district plans. Emphasizing fair representation of women in the expanded planning meetings is a major area of concern for all members of the project team.

Uganda has a predominantly rural population, and many Ugandans seek justice at the local level. These are local tribunals and are state sponsored. The local council courts (LC courts) apply customary norms and provide regional fora for dispute or conflict resolution.[149] Five local government councils or levels exist in Uganda, running from the villages to the district or city level. Local council courts are established at the village level (LC1), to the parish level (LC2), and on to the sub-county level (LC3).[150] The courts only have jurisdiction over limited civil matters and petty criminal offenses.

---

148 Counties remain in many places but in the administrative structure, their numbers are dwindling.

149 During the guerrilla war of the early 1980s, the NRM formed locally elected, nine-person committees known as resistance councils (RCs) in the areas it controlled. The enactment of the Resistance Committees (Judicial Powers) Statute 1987 resulted in the administrative units being vested with judicial powers (now referred to as local council courts since the passing of the 1995 Constitution and the Local Government Act of 1997).

150 LC4 and LC5 are largely administrative.

They also deal with cases governed by customary law including property, intestate[151] inheritance, and marital disputes. There are close to four thousand LC Courts countrywide.[152] At all stages, the constitution and the 1997 Local Government Act require that one-third of the councilor positions be set aside for women. This is in addition to any women who gain seats by open competition.

a) Gender Offices at Local Levels

Under the 1993 National Women's Council Act, women's councils were established. The grassroots gender offices were formed. The ministry of gender was behind this establishment. These councils and structures are charged with the responsibility of fostering the social and economic development of women. However, as more than one respondent from various counties in Mbarara remarked during the research, "women's councils have only been used for political purposes rather than fostering economic development. Women's councils are used as mobilization tools for political campaigns"[153] These councils are composed of five women. They start at local council level one[154] to local council five (district level).

The chairpersons of the women's councils at level one and two become automatic members of local councils one and two respectively. However, when it comes to local councils three and upwards, the two structures are separated, and there is no relationship between them. Indeed, the women's council statute is not provided for in the Local Government Act and is hence not recognized as a structure by the local government. Therefore, women's boards do not receive funding or technical support from the local governments. Under the multiparty system, there have been calls to remove the women's councils.

Yet, local level participation and decision-making is key to national level involvement and decision-making. Thus, women's active participation in

151 Where a person dies without making a will.

152 Republic of Uganda, "*Summary of Background to the Budget 2001/02,* Uganda Poverty Reduction Strategy Paper Progress Report 2002," p. 43.

153 Meeting with council members at Mbarara town in April 2014.

154 This is a smallest government unit of administration also known as a village level, although this also applies to those units in towns.

their grassroots and national organizing are core to democracy in Uganda. They struggle for and give the nation their contribution, which Ugandans can rely on. Women's organizations continue to be the primary avenues through which women address day-to-day struggles on the family, social and political levels. Thereby, they provide social, cultural and economic services that the government or other non-government organizations cannot. Therefore, Ugandan women in their organizations demonstrate a dependable democracy and exercise themselves a process of democracy that Uganda would like to have.

During research, it was observed that some of these offices have remained as a name, they are no longer operational and some have been swallowed by other "traditional" offices.[155] It was found that they are heavily underfunded and because of corruption the little that they did receive has also been swindled.[156] Secondly, it was discovered that in many areas very few women are aware of this national action plan. Many women remain largely ignorant of the activities of these gender offices and in some cases it has been associated with power struggle.

The underfunding and sometimes lack of funds have left these offices by name. This has affected the gender national action plan. It was indeed a plan that was done without any financial considerations or monitoring and evaluation of this framework. As a result, women at the local levels remain largely ignorant of these national policies. Many respondents seemed to know of the existence of such offices and some were indeed elected to these offices, but they appeared to know nothing of their roles and job descriptions.

The research found that often these offices are located funds. These projects do not get enough prior preparation or enough time to enable gender responsiveness. Many of them are time-bound and target-oriented, which reduces the scope for sensitive gender works that often require a lot of time.

Men are often excluded and they distance themselves from women.[157] Without men, this emancipation of women remains an enormous challenge,

155 The word 'traditional' is used here to refer to the conventional offices, e.g. the social development office.

156 Women's leaders' forum meeting on 4th June 2014 in Mbarara.

157 The research found that many men see women's projects as exclusive and they have nothing to contribute to the family or the community. However, this assertion is not backed by facts.

especially in rural areas. A good example was a women's goat project. It was observed that women were given this project with an intention to boost women's economic independence and empowerment but also to look after their families. Unfortunately, men, who in most cases are the owners of land, never co-operated and at the end the women's goat-rearing project failed.[158]

Another challenge is that often a lot of project work is piecemeal and uncoordinated. These are often run by agencies and within communities where little gender sensitization has taken place. In most cases where awareness and understanding of gender inequality are low, it leads to poor results.

Yet another chilling fact was found in the implementation phase. Most women's offices focus on many things at the same time. This is sometimes too ambitious and can in itself be a weakness because the volume of work becomes enormous. Most offices were showing their action plans with so many things to be done but had no concrete actions.

It was also observed that some women were not themselves gender sensitive. In some cases, there were also traditional stereotype women in these offices; it is true that not all women are capable of enhancing the cause of their fellow women. It was observed that some women are even more conservative than men. This too was in many cases a weakness. Not every person working in the public sector has skills in gender analysis, and not everyone is able to identify gender issues and design appropriate interventions to address them. This problem is still faced by many gender offices.

Nevertheless, where the gender offices were still operational, they were very instrumental in gender sensitizing their communities. Where the gender policy plan is known and where able women implemented it, it has borne many fruits. They have somehow undertaken the project and there has been a considerable improvement in the lives of women.[159]

b) Community Based Organizations (CBOs)

Another key area where women have been able to organize themselves and show influence is through local organizations. The ability to unite and form

---

158 Women of Bushenyi, goat rearing project, 2010.

159 This was observed when the author visited a group of women at the district headquarters in Bushenyi on 1st June 2014.

groups help them to have one voice in order to make themselves heard. The research identified the presence of such organizations.

There has been a steady growth of both local and international Non-Governmental Organizations (NGOs) as well as community based organizations (CBOs) in Uganda recently. Many of these have played a critical role in ensuring that rural areas develop. They do that by developing programs that transform communities from miserable to humanly dignifying states. Many of these are directly or indirectly improving women's situation. A common characteristic that cuts across is that many of these are gender responsive and sensitive. In the interest of our project, we shall limit ourselves to those that are directly concerned with women.

4.2.1.4 National Level

It is vital to view women's efforts in a wider spectrum. Women cannot be successful as individual groups in their local level. Women's groups have to be in touch with many other organizations on the national level. The problem that affects a woman on the national level automatically affects her on the grassroots' level. As much as women need to get organized at the base level, they too need big organizations for support. Below are the contributions of some organizations and the challenges that affect women at the national level.

a) Non-Governmental Organizations (NGOs)

NGOs are numerous in Uganda and a big percentage of these have as their mandate or at least part of it to promote gender equality. NGOs are legally constituted organizations that are created by natural or legal persons that operate independently from any government. Essentially, NGOs are organizations that are not based in a government and not created to earn a profit.[160]

Against this background, a few NGOs were considered by this project. This was only intended to assess the impact they have had on women's emancipation since the age of emancipation in Uganda. One of the NGOs directly involved in gender equality is the Federation of Female Lawyers (FIDA). FIDA has played a crucial role in the promotion of women's rights by offering a voice and free legal services to women. FIDA does this on

160 Global Education 2001.

the national and regional levels as well as on the international level (FIDA 2009).[161]

Another good example is the Women's Organization Network for Human Rights Advocacy (WONETHA), which defends women against discrimination, harassment and abuse. Legally formed in 2008,[162] WONETHA has been working to improve the health, social and economic well-being of adult sex workers in Uganda. WONETHA values and respects the rights of sex workers who want to exit, and prepares them to start new livelihood by building skills in leadership, economic empowerment, personal development and entrepreneurship. Importantly, WONETHA provides information on HIV and AIDS, and sexual and reproductive health and rights.

By helping to empower women, NGOs have, in a way, contributed to liberating women and accelerating development faster than ever. Women are now engaged in micro-finance projects to support their families effectively and these organizations have helped to transform men into responsible citizens – in as far as family care is concerned. Important areas have also been supported, such as agriculture, where women remain many, and the health sector.

i) Agriculture Sector

In the area of agriculture, a lot has been done. Agriculture is the backbone of Uganda's economy, and women constitute 80 percent of the workforce. Many organizations have channeled resources to it, for example, the National Agricultural Research Organization (NARO). NARO gives guidance and coordinates all agricultural research activities. Many other NGOs like the Hunger Project and Heifer International have come up with agricultural programs that aim to fight food insecurity. These two NGOs operate in most districts of western Uganda. They provide trainings or awareness programs for sustainable livelihoods and give agricultural aid to farmers to kick-start actual farming practices.

NGOs employ many women since they are in most cases not gender biased. This was attested to by an interviewee who was employed by an NGO and she managed to finance her further studies at university. She further

161 FIDA-http://www.fidauganda.org/ accessed on 23rd July 2014 at 23:17.
162 Company Limited by Guarantee No. 114161.

said that she was not an isolated case since she was employed alongside many other women[163].

With these services, NGOs have evidently reduced poverty, and may have improved food security and nutrition and achieved positive social change as well.[164] The economic indicator as a factor of gender balance will be discussed under economic reality.

ii) Improvement in the Health Sector

Some NGOs in western Uganda have significantly contributed to the health sector in the fight against HIV/AIDS and other sex-related diseases, malaria, TB and reproduction-related complications. Such organizations include The AIDS Support Organization (TASO), and The Elizabeth Glaser Foundation. These NGOs not only conduct counseling and HIV testing, but also empower affected communities with vital health information for prevention and survival. They have networking bodies through which they pool resources to increase the effectiveness of the management of health programs.

They have also contributed to the improvement in water access and sanitation. NGOs develop programs like borehole construction, community cleaning, and microfinance schemes aimed at improving housing conditions and providing access to clean water in areas with the most need of them.

iii) The Challenges of NGOs vis-à-vis CBOs

Most of these NGOs have been criticized for their lack of impact and for being profit-oriented rather than genuine service providers. The high cost of administration makes it hard for organizations to survive. It was found that there was lack of harmony within NGOs. They fail to represent the same virtues they preach when the internal administration is marred by crises. The cause of the crises is normally the struggle for positions that reap enormous rewards. NGOs and CBOs tend to have weak coordination mechanisms, small membership bases, and are dominated by strong personalities. And once funds begin to trickle in, misunderstandings break up even

---

163 Lydia Bakecura, 35, Natural resource researcher, Enschede, Netherlands, 26th July 2014.

164 Zeller, M., Sharma, M., Ahmed, A., & Rashid, S. 2001 cited in "*Role of NGOS in Rural Areas*" by Kigenyi Asifu, Nov. 2011.

more – leading to organization disrepute. Similarly, the mismanagement of funds in mainly smaller organizations threatens the good reputation of NGOs generally[165].

Also, a mentality of over-dependence rather than one of interdependence disables the creative minds of organizations. When projects are either phased out or are no longer of interest to funders, they close easily – a situation that affects beneficiaries fatally. Donor dependency has been cited as a chronic problem that continually compromises CBOs and makes them vulnerable

b) Positive Implications

NGOs of any level or discipline do impact the lives of communities positively. Non-governmental organizations, by the virtue of being small-scale, flexible, innovative and participatory, are more successful in reaching the poor and in alleviating poverty than any other group. Their work, like social mobilization, is a continuous process aimed at changing the minds, attitudes and behaviors of the people to involve in any development process. That, though, has been undermined by some selfish-driven people or groups.

c) Negative Implications

The vast number of NGOs indicates, on the one hand, that the current system of democracy is working to the extent that it makes private organizing possible. But on the other, it means that the Ugandan government is unable to meet its obligations to citizens. NGOs also overshadow women's contributions, particularly at the local level.[166] Most women's organizations at the local level are not registered with the government and are thus not seen as organizations doing fundamental work.

When NGOs collaborate with women at the local level, they project themselves as "rescuers" of women from poverty. This overshadows local women's initiatives, accomplishments, and visions. For example, more often than not, one will find that the government is more concerned about creating a secure environment for the functionality of NGOs than it is about creating more inclusive and efficient policies that would open doors to all

165 Uganda Project Performance Evaluation Report, Kampala, 2001.
166 Tamale, *Women Hens Begin to Crow*, op.cit., p. 4.

citizens' participation – politically, socially and economically. This does not help us build a dependable democracy. Having a reliable democracy that acknowledges women's work at all levels would give all Ugandans assurance and protection of their needs and rights as citizens.

4.2.1.5 Popular Media

In a civilized society media is a vital arm. It puts checks and balances on the government in its own way. It entertains and teaches, it informs and educates. The popular media in Uganda, however, has remained at the level of looking at women as sexual objects. Most tabloids in Uganda remain on the level of objectifying women and portraying them as "meant" for sex.

Furthermore, much of the popular media often maintains a sexist discourse and line by portraying female politicians or leaders as belligerent, incompetent upstarts whose political work is trivial compared with the details of their personal lives.[167] When a story about a female politician comes out, it spreads like wildfire, whereas the same story about a fellow male politician may not be seen as very attractive. For example, at a demonstration against rape, former politician and activist Matembe remarked that rapists' "potentially dangerous instruments [... should] be taken away if not used properly". This statement about the castration of the defilers sparked widespread outrage in the press and among other politicians, while few articles or comments appeared condemning rape or reporting the message of the demonstration against this ill. Because of the limits of 'acceptable' political discourse, many of her female colleagues who agreed with her refused to say so in public.[168]

Recently, the culture of men selling nude photographs of women (their girlfriends) has been growing in the media. The widespread condemnation of such primitive and disrespectful attitudes has not been handled well by the security agencies. This too has shown how the popular media has not been instrumental in the liberation of women. Female leaders and politicians have been a target of these media houses intending to show how weak female leaders can be.

167 Tamale, *Women Hens Begin to Crow*, op.cit., p. 185–187.
168 Ibid., p. 185–187.

4.2.1.6 *Critique of Governance as an Indicator*

Despite Uganda's constitution governance and progress, much key legislation and formulation in Uganda is inconsistent with gender equality. A good example of legislation that is not implemented properly is the Domestic Violence Act, passed in 2009.[169] Due to the Domestic Relations Bill having been on the shelf for half a century, the Domestic Violence Act is rendered useless as it needs women to have knowledge and specific rights that are established in the Domestic Relations Bill. Organizations like the Women's Rights Initiative (WORI) based in Mbarara fight for women's rights, but it is a long and slow process.

Secondly, the government has begun to create mechanisms to operationalize its international and constitutional obligations, including through the national gender policy and the national action plan for women. However, much remains to be done to take forward activities to implement gender equality in Uganda's legal framework. A crucial issue is the need to reform legislation that is unconstitutional because it discriminates on the basis of gender. The Domestic Relations Bill, currently before parliament, would go a long way to addressing many of these issues. Also, Uganda needs to enact legislation that would address critical social problems that affect gender relations and women's position in society and the home.

Enacting laws to implement Uganda's constitutional commitment to gender equality is not only essential for growth but also for stability. Some of the proposals or bills currently under consideration in parliament directly address women's ability to access economic assets, a key issue in the self-reliance of women. For example, Land Allocation Practices also need to be changed.

The legal and political framework has an essential role to play in determining women's access to vital economic resources, including land and property, and credit and other monetary resources. But legislative reform alone will not be sufficient. Something concrete has to be done. The law concerning land is not discriminatory, but it does not address the highly unequal allocation of land between men and women. It also does not address the issue of ongoing unjust inheritance and ownership practices that

---

169 Ellis, A. et al., *Gender and Economic Growth in Uganda*: op.cit., p. 17.

perpetuate this inequality. The central issue is not reforming the legislative structures, but changes in customary practice and attitudes.

It is not only Uganda's legal framework and inheritance and ownership practices that limit women's access to economic resources. Perhaps a more important issue is the fact that Uganda's population remains largely unaware of its legal rights or how to enforce them. This is especially true for women, who have even less access than men to legal advice and representation.[170]

The imbalance between men's and women's rights in Uganda goes beyond the legal emancipation of women. Complex social formation, cultural, and religious issues are at work. This leads to the second indicator of the impact of the emancipation of women.

4.2.2 The Social Formation: The Cultural and Religious Reality

There has been a societal transformation in Uganda. After the takeover of the Museveni regime that ushered in the age of emancipation, a lot has been done. With programs of *mchaka-mchaka*,[171] where there was politicization, the introduction of local courts and local security defense units, the introduction of universal Primary Education (UPE) and other societal structural adjustments, Ugandan society seemed to have taken another direction. There was sanity among the once-traumatized society. The society itself was able to come to terms with its past and face its present squarely. Each citizen identified himself or herself as a Ugandan.

Women too were seen as part of this society. Many women took it for themselves to better their lives, to improve their home situations and develop their communities. This was the fruit of the sanity that was ushered in. This led to the stability and development of many communities in Uganda. The mentalities started changing. How the attitudes changed is not without challenges. The question of culture plays a significant role in people's lives. Where culture remained unchanged, there has always been many hurdles

170 Ellis, A. et al., *Gender and Economic Growth in Uganda,* p. 33.

171 *Mchaka-mchaka* refers to an political and military awareness program introduced by the NRM government when it took power.

with modernity. Modernity seemed not to rhyme with many cultural practices and principles in Africa. These affect the social formation.

The project assessed this phenomenon that seemed inconsistent with women's emancipation despite much effort that has been invested. Avoiding this fact is evading reality on the Ugandan scene. The culture and traditions affect how people react to situations, and the success of any government program has always been dependent on these factors.

4.2.2.1 Strong Cultural Principles

Uganda, like any other African country, is gifted with different ethnic groups with a diversity of languages, cultures, and traditions. As already seen in previous chapters, the main ethnic group in southern Uganda is the Bantu. It comprises eight percent of the population,[172] and it is second largest of the major ethnic groups.

Banyankole is a sub-ethnic group of Bantu. The Bantu, like many other groups across Africa, have long-held traditions, taboos and strong principles regarding gender, sex, and sexuality. This fact affects how people in this region think and behave, how they live and build their lives. Although there has been a big influence of modernity and Christianity, some people still relate to the traditional culture. This is mainly noticeable in the teachings of the African Traditional Religions (ATRs) and other cultural practices. The believers of ATRs firmly believe that physical and spiritual life is a continuum, for which the realities of spiritual and material are not mutually exclusive but merge into one another.[173]

Furthermore, ATRs hail a powerful creator who is most evident in awesome forces such as the sun, moon, stars, thunder and lightning. This powerful creator can become angry if not satisfied with one's behavior, and he controls every aspect of life.[174] John Samuel Mbiti, an African theologian, states that African Traditional Religions permeate all aspects of life. And because of this there is no distinction between the sacred and the secular,

---

172 Otiso, M, K., *Culture and Customs of Uganda.* Greenwood Press, London, 2006, p. 3.

173 Ibid., p. 89.

174 Ibid., p. 86.

between the spiritual and the material areas life.[175] This begins already in childhood and grows with the whole person.

To locate the place of women among the Banyankole, the project made effort to understand today's social strata and formation that still dominates the lives of many women and men. The situation of women today can be understood in the context of these strong cultural principles passed on through early childhood formation and education.

4.2.2.2 Early Childhood Preparation and Education

The formative years of a child are probably the most influential factor on gender structure among the Banyankole but also among most of the African tribes. It is also true concerning the childhood psychosocial development, which stresses that what a child goes through or learns affects the rest of his or her life.

a) Early Childhood

Already at birth, the initiation practices surrounding the child implant a long-lasting effect. This stage has, of course, nothing to do with the differences in class or economic standing. The birth of a child is often surrounded with initiation practices, be it in a religious, traditional or even medical sense. From their day of birth or even before, at the moment the mother is aware of the conception, a child is confronted with the world – a world full of signs and symbols. These are often expressed differently depending on beliefs, faiths and confessions. The longest-impacting are those with cultural intonation, for example, the naming of a child. The initiation practices, such as naming the child, already demarcate a very clear boundary between sexes, sexuality and mentality.

Among the Banyankole, for example, a child is named according to situation and not according to a particular family. Although some people nowadays try to copy the practice from other societies, it was found that many end up having three names: a Christian name, a "real name" and a family name. According to interviews, a family name is "very unpractical"

---

175 Mbiti, S. J., *African Religions and Philosophy*, Heinemann publications, 2nd Edition, Nairobi, 1970, p. 2.

in a society where many children are treasured. This brings about confusion, not only in the school but also at home and among relatives. Christian names remain very foreign, as many do not have Runyankole translations or even an equivalent in the Runyankole language.

More to that, activists believe that a name donates a person, it encompasses the whole character of an individual. Every child born is unique. Many also believed that a name means a unique character. Kinyankole philosophy holds that every person is unique and that two people will never share the same character even when they happen to be identical twins. And from experience, many think that a name forms or destroys someone's character. "*Eiziina ribi ryiinaaza mukama waaryo.*"[176]

But the problem here is that many names are highly gender biased. With modernization, the trend seems to be changing but it is still highly visible. During interviews, for those who live in rural areas this was clear. "A girl should not be given a boy's name because it will affect her in future", said one village leader.[177] Examples include when a child is born during a good time of peace, around things that bring about peace, the name would most likely relate to peace: if the child was a girl she would be named *Kobusingye* and the boy would be *Busingye*. *Kobusingye* is a diminutive form of peace, a small person for peace. The boy receives a full name meaning peace. The gender bias already is in the name. Whether this affects the character of a person remains an issue for psychologists, but the Kinyankole philosophy already gives the background.

b) Informal Education

The upbringing of a child is taken seriously among the Banyankole and the family, which plays a significant role, is the child's first school. This is commonly known as informal education. At this level of education, the mother is the first teacher and in most cases she dominates the life of the early years of the child. As such, female parents are directly responsible for instilling

176 A proverb in Runyankole also shared by Bakiga stresses the need to have a good reputation which should be selfishly protected. But it is also meant in the literal sense of having a bad name.

177 Ahokukiriire D. (Kakunkuna), 68, peasant, Local Council 1 Chairperson, Rubindi B, interviewed 20th May 2014.

behavior, and the male parents directly implement them. The mother introduces the constitution of life, and the father "polices" or enforces it.

Again here, the roles of the future women are clearly outlined and expected behavior is emphasized. Concerning the boys, they will be formed to suit the expected masculine character. Usually, this would be emphasized by his father as his role model. It is important to note that already at this stage, the woman's position and role are clearly articulated in word and action. This is very true in rural as well as urban areas in Uganda.

At this level of upbringing, other family members are also involved. These include paternal aunts charged with tutoring girls in their specific gender roles. This too is in decline due to migration and other factors that have changed society. The major role is for girls to remain feminine, which means they have a certain way of sitting or walking, respect elders, cook and conduct themselves as women at all times.[178] These are useful markers for the expected behavior of young women in the Ugandan context. During interviews, women confirmed that this is still the case in many homes.

However, there has been a change of application. There has been an increase in hired or "professional" aunts – *shwenkazi* or *ishenkazi* – who in most cases take over before marriage to regulate "the ignorance of the educated". Meeting women at Nyarutuntu in Bushenyi and Mbarara Catholic social center shed much light on this issue. These professional aunts do not help girls to gain their esteem, but rather they indoctrinate them to the patriarchal mindset.

But in all, the project found that there is still much influence on the conduct of girls while still young. This is mainly from the whole societal set up. The same happens to male children.

c) Formal Education

The next stage of child growth among the Banyankole is the formal education. However, the two phases are not mutually exclusive. The formal stage continues as long as a child is under her parents and relatives. Therefore, the formation of the child remains the shared responsibility of parents and teachers under normal circumstances.

---

178 Tamale, S. "*Eroticism, Sensuality and 'Women's Secrets' Among the Baganda*" in IDS Bulletin Volume 37 no. 5. 2006, p. 89–97.

The Ugandan system of education is termed as 7-4-2-3, i.e. seven years of primary, four years of secondary, and two years of high school and three years of the tertiary or university level. This system of education is British based, although there have been many adjustments to fit the African context.

There is an enormous difference between schools in rural areas and the schools in urban areas. While the schools in urban areas seem to be well equipped, the schools in rural areas are largely poorly equipped. Many essential requirements are lacking, including electricity, clean water, classrooms and scholastic materials. Also, a big difference was observed that religious-based schools and privately-owned schools seemed to be better in many aspects compared to government-owned schools. There is, of course, a considerable number of reasons for this. Although the school curriculum is the same for all schools, the implementation differs considerably. Whether these variations affect gender remain a question of research.

In any case, formal education is the continuation of the formation already begun at home, especially in the area of morals. The implementation of patriarchal attitudes is ingrained in the minds of a child already at this stage, and new ideas of modernity are further nurtured. The boy or the girl finds yet another new form of identification and association.

In recent years, due to obligatory free universal primary and secondary education programs, the percentage of female learners has increased. The literacy level has also improved and now more than ever, women and girls have a chance to join institutions of higher learning. However, a big gap remains between male and female learners, as shown in the table below.

Figure 1: Percentage of Female Learners in the Enrolment by Year and Education Level

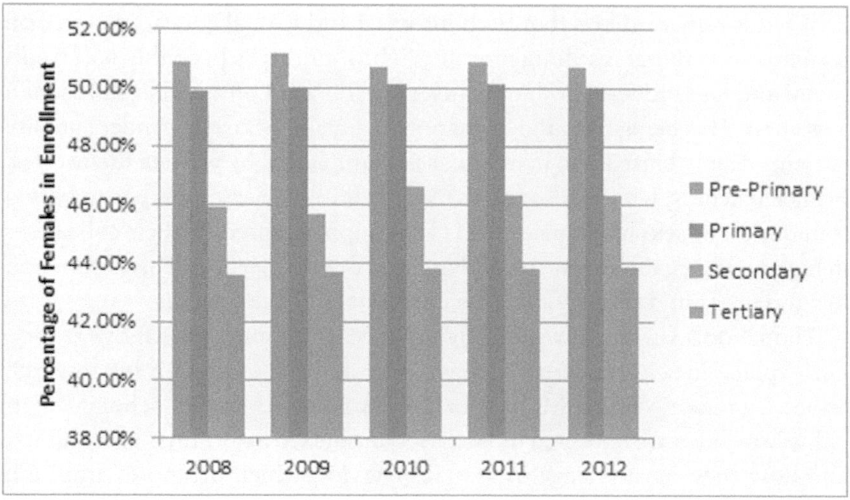

Source: Uganda Bureau of Statistics (UBOS), 2012

Two-thirds of women aged 15–49 in Uganda (64 percent) are literate, compared to 56 percent in 2006. The level of literacy is much higher among women aged 15–19 than among women in other age groups. 86 percent of women in urban areas are literate compared to 59 percent in rural ones. In general, men are more likely to be literate than women. 78 percent of Ugandan men aged 15–49 are literate, a decline from 83 percent in 2006. The pattern of male literacy is similar to that of women. However, there are marked differences between men and women across age groups. 79 percent of men aged 45–49 are literate compared with 50 percent of women in the same age group. The gap in urban-rural literacy among men is smaller than that among women, suggesting that men in rural areas have better access to learning.

UBOS data on literacy and numeracy reveal that, on average, girls are better than boys in literacy in the third year of primary school (P.3), though this advantage fades when reaching primary six (P.6). Numeracy remains a challenge for girls at both P.3 and P.6, hence their needs to be carefully addressed in order to close the gap between girls and boys.[179]

What is remarkable is that both informal and formal education agree on probably one thing: instilling morality. The morality is probably half traditional and half modern, both of which place the man on a higher status than a woman. This being true, the formation of a child regarding gender equality remains deeply biased and in most cases championed by women themselves. Female teachers, who in most cases teach children's classes, prepare a biased foundation of sexual balance that is later supplemented by their colleagues in higher classes, then at the secondary level or even beyond. This is common in rural areas and the schools with confessional backgrounds.

The schools visited in western Uganda seem to confirm the above reality. Girls' place in schools seems to have already been sealed. In his research about Ugandan schools Muhanguzi, a renowned Ugandan scholar, highlights how boys are expected to be masculine and to assert their masculinity, and how they must engage in sexual behavior, which promotes ambition and assertiveness, and be the instigator of sexual relations[180]. Muhanguzi claims that in sexual relations, boys act in a selfish and self-serving way, which girls in their contradictory role must refuse but also submit to in order to avoid being thought of as masculine, and thus lose respect[181].

In rural areas, a gender-biased nature of education is still the way. Although the gender-sensitive curriculum has been given, it "has had no big effect on the rural school" confirmed one of the leaders of the head teachers' association in Mbarara district.[182] It was found that the rate school drop-out was high. This affects both sexes, but girls are more affected because many parents do not value girls' education as highly as that of boys, because girls will marry and leave the cradle homes. This leads to school drop out on the side of the girls or even a lack of motivation.

---

179 http://www.wikigender.org/index.php/Gender_Statistics_in_Uganda, accessed on 13th November 2014 at 11:24.

180 Muhanguzi, F, K., "Gender and sexual vulnerability of young women in Africa: experiences of young girls in secondary schools in Uganda" in *Culture, Health and Sexuality: AN International Journal for Research, Intervention and Care,* 2011, p. 713–725.

181 Ibid., p. 714.

182 Kabigumira D, 50, Head teacher, Bushenyi, 28th May 2014.

Another cause of dropping out of school is pregnancy and early marriage of school girls. The well-established link between education and fertility is confirmed in Uganda. Girls who quit school and get married are likely to produce more children than their classmates who continue their studies at the university or tertiary level. The project found that educated women are seen as more emancipated than the less or not educated. They are more likely to be economically independent and take part in decision-making. Some researchers have affirmed that gender inequality in education, employment, earnings and bargaining power with families plays a significant role in keeping Uganda's fertility rates among the highest in the world.[183]

The reality is that school girls enter into sexual relationships, among other reasons, as a way of obtaining necessities that their poor parents cannot afford. Many of the girls are underage, i.e. below the age of 18 according to the Ugandan law, and this is termed as defilement. Defilement is thus a serious and widespread problem exacerbated by local leaders and parents who make deals accepting compensation from the defilers or marry off the affected girls. By this, the defilers contravene the Ugandan law and often go unpunished because many of these cases remain unreported.

This unequal power balance is well documented as contributing to girls' vulnerability to a range of sexual and reproductive dangers such as unwanted pregnancies, HIV infection, rape, sexual violence and sexual exploitation.[184] It is important to understand that sexuality also can influence gender roles. During the interview with the female leaders at Mushanga in Bushenyi district, they unanimously admitted that these mentalities and expectations remain a "challenge and a loophole" in Uganda's education system[185]

d) Gender Biased or Traditional Roles

With the introduction of affirmative action and consequently availing "equal" employment law, the female workforce has increased in many sectors. This

---

183 Klasen Stephan, *Gender and Growth in Uganda: Some Preliminary Findings and Policy Issues,* prepared for the World Bank and MFPED, February 2004.

184 Bohmer, L and E. Kirumira, E. (2000). "Socio-economic context and the sexual behaviour of Ugandan out of school youth" in *Culture, Health and Sexuality*. Vol. 2:3 p. 270.

185 Interview with female leaders at Mushanga, Kabwohe, on 2nd June 2014.

measure was meant to address past discriminatory practices in Uganda with the hopes of preventing future discrimination by employers and hirers. Research has it that many employers on private and public levels have taken positive steps to end discrimination, including implementing programs to train, hire and promote individuals from disadvantaged groups, especially women.

However, an affirmative action policy in 1995 revolved mainly around allowing women to enter university and did not identify areas of employment, which are vital. As a result, women have remained in their "traditional" roles but evolved into another form.

The project found that many nurses in the hospitals are female. In fact, many people identify the profession of nursing as feminine. Many employed women in Mbarara are nurses, secretaries, teachers, bar/hotel attendants, and accountants. Female workers are hardly ever in top positions and are seldom found in traditional men's jobs, e.g. mechanics.

The traditional hard jobs but in most cases well-paid jobs have remained a preserve of men. The stereotypical gender roles and employment seem to be in another form. On the one hand, a positive aspect is that at least women have come this far, and they can earn something. On the other, it shows how women remain badly paid and remained in stereotypical positions.

Also, women who have other well-paid jobs or responsibilities are often seen through the spectacles of being women in a traditional sense. This affects mainly middle-qualified woman. The big beneficiaries of affirmative action seem to have been women who are highly educated and well placed and in most cases they are politicians. Even then, it was found that women in such big positions are placed there based upon a stereotypical assessment of their strengths and weaknesses based on their gender evaluations.

e) Traditional Women's Wear

While the research valued the innumerable and hypothesized benefits of uniforms in schools, for example reductions in perceived inequality within the school, reductions in aggression and violence, identification of students who should be in school to limit truancy, and the avoidance of unregistered youth entering the school and causing disruption, it found a very big loophole. Girls and boys have different uniforms. The uniforms are designed in traditional female or male forms. In many girls' schools, wearing trousers is still punishable. Many girls wear these trousers at home or during holidays and then at school, it is strictly prohibited. It could be a question of discipline but also a question of the school's mentality.

The efforts of many women and men have led to much advancement but the realities of gender equality issues in clothing remain. Wearing trousers "remains a tolerable evil that is foreign to African culture" as one female leader asserted during an interview.[186] Nevertheless, many women see this as a breakthrough. The society itself seems indifferent to what women wear, although many women have often been harassed or stripped naked by "cultural activists". This was witnessed in Kabale town in 2012. Women's wear is still very much controlled by men; either their husbands or fathers or even by fellow women who see it as "going overboard in quest for women's freedom.

f) Traditional Sports

The project found out that there is inequality in modern sport. The dichotomy between women and men in the understanding of sport remains a clear issue. Inequality in modern sport is deeply rooted in socially constructed cultural norms and expectations of masculine and feminine appropriateness, which have shaped values, attitudes and behavior regarding participation patterns for girls and boys, men and women. While there have been many improvements, there are still structural constraints perpetuating gender inequality that need to be challenged and transformed. For example, many schools still emphasize netball as the only sport for girls and girls' football is unheard of. Girls who wish to take up football or soccer as their game often find resistance and misunderstanding with their parents. "My father beat me up and warned me never to play a men's sport" said a seventeen-year-old girl at Kazo secondary school.

It is true that netball is a popular women's sport in many parts of Africa.[187] Several African nations are ranked among the top thirty-two in the world.

---

186 Kebirungi J, 32, Teacher, Kazo, 2nd June 2014.

187 DaCosta, Lamartine P.; Miragaya, Ana (2002). *Worldwide experiences and trends in sport for all.* Aachen [u.a.] Meyer & Meyer Sport, 2002. Meyer & Meyer Sport. Or Shakespeare, Wilma; Caldow, Margaret (2009). *Netball: steps to success.* Champaign, Illinois: Human Kinetics. xi.

As of July 2014, Uganda was ranked fourteenth.[188] This is of course a good thing. Netball is one of the most popular women's participation sports in schools in Uganda. While participation rates are high, there is no sense of collective identity among the players as netballers nor do they have a dream of being part of a national netball community in future.[189] But they take this as their sport ordained from nature. On the other hand, boys identify themselves with football, even acquiring the names of the renowned footballers and having a dream of one day playing in a national or district team. In 2002, 40 percent of African girls rated netball as their favorite sport and 19 percent of non-African girls liked netball best. Many African girls claimed netball as their favorite sport even if they had never played it.[190]

g) Independent Women

There is a group of women that is coming up in Uganda, especially in urban or semi urban areas, that is known as independent women. They also exist in rural areas but they are often accompanied by abuse and sometimes assaulted. Some of these have never married, others are just single mothers and the rest simply chose this life. The project interviewed some of them and they seem to be traumatized despite being economically stable women in comparison with their counterparts. "What can we do?" said one woman, "life has to continue. They call us names and not only men but also women who are married. It is my choice."[191]

Similar economically independent women in rural areas in some parts of central Uganda were labelled as "*kyeyombekyeire*"[192] (I built my own house), implying both masculine qualities and connoting illicit wealth gained through prostitution. This is true in western Uganda.

188 International Federation of Netball Associations (21 January 2011a). "Current World Rankings". Accessed 4th March 2011 at 22:09.

189 Keim, M., *Nation building at play: sport as a tool for social integration in post-apartheid South Africa*. Meyer and Meyer Sport, 2003, p. 143.

190 Ibid., p. 85.

191 Kobusingye J., 28, housewife, Kampala, 23rd June 2014.

192 The Runyankole word *Kyeyombekyire* means "I built it" (the house or home) myself. In most cases, this is done by women who live a single life.

If market work allows women to challenge traditional role boundaries in the economic domain, even in a limited way, the same apparently does not extend to the domain of sexual negotiation within partnerships.

But in all, the reality is that women have started living their lives instead living the lives the society offers. This is in many cases not fulfilling. While it is good that society puts forward its expectations for its members, it is good that the members choose their own destiny.

4.2.2.3 The Religious Reality - The Input of the Catholic Church

Uganda is a country with three main religious groups. Christians make up the majority, 42 percent of which are Roman Catholics, 40 percent are Protestants and since some years ago, the Pentecostal and independent churches mainly originating from America have been gaining ground in Uganda. Islam constitutes about 13 percent of the total population. Approximately one percent of the Ugandan population are members of African Traditional Religions (ATRs).[193] All these religions have in one way or another contributed to or affected the position of women in Uganda. But this paper will limit its scope to the Catholic Church and its contribution.

4.2.2.3.1 The Catholic Church

The Catholic Church in Mbarara admits unreservedly that women's contribution to the Church in recent years has been enormous. Gender equality has been a topic and has somehow been making steady progress. Unlike in past years, women have somehow played a decisive role, recognized and appreciated by the Church.

The positive impact is irreversibly recommended for the benefit of the Church and the good of the individual women. The positive effect of women's liberation on the apostolate is mainly noticed in pastoral work, small Christian communities, lay apostolate movements, women's groups, economic and material support, inculturation, ecumenism and development-oriented projects.

---

193 Uganda Bureau of Statistics. Uganda Demographic Health Survey 2011 at: http://www.measuredhs.com/pubs/pdf/PR18/PR18.pdf, retrieved 28th May 2014 at 11.23.

a) Pastoral Work

The pastoral work covers all the work of the Church among the people. For a long time, this field that was denied to women. It was reserved for men. After realizing the importance of involving women in pastoral work, the diocesan synod of Mbarara of 1982 decreed and encouraged the participation of women. But this decree was not effected until of late, and women have responded enthusiastically to this long overdue duty.[194]

However, considering the universality of the Church, the synod limited the areas of operation. This limited participation and any other limitation of women trying to act in the Church regarding the pastoral duties should be understood in the context of the universal Catholic Church. "In areas where women have not been permitted by the universal church, the synod of Mbarara did respect the guidelines from the magisterium, said one of the Synod members."[195] Apart from these limitations, women have shown their commitment in the following areas.

b) Small Christian Communities

The small Christian communities in many parishes are active. The communities gather at the home of a member when this is feasible or at a convenient place. When they gather, members discuss what affects or is affecting or has affected their lives and they share it in the light of the gospel. They share their lives in a spirit of brotherhood and sisterhood and translate it to their Christian faith and belief through prayer and conversation. Within such small gatherings, there naturally arises a connection of understanding, acceptance and support. They then support each other and learn in a personal way, the meaning of being a Church. Helping one another also brings them closer to working with each other.

Small Christian communities have been a platform for women's exposure to their faith. They have manifested the true Christian living worthy of imitation. They have also fostered unity.

---

194 Mbarara Archdiocese, The Chancellery Archives, Mbarara, 2013.

195 Behakanira G, 56, Synod member, Nyamitanga, interviewed at Mbarara on 4th June 2014.

One man from Ibanda parish during an interview said that he had been inspired by his wife's preaching and way of life at home. As such, women's emancipation promises unity in the Church.[196]

As a result of liberating and appreciating women at lower levels, they have been given responsibilities such as chairpersons, treasurers, secretaries in charge of liturgy, and so forth.

Still, small Christian communities have been an avenue for liberated women to embrace the long-said active participation. The Second Vatican Council views the Church as a people of God who are to participate fully and actively in the building of the kingdom of God. Thus, active participation has been observed in liturgical worship especially in the mass, prayers and gospel sharing that had been suffocated during "women's absence". Many women participate or lead which was never the case. Slowly, male believers have come to get used to female church leaders.

Besides the religious impact small Christian communities have had, they have endeavored to take up the social dimension. These communities try to look into clan barriers, prejudices, and historical biases. Sensitive issues have been dealt with for the sake of society. These issues range from economic to social and from political to religious issues. In some meetings, they discuss the role of modern women in their communities.

Indeed, small Christian communities have offered an opportunity for women to prove their worthiness that has automatically had an impact on the Church. To the Church, this has added an ecclesial dynamism for the spread of God's word.

c) Lay Apostolate Movements

Of late, the lay apostolate movements have functioned as church pillars in spreading the good news to the grassroots Christians in the Mbarara archdiocese. There are some lay apostolate movements in the archdiocese of Mbarara, but the research will be limited to two: Legio Mariae and Catholic Charismatic Renewal (CCR). The membership of these two movements is largely female.

Ninety percent of the Legio Mariae, commonly known as legionaries of Mary, are female. This is because the legion came into existence as an

196 Baguma Serapio, 49, Peasant, Interview at Ibanda Parish on 28th May 2014.

organization of women, and eight years passed before the first men's presidium was established.[197] Today in the Mbarara archdiocese they still have an upper hand because women consider the Virgin Mary as their role model and mother. Many women have joined the charismatic movement because of its liberating character from the oppression of both satanic powers and bodily sufferings. To many women, the Charismatic Renewal Movement served as an outlet for their freedom. Due to the above intentions, these two female-dominated movements have had a significant impact on the Church.

The Legion of Mary movement is organized in presidia, curia, comitia, senatos and concilia. It has both nominal and active members. Their central theme is to fight Satan, the enemy, using the rosary or other prayers. It is further entrusted with the duty of visiting and consoling the sick, the poor, the weak and the suffering. Women in these movements have testified to this. The Legion of Mary charges members with a duty to love God and others daily, and this is a lived experience for many women.

The Charismatic Renewal Movement celebrated its silver jubilee in Uganda in 1997. In this movement women also dominate. The spirit-filled women echoing Priscilla (Rom. 16:2) and Mary (Acts 12:12) in the apostolic times have become witnesses to the gospel. Some women have been appointed to the diocesan spiritual renewal in the diocese. These charismatic women have done tremendous work. They have attracted many other women to the renewal, and they have inspired many lives.

The CCRM has also acted as a venue for training female public speakers. Women have been challenged to be bold in preaching the word of God. After every "life in the spirit seminar", all the participants are commissioned to go, preach and be salt and light to the world (Mt 5:13–15). Hence, the public speaking skill is a condition without which one cannot preach effectively. Out of the 43 women interviewed in Rubindi, 39 women told the author that they were not able to stand before people even to introduce themselves before they joined the CCRM. With this movement, the Church is blessed with 'sharp' women.[198]

In addition to that, the CCRM has had an active involvement in the apostolate through its outreach programs. They involve visiting the sick,

197 Legion of Mary, Curia Mbarara Archive, Mbarara, visited on 4th June 2014.
198 Kabaguma R, 52, CCRM group leader, Rubindi, on 3rd June 2014.

non-baptized, the people of other denominations, preaching the word of God and praying with people. Since the majority are women, not only does the Church benefit automatically but also society.

The common element among the members of the two movements mentioned above (Legion of Mary and the CCRM) is their courage and freedom.

In conclusion, the lay apostolate movements that are dominantly joined by women contribute significantly not only to the Church's apostolate in Mbarara but also to the liberation of women.

Assuredly, women have come to the stage through the small Christian communities, and they have further demanded their rightful position in the Church. The greatest challenge for the Church is reconciling its teaching of equality and love for all humanity with women's position. Women's emancipation has rung the bell for the Church to revisit its policies.

d) Women and Leadership in the Church

Having women as leaders in the Church was not common. Recently, the number of women in positions of leadership has increased sharply. For example, the Vice-Chairperson of the Council of the Laity at the archdiocesan level is a woman, Mrs. Angela.[199] On the parish, zonal and deanery levels, women are quite well represented. The position of women in the Church in Mbarara has been revisited.

Women have become dynamic points of instilling the values and virtues of a Christian education. The home remains the central point and the very first nursery school of Christian education from which springs the rest of a child's training or education. This has been the impact of women's liberation in carrying out apostolate in the family.

There are other kinds of families where the effect of women's liberation on the Church has been felt. These are widow-headed families, single-mother-headed families, orphanages, women's religious communities, and so on. In all these, women have played the leading and vital role of practicing

---

199 Mbarara Social communications office, Records section, Mbarara Archdiocese, 28th May 2016.

kingly, priestly and prophetic offices as entrusted to all Christians in the Church.[200]

Furthermore, a positive impact has been observed in the areas of the few women who have been given ministries in the Church. A considerable number of women have been installed as extra-ordinary ministers of the Eucharist, lectors, acolytes and some women have been commissioned as catechists. Examples of parishes with female catechists include: Rwera, St. Kaggwa, Rubindi, Mushanga, Nyamitanga and Kioga, each with more than three catechists. In all these parishes, female catechists have even posed a challenge in the preaching of God's word to male catechists.

The author interviewed Mrs. Maria Keebire and Mrs. Y. Kato from Kioga parish about their experiences and they affirmed that they have been a breakthrough to men's mentalities and have acted as a great encouragement to the rest of the women. These, too, have had a great impact on their particular churches.[201]

In addition to that, as cantors, musicians and choir leaders, women have produced useful and inspiring religious hymns. Examples of such women are Sophia Munungu from Kitabi parish, Sr. Theresa Kantarikira, OLGC and Sr Generoza, OLGC. These, together with many others, have composed many hymns, songs and carols that not only make liturgy nourishing but also lively. This music is recorded and transmitted to the local radio stations in the Mbarara Diocese.[202]

More to that, many women, especially religious nuns or sisters, are head teachers of schools where they teach humanistic subjects and preach or teach God's word. Some women show good examples in word and deed, thus inspiring the youth. These are exemplified by the head teachers of Maryhill high school (Mbarara), St. Theresa secondary school (Ibanda), St. Catherine girls school (Kiruhuura), St. Cecilia Vocational Girls' School

---

200 Austin Flannery, *Vatican Council Vol. 2*: Inter Insigniores, Declaration on the Question of the Admission of Women to the Ministerial Priesthood, 1976, No. 4.

201 Mrs Keebire, 31, Mrs Kato, 44, peasants, Kioga, Isingiro, 4th June 2014.

202 Mutabaruka Charles, 47, director and priest, Radio Maria, Mbarara Branch Uganda, 2nd June 2014.

(Bushenyi) and Nyamitaga college (Mbarara), all of which are renowned schools in the western part of the country.

As a result of emancipation, women have become leaders of higher institutions, and it is in these institutions that they have received special credit from the Church. Examples of institutions headed by women are colleges, such as Ibanda where a religious sister is the vice principal, hospitals like Ibanda, which is a model hospital in Mbarara, and the Mushanga social centre. In all these, women's presence has been felt and recognized.

Many more women ran the catechumenates in different parishes and Sunday school programs. Recently, these have been introduced in the Mbarara Diocese.

In the area of mass media, liberated women have had a positive contribution to the Church. A religious sister commonly referred to as "Sr. DJ" works with the diocesan FM radio station – Radio Maria. She doubles as the head of the communications office of the whole archdiocese. Her reflections, news and programs concerning the home have done a lot to build the Church and encourage other women. Obviously, there are massive articles in local and national newspapers written by women and phone calls from women in defense of their beliefs and against ill-treatment from men. "They also defend the Catholic Church against the atheistic tendency today,"[203] said Sr. Keneema during an interview with her.

Finally, in the field of pastoral work, many women are either directly or indirectly involved. Many women serve the Church as catechists, religious sisters or nuns, ushers, cantors, choir mistresses, wives of catechists, housemaids, to mention but a few. The Church cannot remain indifferent to the work and massive contribution done by these women. And to appreciate it approves the positive impact the women's emancipation has brought so far on the Catholic Church.

However, women still lack the power of decision-making at the higher level. Their voices in the Church remain represented by men. They are not allowed to be ordained to ministries reserved for men, and this, of course, lets the Church remain patriarchal in nature. The subject of women being

203 Keneema G., 58, nun, commissioner of social communications, Mbarara archdiocese, Mbarara, 4th June 2014.

involved at the higher level is never an issue to many women as society itself has accepted that way.

4.2.2.4 *Ecumenism and the Anglican Church*

Apart from playing the primary liturgical role as the congregation or the listening, worshipping community, some women associate with, work with and appreciate people of other religions. In fulfilling the ministry recommended by bishops of evangelizing the not yet baptized and the ministry of co-operation and promotion of unity of Christians, women's contribution is felt. Still, they are urged to have a genuine dialog with Muslims and members of other faiths.

In the Mbarara diocese, religious division and conflict have been a reality. This has been evident between Catholics and Protestants since colonial times. Some women's groups such as the Mbarara Young Women Christian Association and the Mothers' Union (from the Church of Uganda, the Anglicans) have struggled and encouraged ecumenism and interreligious dialog.[204] On the individual level, many women visit and support each other despite religious differences, which is a real beginning of ecumenism and interfaith dialog. This has benefited both groups. They learn from each and foster unity among them with a common goal of gender equality in the Church. With the emancipation of women, the wound of religious conflict is also narrowing.

Also, together with their sisters elsewhere in the world especially in the USA, Banyankole women struggle to unite their efforts to bring feminist values of equality and mutuality to mainline Christian denominations. However, they are still blocked by a world dominated and managed by male attitudes.

4.2.2.5 *On the Secular Level*

During the research, it was observed that despite the efforts by the government and the civil society, many women, especially those with little education or those who live in rural areas, remain a disadvantaged group. They

204 Female Representatives of the Mothers' Union, Ruharo Mbarara, 23rd May 2015.

are often poor, with little or no education and they access less rights than their male counterparts.

Women hardly ever have access land and other resources. Despite their big contribution to society's welfare, women remain beneficiaries, not owners. This means that they contribute a great part, and they own almost nothing. They remain at the mercy of the male masters.

Furthermore, the secular society represents values that endorse male domination and a patriarchal mentality, indicating subservient female behavior in all areas of life, including their sexuality.[205] This is not only seen in the experiences of young people in school but also in marriage, the greatest institution in African society. Marriage seems to play a significant role in gender equality.

4.2.2.5.1 The Institution of Marriage and Gender Equality

There are six types of marriage in Uganda: Civil, Christian, Hindu, Baha'i, Islamic and the customary marriage. Although Hindu and Baha'i marriages are also recognized as legal marriages in Uganda, they are rare in western Uganda.

In all these marriages and especially in rural areas, the common denominator remains the discrimination of women. But the fact remains that throughout Uganda, including the southwestern region, gender roles are being negotiated by education modernity and more poverty on the one hand, and as such, marriage too is affected on the other. An indication of this affects women; marriages structures are transforming in Uganda and cohabitation is rising as couples cannot afford the costs involved in weddings, such as bride price and receptions.

Marriage is dealt with in the Ugandan Constitution of 1995. It dealt very precisely with the rights of the family. It states that men and women of the age of eighteen years and above have the right to marry and to found a family and are entitled to equal rights in marriage, during marriage and at

205 Muhanguzi, K. F. Bennett, J. Muhanguzi, H, R, D. (2011). "The Construction and Mediation of Sexuality and Gender Relations: Experience of Girls and Boys in Secondary schools in Uganda", in Feminist Formations vol. 23, 3, p. 132–152.

its dissolution.[206] This article brought about a new understanding of marriage. Marriage is an institution that has a significant impact on men's and women's property rights.

This impact is mainly observable in the three prominent marriage types in Uganda; traditional, religious (Christian, Islamic for example) or civil. Traditional weddings are based on the customs of indigenous Ugandan culture.

Mostly, marriage is an initiative of the man himself or his parents. The parents or the aunties and other relatives are then involved in leading to an introduction stage. From here, the marriage involves many parties. This practice cuts across almost all Bantu groups.[207] In modern times, there are lots of variations but they do not differ significantly.

A religious marriage where the ceremony is presided over by a priest or pastor is only conducted after the customary bride price has been made, as this African tradition has been incorporated into Christian practices.[208] Muslim marriages, like traditional marriages, are commonly arranged by the parents to achieve compatibility. Muslim marriages, like traditional marriages, can be polygamous as the Koran allows men to have up to four wives as long as he can look after them.

In terms of polygamy, the rate has declined nationally from 32 percent in UDHS 2000 to 25 percent in this recent UDHS 2011.[209] It is believed that this is due to the emancipation of women, the awareness of their rights and socio-economic problems.

The third type, civil marriages, are administered by government officials and can be undertaken by couples facing opposition from their families. If couples have had an introduction stage and are cohabitating, the community views them as official, but it is not a legally recognized form of marriage.[210]

In any case, family law in Uganda covers who can get married, the types of marriage that are legal, what makes a marriage legal, marriage rights

206 Constitution of the Republic of Uganda, Kampala, 1995.

207 Tamale, op.cit., p. 89–97.

208 Otiso, op.cit., p. 86.

209 Uganda Bureau of Statistics. (2011). Ugandan Demographic Health Survey 2011 at: http://www.measuredhs.com/pubs/pdf/PR18/PR18.pdf, 30th December 2014 at 12:00.

210 Otiso, op.cit., p. 86.

and responsibilities, as well as marriage breakdown (either by separation or divorce). In practice, customary and religious rules and norms about marriage are applied to family law alongside statutory requirements.[211] Regardless of differences in the written laws and in customary and religious rules, the constitution provides the standard upon which all marriages are based to be fair to both men and women.[212] This can be in a monogamous or polygamous marriage.

a) Monogamy

According to Ugandan law, monogamous marriage means a marriage between a man and woman, neither of whom, during the subsistence of such marriage, shall be at liberty to enter or contract any other valid marriage. This is commonly practiced by the Christian, Hindu and Baha'i marriages. Some Muslims also marry one wife. Monogamy is a form of relationship in which an individual has only one partner during his or her lifetime or at any one time (serial monogamy), as compared to polygyny, polyandry, or polyamory. The term is also applied to the social behavior of some animals, referring to the state of having only one mate at any one time.

It is important to have a clear understanding of the nomenclature of monogamy because scientists use the term monogamy for different relationships. Biologists, biological anthropologists, and behavioral ecologists often use the term monogamy in the sense of sexual, if not genetic, monogamy. Modern biological researchers using the theory of evolution approach human monogamy as the same in human and non-human animal species. They postulate the following four aspects of monogamy:

Marital monogamy refers to marriages of only two people. Social monogamy refers to two partners living together, having sex with each other, and cooperating in acquiring basic resources such as shelter, food, and money.

Sexual monogamy refers to two partners remaining sexually exclusive with each other and having no outside sex partners. Genetic monogamy refers to sexually monogamous relationships with genetic evidence of paternity.

---

211 Property Rights and Gender: A Training Toolkit - Property … (n.d.). accessed from http://www.icrw.org/files/images/Property-Rights-and-Gender-A-Training-Toolkit-P on 13th October 2015 at 21:23.

212 Ibid.

When cultural or social anthropologists and other social scientists use the term monogamy, the meaning is social or marital monogamy. Marital monogamy may be further distinguished between: marriage once in a lifetime or marriage with only one person at a time (serial monogamy), in contrast to bigamy or polygamy.

Human monogamy's legal aspects are taught at faculties of law. There are also philosophical aspects in the fields of interest of such as philosophical anthropology and philosophy of religion, as well as theological ones.[213]

b) Polygamy/Polygyny

Polygamy is a marriage that includes more than two partners.[214] When a man is married to more than one wife at a time, the relationship is called polygyny, and there is no marriage bond between the wives. When a woman is married to more than one husband at a time, it is called polyandry, and there is no marriage bond between the husbands. If a marriage includes multiple husbands and wives, it can be called group marriage[215]

In my research, the noticeable standard type of polygamy in Uganda is polygyny. It should be noted that the use of the term polygamy to mean polygyny is widespread and commonly used. In any case, a polygamous marriage has come to mean a marriage in which the man is married to more than one wife.

Under polygamy is another type known as a "potentially polygamous marriage", which means a marriage between a man and a woman in which the man has the capacity to contract another marriage during the subsistence of the first marriage, but has not yet done so.

A new form of a polygamous marriage before the Ugandan parliament is cohabitation. "Cohabitation" usually refers to unmarried couples who live together without formally registering their relation as a marriage. Such arrangements have become increasingly common in Western countries during the past few decades, led by changing social views, especially regarding

---

213 https://en.wikipedia.org/wiki/Monogamy accessed on 3rd June 2013 at 10:00.

214 Marriage-Wikipedia, retrieved from http://en.wikipedia.org/wiki/Marriage, accessed on 3rd June 2013 at 10:00.

215 Zeitzen, Miriam Koktvedgaard. "Polygamy: a cross-cultural analysis". Berg. p. 3. ISBN 1-84520-2201.

marriage, gender roles, and religion. More broadly, the term cohabitation can mean any number of people living together. To "cohabit", in a broad sense, means to "coexist".[216]

Cohabitation is not yet legally recognized as a form of a marriage in Uganda. Consequently, cohabitating couples do not have the same property rights and legal protections as men and women who are married. For example, unless the land where they stay is registered in her name (either alone or jointly with her partner), a cohabiting woman has no legal protection to stop the man she is cohabiting with from selling, renting out, or giving away the land where the couple stays or farms, whereas a married woman would be protected in that her partner could not take any of these actions without her written consent.[217]

All forms of polygamous marriages have adverse effects on women. The practice in many cases fragments land, shares the meager income of the man and makes it difficult for men to provide for their families. In very few case, where the rich and wealthy men marry to prove their position in society, the issue of meager income may not arise.[218] Women in polygamous marriages or cohabitation end up as family heads with limited resources, sharing scarce resources across many households or with their co-wives. Fertility rates are higher among women in polygamous families, who compete for male heirs. This is evident in rural and slum areas.

Polygynous marriages have reinforced some aspects of male dominance but also have given women an arena for cooperating to oppose male dominance. A man may grant his senior wife "male" status, allowing her to behave as an equal toward men and as a superior toward his other wives.

---

216 http://www.oxforddictionaries.com/definition/english/cohabit?q=cohabitation#cohabit accessed on 3rd June 2013 at 10:08.

217 Property Rights and Gender: A Training Toolkit - Property from http://www.icrw.org/files/images/Property-Rights-and-Gender-A-Training-Toolkit-P accessed on 3rd June 2013 at 10:00.

218 Traditionally, a polygamous marriage was proof that a man is rich and can afford to marry many women and produce many children and provide for them as well. It was also proof that the man was hardworking. But in Uganda this is proving to be very difficult because the standard of living has changed.

However, polygynous marriages have left some wives without legal rights to inheritance after divorce or widowhood.[219]

The common denominator in all these marriages is the payment of bridewealth. The payment of bridewealth as a practice is deeply ingrained, not only in men but also in women.

4.2.2.5.2 Payment of Bridewealth

Among Banyankole, there is no single type of marriage that does not recognize the tradition of bride price. One is expected to pay bride price, also known as bridewealth. Bridewealth is the amount of money or property or wealth paid by the groom or his family to the parents of a woman upon the marriage of their daughter to the groom[220]. It has been a cherished custom among African societies since time immemorial. However, it poses a question on whether a token of appreciation, in this case, bride price, entails the element of a sale. "Bride price operating in a money economy has come to acquire the qualities of a sale – it is now, more than ever before, the price of a woman."[221] In western Uganda, cows or goats are common items of bridewealth. But nowadays, it has evolved to include modern assets such as motorcycles or even cars.

Dowry, which is paid by the family of the woman to the groom on the very day of receiving the bride, is intended to be used by the bride to help establish the new household. This includes ordinary household items. Dowry depends on how much the groom paid. The more he pays, the bigger the percentage he and his wife receive. It should be noted that the Kinyankole culture simultaneously practice both dowry and bride price.[222]

---

219 Culture of Uganda - history, people, clothing, women, beliefs ... (n.d.). Retrieved from http://www.everyculture.com/To-Z/Uganda.html, accessed on 4th June 2013 at 11:03.

220 http://en.wikipedia.org/wiki/Marriage#Monogamy accessed on 3rd June 2013 at 12:20.

221 Corinne A.A. Packer, "Using Human Rights to Change Tradition: Traditional Practices Harmful to Women's Reproductive Health in Sub-Saharan Africa" Vol. 13, *School of Human Rights Research Series*, 2002.

222 Tibebebirwe P, 75, cultural inheritance, Ankole Kingdom, Mbarara, 28th Sept. 2012.

The agreed bride price or dowry may or may not be intended to reflect the perceived value of the girl or young woman. Bride price or wealth received by the parents of the girl and her extended family remain a huge challenge and a point of contention.

Early marriage, especially in the case of girls is a common strategy used by poor families to raise income for the rest of household members, more practiced in rural than urban areas. Many girls perceive marriage as an escape route from family poverty while the common cultural practice of charging bridewealth brings quick and substantial income to her family. Girls sometimes withdraw themselves from school, especially if their needs for supplies like shoes and dresses are not met by their parents or guardians. In other cases, parents encourage girls to drop out or fail to pay their educational costs and arrange marriages for them or encourage them to get married. Most societies define femininity in relation to marriage and girls have been socialized to accept that perspective. This social construction that relates femininity closely with marriage also lowers girls' aspirations for secondary and higher education as most of them do not see the need to excel in education as a value related with marriageability.[223]

Market-related factors lead in determining dropout rates for primary schools for both boys and girls. In the case of girls, however, social relations of gender lead in creating and maintaining the gap between boys and girls dropping out of school.[224] At primary school level, it is the gendered division of labor within the household that affects the girls while at the secondary school level it is marriage norms at community and household levels that adds to the gap already created by differentials due to market-related factors.[225]

---

223 Gender and Education in Uganda - United Nations http://portal.unesco.org/education/en/file_download.php/ accessed on 3rd June 2013 at 10:00.

224 Bright Judith, 58, Headteacher, on Education, Kampala, 5th August 2014 at 14:00.

225 Gender and Education in Uganda - United Nations... (n.d.). Retrieved from http://portal.unesco.org/education/en/file_download.php/ccd0dc371f4712b609604dbf accessed on 3rd June 2013 at 10:00.

a) Pros – For

Many Ugandans esteem the payment of bride price or dowry and see it as integral to the institution of marriage. They are convinced in line with Otiso's commentary; that bride price equates as compensation to the bride's father for the loss of his daughter's labor, as Uganda is a mainly an agrarian society.[226] It was and remains a token of appreciation.

They further argue that this is a sign of respect and recognizes the value of a girl. Tamale, a professor at Makerere University, argues that there are links with bride price to a girl's sexual and reproductive qualities. This is evident as a higher price is given for a girl if she is a virgin, has education or comes from a well-respected family.[227]

While interpreting the constitution of Uganda, the constitution court supported the bride price. Four out of five judges of the constitution court affirmed that the payment of the bride price is imbued in the constitution. Article 37 confirms their argument: "Every person has a right as applicable to belong to, enjoy, practice, profess, maintain and promote any culture, cultural institution, language, tradition, creed or religion in community with others."[228]

In dismissing the petition, the honourable judges led by Deputy Chief Justice Kikonyogo argued that the custom of payment of bride price is not per se unconstitutional as it does not prohibit a voluntary, mutual agreement between bride and a groom to enter into the bride price arrangement owing to the fact that under Article 31 clause 3 of the constitution, marriage shall be entered into with the free consent of the man and woman intending to marry.

Justice Kikonyogo seemed to be in agreement with the petitioners because some of the statements she made gave that implication. "I am in agreement with the view that the customary practice of the husband demanding a refund of the bride price in the event of dissolution of the marriage demeans and undermines the dignity of a woman and it is in violation of Article 33 clause 6 of the constitution."[229]

---

226 Otiso., op.cit., p. 86.

227 Tamale, S. *Out of the Closet: Unveiling Sexuality Discourses in Uganda* in Feminist Africa, Issue 5, 2005.

228 Constitution of the Republic of Uganda, Kampala, 1995.

229 Ibid.

However, she decided that the petition must fail on the grounds that the constitution under Article 50 can adequately cater for the aggrieved victims. In my humble opinion, I think the judge in her judgement of the issues was errant. She ought to have just been straight forward instead giving a false impression of being in agreement with one side and then deciding against it.

b) Cons – Against

Considering the above definition of bride price, in relation to the modern Uganda where constitutionalism is pertinent, a dilemma of sorts is created when archaic customs that cannot fit into the context of modern times are carried on under the umbrella of customary law. A division is created between the conservative and the radical, both using the backing of the Constitution to strengthen their stance.

The argument that the colonial masters made a mistake by tarnishing what was a treasure in marriage, a sign of gratitude to the family of the girl to bad tradition does not hold water. Yes, apparently, it looks so. But on closer inspection, this practice reduces a woman to a commodity sold and a property owned by a man.

It also predisposes girls to early marriage, as some parents want to solve the problem of poverty and this compromises girls' rights as human beings. They become commodities, the property of their husbands to be treated as they wish. Early marriages, which are being fought against, remain a threat to girls who are in school in many parts of the western region. This naturally affects their education opportunities and compromises their health and employment. "We have been in a fight with parents trying to withdraw their girls to marry off," said Sr. Grace, the headmistress of St. Catherine's Girls' School.[230]

Payments for brides confirm women's status as property and lead to the perception among both men and women that men own women and that it is, therefore, a women's job to both provide for and serve men. In a discussion at Kashekuro in Bushenyi, one woman expressed a common

230 Kyomugisha G, 33, ESM nun, Headmistress, St. Catherine's, at Kiruhura on 2nd June 2014.

sentiment when she said, "I was bought by the man, so my body is his asset to use as he wishes."[231]

Bride price is also used to legitimize domestic violence. In a discussion of domestic violence in Mbarara town, a male participant commented, "If you buy a goat, do you not punish it anytime it strays?"[232] The women agreed that as men had paid cows for them, they were property to be used as the men wish.

Finally, the Ugandan Constitution also states that all persons are equal before and under the law in all spheres of political, economic, social and cultural life and in every other respect and shall enjoy equal protection of the law.[233] Article 32(2) states that, "... customs and traditions ... against the dignity, welfare or interest of women ... are prohibited by this Constitution." In my view, the custom ought to have been declared unconstitutional.

c) Human Rights Watch Position

According to the Human Rights Watch, bride price was once a gesture of appreciation to the bride's family; now men literally purchase their wives. As in a commercial transaction, the husband's payment entitles him to full ownership rights over his acquisition. It challenges the government to re-evaluate and put good customs and traditions in place for its citizens.

The position of Human Rights Watch has not influenced in any away the custom of bride price in Uganda. It remains to be seen if their advisory role will affect the decisions of the legislators in parliament to tackle this long-cherished tradition of most tribes in Uganda. The good thing is that individual families have started to negotiate and prepare marriages for their children without involving the issue of bride price.

4.2.2.5.3 Separation and Divorce

The institution of marriage is still highly treasured among the Banyankole, and it is always hoped that couples will be happy in a lasting marriage. But

231 Kentabire C, 57, Housewife, in interview on bride price, Kashekuro Bushenyi, 6th June 2014.

232 Bagumisiriza H, 43, Trader, in interview on domestic violence in families, Mbarara, 6th June 2014.

233 Constitution of the Republic of Uganda, Kampala, 1995, Uganda.

the reality is that sometimes marriages do not work out, and the spouses choose to separate or divorce. This is a bitter reality of any society.

Although Uganda's Bureau of Statistics or any other official agency does not compile national divorce figures, court clerks, academics, activists and lawyers now say they are handling many more divorce cases now than a decade ago.

"The numbers kept going up," said Ismail Jjemba, a clerk at Uganda's High Court, referring to the effect of the Constitutional Court's ruling. "It's almost always the women who complain first."[234]

The situation of family and marriage has changed dramatically in Uganda. There are so many positive things that modernity has brought with it, and there are negatives that accompanied it. This is a sign of changing times in Uganda, where it used to be extremely difficult for a woman to get a divorce. Such proceedings were almost always initiated by men, a legacy of traditional beliefs that stress that women should be submissive and of a now-unconstitutional divorce law.[235]

In a climate of emancipation, the issue of separation and divorce will continue to arise as long as men still oppress women. The fact is the number of separation and divorce cases is going up.

a) Separation

Separation is a situation where a husband and wife stay away from each other for a given period either because they have agreed to (separation by agreement), or because the court has ordered the separation (judicial separation). Separation does not end a marriage, but only suspends certain rights of the husband and the wife. The husband and wife are still considered to be married. Neither can marry another person during the separation. Separation should not go beyond two years.[236] Few people in Uganda know the

---

234 http://www.huffingtonpost.com/2013/04/30/divorce-rate-as-gender-eq_n_3187187.html accessed on 12th May 2014 at 11:10.

235 As gender equity rises, more Ugandan women divorce, from http://bigstory.ap.org/article/gender-equity-rises-ugandan-women-seek-divorce accessed on 3rd June 2013 at 10:00.

236 ICRW, Property Rights and Gender: A Training Toolkit, Kampala, 2010, p. 10.

difference. Many still turn to their parents or religious leaders, who then reconcile or advise on the mode of separation.

A marriage separation agreement is a legal document prepared by spouses contemplating a divorce who have reached an agreement to separate and details how their property, assets, debts and other marital issues will be divided or handled. This agreement can also be used to define child custody, visitation, and child support if the parties have minor children.[237] Although this type of separation is common, few prepare documents. It is usually done through the rulings from local councils or/and parents.

A legal separation that for many is often mistaken as divorce can, in fact, be the first step towards a couple's decision to divorce. In a legal separation, the spouses live apart from one another in an effort to either settle their marital issues or to come to a final determination on how their property will be divided if they proceed to get a divorce. States vary in how they treat spouses who are legally separated and what rights are associated with a legal separation versus a full divorce. The most significant issue is the right to remarry, which is not available to couples who are not divorced. During interviews, it was noted that many women suffer more in this separation than men. Men seem to be accepted in the community more easily than women who live separately from their husbands.

b) Divorce

Divorce is the permanent ending of a marriage. It only applies to legally recognized marriages. The procedure for divorce depends on the type of marriage the parties had. The proper legal procedures have to be followed for a divorce to be valid and for the marriage to be permanently finished. Leaving or chasing away a spouse does not amount to divorce or put a legal end to a marriage.[238]

---

237 Divorce Papers and Free Printable Online Divorce Forms. (n.d.) from http://www.mydivorceusa.com/sample-divorce-forms, accessed on 3rd June 2013 at 10:00.

238 Property Rights and Gender: A Training Toolkit - Property ... (n.d.). Retrieved from http://www.icrw.org/files/images/Property-Rights-and-Gender-A-Training-Toolkit-P, accessed on 13th June 2014 at 10:07.

According to the Divorce Act (Chapter 249), a husband may apply by petition to the court for the dissolution of his marriage on the grounds of adultery. A wife may initiate divorce on several grounds: her husband has changed his profession of Christianity for the profession of some other religion, and gone through a form of marriage with another woman, or has been guilty of incestuous adultery, bigamy, rape, sodomy or bestiality and desertion.

Divorce rates in Uganda are relatively very small compared to other countries. This has two sides. On the positive note, the culture dictates harmony in the family and exalts the beauty of the family. The extended family in many African communities is there to help when a problem arises. On the other hand, it shows the inability of women to escape abusive marriages. Lack of decision and a feeling of helplessness lead women to accept whatever comes their way.

c) The Effect of Divorce or Separation on a Woman in Uganda

Firstly, the process itself is very energy consuming. It takes a lot of courage, determination and pain to begin the process of divorce. It is also hard especially for a woman to receive help. The only help would be to help her to remain submissive. The psychological pain together with the uncertainty of her future is the first consequence of ending the marriage.

Secondly, the question of bride price. When a marriage ends through a divorce at the request of a woman, the bride price that was paid to his parents has to be paid back. The parents of the woman are in most cases very old and payment that was through livestock twenty years ago has now often doubled in worth. Twenty-two years ago there were a lot of cattle and the demand was not like today when those goods are commercialized. It is not only the payment of the court fees, hiring lawyers, transport, etc. but also the bride price. This is a very expensive risk.

But more to that, divorce is still stigmatized in Uganda because of the nature of society. Women who divorce are still seen as "failures" in marriage. It is very hard to remarry. During an interview with female leaders at Mushanga, a woman who divorced said "I am actually surprised that the people still choose me to be a leader and more surprised today to meet a priest to talk about this (marriage and divorce)"[239].

---

239 Asiimwe Robinah, 38, Banker, Kabwohe, on 2nd June 2014.

Also, when a marriage ends or couples separate, the properties that they have must be divided. Women and men may bring their own property into a marriage. They may also acquire or improve property together while they are husband and wife. It is important to understand women's property rights in divorce and separation.[240] It is common for women in Uganda to lose property in a divorce even if it was their personal property or they contributed to it because many cultures and traditions say that only men can own property, or they limit the resources that women can have.[241]

There are, of course, so many consequences of a marriage ending in divorce; some are negative, and others are positive. From the individual perspective, especially on the side of a woman, it is a relief. On the side of children, it is traumatizing. But at the end of the day, one has to choose the lesser evil.

4.2.2.6 Inheritance of Property

Inheritance of family property is possible in two ways. When there is divorce, when the family head dies, and when it is decided willfully by family members.

The last form is usually done at the request of the family head when he is ill or is about to die. The inheritance of property in Uganda remains a very contentious issue on both local and national levels. The question remains, who owns what?

According to Uganda's Constitution and Land Act, both women and men have equal rights to own land and property, either as individuals or jointly with other people[242]. When people get married, they do not lose these rights.

However, because couples tend to share property, what belongs to the husband, what belongs to the wife, and what belongs to both can become confusing. In many cultures in Uganda, most or all property belongs to

---

240 Property Rights and Gender: A Training Toolkit - Property http://www.icrw.org/files/images/Property-Rights-and-Gender-A-Training-Toolkit-P, accessed on 13th June 2014 at 10:07.

241 Ibid.

242 Property Rights and Gender: A Training Toolkit - Property from http://www.icrw.org/files/images/Property-Rights-and-Gender-A-Training-Toolkit-P accessed on 13th June 2014 at 10:07.

men, even those things a wife brought to the marriage. It is important for women and men to know that they can own property before, during and after marriage.

Unfortunately, current marriage laws in Uganda do not clearly spell out the property rights of married men and women. Rather, this information comes from common law (the law passed on to Uganda by the British). Women have equal rights to men in getting married, during the marriage, and if and when they decide to end the marriage. Traditionally, property is still viewed as belonging to the man. He still controls although the modern trend shows that both parties contribute to the acquisition of this property.

Inheritance practices remain a very dangerous signal to the mentality of the father to the daughters. However, this is quite challenging in an African setting when a woman is expected to join the family of a man. When a girl receives a plot of land from her family, it is not usually easy when she marries. Sometimes this affects the parents before they apportion the land. All the same, land inheritance practices perpetuate landlessness, attach little value to women, who are rootless and visitors in their own homes, and reduce the potential productivity of women when they feel like strangers in their home.[243]

4.2.2.7 Widow Inheritance

Widow inheritance is when a male family member of a deceased man marries his widow without her consent. Since it was abolished, it has changed its form. It has now a more subtle form. It is highly secretive and worse than before. This is one of the old traditions of the Banyankole. It is a practice that was abolished and is seen as highly archaic and very unjust.

In any case, widow inheritance practice disempowers women and may entail dispossession of property and children, especially girls. It predisposes women to HIV/AIDS but also the men who inherit them because sometimes the deceased husband had died from it. In any case, the results are often catastrophic, but it mainly reduces the scope for protecting children.

---

243 Mukasa, Stella, Nite Tanzam, Hope Kabuchu, and Santa Vusia Kayonga. 2004. Uganda: Poverty and Gender Assessment: Strengthening Linkages between Poverty and Gender Analysis in Uganda. Copenhagen: Danish Development Cooperation.

The prohibition of widow inheritance has been successful. Many women who still practice it do it of their own will. The "law is there; one may not be forced into it" said one female leader in the Kyabugimbi county.[244] But "circumstances may force one to give in to it" retorted the other.[245] In reality, she was inherited by the brother of her deceased brother.

This cultural practice of widow inheritance has been successfully rooted out with the new legislature of 1995. Therefore, one can say women have been liberated from this practice that is very demeaning and non-compliant to the rights of a woman.

4.2.2.8 Domestic Violence

In November 2009, parliament passed the country's first bill criminalizing domestic violence, the Domestic Violence Act, which was signed into law in 2010. The bill provides a thorough definition of domestic violence that includes physical, sexual, emotional, verbal, psychological, and economic violence as well as harassment. In addition, the bill provides protection orders for abused women, which had not previously existed in Ugandan law. Rape is a criminal offence in Uganda under Chapter 14 of the Penal Code, which also prescribes the death penalty for those convicted of rape.[246]

Spousal rape is not currently recognized as a criminal offence, but the Marriage and Divorce Act and the draft Sexual Offences (Miscellaneous Amendments) bill of 2004 (both pending) recognize spousal rape as a crime and mandate imprisonment, fines, and compensation to the victim as punishment if the partner's refusal to have sex is on the basis of poor health, surgery that affects the capacity to engage in sexual intercourse, childbirth, or "reasonable fear that engaging in sexual intercourse is likely to cause physical or psychological injury or harm".[247]

Domestic violence was and remains a concern of the legislators regarding emancipating a woman. After many years, the project has found that

---

244 An Interview with women "Bakyara Tukore" at Kyabugimbi on 25th May 2014.

245 Ibid.

246 http://www.genderindex.org/country/uganda, accessed on 13th June 2014 at 10:17.

247 Ibid.

domestic violence is still a very serious problem. This knows no age group or level of education. In fact, the first ever female vice president of Uganda openly confessed to having been physically beaten by her husband, a thing that resulted in divorce and later ended her career as a politician.[248] Many women in the focus groups confessed that they have been beaten or slapped at one time or another. "You see us smiling during the day but what goes on in the family is only known by the walls of our bedrooms," said one woman during the group interviews.[249] When asked whether this was true, many others outside the focus groups smiled and agreed in unison.

The problem of gender-based violence is widespread in Uganda. United Nations data suggest that more than 40 percent of Ugandan women have suffered domestic violence.[250]

Field research into domestic violence carried out in the districts of Iganga, Kabale, Kampala and Kitgum by Law and Advocacy for Women – Uganda found that 62 percent of the focus groups identified the payment of bride price as a major cause of domestic violence as it encouraged men to beat wives who did not measure up.[251]

Unfortunately, many women believe or are driven to conform to the cultural imperatives that violence is normal, especially when it comes to the man disciplining his wife over something that she has done wrong. UDHS data has found that 76.5 percent of women believe that wife beating is acceptable for any one of a specified set of reasons. The reasons for wife battering, beating or insulting are diverse. The grounds for domestic violence in rural areas and urban areas differ significantly, but the core source is the same – the superiority of men over women. It is indeed the real source.[252]

In urban areas, where women are more emancipated than their colleagues in the countryside, the situation is not better. They too faced this problem. This was mainly observed among working class women who have to be

---

248 http://news.bbc.co.uk/2/hi/africa/3049833.stm, accessed on 13th June 2014 at 22:07.

249 An Interview with women leaders at Ibanda on 19th May 2015.

250 http://www.un.org/en/events/endviolenceday/pdf/UNiTE_TheSituation_EN.pdf accessed on 21st April 2015.

251 Lisa Karanja, "*Just Die Quietly: Domestic Violence and Women's Vulnerability to HIV in Uganda*" 2003, Vol. 15, no. 15(A).

252 Irene Atumwa, 36, Housewife and Businesswoman, Mbarara, 4th April 2015.

away on different errands as required by the nature of their jobs. The imperative to control the family and consequently the woman is something not to be underplayed. This seemed to be the cause of violence in many cases.

Many men fear that women will become promiscuous and indulge in extra-marital affairs if they are not monitored. In fact, that is a reason why many men would prefer to dictate what type of work his wife should do. One woman in the focus group is a qualified banker, but after two years of conflicts in the family due to working with almost only males and coming home late, she had to resign from her job at the bank to save her marriage. She now runs a shop in her hometown where her husband can monitor her easily.

In the Kinyankole dialect, *okufuuha*[253] as a verb or *obufuuhi* as a noun denotes the "control" a person exercises over another to stop her from extramarital affairs. The negativity within this practice is that it is at the level of suspicion or rumors. Some women use it, but they do not have the capacity to hurt their partners as men do. Therefore, *obufuuhi* is at the heart of domestic violence in many families.

Notably, male to female domestic violence levels in rural Uganda are higher. They have ended up even in death. Between January and April 2013, there were 72 reported cases in the police report of men killing their wives and women killing their husbands.[254] It must be clear here that domestic violence is not one-sided, but in most cases it is male against female violence. This is mainly associated with alcohol consumption and the urge to enforce discipline on the female partner. Almost all women whom the research approached testified to this fact. Either they are victims or their friends are or they know someone who has been assaulted or threatened by her partner. In all these cases, many women prefer to remain silent as they do not trust their justice system or for fear of being ridiculed or divorced. The police spokesperson in Mbarara who preferred anonymity said this.

A similar study was conducted by researchers from the Johns Hopkins Bloomberg School of Public Health in the US highlighted and affirmed this reality of high levels of domestic violence associated with both alcohol

253 *Okufuuha* - a word which has two meanings - a grass thatched house and puffing of smoke. Although many think it is building a house around a person, the new dictionary refers to it as to do with puffing smoke to scare an enemy.

254 *New Vision*, Uganda, 18th June 2013, by Vision Reporter.

consumption and the male partner's perceived risk of HIV and other sexually transmitted diseases (STDs). The study found that approximately one in three women living in rural Uganda reported being physically threatened or assaulted by their current partner. The findings from the study suggest possible links between the risk of domestic violence and alcohol consumption and women's perceived risk of HIV from their male partner. The study was published on 22 January 2003, in the Bulletin of the World Health Organization and is among the first studies from Sub-Saharan Africa to examine domestic violence at a community level.[255]

The authors note that at the same time there is widespread acceptance of domestic violence in this setting. Seventy percent of men, and 90 percent of women viewed the beating of the wife or female partner as justifiable in one or more circumstances. In their opinion, "little progress in reducing levels of domestic violence in settings such as Uganda is likely to be achieved without significant changes in prevailing individual and community attitudes toward such violence." Sixty percent of women aged 15–49 years experienced physical violence, 39 percent sexual violence, and 16 percent have experienced abuse during pregnancy.[256]

Another bad practice that still affects women is domestic violence. Reporting and handling domestic-violence-related problems remain very challenging to low courts who are comprised mostly of men. Domestic violence disempowers women of ability, esteem and affects their health and productivity, sometimes it results in death.

Some local council (LCs) officers who spoke to Human Rights Watch seemed to be unaware of the widespread nature of domestic violence and of the fact that many women did not perceive LCs to be viable sources of support. Isma Tamale, LC1 defense chair in his village, was shocked to hear

---

255 Michael A. Koenig, et al., Domestic violence in rural Uganda: evidence from a community-based study in Bulletin of the World Health Organization: the International Journal of Public Health 2003; 81(1): 53–60 or Domestic Violence Levels High in Rural Uganda - 2003 - News ... (n.d.) from http://www.jhsph.edu/news/news-releases/2003/uganda-violence.html, accessed on 13th June 2014 at 22:23.

256 Uganda Bureau of Statistics, Uganda Demographic Health Survey 2006 at: http://www.measuredhs.com/pubs/pdf/PR18/PR18.pdf accessed on 13th June 2014 at 18:23.

that many women did not feel that the LCs could help them: "We have cases of violence against women but not many. Men leaving their wives in the house without giving them assistance and quarreling with their wives ... Yes, I mean beating ... I'd be surprised to learn that there are many women who are beaten who don't come to the LC. It's probably because they still love their husbands. I don't agree that if they don't come it's because they don't see the LC as a solution ... I won't lie, we have no programs to deal with domestic violence as yet."[257]

The government has failed to ensure that domestic violence is adequately investigated by the police and prosecuted in the courts. Human Rights Watch interviews showed that the belief that domestic violence is a private concern that should not involve the state was prevalent within the police force and at the local council level.

In 2002, a female activist wrote: "[The] application of equality in Uganda is asymmetric. It subjects relations in the public sphere – the world of political participation, employment, and education – to minimum standards of justice. In contrast, it relegates the private sphere of the home and family to an arena that is almost beyond justice."[258] Three hundred and forty-three interviews with police and state prosecutors indicated that women's economic vulnerabilities made efforts to pursue domestic violence cases difficult, and that although a small number who filed charges followed their cases through to their conclusion, most ultimately withdrew their complaints so that their partners could return home and provide for the family. Often this resulted in further violence.[259]

---

257 Strengthening of the Judiciary Project, "The Strengthening of the Judiciary Project, Background," http://www.judicature.go.ug/docs/Thepercent20Strengtheningpercent20ofpercent20thepercent20Judiciarypercent20Project.pdf, accessed on 13th June 2015 at 12:24.

258 Jacqueline Asiimwe, "Co-ownership of Land by Spouses: Should it be in the Land Act or the Domestic Relations Bill?" p. 140.

259 HRW: *Just Die Quietly: Domestic Violence and Women's* ... (n.d.) from http://www.hrw.org/reports/2003/uganda0803/6.htm accessed on 16th June 2014 at 18:07.

4.2.2.9 The Critical Review of Cultural and Religious Reality

The imbalance between men's and women's rights in Uganda goes beyond the legal emancipation of women. Complex social, cultural, and political issues are at work.

Reforming the law has been and remains safe, but above all the cultural and religious setting has to change. This will change the Ugandan society that places a woman in an inferior position in relation to men. The assumption that a woman cannot do what a man can do is entrenched by traditional customs and norms in Uganda. African academics such as Muhanguzi[260] and Nyanzi[261] believe the cultural and religious norms prevalent in Ugandan society pressure women and men to follow specific and rigid gender rules that do not allow an atmosphere of gender quality.

All in all, Uganda is a patriarchal society where the mixture of culture and religion has led to clear distinctions between the gender roles, where females are viewed as feminine, with their sexuality controlled and suppressed and thus female sexuality is constructed as subservient, emotional and caring. A big change in the mindset and mentality of both men and women is needed in order to better the position of women in Ugandan society.

4.2.3 Economic Distribution Indicator

This is probably one of the most considered indicators in the eyes of many sociologists. Under Section 3 of the Employment Act (2006), women are entitled to sixty work days of paid maternity leave at 100 percent of wages paid for by their employer, although leave can be extended in the event of illness of the mother or child.[262] The Employment Act (sections 6, 17) also protects pregnant women from unjust dismissal and guarantees the right to return to their old jobs.

---

260 Muhanguzi, F, K, "Gender and sexual vulnerability of young women in Africa: experiences of young girls in secondary schools in Uganda" in Culture, Health and Sexuality: An International Journal for Research, Intervention and Care, 2011, 13:06, p. 713–725.

261 Nyanzi et al., "Money, Men and Markets: Economics and Sexual Empowerment of Market Women in South-western Uganda" in Culture, Health & Sexuality, 2005, Vol 7. p 13–26.

262 http://genderindex.org/country/uganda, accessed on 20th June 2014 at 11:07.

In addition, women are protected from discrimination in the workplace based on race, color, sex, religion, political opinion, national extraction or social origin, and HIV status under the Employment Act.[263] However, these protections do not apply to the large percentage of employed women in Uganda who work in the informal and agricultural sectors – 42 percent of women in the labor force are unpaid family workers and women account for 75 percent of agricultural workers – which means that the majority of Ugandan women are vulnerable to employment discrimination and are ineligible for maternity coverage.[264]

Uganda relies heavily on agriculture and women contribute largely to it. The day of a woman in Uganda is usually packed with work. It ranges from working in the field or the office, catering for the family, looking after the children or worrying about them, and caring for the weak or old members of the family. Sometimes a woman is responsible for carrying and marketing the produce to get money to sustain her family or the people under her care, but mostly for developing the community or country. Undoubtedly, women are the backbone of the economy. Unfortunately, the facts on the ground show unfair distribution in Uganda's economy. Women are seen as producers or workers whose toil and sweat is usually enjoyed by others. Although women are producers, they are not decision makers in the economic distribution.

Available data indicate that women work considerably longer hours than men, between 12 and 18 hours per day, with a mean of 15 hours, compared with an average male working day of around 8–10 hours.[265] Women bear the brunt of domestic tasks, including processing food crops, providing water and firewood, and caring for the elderly and the sick. Fetching water, collecting fuelwood, and pounding grain involve arduous physical work and must be performed daily, in addition to agricultural and other productive work. The time and effort required for these tasks, in the almost total absence of even rudimentary domestic technology, is staggering.[266]

263 Ibid.
264 http://genderindex.org/country/uganda, accessed on 20th June 2014 at 11:23.
265 Uganda - FH Canada. (n.d.) from http://www.fhcanada.org/About-Us/Uganda, accessed on 13th June 2014 at 10:07.
266 Ibid.

Therefore, to assert that the economic dependence of women lies at the heart of the problem of their liberation is but the bitter reality. Many women look to men for survival. Some get money out of their produce and take it to their husbands who then determine how the money is to be spent. Many women remain slaves in their homes under the cover of the protection from men. They depend on their men for almost everything. This is another indicator that women are still far away in the struggle.

Men control land, capital, and other productive resources, and this renders women economically weak. Being financially strong means one has to control these factors of production. Controlling factors of production means controlling other sectors in society.

More to that, behind women's lack of control over productive resources and assets is a systemic issue; inequity in marital status and property ownership intersects with cultural attitudes and beliefs to create formidable obstacles to change. The imperative to control women – embodied in the question "how can property own property?"[267] – is underpinned by the fear that women will become promiscuous and indulge in extramarital affairs if allowed to work or own money. Men express the view that women will become "uncontrollable," "unmanageable," "unruly," or disrespect men if they gain economic independence.[268] They fear that allowing women to work may lead to family breakups, because women will be able to abandon their husbands once they are no longer economically dependent on them.

However, with the new wave of the emancipation of women, there have been women trying to be self-reliant. This project mentions just a few. There has been an increase in the formation of women's groups known as self-sustaining groups. The intention of these groups aims at empowering women economically. One such group is a church-based group called the Mbarara Catholic Women Organization (MCHWO). This guild has been founded in many parts of Mbarara, Bushenyi, Ibanda, Kiruhura and Buhweju and in other areas where it is still in its infancy stages.

---

267 "*eitungo ritunga rita erindi*?" a common question in the vernacular posed by some men during the interviews. This implies that as soon as the bride price is paid, women automatically become part of their husbands' property.

268 Rutashoka Y, 54, Member of Parliament, Mbarara constituency, Kampala, 6th June 2014.

Like any other women's group, MCHWO came up with a developmental orientation but initially as a reaction to the high illiteracy as well as poverty levels of Catholic women. Many Catholic women were despised by other religious affiliations but also by men, because they were thought to be very backward. Thus, the Catholic Church began and encouraged the move to uplift the economic and social standards of Catholic women. It was meant to make them aware of the possibility of self-reliance and of the role they owe the Church as church mothers.

As a result, the Church has not only gained from this endeavor but has caused other governmental bodies to profit from it. These guilds have benefited both the Catholic women and women of other denominations. To the local population, for example, the projects around Ibanda town have brought employment and development to many people, especially women.

Due to these Catholic women's guilds on sub-parish and parish levels, the Church has called for national and diocesan organization. For example, on the national level, there is Uganda Catholic Women's Bureau based at the Uganda Catholic Secretariat, Nsambya. This means inter-district relations are in place.

Additionally, other women's groups such as *Bakazi Twimukye* in Bushenyi, *Bakazi Tweyombekye* in Kagongi and *Bakazi Twetunguure* in Ntungamo, are involved in economic activities[269]. They lay out economic strategies and actively implement them. Also, many women run income-generating projects. Hence, their communities benefit by receiving good business women together with income.

No doubt, as women break the vicious circle of poverty, the population benefits financially and materially; financial support is usually channeled through taxes and donations. Also, some women's groups operate on church lands on a land lease basis. Hence, they pay rent. As women constitute the majority of church-goers, Sunday offertory collection mainly depends on them. The author observed that women are the majority of those who ask for mass intentions and consequently mass stipends. This partly sustains the Church but also the whole community because many parishes employ

269 These women's groups mostly engage in economic activities to support each other for the household up-keep.

on average seven to ten workers in their banana plantations or farms or as parish house cooks.

More so, women's projects of tree planting, milling machines, farms and granaries have contributed to the economy in one way or the other. Timber and building materials to build towns and villages have been obtained from the forests planted and owned by women, for example, in Ibanda parish.

Finally, women's religious groups or nuns are one of the better-organized women's groups. These not only contribute to the Church's apostolate, but to the entire population in which they live. In Mbarara, the sisters of Our Lady of Good Counsel (OLGC) have farms, dairy projects, milling projects, candle-making and sweater-making projects.

Many kinds of projects have been mentioned in the subject of the work done by women's guilds. Other important projects include educational projects, where vocational training has been undertaken to try to uplift and solve the imbalance of education for girls, such as secretarial colleges in Nyamitanga. Another good example is the scholarship foundation fund project for women's education. These have an effect on the Church, as it is provided with educated people, secretaries, social workers, therapists, and psychiatrists, etc.

Still, women are engaged in money-generating projects, for example poultry, bridal salons, coffee and tea rooms, sewing, shoe making, tailoring, handicrafts, making garments and knitwear, candle making, vegetables and mushroom projects (in Rubindi) and tree planting. All these help women to develop the country's economy, their own economy and consequently they are becoming economically independent. However, access to some resources such as land and capital remains an uphill task.

4.2.3.1 Access to Land and Finance

One of the challenges women in western Uganda face is access to land. Most of the projects mentioned above come from their own sweat and pulling together to get enough credit. Some of these projects are still run on leased lands. Land is a resource still inaccessible to many women or women's groups. The late President Nyerere of Tanzania once observed:

> Women of Africa toil all their lives on land that they do not own, to produce what they do not control, and at the end of their marriage, through divorce or death, they can be sent away empty handed.[270]

However, before the law women are allowed to own land or property as men. The bitter reality is that ownership of registered land remains for women and men at seven percent and 93 percent respectively, which means that women remain economically behind men.[271] Land is a sign of power and control but also wealth. Land inheritance remains mainly patrilineal and as such women have no other option but to depend on men.

The second indicator of why women largely depend on men is that women work mostly at home and have limited job opportunities. In the formal labor force, women remain disadvantaged. No emphasis is placed on preparing them for the workplace. Women are exposed to heavier workloads and face hazardous conditions. Women stand at 32 percent to 24 percent of the adults within households likely to becoming sick.[272] They undertake household chores, which means looking after the family but also trying to earn something for sustenance.

According to research on people that receive wages of less than 40,000 Ugandan Shillings a month (11.74€ as of 13th July 2014), women stand at 51 percent compared to male compatriots at 49 percent. The fact is that less value is placed on women's work. A lack of credit limits women's economic independence and then affects gender relations. Distribution of credit stands at 91 percent for men compared to nine percent for women.[273]

4.2.3.2 Literacy Factor and Access to Education

Another critical factor is literacy. In Uganda the literacy rate – those can write and read – stood at 87 percent in 2012, an increase of 66.8 percent

270 Nyerere, Julius, former president of Tanzania at Third World Conference on Women, 1984/HRW: Just Die Quietly: Domestic Violence and Women's Retrieved from http://www.hrw.org/reports/2003/uganda0803/5. accessed on 13th July 2014 at 10:07.

271 Ellis Amanda, Eds: GENDER AND ECONOMIC GROWTH IN UGANDA: unleashing the power of women, Washington DC, World Bank, 2006, p. 22.

272 Ibid., p. 22.

273 Ibid., p. 22.

from 2006.[274] Women stand at 63 compared to men 77 percent.[275] This has already been covered in the previous chapter. Literacy is vital to the development of a human person but also to national development.

Credit should be given to the affirmative action and the campaign of girls' education. Literacy rates reflect the low value placed on people. Grooming women for marriage was (and is in many rural parts of western Uganda) a factor in limiting schooling and, therefore, a backlash to literacy. This is true in Kiruhura, where it was observed that girls are groomed to receive the quickest qualification possible or even to drop out of school in view of marriage (meaning sometimes in view of bridewealth).[276] The allocation of gender roles also affects girls' progression in formal education, the primary channel for literacy. Naturally, poverty interacts with negative attitudes and makes the situation worse.

The enrollment of girls at a tertiary level is another key factor. It stands at 38 percent compared to males' 62 percent.[277] But unfortunately, many people still think that an investment in girls' education is a loss. Many believe that a girls' education is an investment that goes to the family where she will be married or to the clan of the girl's husband. This discourages many families from educating their daughters. Early marriage also keeps tertiary enrollments low. Such negative attitudes and thinking make it hard for women to progress.

Education remains key in the gender equality campaign. It is the beginning of the way to women's independence in almost everything. One becomes independent, can receive a salary, or be an entrepreneur herself, thus breaking the male dominance in this area.

---

274 http://en.wikipedia.org/wiki/List_of_countries_by_literacy_rate accessed on 1st February 2014 at 14:00.

275 Uganda Bureau of Statistics, Uganda DHS Ed Data Survey, 2011. Education Data for Decision Making. UBOS, Entebbe, Uganda.

276 Interview with female leaders at Kazo parish, Kiruhura District, 29th June 2014.

277 Uganda Bureau of Statistics, Uganda DHS Ed Data Survey, 2011.

4.2.3.3 *Labor Exploitation*

Apart from being dependent on men, women still face exploitation by employers. This, however, seems to be a big problem for women almost on the global scale.

Women who have received little education or have not received qualifications are hired and paid very little money. Although there are laws in place, many women do not use them. They are either ignorant of them or they are afraid of being fired. Thus, they work very hard but also do overtime with tiny pay compared to their male colleagues, because this all depends on the power to bargain, which many women still lack.

Inadequate education leads to underemployment and sometimes to unemployment. As a result, many people resort to going and working for employers who in turn determine their wages or salaries. And in a society that is predominantly patriarchal, women are at a disadvantage.

The focus on women's overburden in the UPPAP (Ugandan Participatory Poverty Assessment Project) recognized explicitly that market and household economies are intertwined. It further holds that this has critical implications for both the allocation of labor – and its productivity – across the full range of tasks that disproportionately fall on women. Some specific adverse effects of time poverty were identified in some key areas, in a way that insightfully captures the cross-cutting nature of this issue.[278]

4.2.3.4 *An Analytic Look at Economic Reality*

Although economic or financial autonomy was not the sole factor limiting women's capacity to leave abusive relationships, many of the women experienced poverty. So severe was it for them that they had literally no any other option apart from remaining with husbands who routinely beat them. Their worth and social acceptance was found in marriage and children, making the separation or divorce almost impossible. Although returning to their parents' home was an option for a few women, some encountered male relatives or friends who either did not wish them to return home or were unable to repay the bride price.

278 UPPAP, 2002.

Lack of education undoubtedly contributes to women's economic dependency. The Rakai study found that women with secondary schooling experience had "significantly lower risks of violence."[279] Out of fifty women interviewed by Human Rights Watch, only twenty-one had continued to secondary school.[280]

From the above facts, together with many findings of the project, one can conclude that dependence on men deprives women of influence in family and community matters, and ties them to male relationships for sustenance and the survival of their children.[281]

Women's lack of access to finance affects not only the process of gender mainstream but also the economic progress of the country. The empowerment of women in the field of agriculture will be a great benefit to the country in the area of the economy.

Secondly, there are many businesses run by women that need a financial boost. Women make up nearly 40 percent of businesses with registered premises. Unfortunately, they receive only nine percent of all credit. Banks often require land as collateral, but as a result of land allocation practices that favor men, women hold only seven percent of registered land.[282]

Land is vital in Uganda's economy. However, land allocation practices in Uganda remain unfair, and this poses a fundamental constraint to female entrepreneurs, affecting not only their access to credit but also their ability to find business premises. Although formal succession laws give women inheritance rights over land, customary patrilineal practices (and the inability of many women to assert their legal rights) mean that formal laws are rarely adhered to. Only about 15 percent of the land is actively registered

---

279 Michael A. Koenig et al., "*Domestic Violence in Rural Uganda: evidence from a community-based study*", op.cit., p. 56.

280 HRW: *Just Die Quietly: Domestic Violence and Women*, from http://www.hrw.org/reports/2003/uganda0803/5.htm, accessed on 11th August 2014 at 00:07.

281 Culture of Uganda - history, people, clothing, women, beliefs ... (n.d.) from http://www.everyculture.com/To-Z/Uganda.html, accessed on 14th September 2014 at 10:07.

282 Amanda, E., et al., p. 29.

in Uganda[283], and it is rare for women to be registered as owners or for their rights to be noted on the register. This has to be dealt with decisively.

Many female entrepreneurs or women who engage in businesses still face particular difficulties with taxes and customs. Recent evidence suggests that businesses headed by women are forced to pay significantly more bribes and are harassed more than businesses run by men. This is because Ugandan women are less educated and have fewer formal business skills than men, and they find it harder to deal with tax issues, and time. Poor women find it difficult to comply with complex tax registration requirements. It is recommended that the Ugandan Revenue Authority develop policies for assisting women entrepreneurs, through tax clinics and open discussions, for example.

Women who live in the countryside often lack control over their income, even when they provided the labor for it. Women lack incentives to raise cash crops because men tend to control the resulting income.[284] This itself has a cultural background. It is to be noted that some justified cultural and customary practices pose not only a threat to women's safety and security but also limit the economic input.

All in all, culture has a pervasive impact on social and economic life. It is a cross-sectorial issue that influences the roles and status of men and women in different sectors. Cultural factors inhibit Ugandan women from realizing their potential in business. A woman involved in a business is frequently referred to as an immoral person.[285] A married woman must normally seek permission from her husband to conduct business, and particularly in rural areas women occasionally have to give up income from their enterprises to their husbands. This is not only against women rights but also counterproductive to the country's economy.

---

283 Middle East: Economy | Scholastic.com. (n.d.) from http://www.scholastic.com/teachers/article/middle-east-economy accessed on 11th August 2014 at 10:07.

284 World Bank 2005b, "Uganda: From Periphery to Centre: A Strategic Country Gender Assessment." Poverty Reduction and Economic Management, Africa Region. Washington, DC.

285 Lubega, Sarah. "Law Reform and Effective Implementation as the Means to Economically Empower the Ugandan Woman." In Bond, Johanna, *Voices of African Women: Women's Rights in Ghana, Uganda, and Tanzania*, Carolina Academic Press, North Carolina, 2005, p. 379ff.

4.2.4 Health and Welfare Indicator

The government of Uganda has made progress in this area. It has tried to establish a system and has abolished the user fees in health. This has, of course, strong pro-poor and pro-women effects. This means that poor people, especially women, have increased access to health facilities since the abolition of user fees. This has of course its weaknesses and strengths. In this indicator, the project researched the implications it has had in the lives of women. Women's health is vital to their liberation. Emancipation must be integral, and a healthy person is easier to liberate than a sick person.

Uganda's health system is divided into different levels at the national and district levels. At the national level, there are the National Referral Hospitals, Regional Referral Hospitals and semi-autonomous institutions including the Ugandan Blood Transfusion Services, the regional or National Medical Stores (NMS), the Ugandan Public Health Laboratories and the Ugandan National Health Research Organization (UNHRO).[286]

At the district level in a decentralized form of governance, the lowest district health system consists of Village Health Teams (VHTs). These are quite numerous and are volunteer community health workers who predominantly deliver health education, preventive services, and simple caring or curative services in the communities they are assigned too. They constitute level one health services. The next level is Health Center II (HC II), which is an outpatient service run by a nurse or any designated medical person. It is intended to serve around 5,000 people. After HC II is Health Center III (HC III), which should serve around 10,000 people and provides, in addition to HC II services, in-patient and simple diagnostic and maternal health services. It is managed by a clinical officer. Above HC III is the Health Center IV (HC IV), run by a medical doctor. It provides surgical services in addition to all the services offered at HC III. HC IV is also intended to provide blood transfusion services and comprehensive emergency obstetric care.[287] In all these, women receive special treatment, for example, of prenatal, postnatal care.

286 Ministry of Health, Government of Uganda. The Second National Health Policy. Promoting People's Health to Enhance Socio-Economic Development. Kampala, Uganda, July 2011.

287 Ministry of Health, Government of Uganda. Health Sector Strategic Plan 2000/01 – 2004/05. Kampala, Uganda, 2000.

4.2.4.1 *Physical Reality*

Uganda has one of the fastest growing populations in Africa. It currently has a population of around 34.9 million[288] and its fertility rate is placed among the highest in the world.[289] Uganda has several good policies and action plans that address its primary population and development issues, yet none adequately address the country's fertility. This mostly affects women.

a) Women and Birth

The fertility rate (the total births per woman) in Uganda was 6.05 as of 2011. Over the past fifty-one years, this indicator reached a maximum value of 7.12 in 1969 and a minimum value of 6.05 in 2011. The total fertility rate represents the number of children that would be born to a woman if she were to live to the end of her childbearing years and bear children in accordance with current age-specific fertility rates.[290]

According to estimates from UNICEF, Uganda's maternal mortality ratio, the annual number of deaths of women from pregnancy-related causes per 100,000 live births,[291] stands at 435[292] after allowing for adjustments. Women die as a result of complications during and following pregnancy and childbirth, and the major complications include severe bleeding, infections, unsafe abortion and obstructed labor.[293]

Most women in developing countries have at least four antenatal care visits, are attended to by a skilled health worker during childbirth, and receive postpartum care. In contrast, only 47 percent of Ugandan women receive antenatal care coverage, and only 42 percent[294] of births are attended

---

288 http://www.redpepper.co.ug/ugandas-population-now-at-34-9-million/ citing National Housing and Population Census released on 17th November 2014 by the Uganda Bureau of Statistics.

289 http://www.prb.org/Publications/Datasheets/2011/world-population-data-sheet/uganda.aspx

290 http://www.indexmundi.com/facts/uganda/fertility-rate.

291 Women; Definitions; UNICEF. Retrieved 20th February 2012 at 10:09.

292 Uganda; Statistics; UNICEF. Retrieved 20th February 2012 at 10:55.

293 Health in Uganda - Wikipedia, the free encyclopaedia. (n.d.). Retrieved from https://en.m.wikipedia.org/wiki/Health_in_Uganda on 20th February 2012 at 11:15.

294 Ibid.

by skilled health personnel. Among the poorest 20 percent of the population, the share of births attended by skilled health workers was 29 percent in 2005/2006 compared to 77 percent among the wealthiest 20 percent of the population.[295]

During the interviews, personal testimonies from different women were narrated. One woman narrated how she witnessed her friend bleed slowly to death in the maternity ward in a major hospital, citing the poor state of maternal health care that is provided to some women. This sometimes happens even in some major urban healthcare facilities.

Many women in rural areas or even urban areas tend to produce more than four children and in most cases do so without full proper medical attention resulting in a long-term risk to their lives. Moreover, there is still a high prevalence of diseases such HIV/Aids, domestic violence and other associated problems that greatly affect their health.

b) Girls in School and Personal Hygiene

One of the most uncomfortable topics in Uganda is this area. During the research, the project found the hard reality that can drastically affect the self-esteem of a girl in school. One of the causes of girls dropping out of school is the menstrual period that is natural to women. In Uganda, where sex and sexuality issues are not discussed in the public and remain very secretive, young women or girls suffer psychological trauma during their first experiences. This normally happens in their last years of primary school and at the beginning of secondary school. With the Ugandan 7-4-2-2 system of education, a girl who starts school at the age of four or five is likely to complete her primary education at the age of twelve or thirteen. This is a typical age for many girls to transition to womanhood. This is our fate as women, says a senior female teacher. We try to help girls but sometimes they land in poor hands.

While macro-level data are available on sanitation access and gendered school attendance, the everyday 'lived experiences' of schoolgirls with poor

295 "Millennium Development Goals Report for Uganda 2010". United Nations. Retrieved 20th February 2012.

sanitation access are poorly understood.[296] Reflecting on the difficulties of obtaining information on such sensitive issues,[297] academic research on the influence of puberty (and the risk of sexual harassment that can accompany this) and menstruation on girls' school attendance has been quite scarce.[298] Nevertheless, interest in menstruation and poor sanitary product access as possible causes of female pupils' absenteeism has attracted attention from the media, NGOs and policy-makers following efforts to track progress towards the millennium development goals.

As if that is not enough, sanitary pads cost money. In village shops, it is not in the interest of the sellers to offer them. The young girls look at them as something shameful and they resort to using "raw cotton" or some "rugs" or pieces of clothes which they usually learn from their peers or their mothers. The openness on such issues in the lives of women remains a challenge to Ugandan society. One can note that there is a link between gender, sanitation and education; for example, a girl who is not comfortable with her periods may remain absent from school for fear of being bullied.

Emphasizing linkages between girls' absence from school and poor sanitation provision, several studies in South Africa have highlighted important everyday challenges associated with managing menstruation in school environments. Sommer's research in Tanzania emphasises the difficulties created by a lack of access to private toilets with water supplies,[299] sanitary products, painkillers for menstrual cramps, and spare clothes if leaks occur. Long school days (typically eight hours in Kenya and Uganda) that increase the risk of menstrual leaks coupled with frequent harassment by boys in and around school toilet areas add to the shame and embarrassment experienced

296 M. Sommer, "Where the education system and women's bodies collide: the social and health impact of girls' experiences of menstruation and schooling in Tanzania J. Adolescence", 33 (4) (2010), p. 521–529.

297 McFarlane, C., Desai, R., Graham, S., "Everyday Geographies of Sanitation: Politics and Experience in Mumbai's Informal Settlements". <http://www.esrc.ac.uk/my-esrc/grants/ accessed 4th September 2013 at 10:12.

298 McMahon, S., Winch, P., Caruso, B., A. Obure, E., Ogutu, Ochari, RRheingans "'The girl with her period is the one to hang her head.' Reflections on menstrual management among schoolgirls in rural Kenya" Biomedicalcentral, 11 (2011), p. 1–10.

299 Although it should not be overemphasized that many girls may not have access to such facilities in their homes either, that is the fact on the ground.

by many post-pubescent girls. Where it is difficult to change sanitary products, infection (and the odour of menstrual blood being detected by others) are likely to be higher and girls may suffer discomfort and stigmatization as a result.[300] Given such constraints, it is unsurprising that many Kenyan girls view "menstruation as the most significant social stressor and barrier to schooling"[301] and prefer to manage their menses at home.

The pan-African NGO FAWE (Foundation for African Women Educationalists) found that a "culture of silence" surrounding menstruation in rural Uganda resulted in it being "ignored in families, schools and communities."[302] This remains a thorn in the side of the fight for women's equality in Uganda.

Also, the cultural sensitivity and taboos and etiquette surrounding menstruation coupled with the "great distaste" associated with sanitation more generally have long resulted in the neglect of such issues within development initiatives and wider academic research.[303]

The consequences are that the young women become insecure in the company of men. Girls in mixed schools are often bullied by boys, and they never report these incidences, especially to male teachers. As a result, they feel dirty, and as already said, in extreme cases they leave school – the reason for school drop-out. At home, daughters never share these challenges with their male parents and when their mothers must work far from home, or they are not "friendly to their daughters", they take it up themselves.

---

300 Muito, M., 2004. "Gender equality in the classroom: reflections on practice." Paper presented at the Beyond Access: Gender, education and development project seminar on pedagogic strategies for gender equality and quality education in basic schools 2004 from: http://www.ioe.ac.uk/schools/efps/GenderEducDev/Muitopercent20paper.pdf accessed 12th May 2009 at 13:10.

301 McMahon, S., Winch, P., Caruso B., A. Obure, E. Ogutu, I. Ochari, R. Rheingans "'The girl with her period is the one to hang her head'. Reflections on menstrual management among schoolgirls in rural Kenya", Biomedicalcentral, 11 (2011), p. 1–10.

302 FAWE Uganda, Creating Opportunities for Girls' Participation in Education in Uganda Presentation at Transforming Spaces: Girlhood, Action and Power Conference, Montreal, November 2003.

303 George, P., The Big Necessity: Adventures in the World of Human Waste, Portobello Books, London, 2008.

Additionally, the research found out that many school girls who were interviewed never wanted to identify themselves with this "period of time" in their lives. They are shy and feel that being a woman in this context is something that belittles them. Although this cannot be equaled with self-denial in the sense of the word, it affects the psychological balance of a woman.

The project further interviewed the male teachers who in most cases never wanted to discuss the issue. They harness the typical stereotypical theories of African as well as Europeans origins – women are seen as unclean during this period. A whole chapter of Leviticus, which in fact one of the teachers quoted, is dedicated to that prejudice. The African tradition also held women during this time as sick. In any case, men distance themselves from this talk or from merely thinking about it, and the senior women are left alone.

However, girls in educated families and from township schools seem to be at an advantage. Some who were asked in Mbarara, Bushenyi and Ibanda township schools had mixed reactions. Some confessed that they hide these revelations from their parents, and they manage alone or with the help of school mates. But one underlying factor was that these girls in urban schools can afford to buy pads or some painkillers. Their counterparts in rural areas stay with their parents or are in poor schools where they are never given enough pocket money. Those still in primary seem to have it rough.

The current legislation against gender inequality has not served these poor girls or young women because this matter lies in the private sphere.

4.2.4.2 Psychological Reality

Women not only face physical health problems, but more tormenting is probably on the psychological level. While interviewing groups of women, it was clear to many that the liberation of women is a threat to the "stable long-held African culture", community, and they feel "guilty" that they must break it.[304] Others cite the many incidences of the family breaking up, spouses killing each other in fights and spouses running away from their homes.

However, this could be easily understood because this is a situation where two parties are facing each other; one for liberation (a woman claiming her

304 A female lawyer, 34, on the question of the negative side of gender equality, Kampala, 2nd June 2014.

rights) and another for non-liberation (one clinging to the oppressive status quo). There is nothing good that comes easy.

Women's liberation has not been "heaven on earth". It, too, has had an adverse impact on other aspects of life. The emancipation of women was never served on a silver platter but in some areas, especially in Mbarara where there was not enough sensitization, it was accompanied by some kind of martyrdom.

When the author approached the Diocesan Peace and Justice Office in Mbarara, he noted that they currently have 167 cases between women and their husbands, of which 48 cases file for separation if not divorce. In all 48 cases, there was a charge of "women of today are a problem".[305] The Church is striving for reconciliation.

a) Male Attitudes

Many men are not yet comfortable with women's emancipation. The author noticed that many men and even some church leaders had ill-feelings about the whole project of gender mainstreaming.

Some men oppose even the government or church policies openly without facing justice. In Kyarwehunde, Rwera parish, Ntungamo district, for example, a prominent man stopped going to his local church just because a woman catechist was put in charge. He even persuaded the assistant catechist, who was a male, to resign.

Such naivety and ill-feelings result from conservatism and lack of sufficient sensitization. As a result, some female leaders have been abused, despised and molested in some villages. It was noted that in Kibingo, Rubindi parish, some men chased away a female representative under the excuse that she was a "curse" to the area. Although this group of men was apprehended and punished, it remains to be seen how many share this radical and archaic mentality.

On the other hand, there has been a steady increase in male activists for gender equality. During interviews, men were in most cases invited, and they contributed. Some men are even shareholders of office bearers of the projects of women. Julius Tunanukye, a lay leader, said in one of the interviews: "the

---

305 Peace and Justice Tribunal Offices, Mbarara Archdiocese, Archives, File No. 7 visited on 3rd June 2014.

success of our families and our communities depends largely on women. Cooperating with women is the only way for the future of our country and the Church."[306]

b) Women Used for Political Ends

Uganda has a multiparty political system of government. As already discussed, the movement system of governance paved the way for women's rights. A few years ago, Uganda adopted the multiparty system. Under the multiparty system, almost all political parties came up with manifestos and charters that reasonably promised to handle women and gender issues, including promoting the involvement of women in their decision-making,[307] as well as advancing women's problems and concerns. They too promised to end all forms of injustices against women.

During the research evaluation of what women have gained under this system of governance, the main question put was: how far have the political parties implemented these commitments to include women and handle gender issues in their party agendas? Have women gained anything or these are empty promises? An excellent source of the evaluation was the Forum for Women in Democracy (FOWODE), which commissioned a study in 2007 to analyze gender issues in political party agendas in Uganda. A study titled "Dancing to the Tunes of Democracy: Women and Political Party Agendas" found that despite the modest commitments to women and gender issues by all leading political parties, they have not done enough to ensure sufficient female representation in their structures and gender mainstreaming.[308]

"Most political parties through the structures, processes and practices do not promote gender equity and equality and as such are discriminatory to women hence the need for more gender sensitivity and strategic interventions

306 Tunanukye J, 49, Parish Head Catechist, Buhimba, Bushenyi, 28th May 2014.
307 UGANDA: Long Way to Go for Uganda Women in Political Parties. (n.d.). Retrieved from http://makeeverywomancount.org/index.php?option=com_content&view=article accessed on 5th December 2012 at 12:30.
308 Forum for Women in Democracy (FOWODE) Kampala, 2007 at: http://www.peacewomen.org/news_article.php?id=2887&type=news 2005 accessed on 12th February 2014 at 14:04.

so that multi-party democracy indeed benefits women,"[309] the report reads in part. The study notes that women's issues and commitments in political parties were "were lost in the mainstream"[310]. And yet, many political parties still use these promises to get more votes from women.

Furthermore, the study report shows that all political parties fell short of the required 40 percent female representation in the party's governance structures that most political parties had committed to.[311] Even then, the study notes that the deputizing syndrome has continued in most political parties with women taking up positions of deputy or vice. It is unfortunate that most political parties consider women together with other special interest groups, which limited their ability to focus effectively on addressing gender issues.

Lastly, it was also noted that most political parties preferred to field male candidates than female candidates as party flag bearers. The assertion was obtained from some of the political party officials, men and women; and from reading relevant literature that included political party manifestoes, constitutions, and press reports. This shows that many political parties take advantage of women who form the majority of the population of Uganda.

c) Notable Extremes

In 2014, an Anti-Pornography Bill was passed.[312] The law was criticized as infringing on women's rights and freedoms, and called the "mini-skirts bill".[313] The bill bans "indecent" dressing including any skirt that falls above the knee and any form of dress that may "sexually excite".

Naturally, any new thing brings with it some excitement, mistakes, and shortcomings. The liberation of women was long overdue, and when it came, some women received it with enthusiasm and have exaggerated it. Some activists have gone overboard and look like extremists.

Some women have equated emancipation to becoming men or manly women. Some women think that freedom means behaving like men, limiting

309 http://www.genderlinks.org.za/article/dancing-to-the-tunes-of-democracy-women-and-political-party-Agendas accessed on 25th January 2011 at 11.45.
310 Ibid.
311 Ibid.
312 http://www.genderindex.org/country/uganda#_ftn46 accessed on 17th April 2016 at 17.57.
313 Ibid.

to dressing like men or even speaking like them, becoming authoritarian and aggressive. This has affected not only men but also their fellow women. As such, some other women find themselves getting loose from the bondage of men and falling prey to a new trap of fellow women. Here they were singling out their "overzealous" leaders. This was often stated in almost all interviews.

Also, some women have gone to extremes by thinking that emancipation could be achieved immediately. As a result, there has been frustration or friction and conflict. In fact, one of the reasons why the majority of the followers of the cult of the restoration of the ten commandments were women is that many women thought they had been liberated fully, which caused commotion in homes, hence they had to take refuge. Unfortunately, many women and men perished in the Kanungu inferno on 17 March 2000, and others were either strangled or stabbed by the cult leaders.[314]

Furthermore, there has been an extremism of mistaken equality with authority that has been one of the greatest roadblocks to gender quality. Some women have posed as husbands, taking up roles of men and not entertaining any discussion. For example, a certain woman in Ibanda parish told other women in the meeting that she had to "beat" her husband because he had refused to wash their child and to cook.[315]

All these find their bearing in the gender mainstreaming process. This requires the empowerment of women while still involving men.

4.2.5 Observations and Conclusion

4.2.5.1 Observations

The four indicators of the situation in Uganda give a clear picture of the successes and the remaining challenges of this project. On the level of governance, a lot has been achieved concerning gender equality. The political

314 On 17th March 2000 at Kanungu in Rukungiri district in western Uganda, about 1,000 people belonging to the Movement for the Restoration of the 10 Commandments of God cult were killed, many of whom were women.

315 Interview with a group of women at Ibanda parish, Ibanda District on 28th May 2015.

climate and the legal framework emancipate women. However, in other indicators the project portrays and still faces many challenges.

Despite the fact that the number of women participating in politics and governance has been steadily increasing, their participation or involvement has not had the desired impact on women's situation. It has not had a big effect on the implementation of legislations and policies to make them gender sensitive, human rights compliant and responsive to women's rights, interests, and needs.

The research has found the following reasons for this inability. First, women as direct beneficiaries of affirmative action have not done enough to interpret it in their lives, monitor its implementation and ensure that its provisions and proposal are enforced. Also, the government has demonstrated on several occasions its reluctance, which is mostly seen as a lack of political will to operationalize the constitutional provisions for gender equality and women's empowerment. Thirdly, the institution of patriarchy is still active, and this makes the conditions for women's empowerment in Uganda very problematic.

However, the paper has recognized some achievements in terms of the constitutional provisions, the institutional and political framework in place that women and society can build on to achieve greater gender equality and female empowerment. The project further proposes policy recommendations, which, if properly implemented, would contribute substantially to scale up women's impact on policies, bills and legislations for gender equality and women's empowerment.

In all, gender inequality is still to be felt in these areas, and gender inequality encompasses the principle that men and women are unequal and the notion that men are innately superior, occupying positions of authority. This is due to the strong social patriarchal structures and long held cultures.

The research further found that the momentum and untenable zeal leading to the unity of purpose and effort by women, which was depicted immediately after the takeover of the NRM regime, the age of emancipation during the constituent assembly process that resulted in the positive impact on the constitution-making process was not sustained after the passing of the constitution. The fire of affirmative action was soon ignited. The sustainability of the project was wanting. It only continued in some sectors where bills were already in place, but still faced the danger of being weakened.

The problem was that men and women got this affirmative action as a reward or gift. They never looked at it as their right. This issue also influenced the way women operated. This created another problem whereby women's organizations and networks mobilized and organized on an ad hoc basis for particular issues or problems rather than having a sustained and focused struggle for liberation and empowerment of women. As a result, women as direct beneficiaries of affirmative action have not done enough to shape its interpretation, supervise and monitor its implementation and ensure that its provisions are enforced.

As Kharono observes:

> The weak sense of ownership of affirmative action among women and their various organizations and networks has contributed to the continued perception that affirmative action is a gift from the NRM government rather than a right. That this attitude persists, notwithstanding the constitutional provisions, illustrates the failure of its proponents to own, engage and define its content and develop a coherent and strategic agenda for its implementation.
>
> Given this failure, it is not surprising that a large number of women beneficiaries of affirmative action not only feel obliged to the NRM government but also dare not challenge the status quo. They find it easier to fit into, rather than transform systems cultures and structures that have marginalized them, which is the intended purpose of providing for affirmative action in the constitution.[316]

This, however, is not the only challenge. Another problem or even the greatest challenge to affirmative action is compounded by the institution and practices of patriarchy that are still influential in Ugandan society. Patriarchy here is understood as a systemic male dominance in economic, social, cultural and political spheres. It validates male values, behavior, and privilege and devalues the position of a woman in that particular set-up.

4.2.5.2 Conclusion

The situation of women is not yet up to the required standard, but gender mainstreaming remains one of the ambitious projects in Uganda. The biggest challenge of this project remains the complicated social set-up, strong cultural institutions and long-held traditional practices imbued with laws and acceptable customs but also the mindset of the people.

---

316 Kharono, 2003, opt.cit., p. 11.

However, the ambitious project remains focused and feasible due to the awakening of human rights and the young emancipated generation of women. Special credit is also attributable to the international exposure of young women. Uganda in particular and Africa in general can no longer remain in isolation. As such there is a big hope for the gender equality and equity in Uganda soon. This requires, though, a concerted effort from men and women in empowering women of all ages.

In conclusion, therefore, empowering women is a way forward for women's liberation in Uganda. This requires empowering women not only as a group but also as individuals. The empowerment of women will be dealt with in the next chapter.

Chapter Five: Women's Power and Empowerment

5.0 Introduction

Without any doubt, the project of women's emancipation and gender equality in Uganda has been one of the successful ventures of an African state. Even more impressive is the fact that it has been possible in an environment of a very solid gender-biased cultural institution. Uganda has been one of the front-runners of women's rights in Sub-Saharan Africa.[317] However, despite these efforts, women have not yet achieved their rightful position in Uganda. Does it mean women's emancipation is an illusion in Uganda? What of the future of this project? Why is the realization of this dream taking so long? Where is the problem?

Uganda's legal framework has been highly improved, and many avenues and opportunities have been availed to enable women to enforce their rights and obtain their rightful position in society. The political climate remains that of respect and encouragement towards women's rights. The women too somehow have something to be proud of.

On the other hand, the research found that the process of improving gender equality and equity has a long way to go. Very few women feel they have been emancipated. Women, especially in rural areas, still live in a kind of servitude despite the measures in place. The reasons for this reality are diverse and vary from place to place. These must be dealt with decisively and concretely to achieve the intended goal.

The research, therefore, identified a key area where a lot of effort is required to bring about change in western Uganda and the rest of Uganda. The recommendation of the research is that women need empowerment and power to overcome all these obstacles that hinder gender equality.

317 Mushemeza E. Dickens, "Contribution of Women in Influencing Legislation and Policy Formulation and Implementation in Uganda", op.cit.

5.1 Definition of Terms: Power and Empowerment

The definitions of the two terms remain subject to continuing debate in the social as well as political sciences. Thus, these two principal terms have been used differently by many people from different walks of life. Although they have been used loosely in different situations, these terms are technical and academic in nature. They, too, are closely related but for the purposes of good research they will be first defined and then applied.

It is good to note that these two terms are used in the social context but more specifically in an environment where governance and control depend on how much influence a particular group has at a given time. Therefore, the two terms will be limited in this context.

5.1.1 Empowerment

Empowerment has been and still is a wide, complicated and highly debated term in academic circles and especially at the international development level. The problem is that empowerment, as a term, is very diverse and can be applied in many different situations. Thus, one can refer to empowerment to mean social, cultural, political or economic empowerment. Its theoretical application poses a rather complicated practical reality. It has been applied by different branches of philosophies and as well as other scientific researches. This means there are different usages and definitions. It is, therefore, worth differentiating between the technical and working definitions.

5.1.1.1 Technical Definition

Amidst a vast number of different definitions, a more generally acceptable term defines empowerment as the multi-dimensional social process that helps people gain control over their own lives.[318] However, it should be noted that not everyone accepts that empowerment can be clearly defined, let alone measured, and for many feminists, the value of the concept lies precisely in

318 Page, N., & C. E. Czuba., *Empowerment: What is it?* Journal of Extension, vol. 37(5), 1999, p. 24–32.

its "fuzziness".[319] Nevertheless, while acknowledging such limitations, for the purposes of this research the need for definition and measurement is self-evidential. In any case, the research should define the term and its usage.

Important to note, there are four other terms that are most often included in technical definitions of empowerment. These are: options, choice, control, and power.[320] These are very important elements in defining empowerment.

Empowerment should incorporate the integral person. Empowerment should embrace all spheres of women. Here the usage of Oakley's work offers a significant impulse to the process of gender mainstreaming. Oakley identifies five key uses of the term empowerment in development studies. These are: empowerment as participation; empowerment as democratization; empowerment as capacity building; empowerment through economic improvement; and empowerment and the individual.[321] He identifies the link between empowerment and involvement as the strongest in practice. The World Bank, for example, "began to recognize several stages of participation: information sharing, consultation, collaboration and finally, empowerment."[322]

From the above, different definitions and efforts have been attempted to make the term empowerment understood. It should be conceptual to the women seeking equal treatment as men. Thus, a working definition of this term is of vital importance.

5.1.1.2 Working Definition

The definition of empowerment adopted in this dissertation is the process through which those who are currently disadvantaged achieve equal

---

319 Kabeer, N., *Gender Equality and Women's Empowerment: A Critical Analysis of the Third Millennium Development Goal*, in Gender and Development, Vol. 13, No. 1, 2005, p. 18.

320 Petesch P., C. Smulovitz & M. Walton, *Evaluating Empowerment: A Framework with Cases from Latin America. In D. Narayan, ed. Measuring Empowerment: Cross-Disciplinary Perspectives*, The World Bank, Washington, DC. 2005, p. 40.

321 Oakley, P. (Ed)., Evaluating Empowerment: Reviewing the Concept and Practice. Oxford: INTRAC, 2001, p. 43.

322 World Bank 1998; op.cit., p. 19.

rights, resources and power.[323] Thus, women in western Uganda will only be fully emancipated when they are empowered. This empowerment involves achieving equal rights as men, achieving resources such as land, credit and property but above all, acquiring power. This can only be achieved through participation.

In this chapter, the concept of empowerment will be explored through some theories, especially those of Kabeer and Rowlands. These theories deal with "power within", "power from/over, power to" and "power with", using the dimensions of resources, agency and achievements. That means that women of western Uganda will undergo a particular transformation in order to be fully emancipated. This transformation is, however, a process that takes some time, if not a couple of years.

In supporting the working definition, another theory propounded by Paulo Freire will be applied. This is a "Pedagogy of The Oppressed". This is supplemented with Rowlands' "collective" and "personal empowerment" theory. As an example, empowerment will be tackled in the areas of culture and education, economic independence, and political control. At the end of this study, concrete recommendations will be offered to make the process of women's empowerment in the western region of Uganda a reality.

5.1.2 Power

In the first place, empowerment is about power. Empowerment is a process of changing power relations in favor of those who had previously exercised little power over their own lives. Power is an essential tool for empowerment. One cannot talk of empowerment without implying power and one cannot talk of power without talking of a certain control.

Further, women's intrinsic mistrust of and discomfort with masculine hierarchy has led to some discussion about the meaning of power itself. Thus, there has been a questioning of the ethics of power over others, be it people or nature, and its substitution by a notion of power as the ability to be, to express oneself. In this sense, the concept of power or authority is quite close

---

323 Mayoux, L., *Empowering Enquiry: A New Approach to Investigation*, 2008 from: http://www.kepa.fi/tiedostot/empowering-enquiry.pdf accessed on 12th August 2014 at 09:00.

to the concept of human capability. In craving to define their position, the women of Uganda began to discuss and face the reality of control in Ugandan society. Meeting this challenge occurred after a long struggle. Thus, the question of control and eventually power took center stage. What is power?

5.1.2.1 *Technical Definitions of Power*

Almost all dictionaries have tried to define the term power. Different definitions have been given and further defined. But for this research, one has been of interest and is defined as "the ability or capacity to perform or act effectively".[324]

Within social sciences studies, power was first identified as power over. As Robert Dahl defined it, "A has power over B to the extent that he can get B to do something that B would not otherwise do".[325] It further assumes "In this approach, power is understood as a product of conflicts between actors to determine who wins and who loses on key, clearly recognized issues, in a relatively open system in which there are established decision-making arenas".[326]

Eventually, a second dimension or face of power was recognized – the ability to prevent certain people or issues from getting to the decision-making arena in the first place. Bachrach and Baratz argued that political scientists must focus[327] "both on who gets what, when and how and who gets left out and how".[328] This dimension of power is concerned with the rules and methods of legitimizing some voices and discrediting others, or even silencing them.

Stephen Lukes then suggested that perhaps "the most effective and insidious use of power is to prevent such conflict arising in the first place."[329]

---

324 http://www.thefreedictionary.com/power, accessed on 11th August 2015 at 00:07.

325 Dahl. R., *The Concept of Power Behavioural Science*, Vol. 2, 1957, p. 202–203.

326 Ibid.

327 http://ageconsearch.umn.edu/bitstream/30578/1/ia030003.pdf, accessed on 12th August 2014 at 09:00.

328 Bachrach, P. and Baratz, M. S. (1970) *Power and Poverty: Theory and Practice*. New York: Oxford University Press, 1970, p. 105.

329 Lukes, S., Power: A Radical View, Macmillan Lukes, London, 1975, p. 24.

From this perspective, the powerful may win battles not only by doing so in open conflict or by preventing opposing voices from being heard. They may also get their way by manipulating the consciousness of the less powerful to make them incapable of seeing that a conflict exists. As Sen observes, "There is much evidence in history that acute inequalities often survive precisely by making allies out of the deprived. The underdog comes to accept the legitimacy of the unequal order and becomes an implicit accomplice."[330] This is true of many women who desperately accept the status quo as divinely programmed.

In this regard, there are three dimensions of power that consist of one party or a group of people getting their own way against the interests of another party or another group. They achieve this either by winning in open conflict, preventing their opponent from being heard or preventing their potential opponent from even realizing that there is a conflict of interests. These are all examples of a zero sum game, i.e. by definition one person's gain is another's loss (even if, as in the third dimension above, the loser is not even aware of her loss).[331]

5.1.2.2 Working Definition

In this research, the definition of Srilatha Batliwala would be adopted and supplemented with the definitions mentioned above. Batliwala defines power as having two central aspects – control over resources (physical, human, intellectual, financial, and the self), and control over ideology (beliefs, values, and attitudes).[332] This means power, which means control over the acts and thoughts of others.

If power means control, then empowerment could be understood as the process of gaining control. Therefore, women need power to acquire control: control of resources and control of ideology. For the Banyankole

---

330 Sen, A. Gender and Cooperative Conflict In Tinker, I. (Ed) Persistent Inequalities, Oxford University Press, Oxford, 1990, p. 26.

331 Ibid.

332 Batliwala, Srilatha. 1994. "The meaning of Women's Empowerment: New Concepts from Action." in Population Policies Reconsidered: Health, Empowerment and Rights. G. Sen, A. Germain, and L.C. Chen, eds. Cambridge, MA: Harvard University Press, 1994, p. 127–138.

women, that will be the decisive path to gaining their rightful place in society. During the research, it was evident that women generally have no control over resources and ideology or even policies in Uganda.

5.2 Contextualizing Power and Empowerment

There are as many reasons as they are many women that explain why many Ugandan women remain in powerless situations. Despite the admirable efforts of the government and other agencies – both national and international – to avert this position, it remains a problem. The research will limit itself to what women have in common and to a certain context.

In western Uganda, there is a common factor that all women share. As women, they are all constrained by "the norms, beliefs, customs and values through which societies differentiate between women and men."[333] This is not only true of women in western Uganda, but it also cuts across the whole of Uganda.

Naturally, the particular ways in which this operates vary from tribe to tribe, from culture to culture and from time to time. This is true among the Banyankole. This can be exemplified by the lower incomes of women compared to men and their dependence on men. Boys also get better education compared to girls and the severe restrictions on women's mobility by their husbands or parents. This powerlessness is also visible among the Banyankole in domestic violence cases, male-dominated decision fora and women's inferior access to assets and property, especially land. Women would therefore require this prerequisite – power – in order to be empowered.

5.2.1 Women and Power

The notion of women's emancipation deals with the level of control and power that women are able to achieve. There are different faces of power, but women require the face of power that is liberating in nature. Power has been associated with men from time immemorial. In order for women to be powerful they require this liberation. It is in itself a movement from one point to another.

333 Kabeer, N. *The Power to Choose: Bangladeshi Women and Labour Market Decisions in London and Dhaka,* London: Verso, 2000, p. 22.

Women in western Uganda need the force that pushes them from their current status quo to another higher level. This kind of power brings about the ability to make their own choices and independently start living the lives they choose. Below are steps that illustrate this upward movement.

5.2.1.1 Power Within

The "power within" is probably the most important step in empowering women. The process of empowerment begins with the resource stage that provides the ability for the women in the women's groups and movements to achieve their self-worth before challenging the structures around them. As Batliwala states: "women must first recognize the ideology that legitimizes male domination and understand how it perpetuates their oppression."[334] Women in Uganda must first appreciate the social strata and identify where they are marginalized before they can proceed with their freedom. This is a resource stage. Concluding from Kabeer, resources refer to the material and financial circumstances available, as well as the varying human and social resources that develop an individual's ability to exercise agency.[335] Women must be aware of their surroundings and the immense power within them to overcome it.

In line with Batliwala's term "oppression" and the need for knowledge, the research employs Paulo Freire's work and his discussion on education and oppressors.[336] Freire's work has been viewed by many as key to liberating the oppressed. This resource knowledge is called pedagogy of the oppressed. Women, too, are seen in this study as the oppressed.

The theory came into existence in 1968 after Paulo Freire began to see the potential for education to enlighten impoverished and illiterate peasants in Latin America.

Critical pedagogy can be viewed as a theory for the education of the marginalized, the excluded and, in this case, women.

It should be noted that this theory is based on the principle that through a lack of resources for knowledge, oppressed groups examine their world

334 Batliwala, 1994, op.cit., p. 131.

335 Kabeer, 1999, op.cit.

336 Freire, P., *Pedagogy of the Oppressed*. Intro by Ramos, B, M. (1996 edition), Penguin, London, 1968, p. 32.

through critical eyes. Once provided with these tools, the marginalized are able to build a critical consciousness or conscientization as Freire describes it,[337] then being able to see and wish to change the structures around them that function to restrict and contain them. It is clear that in this study, once the women gain knowledge from resources available at the groups, they will be able to develop. They develop what Kabeer calls "power within"[338] to make choices that will be part of their process of empowerment. Thereby as Freire states, equipping them with self-awareness as well as awareness of the world in which they exist and function.[339] By doing so, Freire claims, one can act upon and transform his or her world, moving towards new possibilities and a richer, more satisfying life as an individual and as a collective.[340]

The work of Freire is employed in this study because he refers to the essence of education as the practice of freedom through participatory methods. This research has found that his work is a great help in gender streamlining. After gaining full participation, women will no longer be just data to be analyzed but a reality to understand the world through their eyes. Women in western Uganda will know their worth as individuals and begin to move towards freedom.

Freire believes that students should be able to realize that there are unequal power relations at work, and the research should assess whether the women believe this to be true in Uganda and most especially in the western part of the country. Therefore, through education, teachers and students incorporate knowledge of diverse racial and ethnic minorities' as well as social classes and, importantly for this research, gender[341]

Although this study does not focus on formal educational institutions as such, all women's groups involved in this study have some kind of teacher-student type structure and a set of learning objectives are incorporated into the groups. Thus, Freire's theory is relevant for examining how each group deals with the access of knowledge, and how the groups work with the

---

337 Ibid.
338 Kabeer 1999, op.cit.
339 Freire 1968, op.cit., p. 32.
340 Ibid, as cited in McIntyre 2008, p. 3.
341 Freire 1968, op.cit., p. 53.

structures and agency involved in empowerment within this region. In this study, Freire's reference to "oppression" is used to describe women's ordeal.

This study refers to women as the "oppressed" because the very structure of their thought will have been conditioned by their existential situation and their perception of themselves has been influenced by their adoption of the oppressor's guidelines.[342] In this study, no one specific "oppressor" is named; instead the social institutions and traditions including men and the violence they may enact, which may be embedded into the unspoken structures within the groups, will be explored. It is not easy to identify any single oppressor in a very long-held tradition that has been cobwebbed with both internal and external influences.

Power within, for example, refers to qualities such as self-unfolding, self-esteem, self-driving and self-confidence[343]. In a sense, all power starts from here – such qualities or assets are necessary before anything else can be achieved. "[A] woman who is subjected to violent abuse when she expresses her own opinions may start to withhold her opinions and eventually come to believe she has no opinions of her own. When control becomes internalized in this way, overt use of power over is no longer necessary."[344] The internalization of such feelings of worthlessness is a well-recognized feature of women's oppression and, therefore, many development interventions seek to bring about changes at this level. Women have to be set free from the inside out.

Furthermore, Joke Schrijvers uses the term "autonomy" and defines it to mean, "a fundamental criticism of the existing social, economic and political order ... an anti-hierarchical concept, which stimulates critical and creative thinking and action ... transformation which comes from within, which springs from inner resources of one's own as an individual or a collectivity."[345]

---

342 Ibid., p. 29.

343 Kaber, op.cit.

344 Rowlands, J., "A word of the times, but what does it mean? Empowerment discourse and practice of development," in Women and Empowerment in the Third World Illustrations. Cf. Sayer, A. *Realism & Social Science*. London: Sage, 1998, p. 12.

345 Schrijvers, quoted in Stromquist, Nelly P., "The Theoretical and Practical Bases for Empowerment." Women, Education and Empowerment: Pathways

Power within is therefore a realization of self and the capability of an individual. This is like the resource stage. It is a springboard for all the transformation. It is vital for women to kick-start this upward movement.

5.2.1.2 Power From / Over

Once one has gained self-discovery and awareness, then one can act or react. The terms "power from" and "power over" are intrinsic to women striving for empowerment as a way to challenge the structures around them. In this regard, it is important to mention women whose power is external, derived from laws, social empowerment groups like mothers' unions or financial SACCOS that women normally belong to. I think these tend to give them empowerment.

Women in Uganda should shed all those things that chain them, hence blocking them from achieving their freedom. This is the first step, "a move from". Power from and power over are an overriding dimension of empowerment that constitute agency.[346] Kabeer states that agency is inexorably tied to power, as "it represents the processes by which choices are made and put into effect".[347] It further explains how there are two faces to agency. The combination of Freire's argument of the oppressed and the role of the oppressor is also of great help.

This means women will identify and try to negate the authoritarian control, for example, the patriarchal rules at play in Uganda that legitimize gender-based discrimination and gender inequality. Once that is done, women will be moving forward. Thus, the usage of the term "power to".

5.2.1.3 Power To

"Power to" is defined as "generative or productive power (sometimes incorporating or manifesting as forms of resistance or manipulation) which creates new possibilities and actions without domination."[348] It is not enough to challenge the structures and moving out of them without knowing what

---

Towards Autonomy. United Nations Children's Fund (UNICEF), *The Women's Equality and Empowerment Framework*. 1995, Pp.15–16.

346 Kabeer 2005, op.cit.

347 Ibid.

348 Rowlands 1997; op.cit., p. 13.

next. In this next step, "power to" implies treading into or leaping into another sphere. It is being down to earth, being hands on.

In other words, this is the power that increases the boundaries of what is achievable for one person without necessarily tightening the limits of what is achievable for another. For example, if someone learns to read, it makes many more things possible for him or her. It does not restrict others. This means that women redefine their borders and this does not mean to infringe on the rights of men. On the contrary, it places men in their rightful position.

5.2.1.4 Power With

"Power with" refers to a collective action, recognizing that more can be achieved by a group acting together than by individuals alone. Many interventions aim to empower women, and create opportunities for women to spend time with other women in order to reflect on their situation, and to recognize their strengths[349] so as to devise strategies to achieve positive change. Women in western Uganda or even Uganda as a whole need each other.

It is already clear that groups of women have had a greater impact on their societies than individuals who have struggled alone. It is of great importance that women unite in groups and associations in western Uganda and share their collective dream. This helps women to develop critical minds to discuss new ideas and work out new strategies.

Above all, women need a network through which a new interpretation can be given and spread, activating a social movement and a together-oriented empowerment. Fighting against an immemorial time structure requires a lot of energy and effort. Therefore, women need power as individuals and collectively as groups. "Power with" is key to women especially in rural Uganda where a concerted effort is required to challenge the status quo of their communities or societies. This is will create a road to empowerment.

---

349 Development of "Power within' among the Women: A Road to ..." (n.d.) from http://www.ccsenet.org/journal/index.php/ass/article/viewFile/9794/9776, accessed on 13th July 2014 at 22:02.

5.2.2 Women and Empowerment

Once women have gained power, then empowerment becomes a necessity. Women's emancipation can only be feasible and achievable when women are empowered. This is, however, a long and tiring process. A good example is teaching a village woman how to farm in a modern way, which automatically empowers her to achieve more from her produce but is very difficult. The empowerment of women must be integral, which means one has to be economically, politically, culturally as well as socially empowered.

The vision of this project is to fuel this empowerment of women as individuals as well as a group. It is also to strengthen and mobilize female leaders for rural development. The rural part of western Uganda is most affected. Empowerment presupposes some conditions, though.

5.2.2.1 Conditions for Empowerment

There are different conditions required for successful empowerment. These different conditions relate to the meaning of empowerment in one way or the other. Although different people use empowerment to mean different things, they generally agree on the ontological meaning of the word. The four aspects, too, seem to be generally accepted in the literature on women's empowerment.[350]

Firstly, to be empowered one must have been disempowered or powerless or at the risk of becoming so. This research, for example, speaks of empowering women in Uganda because, as a group, they are disempowered compared to men.

Secondly, empowerment cannot be given or even bestowed by a third party. It must be claimed by those who wish to become empowered. The Ugandan government or other governments, international academicians as well as development agencies cannot therefore empower women on a silver plate. The best they can do is to enlighten them of their plight and facilitate them to empower themselves. This means they may be able to create climates and conditions favorable to the process of empowerment to take place. They cannot make it happen. This has been an illusion of so many feminists and human rights activists in Uganda and on the international scene.

---

350 Siwal B.R., Empowerment of Women-Conceptual Framework, New Delhi.

Thirdly, empowerment usually includes a sense of people making decisions on matters that are significant and vital in their lives and being able to carry them out. As a reflection, analysis and action are involved in this process that may happen at an individual or collective level.[351] There is some evidence that while women's own struggles for empowerment have tended to be joint efforts, empowerment-orientated development interventions often focus more on the level of the individual.[352]

Empowerment is not an end in itself, and there is no final goal. It is an ongoing process, not an end product. One does not arrive at a stage of being empowered in some absolute sense. People are empowered or disempowered, compared to others or, importantly, compared themselves at a previous time.[353] This is almost an eternal process.

Behind these four aspects, a very important fact is vital and that is power. Power plays a key role in the process of empowerment. Power enables things and power must be translated for the good of the community or society and never be abused. This leads to empowerment. Empowerment can be observed at different levels.

5.2.2.2 Levels of Empowerment

There are essentially two main levels of female empowerment: individual and collective empowerment. Other scholars prefer subjective and objective terms but for this research, the terms individual and collective will be applied.

a) Individual Empowerment

Individual empowerment is key to the gender balance in the Ugandan context. The particular subject has to know itself first, and then its immediate and remote surroundings, the mentality and biases, prejudices and structural

351 Impact Assessment Research Centre Working Paper Series. (n.d.). accessed from http://ageconsearch.umn.edu/bitstream/30578/1/ia030003.pdf, on 24th September 2015 at 21:09.

352 Empowerment of Women -Conceptual Framework - Scribd. (n.d.) from https://www.scribd.com/doc/19166610/Empowerment-of-Women-Conceptual-Framework, accessed on 24th September 2015 at 21:09.

353 Impact Assessment Research Centre Working Paper Series. (n.d.). accessed from http://ageconsearch.umn.edu/bitstream/30578/1/ia030003.pdf on 24th September 2015 at 21:09.

weaknesses before it begins to strive for change. An individual has to know herself, her values, beliefs, goals, the influences from social, environmental and economic limitations, the possible solutions in order to effectively demand her new rights. Self-knowledge or self-awareness is not easy to install, but it is possible. The nurturing of the girls must be dealt with just right from the moment of their birth. The Runyankole proverbs "*akati kainikwa kakiri kabitsi*" transliterated as "trimming a plant must start in the early stage brings this to clarity." Child formation has to begin early enough and be geared towards an independent mind.

It is vital that empowerment begins with an individual before it is applied to the group. Empowerment at the individual level includes consciousness raising and the development of a critical faculty.[354] The development of a critical faculty of conscience in an individual will lead to an independent mind.

However, despite it's having "identified empowerment as a ... primary development assistance goal ... neither the World Bank nor any other major development agency has developed a rigorous method for measuring and tracking changes in levels of empowerment."[355] Uganda as a government and the different agencies that fight for human rights are challenged to think anew in this case. The emancipation of women is only possible when the women are empowered right away from childhood.

The final stage in Kabeer's empowerment structure relates to achievements; the potential for people to attain the life they desire. "Achievements have been considered in terms of both the agency exercised and its consequences."[356] For example, an empowered woman is influential in leadership positions and her opinion is often valued. She can effectively financially support the family. Rowlands identifies empowered women as demonstrating the product of empowerment processes as opposed to describing the empowerment processes itself[357] and as an individual. The result is what is seen rather than the means.

---

354 Freire 1974, op.cit., p. 34.

355 Malhotra, A. & S. R. Schuler., Women's Empowerment as a Variable in International Development. In: D. Narayan, ed. Measuring Empowerment: Cross-Disciplinary Perspectives, The World Bank, Washington, DC, 2002, p. 3.

356 Kabeer 2005, op.cit., p. 15.

357 Rowlands, op.cit.

However, individual empowerment cannot go far without collective group empowerment. The two types of empowerment are not mutually exclusive though; they are interlinked. But the individual comes first, for example a rural housewife attempting to change culture and imposing opinions on the man or family. It is from village societal groups that they gain the requisite knowledge and skills to enable them to boldly stand up to discrimination.

b) Collective Empowerment

Probably, that is what many writers mean when they write about empowerment. Many still believe that group empowerment leads automatically to individual empowerment but in the context of western Uganda, the study has found that without individual empowerment, group empowerment remains wanting. Rowlands discusses two types of empowerment, "collective empowerment" and "personal empowerment".[358] Under "personal empowerment" there is a link with Christen's work on relational empowerment and personal empowerment. Christen states that relationships, especially sexual and intimate, play a crucial role in the empowering process.

Christen's claims that relational empowerment gives a feeling of belonging and confidence derived from group solidarity that is then transferred into intimate relationships.[359] In the case of this study, it is to be understood that the relationships between women, their parents, partners and husbands are affected by relational empowerment attained from the group. That is to say, Christen has in mind that one can see the link with relational empowerment theory as "self-confidence, sense of agency and sense of self in a wider context" as fundamental concepts involved in the empowerment process.[360] Rowlands discusses group identity, collective sense of agency and group dignity as core notions of "collective empowerment" and Freire's discussion on education is reminiscent of these concepts.

More to that, Freire's theory concerns the empowerment of the masses through knowledge: "Education [...] becomes the practice of freedom, the

358 Ibid.

359 Christens, B, D., *Toward Relational Empowerment* in Am J Community Psychology, 2012, Vol. 50, p. 114–128.

360 Rowlands, op.cit., p. 23.

means by which men and women deal critically and creatively with reality and discover how to participate in the transformation of their world."[361] Freire's theory and collective empowerment are thus a process of revolution, the ability for all the "oppressed" to open their eyes to the structures around them and demand a change. This is done as an individual but also as a group.

In addition to that, Rowlands discusses the "ability to negotiate, communicate, get support, and defend 'self' in relationships."[362] And these are essential elements of individual as well as collective empowerment in western Uganda.

5.3 Women's Empowerment and Integral Development

This study affirms that both individual and collective empowerment of women lead to societal transformation. Women's empowerment brings about development. This change calls for two distinct forms of agency; "transformative and effectiveness".[363] Transformative agency is more in line with "power from and to". It discusses the agency of the women to suggest a greater ability for them to question, analyze and act on the structures of patriarchal constraint in their lives.[364]

This transformation will automatically lead to the development of the society. A country cannot develop unless it engages the efforts of its entire citizenry. That is why economic development goes hand in hand with social development. Thus, economic development will expand opportunities and increase productivity and raise the GDP for Uganda or even other developing countries. Women's empowerment in Uganda leads to a stable and integral development of the country. Therefore, by empowering women, one is transforming and developing society. Below are suggested areas of empowerment.

---

361 Freire, op.cit., p. 67.
362 Rowlands, op.cit., p. 24.
363 Kabeer 2005, op.cit.
364 Ibid., p. 15.

5.3.1 Key (Main) Areas of Women's Empowerment

5.3.1.1 Social Empowerment

This should be characterized by the following: a rise in the number of women in local arrangements or institutions, for example women's associations, income-generating groups and in positions of power in local councils beginning with the lowest level. Some extent of training or networking among local women compared to men should be encouraged. Women's mobility within and outside their residential locality should no longer be controlled by men. There should be a degree of independence.

This is, however, somewhat sensitive among Banyankole ethnic tribes. This is because men have "sex objectified" women for long. Hence a common saying "*omukazi tayanga*", which transliterated reads "a woman never refuses" or "a woman's no is a yes".[365] Over-protectionism has been identified as one of the ways of oppressing women. Therefore, on the socio-cultural platform empowerment is a necessity. Women's freedom of movement should be respected, and discrimination against women and their daughters should be abolished.

Women's visibility in and access to social spaces is a sign of independence.[366] By accessing modern transportation, by their participation in extra-familial groups and social networks, meetings and gatherings without first seeking men's permission lead to building their self-worth and this helps them to be self-reliant and independent.

Women's literacy and access to a broad range of educational options should be key to their empowerment. There should be positive images of women and their roles and contributions in the media or other social communications.

On the family level, women should be empowered. They should have control over fertility decisions, control over sexual relations, the ability to make childbearing decisions such as the number of children they want and

---

365 An expression that women are weak in defending themselves against men's advances and they should be therefore controlled or accompanied to avoid being used.

366 Anju Malhotra, PhD, Director, Population and Social … (n.d.) accessed from http://siteresources.worldbank.org/INTEMPOWERMENT/Resources/ on 23rd March 2014 at 03:34.

their family decisions. They should participate in domestic decision-making. They should have control over spouse selection, courtship arrangement, and marriage timing. Finally, they should have freedom from domestic violence.

5.3.1.2 Economic Empowerment

As already seen, women's dependence on men is one of the root causes of women's subjugation in Uganda. Economic dependence on men has been identified as a key structural factor at the root of women's vulnerability to poverty, sexual violence, unwanted childbirth, sexually transmitted infections, and a range of other negative outcomes[367]. However, it remains a subject open for debate as to whether empowering women economically alone will improve their situation. But as it stands now, it is a big challenge hindering the efforts of women's emancipation and hence catapulting the gender equality in Uganda.

Nevertheless, the project sees it as vital to empowerment integrity that helps a woman in a milieu such as Uganda, where decision-making depends on how much you have not how much you know. Therefore, the projects affirm that there is a need to enable women to access the same amounts of cash as men to be on the same level when it comes to decision-making.

This research recommends that there should be changes in employment policies. There should be changes in selected activities, particularly greater sharing of unpaid housework and child-care among household members; salary or wage differentials between women and men; changes in mentality and in the percentage of property owned and controlled by women and men, such as land, houses, livestock and they should have equal rights to own property.

It is important that women are enabled to make small or large purchases independently and are encouraged to and taught how. Women should have access to a percentage of available credit from money lending institutions and should be able to receive financial and technical support services from government and non-government sources.

367 Bassett and Mhloyi 1991, Ulin 1992, de Zoysa et al., 1996, Heise and Ellsberg 2001.

Also, women should be able to have control over their income just as men do. They should make relative contributions to family support and be able access and control family resources, especially land and livestock.

On the community level, women should be able to access employment and be involved with and represented by local trade associations. They should be able to own and access markets.

On the national level, women's representation should equal to that of men: women should be in high-paying jobs, be managers, have their economic interests represented in macroeconomic policies and their budgets respected at district as well as state levels.

5.3.1.3 Legal Empowerment

Although Uganda is faring well from a legal perspective, this framework has to be translated in the interest of gender equality. In chapter four of the Ugandan Constitution, a lot has been dealt with. This has been discussed in the previous chapters. What is important here is the application of law.

Firstly, women should be mobilized and empowered to know their legal rights and how to exercise them. This will require: community mobilization for rights; civic campaigns, awareness campaigns for rights awareness; effective local enforcement of legal rights; laws supporting women's rights, access to resources and options; advocacy for rights and legislation; use of the judicial system to redress rights violations.[368] The Federation of Female Lawyers, Uganda (FIDA) is already doing a lot of work, many more NGOs and government institutions should also join the cause.

Secondly, there should be enforcement of legislation related to the protection of human rights, especially those of women. Many cases related to women's rights are heard in local council courts, technically called magistrate courts. Most of these cases are linked to the legal rights of abused, assaulted, divorced or widowed women, and this requires impartiality. There should be an unbiased enforcement of legislation in terms of the treatment of offenders. There should be measures against violence against women. But most importantly, there should be an increase in the number of

---

368 Anju Malhotra, PhD Director, Population and Social … (n.d.) accessed from http://siteresources.worldbank.org/INTEMPOWERMENT/Resources/486312-1095970750368 on 23rd March 2014 at 03:34.

local justices, prosecutors and lawyers who are women, but also an increase in the number of women in the local police force and local defense units. Promotion should be on merit.

5.3.1.4 Political Empowerment

According to a 2007 Pew survey, 65 percent of respondents believed that men and women were equally capable as political leaders, while 27 percent thought that men were better than women.[369]

Women should be mobilized to have knowledge of the political system and means of accessing it. Women's participation, involvement or mobilization in the local political system and campaigns, support for specific candidates – especially fellow women – or legislation, and their representation in local bodies of government is essential. Women's representation in regional and national bodies of government, strength as a voting group, the representation of their interests and efforts in active lobbies and interest groups is part of their empowerment. There is the two-thirds gender rule that has now made it mandatory to designate seats for female representatives not just in parliament but in all employment organizations.

This is due to the fact that the current percentage of seats held by women in local councils and parliament is still very small, and yet these are decision-making bodies. In order to empower women, there is a need to increase the percentage of women in decision-making positions in local government, in the local civil service and to increase the proportion of women who are registered as voters and encouraged to vote. The involvement of women who participate in the public progress and political campaigning as compared to the number of men should be promoted.

5.3.1.5 Psychological Empowerment

Women should be empowered to regain their self-esteem, self-efficacy and self-reliance. The undoing of a long-held tradition should be a kind of healing process. This will lead to psychological well-being that in turn can free women from all forms of servitude or oppression. This empowerment can

369 http://www.genderindex.org/country/uganda#_ftn65, accessed on 23rd March 2014 at 03:34.

also be achieved through education for example, starting with ensuring that girls know their worth and ability to contribute to societal development.

Once that is done, there should be collective awareness of injustice, not only to women but the whole community. This naturally leads to mobilization against injustice against women.

As a result, women would feel a sense of inclusion and entitlement and this is a step forward towards empowerment of women. In order to make women's empowerment a reality, the research gives its recommendations.

5.3.1.6 Sexual Empowerment

As already noted, Uganda has one of the highest birth rates in the world. Mbarara, which is the case study of the present work, is one of the areas with high fertility rates. The project found that one of the reasons for many children in a home is the inability to plan. Many family planning programs have been undertaken by NGOs in Uganda in addition to the national campaign, but the problems still persist. Of course, there are a number of reasons. But one of the problems contributing to the production of so many children is the inability to refuse or negotiate with male partners.

Many of the women interviewed agreed that it is not easy to refuse a man on the pretext of "not wanting" children. Some of the women often gave "false but convincing" reasons for refusing sex. The biggest reason was to pretend that they were sick.

When women are emancipated, they will see themselves as equal partners in marriage and they will always negotiate issues at home. Sexual empowerment has to do with liberating women from this servitude of being seen as sex toys for men. Sexual empowerment goes with respect of the other when it comes to his or her body. This will empower women either practically or strategically within the family or relationships to influence the timing or conditions of sex, or protect themselves better from HIV/AIDS and other sexually transmitted diseases.

This means, however, that the "*swenkazi*" (girls' tutors) from the initiation period must be aware of this fact. Likewise, the Church, through its ministers during the preparation before marriage, has to empower women and men about the importance of respect in this matter. There are, of course, many interventions in all stages of women's growth.

In all, sexual empowerment is not mutually exclusive to other empowerments. For example, there is a very big difference between women who are economically independent with regard to sex compared to rural women who are almost totally dependent on their husbands. They say, "How can I refuse?" For them, it is batter trade. "I give he gives", said one woman.[370] There is a relational challenge between sexual influence and economic dependence.

370 This was one of the women in a meeting with some female leaders at Ibanda, Ibanda District, 2nd June 2014.

Chapter Six: Research Recommendations and General Conclusion

6.1 General Research Findings

This research together with the findings of different development agencies and organizations, both local and international, show that by respecting the rights and freedoms of women and by giving them the ability to choose their partner, to have fewer children, more time between births, investing in children's education as well their food and health needs, less demand will be made on the families' resources, thus helping to reduce poverty[371].

Still, the ability for women to decide when and with whom to have children will supposedly generate opportunities for them to gain education and employment, thus contributing to the development of their country as well as attaining economic empowerment for themselves. Interestingly, however, the Ugandan Demographic Health Survey (UDHS) highlighted how women who are involved in all household decisions desire the most children, whereas women who participated in one or two decisions desired the least.[372] From this data, it can perhaps be suggested that Ugandan women who are involved in all decisions are also accounting towards the household income and feel they would be able to afford more children.

As already highlighted, economic empowerment is linked with gender equality as highlighted by the patrilineal structures in Uganda where women are not able to obtain land rights. So the link between gender relations and economic empowerment is considered a fundamental human right by international development bodies.[373]

371 UNFPA (2011). HUMAN RIGHTS: Supporting the Constellation of Reproductive Rights. at: http://www.unfpa.org/rights/rights.htm on 20th March 2014 at 13:34.

372 Uganda Bureau of Statistics: Ugandan Demographic Health Survey 2011, Kampala, Uganda.

373 OCED 2011, op.cit., Pp.9–10.

6.2 Concrete Research Recommendations

To achieve the full liberation of women in Uganda, all Ugandans will have to unite to foster social, economic, cultural and political as well as educational liberation. There is a need to re-awaken, realize and reinforce affirmative action for women's issues in both official and non-official fora. In this regard, the research recommends the following concrete measures:

6.2.1 Girls' Education

Education is key to transforming society. Generations come and go, and generations bring about different changes. The modern status quo can only be effectively changed by another generation of women. The transformative power of a woman will be productive with a new generation. But this generation has to be prepared for it. The program of girls' education, which has already began in Uganda, should be given more emphasis and the study of human rights, values and awareness should be included.

This is not the concern of only Uganda as a country but also the whole of the sub-Saharan region. Already, many scholars and people of vision have brought this urgency to the forefront. In 2003, the former UN Secretary General Kofi Annan remarked that "there is no tool for development more effective than the education of girls."[374] Indeed, in Uganda there will be no effective empowerment of women or even gender equality without the education of girls. As cited in UNICEF, no other policy or venture is as likely to raise economic productivity, reduce infant and maternal mortality, improve nutrition and promote health.[375]

Still there, other key benefits associated with girls' education include protection against early pregnancy and other sexual/reproductive risks or dangers such as HIV/AIDS.[376] Girls in Sub-Saharan Africa (SSA) bear a disproportionately high burden of such risks,[377] and although girls' school

---

374 UNICEF, 2008. Girls; Education Campaigns. <http://www.unicef.org/education/campaign.html> accessed 4th February 2012.

375 Ibid.

376 Mason et al., 'We Keep It Secret So No One Should Know'- a qualitative study to explore young schoolgirls' attitudes and experiences with menstruation in Rural Western Kenya, 8 (11) 2013, p. 1–11.

377 Ibid.

enrolment ratios in the region have increased in recent years,[378] large inequality gaps in primary education remain.[379] Gender gaps are even more pronounced in secondary education.

The research found that there is a big relation between poor school-based sanitation and girls' low attendance rates or school dropout. Unfortunately, comprehensive research has not been done and relevant information is only provided by personal research and through interviews. "Nevertheless, the interdependence of the gender, education and sanitation Millennium Development Goals"[380] has received increased interest from donors and NGOs. According to Barbara Frost, without sanitation "you cannot achieve universal primary education, you cannot promote gender equality and empower women, you cannot reduce child mortality."[381]

This will be done with the rethinking of programs of health and reproduction in schools following the model of the AIDS campaign, which was very successful in the early 1980s. There should be a consistent program of providing free sanitary kits or tools to schools or of starting the projects of making local sanitary pads. As already seen, girls' lack of knowledge and sanitary pads during their periods affects their self-esteem, especially those girls who happen to be in mixed boarding schools. It is no wonder that girls in mixed schools do not compete favourably with their male schoolmates. Of course, this is not the only problem. Other problems originate from the gender gaps that are found in the school curriculum.

Moreover, the prototype education that is mainly biased as already discussed has to be reviewed, and a school curriculum that places all children under equal treatment should be resolutely adopted.

---

378 World Bank, 2011. World Development Report 2012: Gender Equality and Development. <http://wdronline.worldbank.org/> on accessed 15th March 2012 at 15:00.

379 UN, 2012. Millennium Development Goal 3: Where do we stand? <http://www.undp.org/content> accessed 15th March 2012 at 15:00.

380 Ten, V.T.A., 2007. Menstrual Hygiene: A Neglected Condition for the Achievement of Several Millennium Development Goals, <http://www.eepa.be/wcm/dmdocuments/BGpaper_Menstrual- Hygiene.pdf> accessed on 9th July 2012 at 15:00.

381 Melik, J., 2011. Poor Sanitation Stifles Economic Growth [online] BBC News, 18th November. <http://www.bbc.co.uk/news/business-15552967> accessed on 12th December 2012 at 15:08.

Also, the educational imbalance between boys and girls that still exists on the tertiary level of education should be addressed. Parents who prefer educating boys to girls should be held accountable or even be brought before courts of law to face justice.

Teachers should be offered new opportunities to attend refresher courses to go with the modern thinking of women and gender rights. Boys and men in any institution of learning should be given opportunities to learn more about women and be held culpable when the red line is crossed without any protection from the system. Teachers and lecturers who have abused girls in schools, colleges and other higher learning institutions should be held accountable. The victims who are still alive should be helped. This would require a very strong team of lawyers and female activists to champion this cause. Also, girls or women who offer sexual favors in exchange for grades or marks should be held responsible.

Above all, one needs to know that history has shown that mere community sensitization or girls' education campaigns do not produce the desired impact. This is mainly because the girls are officially enrolled in school but in practice they learn or benefit less than boys. The real cause of this scenario is the existence of unfavorable conditions within these children's circumstances. A theory is one thing, and practice is another.

Therefore, girls' education should not only be a popular movement, a rhetoric or promise of the politicians or a sensitization program that cost the country many shillings only to see the girls remain in a less privileged position. It should be a concrete project with foreseeable fruits.

6.2.2 Employment for Women

As already discussed, the heart of the problems of women in Uganda is their dependence on men. This explains why many women are abused and taken advantage of. The mentality of women looking to men for money or survival has to stop. This should start from the families, indeed the whole upbringing. Secondly, women should be provided with employment opportunities and be independent in their financial status. One cannot be liberated and free when one is a dependent or even a beggar. The dependence syndrome of women on men must be wiped out of the minds of many.

This same issue has been a concern of civil as well as religious leaders including the Pope. Speaking to his weekly audience recently at St Peter's Square, the pontiff said "as Christians we must become more demanding, for example, by supporting the right of equal pay for equal work, why should it be taken for granted that women must earn less than men? The disparity is pure scandal."[382]

As far as personal rights and privileges are concerned, there is an urgent need to achieve real equality in every area: equal pay for equal work, protection for working mothers, young and old, fairness in career advancements, equality of spouses with regard to family rights and the recognition of everything that is part of the rights and duties of citizens in a democratic state.[383] Real equality is not a privilege but a right.

The public service committees in different districts should be gender-balanced. The reality today still shows a different picture. The "deputizing syndrome" should be discouraged. Women should be employed to narrow the gap in employment. Women should be given special attention, not favored attention, and ensure their security, especially when bribes or favors are demanded. Women, too, should be aware of the dangers and report such cases to police.

6.2.3 Protection of Women

The government has to provide security for women, especially against domestic and extra domestic violence. Legal actions should be taken against rapists, molesters, defilers and other criminals who tread on the rights of women. The challenge remains with the government but also with all other bodies, institutions, community-based organizations (CBOs), NGOs and women's groups. In fighting against extra violence and domestic violence, the security forces and the courts have to be vigilant against the sexual harassment and sexual assault that is still observed in some sectors and public places. This, however, has somehow been a success story of the government. This has been achieved through awareness programs and seminars.

---

382 http://www.ansa.it/english/news/vatican/2015/04/29/scandal-women-earn-less-than-men-pope, accessed on 15th March 2012 at 15:00.

383 http://w2.vatican.va/content/john-paul-ii/en/letters/1995/documents/hf, accessed on 15th March 2012 at 15:00.

However, domestic violence still poses a significant challenge as it is largely a private matter that many women keep quiet about to protect their families and for fear of stigmatization. Therefore, the passing of the Domestic Relations Bill is crucial.

6.2.3.1 The Domestic Relations Bill

Although the Domestic Relations Bill (DRB) has been talked of in recent years, this bill is not sufficiently known. It has a relatively long history that dates back to the 1960s. During this period, the government of Uganda (GoU), together with different groups of women under the umbrella of the women's movement, has been working on a just family law. The DRB is, therefore, a reflection of a sustained and comprehensive consultative process that aimed and still aims at consolidating all domestic related statutes, namely marriage, divorce, separation, inheritance and property rights. The proposed law is intended to regulate relations in marriage and the family and will be crucial in determining particularly the legal status of women and children, not only enhancing family but also national stability and ultimately poverty reduction.[384] This, of course, offers women security and protection against the perpetrators who abuse their rights and go unpunished.

In addition, this bill addresses women's property rights in marriage and women's right to negotiate sex or the number of children they have on the grounds of health, sets the minimum age for marriage at eighteen, criminalizes widow inheritance and offers women protection in marriage. Putting into consideration the cultural implication and as a compromise measure, bride price is not prohibited, but the payment of bride price is no longer a condition for the "formalization of customary marriages, and any demands for the return of marriage gifts will be an offence. The bill criminalizes marital rape and provides for civil remedies, such as compensation and restricting orders. The grounds for divorce are equally applicable to both spouses and alimony is provided for."[385]

The DRB further excludes cohabitation from the presumption of marriage, but provides "parties to such relationships with certain rights, including the

384 UWONET 2004.
385 Ibid.

right to register the fact of cohabitation and particulars of any monetary or non-monetary contributions made."[386] "A competent court may then distribute the property equitably in accordance with those contributions, and may do so even when registration has not taken place. Polygamy is also strictly regulated by guidelines that provide for the economic support of all wives."[387] The bill also provides for equal sexual rights and establishes more equitable grounds for divorce.

Finally, the bill has been received with mixed feelings, but in a strong patriarchal society, this was expected. The religious leaders were against it, claiming that it was a threat to the stability of the family. Most of the resistance was received from the Muslims whose institution this bill seemed to have directly attacked.

6.2.3.2 Domestic Violence Act

The Domestic Violence Act was yet another concrete measure in the emancipation of not only women but also all victims. In November 2009, the Ugandan Parliament passed the country's first bill criminalizing domestic violence, which was signed into law in 2010. The bill provides a thorough definition of domestic violence that includes physical, sexual, emotional, verbal, psychological, and economic violence as well as harassment. The bill also provides protection orders for abused women or girls, which had not previously existed in Ugandan law.[388]

Here is yet another important factor that has been dealt with – rape. Rape is a criminal offence in Uganda under Chapter 14 of the Penal Code, which also prescribes the death penalty for those convicted of rape.[389] However, very few cases are fully investigated and others are never investigated at all.

Although spousal rape is not currently recognized as a criminal offence in Ugandan law, "the Marriage and Divorce Act and the draft Sexual Offences (Miscellaneous Amendments) bill of 2004 (both pending) recognize spousal

386 The Domestic Relations Bill in Uganda: Addressing ... - SSRN. (n.d.) from http://papers.ssrn.com/sol3/papers.cfm? Accessed on 12th March 2015 at 15:00.

387 Ibid.

388 http://www.genderindex.org/country/uganda#_ftn21, accessed on 15th March 2012 at 15:00.

389 Ibid.

rape as a crime and mandate imprisonment, fines, and compensation to the victim as punishment if the partner's refusal to have sex is on basis of poor health, surgery that affects the capacity to engage in sexual intercourse, childbirth, or reasonable fear that engaging in sexual intercourse is likely to cause physical or psychological injury or harm."[390]

However, the inclusion of marital rape in the Marriage and Divorce Act has been met with a lot of resistance and has been a source of heavy controversy. This controversy, according to the media, is one of the major contributors to the delay in the passage of the Act, with others arguing that the failure to pass the Marriage and Divorce Act affects the realization of the Domestic Violence Act, rendering it an Act in "name only" that fails to actually protect women.[391]

According to the US Department of State's human rights report for 2012, the law is not effectively enforced; most cases of rape or sexual violence go unreported, and the police lack the resources and capacity to investigate such cases.[392] There were a number of women during interviews who subscribed to this theory. Many never wanted to be quoted or even give concrete examples.

Although there is no nationwide data about rape, it is believed that rape is very common in Uganda, and the enforcement of existing laws is inadequate. According to the 2011 DHS, 51 percent of women reported having experienced some form of sexual and/or physical violence in their lifetime. Among married women, the victim's husband or partner was the perpetrator in more than 55 percent of these cases, reflecting a widely-held belief that spousal rape is a husband's prerogative.[393]

Sexual harassment is a criminal offence, with penalties of up to fourteen years of imprisonment, but the law is not effectively enforced. According to the US Department of State, "sexual harassment is reportedly widespread in schools, hospitals and workplaces. 2011 Allegations that female students from Makerere University were expected to provide sexual favors in return

---

390 Ibid.
391 Ibid.
392 Ibid.
393 Ibid.

for good grades were being continued to be investigated, according to the Department of State's 2012 human rights report."[394]

The rule of law also demands that a state respects and enforces international law. Under the Convention on the Elimination of all Forms of Discrimination Against Women (CEDAW), a treaty adopted by the United Nations Assembly, state parties are required "to embody the principle of equality of men and women in their national constitutions".[395] This has been fulfilled by presence of provisions on equality in the constitution like articles 28 and 33.

In my opinion, the principle of equality between men and women was not satisfactorily observed in this case because the ruling was in favour of the respondents who were in support of an unfair custom. CEDAW also requires state parties to "modify the social and cultural patterns of conduct of men and women with a view to achieving the elimination of prejudices and customs and all other practices which are based on the idea of inferiority or the superiority of the sexes or on stereotyped roles for men and women."[396]

6.2.3.3 Public Space/Public Domain

Concerning access to public space, there are no reported legal limitations on women's freedom of movement, and women's right to travel is guaranteed under the constitution.[397] In Banyankole culture, there are no explicit restrictions. It seems to be something already embedded in the upbringing and formation of female children. Home responsibilities of producing food and caring for children effectively keep most women close to home most of the time. There was therefore no sufficient cultural or social barrier to limit women's movement.

However, it was observed during the research that women seek permission from their husbands in order to travel. Also, according to data from the 2006 UDHS, "35.8 percent of married women who were interviewed

---

394 Ibid.

395 Buergental T., "International Human Rights in a Nutshell" (2nd Edition), West Publishing Co., St. Paul Minn, 1995, p. 69.

396 Ibid.

397 http://genderindex.org/country/uganda#_ftn68, accessed on 2nd January 2015 at 13:08.

reported that their husbands had the final say as to whether or not the wife could leave to visit family or relatives, a percentage that slightly increased according to the 2011 UDHS data, which found that 39.9 percent of married women were the main decision-makers in respect of visits to family members."[398] A significant number of women who were interviewed wondered why this question was even asked. "It is the right of a man to give his wife permission if she has to go anywhere", said Maria Kobubire.[399]

Access to the public domain is another area of women empowerment. Women meet and discuss issues with either men or women. Women's mobility and general access to the public domain is something that empowers women. Many men remain largely uncomfortable because of the misconceptions from time immemorial.

6.2.3.4 Anti-Pornography

Every country in the whole world has an obligation to protect its citizens against immorality and to preserve good cultural values. In this regard, some bills and laws have been passed in Uganda. One of the challenges faced by lawmakers has been the issue of pornography. Uganda is known as a country that is proud of its rich cultural diversity and its preservation of its moral values. Pornography is, therefore, a very big threat.

Pornography also known as *pono* in Uganda "is the portrayal of sexual subject matter for the purpose of sexual arousal. Pornography may be presented in a variety of media, including books, magazines, postcards, photographs, sculpture, drawing, painting, animation, sound recording, writing, film, video, and video games."[400] With the advancement of technology, these are easily accessed even by a ten-year-old primary school child who lives deep in the village.

In 2014, an Anti-Pornography Bill was passed. However, this law was criticized as infringing on women's rights and freedoms, and was called the "mini-skirts bill". The bill bans "indecent" dressing including any skirt that

---

398 Ibid.

399 This was a focus group of women who were in civil service at Mushanga social center Shema on 3rd June 2014.

400 https://en.wikipedia.org/wiki/Pornography accessed on 17th August 2014 at 09:19.

falls above the knee and any form of dress that may "sexually excite".[401] This has put into question the emancipatory role of the parliament to protect all its citizens in Uganda.

It remains to been seen how the other arms of the government – namely the judiciary and the legislative – will react to the calls of many Ugandans and the international community. The calls to revoke the bill still echo from within and outside Uganda. Human rights activists are busy laying strategies to approach the important entities to look for the way forward.

6.2.3.5 International Criminal Court Act

Although there has been tension between the ICC (International Criminal Court) and many African leaders, there have been many positive developments in many countries since the inception of the ICC. In 2010, the Ugandan government passed the International Criminal Court Act, which categorizes rape, forced marriage and sexual slavery as war crimes chargeable under the Ugandan legal system.[402] This too was a milestone in the liberation struggle of the women who were and are mostly the victims of sexual violence especially rape.

Rape, forced marriages and other forms of sexual violence are not new in Ugandan society. A concrete example has been observed by several human rights groups. It was observed that rape and other forms of sexual abuse have been ongoing features of the conflict in northern Uganda over two decades.[403] The Lord's Resistance Army (LRA), a rebel group that has plunged northern Uganda into terrible misery and extended their activities to the neighboring countries such as the Democratic Republic of Congo, the Central African Republic, and Sudan, used rape, sexual mutilation, and the abduction of male and female children for sexual slavery.[404] The LRA must face justice and be tried in courts of law.

---

401 http://www.genderindex.org/country/uganda#_ftn48, accessed on 2nd January 2015 at 13:28.

402 CEDAW (2010), p. 15.

403 http://www.genderindex.org/sites/default/files/datasheets/UG.pdf n 7th December 2015 at 22:14.

404 Ibid.

Therefore, the efforts of the Ugandan Parliament to pass the International Criminal Court Act to make these crimes chargeable under the Ugandan legal system is a concrete step towards justice but also a breakthrough for the emancipation of women. As already observed, what happened in northern Uganda can happen anywhere in Uganda. The International Criminal Court Act is one of the concrete measures to curb sexual violence against women.

6.2.4 Health Facilities

Special consideration should be given to women, especially pregnant women and mothers, but also protection against abusing their rights. The issue of health is a public issue, and it is not limited to women alone, but women need this particular attention.

The research found that maternal mortality is one of the causes of women's death in Uganda. Unfortunately for such an important indicator, there is conflicting data on the maternal mortality ratio (MMR) for Uganda. The WHO estimate of MMR in Uganda in 1995 was very high – 1,056 per 100,000 live births – which places Uganda in the bottom third of SSA (Sub-Saharan Africa). According to the UDHS data for 1995 and 2000, the MMR estimates for Uganda were 527 and 504 maternal deaths per 100,000 live births respectively. Using the example of questions and interviews, the reality on the ground shows that women still die during pregnancy or during birth.

The majority of deaths during birth occur outside hospitals and especially in rural areas. This means that many women seek medical care too late or that this medical care is even delayed in reaching places where women could be helped. Of the deaths that occur in the hospital, many of the women arrived at the hospital moribund. In one study, 86.1 percent of maternal deaths in seventy-four facilities occurred within an hour of arrival.[405] This means there is a need for improvement of in-patient management.

Also, according to the study women lack the resources and decision-making power over when and how to seek medical care since they depend largely on the decisions of the man who would also shoulder the costs of either transport or medical treatment.

---

405 World Bank, Uganda: From Periphery to a Centre: A strategic country gender assessment, accessed on 2nd March 2005, p. 8.

This means effective health services should be extended to rural areas where women remain less privileged and remain at the mercy of men and traditional or even quack doctors who take advantage of them. This came out of the meeting with women at Bushenyi during interviews.[406]

Awareness programs against the deadly HIV/AIDS problem should continue in the population of Uganda. Due to their position in Uganda, women are more likely to be infected with AIDS than men. This is due to the structure of polygamy and drunkenness of some men. This, coupled with women's lack of decision over their sexuality, means they are likely to be forced into sex even when they know the inherent dangers.

Finally, as already discussed, most of the structures are already in place, and they need improvement.[407] The extension of these facilities to rural women will help to understand the plight of the women there and then it will be easy to help them.

6.2.5 Religious Intervention

John Mbiti once said that "an African is religious through and through,"[408] so is the reality among the Banyankole but most especially among the women. It is not easy to separate religion and the life of an African. Unfortunately, religion has been used to enhance the position of a man at the expense of a woman in most cases. It is high time that the same religion be used for the benefit of the woman.

The religious institutions in Uganda should take up this responsibility starting with the traditional mainstream churches, who have a large number of followers. According to the world population review on Uganda of 2014, the Catholic Church accounts for 39.3 percent of the total population followed by the Anglican Church, with 32 percent. Muslims represent 13.7 percent of the population.[409] Other religions must also follow suit.

---

406 Interview with BAKAZI TWEYOMBEKYE at Bushenyi on 29th May 2015.

407 This was already discussed in chapter four. The health system in Uganda is partly decentralized.

408 Mbiti John, op.cit.

409 http://worldpopulationreview.com/countries/uganda-population/ accessed on 21st June 2016 at 12:32.

6.2.5.1 The Catholic Church

The Catholic Church has already issued a number of documents on women's emancipation. In all these they recognized the unique role and the position of women in the society and most especially in the Church. In his apostolic exhortation to the African clergy, religious and the lay faithful, Pope Benedict XVI wrote:

> The Church has the duty to contribute to the recognition and liberation of women ... Giving women opportunities to make their voice heard and to express their talents through initiatives which reinforce their worth, their self-esteem and their uniqueness would enable them to occupy a place in society equal to that of men ... Bishops should encourage and promote the formation of women so that they may assume their proper share of responsibility and participation in the community life of society and ...of the Church.[410]

The African synod echoed the Church's teaching on women. The synod Fathers wrote unanimously. The Synod wants to see women being fully involved in decision-making within the Church, and to assume positions of leadership within the Church, new ministries for women in the Church were recommended and just wages to women workers and women pastoral agents were emphasized.[411] The Catholic Church must ensure the position of a woman in the Church. The work of the Church is a liberating one. Although women are the majority, their position remains that of a subject.

However, most of these documents have remained on paper and have not been translated into practice. Leaders in the Church are mainly men, and they make decisions for their flock. It is high time that church leaders begin to involve women in decision-making. The Church, too, has an obligation to protect the oppressed and protect the downtrodden. The Church should boldly and openly condemn social evils, the suffering of women, injustices against them in many situations and enhance their good.

---

410 Post Synodal apostolic exhortation Africae Munus of his holiness Pope Benedict XVI, to the Bishops, Clergy, Consecrated persons and the lay faithful on the Church in Africa in service to reconciliation, justice and peace, 2011, part 1, chapter 2.2.

411 Uganda Episcopal conference: Be My Witnesses: The Vocation and Mission of Women in Church and Society Today: A Pastoral Letter of the Catholic Bishops of Uganda - August 1996, Kampala.

The project concretely recommends the participation of women in decision-making in the Church. This should be done by their presence in leadership roles. They should not only be seen as deputies of councils but also take up leadership. In some plenaries of bishops, women's groups under the catholic umbrella should be given a forum to bring forward their views.

Secondly, women should be given more leadership roles in the Church. This should be contextual and done with care to avoid any division or confusion of the Church. Female leaders should be motivated and encouraged in their services and be given protection against their colleagues who marginalize them looking at their gender.

Thirdly, female leaders should be given leadership programs. Female catechists and other lay church leaders should be given the support they need. Individual dioceses should take up responsibilities but also such courses, seminars and studies could be arranged on a national level by the episcopal conferences.

Lastly, the lay faithful should also ardently prepare for the changes with due respect. This could already begin in schools. Church leaders should be at the forefront enhancing this noble cause.

6.2.5.2 Other Religions

Religious groups and sects that encourage the oppression of women and abuse women in the name of religion should be put to task. The secretive sects that preach women as evil and use them as temple prostitutes should be prosecuted. Witchdoctors and other traditional medicine men who take advantage of the helplessness of women, especially before the ruthless jaws of men, should face justice.

The government should take responsibility for ensuring the security of its citizens against the injustices from criminals who pose as religious leaders. Without fear or favor, the government must prosecute any person who treads on the rights of people, especially on the rights of women who are mostly victims of such behavior.

On the other hand, the government should encourage and promote other good social values in some religious affiliations regarding women. For example, some religious groups have made women their leaders, especially evangelicals. Many of these female leaders own churches and they, too, have a following. Many of these are registered as NGOs and this offers an opportunity for the government to oversee them.

In all, religious intervention should strive for gender equality in its evangelization, recruitment, training and education. It should aim at equipping women with skills, development practices and promote awareness in its strategic planning and decision-making processes. Religion should strive to build gender awareness and equality in its flock, management and organizational structures, and everyday working practices.

6.2.6 Appreciating and Celebrating Female Sexuality

This research tries to differ from many previous scholars who propend the view that there is no difference between the sexes. Sex differences are in nature; they are not man-made. This research emphasizes male and female sexuality. Men and women live on this planet earth. The mentality of one gender dominating other is what is man-made. Otherwise, no gender is superior to another. No gender should eradicate the other.

Therefore, women and girls of every age, time, place, race, and culture are exhorted to accept and appreciate female sexuality as a god- or nature-given gift. That is the best gift women have that men do not. It is a gift that this research has been aiming to save.

Women who wish to be like men "belittle" themselves and lose their worth. It is self-deception and not the design of the author of life.

Only when women have appreciated what they are will their full liberation come. Where there will be gender balance, and then oppression, discrimination, and other associated evils have no place. Appreciating female sexuality is the first step to liberation. Kiura writes that the basic role of a woman before other things is to be a woman according to the natural law; woman's behavior and mannerisms should be feminine.[412]

Assuredly, this does not mean an inferiority complex as many people have always associated with femininity. Masculinity and femininity deserve the same value and dignity in the eyes of humanity and God.

412 Kiura M. Jane, About Women, St. Paul's Publications, Nairobi, 1991, p. 11.

6.3 General Conclusion

The ultimate level of equality and empowerment is achieved when there is a balance of dignity and power between women and men, and neither has dominance. Then one can speak of women as having their rightful place in society, then women can make decisions regarding their lives, their families and the lives of their children. They, too, can continually play an active role in the development process in their given communities. The contributions of women are unbiasedly recognized and appropriately rewarded. When this happens, gender mainstreaming will have achieved its goal.[413]

In conclusion, women's emancipation is both a reality and an illusion. On the one hand, a lot has been achieved, and on the other more could be done. Women's subjugation seems to go on in several communities unabated despite so much effort to counteract it. It is true, this has been going for centuries and this has been substantially anchored, so much so that one is tempted to believe that it is within nature itself. The perpetrators have been not only men but also women who have nurtured this unfortunate human-made tradition for centuries, from generation to generation. It cannot be eradicated in a day, not even in months or years. Women's emancipation and empowerment is a process that requires time and patience. But it is possible, and one day, women, mothers, and daughters will not only smile but with relief, they will enjoy their God-given rights.

---

413 Empowerment of Female headed households | socialsciences.in. (n.d.) from http://socialsciences.in/article/empowerment-female-headed-households accessed on 2nd December 2015 at 17:22.

Selected Sources and Bibliography

Literature and Books

ABID A.H, Ugandan Women in development: African development Series 1, Foundation for African development, Kampala 1990.

ALLMENDIGER J., Frauen auf dem Sprung, Pantheon Verlag, München, 2009.

AMANDA, E (ed.), Gender and Economic Growth in Uganda: unleashing the Power of Women, Washington DC, World Bank, 2006.

BACHRACH, P. & BARATZ., Power and Poverty, Theory and Practice, Oxford University Press, New York, 1970.

BATLIWALA, S., "The Meaning of Women's Empowerment: New Concepts from Action." in Population Policies Reconsidered: Health, Empowerment and Rights. G. Sen, A. Germain, and L.C. Chen, eds. Cambridge, MA, University Press, Harvard, 1994.

CURLEY, R., Elders, Shades and Women: Ceremonial Change in Lango, Uganda. University of California Press, Berkeley, 1973.

DRIBERG, J, "The Status of Women among the Nilotics and Nilo Hamitics." Africa, Vol. 5, no. 4, (1932), 5 no. 4: 409.

ELLIS, A. MANUEL C. & BLACKDEN M, Gender and economic growth in Uganda: Unleashing the power of women. New York. 2006.

FRANCIS B., O'CONNOR, CSC, Like Bread, Their Voices Rise: Global women Challenge the Church, Ave Maria Press, Notre Dame, 1993.

FREIRE, P., Pedagogy of the Oppressed. Intro by Ramos, B, and M. (1996 edition), Penguin, London, 1968.

GRAHAM, C.K. The History of Education in Ghana from the Earliest Times to the Declaration of Independence, F. Cass, London, 1971.

Grubitzsch H., Lagpacan, C., Freiheit für Frauen-Freiheit für das Volk. Frankfurt: Syndikat 1980.

GOULD J. A., Classical Philosophical Questions, 4th Ed., Charles E. Mern Publications Co., Ohio, 1982.

TURPIN, J., Women in Church History, St. Anthony Messenger Press, Ohio, 1990.

KABEER, N. The Power to Choose: Bangladeshi Women and Labor Market Decisions in London and Dhaka. London: Verso, 2000.

KARUGIRE, S., A Political History of Uganda. Nairobi: Heinemann. 1980.

KATATE A.G. & KAMUGUNGUNU L. Abagabe b'Ankole, Eagle Press, Dar-es-Salaam, 1955.

COFFEY, K., Hidden Women of the Gospels, The Crossroad Publishing Co., New York, 1996.

KIURA, J. M., Women's Dignity, Paulines Publications Africa, Nairobi, 1995.

LLOYD FALLERS, (ed.), The King's Men: Leadership and Status in Buganda on the Eve of Independence. London: Oxford University Press, 1964.

LUKES, S., Power: a Radical View, Macmillan Lukes, London, 1975.

MALHOTRA, A. & SCHULER S. R., Women's Empowerment as a Variable in International Development. In: D. Narayan, ed. Measuring Empowerment: Cross-Disciplinary Perspectives, The World Bank, Washington, DC, 2002, 3.

MATEMBE, M., Gender, Politics, and Constitution Making in Uganda, Fountain Publishers, Kampala, 2000.

MBITI, S. J., African Religions and Philosophy, Nairobi, Heinemann publications, 2nd Edition, Nairobi, 1970,

KARL, M., Die Geschichte der Frauenbewegung, Reclam, Stuttgart, 2011.

MORRIS, H., & READ J., Uganda: The Development of its Laws and Constitution. London: Stevens and Sons, 1966.

MUGYENYI, M. R. "Towards the Empowerment of Women: A Critique of NRM Policies and Programmes" in Hansen (Ed). Developing Uganda. Oxford: Ohio University Press, 1998.

MUSHANGA M., et al., Kashoboorozi y'Orunyankole, MK Publishers, Kampala, 2006.

NJINYA NJINYA, L., African Mind: A Journal of Religion and Philosophy in Africa, Vol. 1, No. 1, 1989.

NZITA, MBAGA-NIWAMPA, R., Peoples and Cultures of Uganda. Kampala, Fountain Publishers, Kampala, 1998.

OAKLEY, P. (Ed). Evaluating Empowerment: Reviewing the Concept and Practice. INTRAC, Oxford, 2001.

OTISO, M, K., Culture and Customs of Uganda, Greenwood Press, London, 2006.

PLUME, D., (ed.), Women of Tropical Africa. Berkeley: University of California Press, 1963.

ROBERTS, P., "Feminism in Africa: Feminism and Africa." Review of African Political Economy, 1984.

ROSCOE J., The Baganda: An Account of Their Native Customs and Beliefs. Macmillan, London, 1911.

SAYER, A., Realism & Social Science. London: Sage, 1998.

SEN, A., Gender and Cooperative Conflict in Tinker, I. (ed.) Persistent Inequalities, Oxford University Press, Oxford, 1990.

TAMALE, S., When Hens Begin to Crow, Westview Press, Oxford, 1999.

TOSH, J., Clan Leaders and Colonial Chiefs in Lango: The Political History of an East African Stateless Society, 1800–1939, Clarendon Press, Oxford, 1978.

WEBSTER, N., Webster's New International Dictionary, G&C Merrian Co., Second Edition, 1939.

ZEITZEN, M. K., Polygamy: a cross-cultural analysis. Berg. ISBN 1-84520-220-1.

Other Sources

Amnesty International, Uganda: The Human Rights Record.

Annalise Moser; Gender and Indicators: Overview Report. London, England: UNDP. http://www.bridge.ids.ac.uk/reports/IndicatorsORfinal.pdf. Morse, Stephen, and Ernest Tollner, 2007, "Development Indicators and Indices."

Austin Flannery, Vatican Council II Vol. 2: Inter Insigniores, Declaration on the Question of Admission of women to the Ministerial Priesthood, 1976.

Ban Ki-moon, Secretary General's Message on the International Women's Day 8 March 2011.

Beck, T., Using Gender-Sensitive Indicators: A Reference Manual for Governments and Other Stakeholders, London, England, Commonwealth Secretariat, CIDA (Canadian International Development Agency), 1997.

Bohmer, L & Kirumira E., 'Socio-economic context and the sexual behaviour of Ugandan out of school youth' in Culture, Health and Sexuality. Vol. 2:3, 2000.

Christens, B, D., "Toward Relational Empowerment" in Am J Community Psychology. 2012, Vol. 50.

Craig Ham, John F, Esther, "A Fully Liberated Woman", in The Bible Today, Vol. 24, No. 1, January 1986.

Dahl. R., The Concept of Power Behavioral Science, Vol. 2, 1957.

Econ. Commission for Africa, 1975

FIDA-http://www.fidauganda.org/

Flannery Austin, Vatican Council II Vol. 2: Inter Insigniores, Declaration on the Question of Admission of Women to the Ministerial Priesthood, 1976, No. 4.

http://www.peacewomen.org/news_article.php?id=2887&type=news

Graeme Irvine "A New Day for Women." In Together: A Journal of World Vision International, New York, October-December, 1992.

http://en.wikipedia.org/wiki/List_of_countries_by_literacy_rate

http://en.wikipedia.org/wiki/Marriage#Monogamy

http://plato.stanford.edu/entries/affirmative-action/

http://www.ec.or.ug/

http://www.genderlinks.org.za/article/dancing-to-the-tunes-of-democracy-women-and-political-party-agendas-2011-01-25

http://www.huffingtonpost.com/2013/04/30/divorce-rate-as-gender-eq_n_3187187.html

http://www.indexmundi.com/facts/uganda/fertility-rate

http://www.measuredhs.com/pubs/pdf/PR18/PR18.pdf

http://www.oxfamblogs.org/eastafrica/?p=5641

http://www.oxforddictionaries.com/definition/english/cohabit?q=cohabitation#cohabit

http://www.prb.org/Publications/Datasheets/2011/world-population-data-sheet/uganda.aspx

http://www.redpepper.co.ug/ugandas-population-now-at-34-9-million/

http://www.thefreedictionary.com/power

http://www.ubos.org/2014-census/census-2014-final-results/,

http://www.un.org/en/documents/: The Universal Declaration of Human Rights.

http://www.un.org/en/documents: The Universal Declaration of Human Rights.

https://en.wikipedia.org/wiki/Berlin_Conference

https://womenourroots.wordpress.com. Mbowa Rose, Uganda Women Anthem, 1986.

ICRW, Property Rights and Gender: A Training Toolkit, Kampala, 2010.

Jamal, V., "Taxation and Inequality in Uganda, 1900–1964." Journal of Economic History 38, no. 2: 1978.

John Paul II, Message of His Holiness, World Day of Peace 1 January, 1995.

Kabeer, N., 'Gender Equality and Women's Empowerment: A Critical Analysis of the Third Millennium Development Goal,' in Gender and Development, Vol. 13, No. 1, 2005.

Kakwenzire Joan, "Concessions given to Ugandan Women," in the New Vision, Kampala, 16 March 1989.

Lubega, Sarah, "Law Reform and Effective Implementation as the Means to Economically Empower the Ugandan Woman", In Bond, Johanna, Voices of African Women: Women's Rights in Ghana, Uganda, and Tanzania, Carolina Academic Press, North Carolina, USA, 2005.

Mayoux, L., Empowering Enquiry: A New Approach to Investigation, 2008 Available at: <http://www.kepa.fi/tiedostot/empowering-enquiry.pdf.

Mbarara Social Communications Office, Records Section, Mbarara.

Michael A. Koenig, et al., Domestic violence in rural Uganda: evidence from a community-based study in Bulletin of the World Health Organization: The International Journal of Public Health 2003; 81(1).

Millennium Development Goals Report for Uganda 2010.

Ministry of Gender, Labour and Social Development, 1999, The National Action Plan on Women, Kampala: Uganda, 1999.

Ministry of Health, Government of Uganda. Health Sector Strategic Plan 2000/01–2004/05. Kampala, Uganda. 2000.

Ministry of Health, Government of Uganda. The Second National Health Policy, Promoting People's Health to Enhance Socio-Economic Development, Kampala, Uganda July 2011.

Muhanguzi, F. K., (2011) 'Gender and sexual vulnerability of young women in Africa: experiences of young girls in secondary schools in Uganda' in Culture, Health and Sexuality: AN International Journal for Research, Intervention and Care.

Mukasa, Stella, Nite Tanzam, Hope Kabuchu, and Santa Vusia Kayonga, 2004, Uganda: Poverty and Gender Assessment: Strengthening Linkages between Poverty and Gender Analysis in Uganda. Copenhagen: Danish Development Cooperation.

Museveni, Yoweri, Selected Articles from the Ugandan Resistance War, NRM Publications, Nairobi, 1985.

Mushemeza E. Dickens, "Contribution of Women in Influencing Legislation and Policy Formulation and Implementation in Uganda (1995–2005)"

National Objectives and Directive Principles of State Policy No. XV.

New Catholic Encyclopedia, 2002, Vol. 15.

Nyanzi et al., "Money, Men and Markets: Economics and Sexual Empowerment of Market Women in South-western Uganda" in Culture, Health & Sexuality, 2005, Vol 7.

Nyerere, Julius, former president of Tanzania at the Third World Conference on Women, 1984.

Page, N., & C. E. Czuba, Empowerment: What is it? Journal of Extension, vol. 37(5), 1999.

Peace & Justice Tribunal Offices, Mbarara Archdiocese, Archives, File No. 7 visited on 3rd June 2014.

Pearson, Amber L. Muchunguzi, Charles, The International Journal of African Historical Studies; January 1, 2011.

Petesch P., C. Smulovitz & M. Walton, Evaluating Empowerment: A Framework with Cases from Latin America. In D. Narayan, ed. Measuring Empowerment: Cross-Disciplinary Perspectives, The World Bank, Washington, DC. 2005.

Rowlands, J., 'A word of the Times, but what does it mean? Empowerment discourse and practice of development,' in Women and Empowerment in the Third World Illustrations.

Sabiiti Richard, The Situation of Women in Fortportal Diocese: A Pastoral Approach to the Dignity and Liberation, MA Dissertation, Nairobi, July 1994.

Schrijvers, quoted in Stromquist, Nelly P., "The Theoretical and Practical Bases for Empowerment", Women, Education and Empowerment: Pathways towards Autonomy. United Nations Children's Fund (UNICEF), 1994, The Women's Equality and Empowerment Framework, 1995.

Siwal B.R., Empowerment of Women-Conceptual Framework, New Delhi.

Smock, Audrey. "Ghana: From Autonomy to Subordination", in Janet Giele and Audrey Smock, eds., Women: Roles and Status in Eight Countries, John Wiley, New York, 1977.

Staudt, Kathleen, 1989, "The State and Gender in Colonial Africa." In Sue Charlton, Jana Everett, and Kathleen Staudt, eds., Women, the State and Development, Albany: State University of New York Press, 1989.

Tamale, S., Out of the Closet: Unveiling Sexuality Discourses in Uganda in Feminist Africa, Issue 5, 2005.

Tamale, S., "Eroticism, Sensuality and 'Women's Secrets' Among the Baganda" in IDS Bulletin Volume 37 Number 5, 2006.

The Making of Ankole, "Uganda Journal", vol. 20, No. 1 (1957).

The New Vision, Uganda's Leading Paper, Oct 2011.

Uganda Bureau of Statistics, Uganda Demographic Health Survey 2006 at: http://www.measuredhs.com/pubs/pdf/PR18/PR18.pdf

Uganda Bureau of Statistics, Uganda DHS Ed Data Survey, 2011. Education Data for Decision Making.

Uganda Bureau of Statistics, Uganda Demographic Health Survey 2011 at: http://www.measuredhs.com/pubs/pdf/PR18/PR18.pdf

Uganda Bureau of Statistics: Uganda Demographic Health Survey 2011, Kampala, Uganda.

Uganda Project Performance Evaluation Report, Kampala, 2001.

Uganda. The Uganda (Constitution) Order in Council. London: H.M.S.O., 1962.

Uganda. The Constitution of the Republic of Uganda, Kampala, 1995.

Uganda; Statistics, UNICEF. Retrieved on 20th February 2012.

UNFPA HUMAN RIGHTS (2011): Supporting the Constellation of Reproductive Rights. at: http://www.unfpa.org/rights/rights.htm

Women; Definitions. UNICEF. Retrieved on 20th February 2012.

World Bank 2005b, "Uganda: From Periphery to Centre: A Strategic Country Gender Assessment" Poverty Reduction and Economic Management, Africa Region, Washington, DC.

Zeller, M., Sharma, M., Ahmed, A., & Rashid, S., 2001, cited in "Role of NGOS in Rural Areas" by Kigenyi Asifu, Nov 2011.

Abbreviations

AIDS	Acquired Immune Deficiency Syndrome
ATR	African Traditional Religion
C.C.R.M	Catholic Charismatic Renewal Movement
CBO	Community Based Organization
CEDAW	Convention on the Elimination of all Forms of Discrimination Against Women
CIDA	Canadian International Development Agency
DP	Democratic Party
DRB	Domestic Relations Bill
FAWE	Foundation for African Women Educationalists
FIDA	The Federation of Women Lawyers
FOWODE	Forum for Women in Democracy
GDP	Gross Domestic Product
GoU	Government of Uganda
HC	Health Centre
HIV	Human Immunodeficiency Virus
ICRW	International Center for Research on Women
ICC	International Criminal Court
ICCA	International Criminal Court Act
IGG	Inspector of Government
KY	Kabaka Yekka (The King Alone)
LC	Local Council
LEGCO	Legislative council
LRA	The Lord's Resistance Army
MMR	Maternal Mortality Ratio
MP	Member of Parliament
NARO	National Agriculture Research Organization
UNHRO	Uganda National Health Research Organization
NGO	Non-Government Organization
NMS	National Medical Stores
NRA	National Resistance Army
NRC	National Resistance Council

NRM	National Resistance Movement
OLGC	Our Lady of Good Counsel
PAR	Participatory Action Research
SACCOS	Savings and Credit Co-operation
SSA	Sub-Saharan Africa
STDs	Sexually Transmitted Diseases
TASO	The AIDS Support Organization
UBOS	Uganda Bureau of Statistics
UDHS	Uganda Demographic and Health Survey
UNDP	United Nations Development Program
UNDP	United Nations Development Program
UNHRO	Uganda National Health Research Organization
UNICEF	United Nations Children's Fund
UPE	Universal Primary Education
UPC	Uganda People's Congress
UPPAP	Uganda Participatory Poverty Assessment Project
VHT	Village Health Team
WHO	World Health Organization
WONETHA	Women's Organization Network for Human Rights Advocacy
WORI	Women's Rights Initiative
MCHWO	Mbarara Women's Catholic Organization

Index

African Theological Studies
Etudes Théologiques Africaines

Edited by Gerhard Droesser and Chibueze Udeani

Vol. 1 Blaise Okachibe Okpanachi: Nigerian-Vatican Diplomatic Relations. Evangelisation and Catholic Missionary Enterprise 1884–1950. 2013.

Vol. 2 Fidelis Chineme Bayo Kwazu: Developing a Viable Strategy of Solving the Problems of Poverty in the Light of Human Rights. A Case Study of Igboland in Nigeria. 2013.

Vol. 3 Onyenali Rowland: The Trilogy of Parables in Mt 21:28-22:14. From a Matthean Perspective. 2013.

Vol. 4 Paulinus Chibuike Nwaigwe: Canonical Marriage Preparation in the Igbo Tradition in the Light of Canon 1063 of the 1983 Code of Canon Law. Canonical Norms and Inculturation. 2013.

Vol. 5 Philip Chika Omenukwa: An Ecclesiological Exploration of the Four Marks of the Church. An Ecumenical Option for the Church in Nigeria. A Study in the Ecclesiology of Francis Alfred Sullivan. 2014.

Vol. 6 Anthony Ikechukwu Chimaka: Formal Education: A Catalyst to Nation Building. A Case Study of Nigeria. 2014.

Vol. 7 Sylvester O. Ajunwa: HI-Touch Pastoral Approach in the 21st Century. A response to the problem of insufficient organic link between faith and daily life in Nigeria. 2015.

Vol. 8 Chizurum Ann Ugbor: Living the Future in Dialogue. Towards a New Integral and Transformative Model of Religious Education for Nigeria in the 21st Century. 2015.

Vol. 9 Damian Emeka Ikejiama: Social Conflicts and Violence among Christian Churches and Denominations in Igboland. 2016.

Vol. 10 Stanislas Jean Abena Ahogni: Solidarité et Enseignement Catholique au Cameroun: L'implication des Parents. Approche Analytique et Enjeux Ethiques à la Lumière de l'Enseignement Social des Evêques du Cameroun de 1955 à 2005. 2016.

Vol. 11 Kizito Chinedu Nweke: Dialogues and Conflicts among Religious People. Addressing the Relevance of Interreligious Dialogue to the Common Public. 2017.

Vol. 12 Mark S. Aidoo: Shame in the Individual Lament Psalms and African Spirituality. 2017.

Vol. 13 Paul Mutume: Women's Emancipation in Africa – Reality or Illusion? A Case Study of Mbarara, Western Uganda. 2017.

www.peterlang.com

www.ingramcontent.com/pod-product-compliance
Ingram Content Group UK Ltd.
Pitfield, Milton Keynes, MK11 3LW, UK
UKHW041828100926
8556IPUK00002B/67

9 783631 723029

Unfolding the Layers of Social Entrepreneurship in Turkey

Burçak Cebeci Perker / Bilge Uyan Atay
Bahar Köseoğlu / Elif Yolbulan Okan (eds.)

Unfolding the Layers of Social Entrepreneurship in Turkey

Discover the Transformative Power of Social Entrepreneurship in Turkey

PETER LANG

Berlin · Bruxelles · Chennai · Lausanne · New York · Oxford

Bibliographic information published by the Deutsche Nationalbibliothek
The Deutsche Nationalbibliothek lists this publication in the Deutsche Nationalbibliografie; detailed bibliographic data is available on the Internet at http://dnb.d-nb.de.

Library of Congress Cataloging-in-Publication
A CIP catalog record for this book has been applied for at the Library of Congress.
LCCN: 2025002457

ISBN 978-3-631-91511-0 (Print)
ISBN 978-3-631-93522-4 (E-PDF)
ISBN 978-3-631-93523-1 (E-PUB)
DOI.10.3726/b22746

Published by Peter Lang GmbH, Berlin, Germany

info@peterlang.com

This publication has been peer-reviewed.

www.peterlang.com

Contents

Ezgi Özkök Sefer
Country Director – Ashoka Turkey

Introduction: Compassionate Changemaker

Turkey's social entrepreneurship scene takes center stage in this book, a collaborative effort by leading academics and practitioners. You will dive into a wealth of knowledge—the evolution of social entrepreneurship, its ongoing challenges, and the impact it generates within this dynamic, fast-changing landscape. As a passionate advocate for social good for the whole, I'm thrilled to introduce this insightful work to those eager to understand and contribute to this movement.

This book celebrates the historical significance and enduring relevance of social entrepreneurship. I believe it will urge you to explore the idea and the need for a "systems change mindset" within social entrepreneurship ecosystem. Superficial interventions and ideas that touch only to the symptoms of social and environmental problems don't bring long-lasting and sustainable solutions. They don't reach the whole society, either. Therefore, today's social entrepreneurs should champion a holistic, systemic approach. By tackling root causes, challenging entrenched systems, and fostering cross-sector collaboration, these changemakers redefine what's achievable in the pursuit of social and environmental justice. As articulated by Ashoka's Founder and CEO, Bill Drayton, "Social entrepreneurs are not content just to give a fish or teach how to fish. They will not rest until they have revolutionized the fishing industry."

This book also unfolds a rich tapestry of case studies. Examples and insightful analyses guide you through the diverse landscape of social entrepreneurship in Turkey. From healthcare and education initiatives to projects focused on environmental sustainability and economic empowerment, each narrative sheds light on the creativity, resilience, and impact-driven spirit of social entrepreneurs. These individuals drive positive change across critical fronts.

The impact of social entrepreneurship extends beyond theory; it's tangible, measurable, and transformative. Through compelling statistics and real-world accounts, this book brings to life the stories of individuals and communities profoundly affected by innovative solutions and compassionate initiatives spearheaded by Turkish social entrepreneurs. Heartfelt testimonials illustrate the profound difference these social innovators are making.

As Ashoka, we have seen a pattern from our more than 4,000 social entrepreneurs in 90+ countries: They were changemakers in their youth years. At the heart of this insights brought us a powerful vision—one championed by Ashoka—that envisions everyone as a changemaker. This vision isn't an abstract idea but a call to action. It urges individuals to harness their unique talents and passions to drive positive change and contribute to a just, equitable, and sustainable society—for the good of all.

In this vision, we can frame social entrepreneurs as the enablers of changemakers. In a world defined by polycrisis, radical uncertainties and deepening inequalities, I believe it is a powerful idea. Before concluding, I'd like to highlight specific facets pertinent to the present state of the social entrepreneurship ecosystem in Turkey, as well as elucidate the pivotal role social entrepreneurs play in activating changemakers:

Challenges and Opportunities: Social entrepreneurship in Turkey faces challenges. This book tackles some of the most pressing issues, like access to funding, navigating complex legal frameworks, and balancing social impact with financial sustainability. However, it also highlights solutions, empowering future changemakers with the knowledge and resources they need.

The Power of Collaboration: Social entrepreneurs don't operate alone. This book emphasizes the importance of collaboration within the Turkey's social entrepreneurship ecosystem. Partnerships between NGOs, government agencies, businesses, and academia magnify impact and create lasting change. The book explores successful collaborative models, serving as a blueprint for future collaborations.

Beyond Borders: Global Impact: The impact of Turkey's social entrepreneurship extends beyond national borders. This book sheds light on how Turkey's social entrepreneurs are addressing global challenges and inspiring others. By sharing innovative solutions and best practices, they contribute to a more equitable and sustainable future for the good of all.

This book is not only a celebration but also a roadmap for future changemakers—whether they are social entrepreneurs or not. May the stories, insights, and lessons shared within these pages inspire you to embark on a changemaking journey or to leverage your ongoing journey of social innovation and positive impact. This book is a call to action. It encourages you to identify a cause you care about, develop innovative solutions, and become a changemaker in your own community. Let this book be your guide as you embark on your own changemaking journey—a journey that starts with a single step that finds its energy in your inner self and has the potential to create a ripple effect of positive change for the good of all.

Banu Demirel
Dokuz Eylul University

Yasemin Ulker
Bahcesehir University

Chapter 1 Sustainable Business Models: Directions for Social Entrepreneurs

Abstract: This chapter emphasizes the urgent need for radical reforms on a global scale to address pressing environmental and social challenges. Focusing on sustainable business models from the perspective of social entrepreneurs, the study aims to contribute insights into strategies and models for start-ups. It explores the nexus between social entrepreneurship and sustainable business models, providing guidance for social entrepreneurs during the startup phase. The chapter covers the imperative for sustainability, the global landscape of social entrepreneurship, its status in Türkiye, the challenges and opportunities faced, and it delves into sustainable business models. The discussion provides strategic and business model directions for social entrepreneurs, emphasizing the interconnectedness of social, economic, and environmental aspects for comprehensive and lasting impact.

Keywords: sustainability, social entrepreneurship, sustainable business models, social innovation

1. Introduction

Humanity needs radical reforms on a scale never previously witnessed in human history due to the gravity and scope of the problems faced globally. Low-carbon, resilient, and inclusive courses of development must be pursued which would eventually lead to a reduction in carbon emissions, protection of natural resources, shifts in the food systems, more employment, and the transition to a greener, more inclusive, and equitable economy (United Nations, 2022).

Environmental and social awareness which create understanding and implementation in sustainable business practices accelerated with the upsurge of sustainable business models which is a paradigm in which sustainability concepts influence the firm's driving force and decision-making. Besides, there is an increasing pressure that is placed on businesses to address sustainability concerns. Organizations are expected to address environmental, social and economic issues such as economic and social inequalities and financial and climate crisis with greater vigor.

Although there is a considerable body of literature on various frameworks and models of sustainability (Joyce & Paquin, 2016; Biloslavo et al., 2018; Morioka et al., 2018; Sparviero, 2019) understanding of sustainable business models and the operationalization of sustainable development in start-ups is limited. To remedy this void, this chapter focuses on sustainable business models from social entrepreneurs' perspective and aim to contribute to a deeper understanding by providing directions for the start-up phase. More specifically this study endeavors to determine:

(a) strategies to be followed to support the start-ups
(b) the sustainable business models that can be adopted

Aligned with these objectives, the subsequent sections of the chapter delve into the imperative for sustainability, the landscape of social entrepreneurship globally and in Türkiye, sustainable business models, and guidance for social entrepreneurs. This chapter is anticipated to illuminate the nexus between social entrepreneurship and sustainable business models, offering strategic directions and recommendations to guide social entrepreneurs during the startup phase. The literature review approach was employed to accomplish this goal. Google Scholar was used to search for social entrepreneurship, sustainable business models, social entrepreneurship in Turkey, and ultimately social entrepreneurship and sustainable business models together.

2. The Urgent Need for Sustainability

The inception of the first industrial revolution was marked by the introduction of water and steam power, coupled with the implementation of mechanical production systems. Subsequently, the advent of electric power in manufacturing processes heralded the second industrial revolution, characterized by a transition to mass production. When electronics and information technology became prevalent in production, a digital revolution known as the third industrial revolution resulted. Conversely, the concurrent connections between the virtual and physical domains define the fourth industrial revolution, which is identified by the integration of cyber-physical systems. Scientific and technological developments have sparked many industrial revolutions, improving manufacturing techniques across ages and creating systems of production that are more productive and efficient than those of previous eras. The increase in supply, especially during the second industrial revolution, has led to increased rivalry, which has over time transformed into a violent worldwide struggle. The escalating consumption patterns, concomitant with the rapid population expansion, exert deleterious effects on the surrounding natural environment, precipitating a depletion of finite resources and posing a formidable threat to the prosperity and quality of life for subsequent generations. The exigency of the circumstance becomes evident when one considers the socio-economic ramifications instigated and potentially exacerbated by the climate crisis, alongside the profound global repercussions, encompassing diminished biodiversity, irregularities in seasons, climatic extremities, inundations, protracted and more recurrent droughts, and the attenuation of water reservoirs (WHO, 2023). Thus, the health and integrity of the society should be safeguarded, and the planet's ecosystems should be preserved. Sustainability, serving as the descriptor for all these concepts, has been defined as "coordinated interconnections facilitating the understanding and effective communication of the concept in the process of achieving sustainable development and directing society towards it" (Glavič & Lukman, 2007: 1884). Sustainability assumes a pivotal role in the implementation of judicious resource management, the reduction of pollution, and the conservation of biodiversity in terms of environmental sustainability. Besides, sustainability underscores the imperative of social inclusivity and equity which is the second pillar of sustainability. It seeks to rectify disparities in the access to resources, opportunities, and benefits, thereby promoting social justice and ensuring that the fruits of development are equitably distributed across all strata of society. The third pillar of sustainability suggests economic stability. Through the cultivation of innovation, efficiency, and responsible governance, sustainability augments economic resilience and mitigates risks associated with resource scarcity and environmental upheavals.

Sustainable development, proposed as a development model and initially defined in 1987, has gained widespread acceptance, particularly in advanced economies, and subsequently in developing countries and markets. Over the past three decades, this model has rapidly disseminated and engendered discussions in various sub-domains of economics and development. Consequently, it has given rise to the emergence and experimentation of numerous new concepts, theories, and practices. In the field of business management, where key stakeholders of the sustainable development model are situated, the post-1990 era witnessed the development of sustainable business management, sustainable production, sustainable consumption, sustainable supply chain management, and various other novel theories and applications. The domain of social entrepreneurship has also emerged as a highly significant area of research for both businesses and scholars (Kannampuzha & Hockerts, 2019). The unique characteristic of social entrepreneurship lies in the establishment of social enterprises that utilize business models to tackle societal problems and generate a positive social influence (Selsky & Parker, 2010).

3. Social Entrepreneurship in the World

Globally, the idea of social entrepreneurship is growing in significance. A novel approach to business, social entrepreneurship successfully tackles societal issues on a worldwide scale while fostering steady economic expansion (Osyka, 2021). Social entrepreneurs develop cutting-edge company strategies that satisfy fundamental human needs and encourage corporate social responsibility (Seelos & Mair, 2005). The goal of social entrepreneurship is to find, assess, and take advantage of opportunities that address fundamental and persistent needs in society in order to generate social value as opposed to financial gain for individuals or shareholders (Certo & Miller, 2008). Noruzi et al. (2010) state that it has several social, economic, and environmental objectives. This is particularly true in light of the issues and requirements faced by the world's impoverished (Bedi & Yadav, 2019). Key features of social opportunity affect how social projects spread internationally (Zahra et al., 2008). By fusing economic acumen with inspiring leadership to accomplish social objectives and enhance sustainability, social entrepreneurship presents a novel approach to management education (Muscat & Whitty, 2009). Through the combination of entrepreneurship's financial gains with the realization of social and environmental goals, social entrepreneurship has the potential to promote social and economic development for people and communities globally. Effective reasoning, increased legitimacy, and information technology—which can be strengthened by information technology and suitable reporting metrics—are the means by which social entrepreneurs can advance society (VanSandt et al., 2009). Above all, social entrepreneurship can be a helpful tactic to address unfulfilled personal and societal demands (Haugh, 2007). To completely comprehend this idea, its origins, and its implications, more study is required (Bedi & Yadav, 2019).

Li (2014) and Agrawal and Gugnani (2014) both stress how crucial it is for social entrepreneurs to have a sustainable business plan. Agrawal searches especially for technologies that are dynamic and financially viable. Li (2014) explores this concept further in her case study of TerraCycle, a social entrepreneurship business that effectively struck a balance between long-term financial viability and social purpose. Mefi (2020) expands on the discussion and adds sociological and cultural viewpoints by emphasizing social values and support as critical elements affecting the prosperity of social entrepreneurship in South African slums. More than a third of the world's population resides in the 15 countries that make up the Regional Comprehensive Economic Partnership Agreement. These nations also produce 29 % of the world's GDP, foster social entrepreneurship to promote innovation, and indirectly influence innovation through sustainable development (Al-Qudah et al., 2021). These studies all emphasize how crucial adaptable, imaginative, culturally sensitive, and long-lasting business methods are for social entrepreneurship.

4. Social Entrepreneurship in Türkiye

According to a study on social entrepreneurship done in Türkiye, civic participation is very common there, while education is heavily downplayed (Inci, 2016). Pro-social elements and individual motives play a major part in the formation of social entrepreneurs in Türkiye, who are motivated by societal vision and personal fulfillment (Ozbay & Çelikel, 2022). Turkish owners of Small Medium Enterprises (SMEs) are motivated more by financial benefits than by intrinsic motivation. The entrepreneurs' reputation for friendliness and sincerity are the most crucial factors in their company's success. Other important elements of achievement mentioned were social skills and providing excellent customer service. The convoluted and perplexing tax code is the biggest issue Turkish entrepreneurs confront. A slow pace economy, unstable staff, and the incapacity to keep accurate records are some other significant issues (Benzing et al., 2009). Bascavusoglu-Moreau (2010)'s research also looks into the factors that influence innovative capabilities in Turkish SMEs and finds that R&D investments, the use of ICTs, exporting, outsourcing, and staff education all contribute to innovation. Interestingly, the most important factor influencing inventive performance is the possession of quality labels and certificates, which demonstrate a company's capacity to learn and use specialist information. The examination emphasizes the inadequacies of organized industrial areas and the shortcomings of the Turkish national innovation system and entrepreneurial activity. There are also acknowledged financial obstacles and a dearth of private finance options for small businesses, yet regional entrepreneurship capital enhances SMEs' capacity for innovation. The research indicates that Turkish SMEs' failures to become knowledge-based, and globally competitive are mostly caused by policy-related problems rather than a lack of entrepreneurial behavior.

With the use of annual data from 1985 to 2016, Philip et al. (2021) study's findings show that regardless of the type of shock, entrepreneurial activity, energy use, financial development, and economic expansion continuously exhibit a detrimental impact on environmental quality. On the other hand, trade openness shows both shortand long-term benefits. The research verifies the existence of Türkiye's environmental Kuznets curve, which indicates that environmental quality first declines before strengthening as the economy grows. The results highlight the necessity of providing incentives to encourage environmentally conscious enterprises, technological advancement, and the creation of smart cities in Türkiye to mitigate the detrimental effects of entrepreneurship on the environment. Uslu et al. (2015) mentioned there has been an increase in environmental and entrepreneurial focus in Türkiye in recent years, as evidenced by the 15 % increase in research and development and entrepreneurial activity pertaining to environmental issues. This change is viewed as an opportunity to improve the ecosystem of green entrepreneurship. Organizations, networks, non-governmental organizations, and structural funders play a critical role in Türkiye's entrepreneurial environment by offering incentives such as tax cuts and exemptions. Nevertheless, several factors, including a need for sufficient information on green entrepreneurship and a lack of regulation at the appropriate levels, prevented green entrepreneurship from reaching the required level in the nation.

Ashoka, with over 3,000 fellows across 70 countries, is the largest global network of social entrepreneurs. These fellows provide creative fixes for societal problems that could have a big influence. Inci (2016) concentrated on Türkiye's Ashoka fellows (in total 35 fellows in 2015), a preeminent cohort of social entrepreneurs in the country. According to this study there is no discernible relationship between the quantity of social entrepreneurs in a nation and its degree of development. Human rights (18 %), civic engagement (17.2 %), and economic development (19.8 %) are the three fields where social entrepreneurship is most prevalent worldwide. On the other hand, civic involvement (40 %) is noticeably more common in Türkiye, whereas social entrepreneurs—who make up 16.2 % of the global workforce in the learning and education sector—are surprisingly absent.

Despite the significant progress Türkiye has made in promoting entrepreneurship, more has to be done to encourage innovation and entrepreneurship in order to create new technologies for sustainable development (Aydoğan & Diallo, 2020). All of these studies highlight the need for additional investigation and assistance with social entrepreneurship in Türkiye, especially with regard to women's empowerment and education.

5. Sustainable Business Models

The concept of the business model has garnered increased prominence, particularly since the 1990s, leading to a notable surge in the engagement of both researchers and practitioners in this domain (Peric et al., 2017; Trapp & Kanbach, 2021; Kubli & Puranik, 2023). The proliferation of factors such as the advent and swift proliferation of the Internet, advancements in communication and information technologies, exemplified by the precipitous decline in computing and communication costs, shifts in consumer profiles and behaviors, technological progress, and infrastructural deficiencies, has precipitated the evolution of novel methods for conceiving and delivering value. Moreover, it is evidently imperative to align efforts with the sustainable development goals articulated by the United Nations, aimed at mitigating or eradicating economic, environmental, and social challenges that pose threats to the well-being of future generations and humanity at large. Corporations, as pivotal contributors to social and economic spheres, bear a profound responsibility in this context. Particularly within the purview of sustainable entrepreneurship, the significance of sustainable innovations and business model innovations geared towards sustainability is markedly substantial in advancing the cause of sustainable development. Within this context, the present section initially provides a definition of the business model concept, delineates the constituent elements of a business model, and elucidates frameworks pertaining to sustainable business models.

While business models have been integral to trade and economic practices since pre-classical times, the widespread recognition and dissemination of the business model concept occurred in the mid-1990s with the advent of the internet, subsequently gaining significant traction. The business model serves as a visual representation of the operational processes within a business, aiding in the comprehension of the determinants that steer company objectives and articulates the value proposition that an organization provides to its customers. It delineates the requisite capabilities and resources necessary for the creation, marketing, and delivery of that value, ultimately fostering the generation of profitable and sustainable revenue streams. The fundamental components of a business model encompass the articulation of a value proposition, the processes involved in its creation, delivery, and the subsequent capturing of value. The conceptualization of a business model emerged with the primary objective of expediting the elucidation of intricate business concepts in a more efficient manner. Over the course of decades, crucial sustainability concerns, with pronounced societal and environmental ramifications affecting both humanity and the natural world, were not given precedence in the majority of business model paradigms. Nevertheless, business models, in order to align with the sustainability objectives of enterprises, are now facing compelling imperatives to evolve towards a more sustainable economic system. Goni et al. (2021) suggest that Sustainable Business Models exhibit three distinctive characteristics that set them apart from conventional business models:

i. generating value for multiple stakeholders, encompassing society and the environment.

ii. envisioning non-financial forms of value, incorporating social and environmental considerations.
iii. considering value destruction, acknowledging negative impacts on society and the environment, such as resource depletion or social dislocation.

There have been different approaches to the conceptualization of sustainable business models. Bocken et al. (2014), for example, investigated at and divided patterns of sustainable business models into three groups: technological, social, and organizational. The classification of the Technological Model produced three distinct patterns for long-term business models. The first pattern, "efficient use of materials and energy," is centered on utilizing resources as efficiently as possible while lowering waste, emissions, and pollution. Two examples of this movement are low-carbon production and lean manufacturing. The process of turning waste streams into valuable inputs is known as "creating value from waste," or the second pattern. This disproves the notion that waste exists by converting garbage into valuable resources and increasing productivity. This pattern transforms raw materials into inputs for a specific process or product line. It is a process-oriented approach. Its main concerns are the elimination of waste and the transfer of waste products from one process to another. Sectoral symbiosis is one instructive illustration of this pattern.

Under the Social patterns category, the first pattern is characterized as "functionality instead of ownership." This pattern explains business strategies that combine several products and services in an effort to enhance customer satisfaction while upholding the significance of the product. The pay-as-you-go, rental, and sharing models are representative instances that are intentionally designed to offer services that meet customer needs without needing ownership of physical goods. In the Social Models category, the "taking responsibility" pattern is defined by proactive engagement with stakeholders to ensure their long-term welfare and well-being. Business models that fit this pattern might include supplier accreditation schemes that promote moral or sustainable community-based activities, workplace health and safety programs, or the early detection and remediation of consumer health problems, especially in developing countries. However, Geissdoerfer et al. (2018) used a categorization method to organize sustainable business models into four categories. These include social enterprises, which are business models that aim to create social impact through the generation of profits from economic activity or their complete reinvestment; bottom-of-the-pyramid solutions, which are business models designed for customers at the lower echelons of the income pyramid; and product-service systems, which are business models that seamlessly integrate products and services into customer offerings, producing products, functionality, or desired outcomes. It is interesting to note that discussions of sustainable business models in relation to the circular economy are common in the literature. According to Comin et al. (2020), new designs are essential for promoting creativity in business models as they place a strong emphasis on sharing and cooperation as key components of model creation.

6. Directions for Social Entrepreneurs

6.1. Strategic Directions

The notion of social entrepreneurship is a multifarious and intricate construct encompassing moral conduct, goal coherence, and the capacity to recognize viewpoints that provide social advantages (Mort et al., 2003). But the discipline is very young, and there is ongoing discussion about its definition and bounds (Dacin et al., 2011). For socio-economic development, it is imperative to refocus macroeconomic policies, remove obstacles to entrepreneurship, and support social entrepreneurship as a job that cultivates an entrepreneurial culture (Davis, 2002). According to Prabhu (1999), social entrepreneurs play a crucial role in the establishment and management of innovative organizations that prioritize social development and transformation.

Social entrepreneurs must strike a balance between generating social value and achieving economic goals. Entrepreneurs need to use social capital, form robust social networks, and collaborate across sectors to accomplish objectives (Kulshrestha et al., 2022). In addition, they ought to put social justice and fairness as well as ethical sustainability above. The development of entrepreneurial skills that influence social entrepreneurial behavior can help reach goals (Mathur, 2011). Distinct psychosocial characteristics of social entrepreneurs is evident in their self-direction, empathy, high entrepreneurship orientation, generosity, altruistic-like social motives, and a service- and entrepreneurial-based job identity (Bargsted et al., 2013). In cases of market and governmental failure, social entrepreneurship seeks to balance value creation and value capture to offer long-term solutions to overlooked issues with beneficial externalities (Santos, 2010). Social entrepreneurship promotes decision-making, human capital, and social impact, hence improving human well-being and social progress (Jiao, 2011).

Moreover, social entrepreneurs can create social value while promoting social change by utilizing their inventiveness, proactivity, and willingness to take risks within a market orientation (Mort & Hume, 2009). Lamy (2019) proposes institutional reforms that encourage entrepreneurs to promote socially conscious actions to make social entrepreneurship sustainable.

Social entrepreneurs can optimize their influence by concentrating on three major directions from the standpoint of sustainable development. First and foremost, it is imperative to take a comprehensive strategy that takes into account how social, economic, and environmental aspects are interconnected. Utaminingsih et al. (2023) state that the following internal and external elements influence SMEs' adoption of innovations in sustainable business models: hedonic motivation, internal speed, facilitating conditions, social influence, effort expectation, and dynamic performance expectancy. Through coordinated action throughout institutional contexts, policy entrepreneurs can stimulate shifts to accomplish the sustainable development goals of the United Nations (Mintrom & Thomas, 2018). During the COVID-19 epidemic, social entrepreneurship was vital in handling the situation and making a significant and creative contribution to sustainable development (Padhiary & Patel, 2022). A comprehensive and cooperative strategy that integrates creativity, technology, community engagement, and continuous assessment can direct social entrepreneurs into more significant and long-lasting projects that improve the environment and society.

6.2. Business Model Directions

Innovation stands as a foremost catalyst facilitating social entrepreneurship. In their research, Gasparin et al. (2021) formulated a strategic framework for social entrepreneurs to innovate. The first steps in the process involve determining societal requirements and developing innovative remedies for them. The second component, Network, requires that networks made up of consumers and beneficiaries be mobilized both inside and outside. In order to provide social and cultural advantages, mobilization is essential for co-creating values in both the cultural and social realms as well as for maintaining, acquiring, and holding onto commercial value. The third factor, economic value, is concerned with assisting the company's financially sustainable expansion. The creation of systems to measure the social, economic, ecological, and cultural effects on society and small and medium-sized enterprises (SMEs) is the final task for the fourth component, Impact. It is emphasized how crucial it is to have a strategy in place and how it helps with the creation and use of business models. The goal of this section is to provide sustainable business models that social entrepreneurs may use to structure and improve their creative ideas when they are just getting started.

As a result, the Triple Layered Business Model Canvas (TLBMC), which considers an organization's social, environmental, and economic aspects and offers a conceptual framework for developing business models that support more sustainable practices, is one of the most well-known tools for business model innovation. By creating and adding stakeholder-based environmental and social canvas layers, as well as life-cycle and stakeholder-based environmental layers, to an extended business model canvas, the TLBMC builds upon the conventional economic-focused technique of a standard business model. Joyce and Paquin (2016) claim that this improved canvas facilitates the development of more thorough and persuasive opinions about the creation of business models with a sustainability-focused perspective.

The Social Enterprise Model Canvas (SEMC), developed specifically to solve the difficulties faced by social entrepreneurs, is introduced by Sparviero (2019). These challenges include the complexities of combining social and economic goals, effectively communicating goals and how they relate to the use of resources and overall strategy, measuring results in terms of output, outcomes, and impact, and implementing the best governance structures that support the mission values and goals. Based on fundamental "instrumental" concepts, SEMC is built. These include explicitly defining and prioritizing mission values and objectives, translating them into measurable impacts and targets, distinguishing between non-targeted (partners and affected stakeholders) and targeted stakeholders (customers and beneficiaries) for a systemic approach to business model design, incorporating the involvement of targeted stakeholders in value co-creation, and accounting for governance elements crucial to achieving mission values and objectives.

The Sustainable Value Exchange Matrix (SVEM) is a visual framework based on rigorous theoretical analysis and practical application. By providing a multi-stakeholder and value-exchange viewpoint, this tool supports discussions on sustainable business models among academics and practitioners. It is structured into four stages: (A) Delimitation of the business's raison d'être: These stages provide input for defining the business purpose and competitive advantage, manifested through the organization's offerings such as products and services; (B) Practices, processes, and resources supporting the creation and delivery of the value proposition: Participants identify key practices, capabilities, and resources for each process; (C) Stakeholders' value captured: Starting with identifying primary stakeholders, this stage seeks to pinpoint the sustainable value captured by each stakeholder; and (D) Matrix critical analysis. Stages A, B, and C aim to delineate the organization's key aspects, fostering reflection during their execution. This serves as preparation for Stage D, which prompts more profound reflections by highlighting the contribution of sustainable business model innovation guidelines to the existing business model (Moriokaet al., 2018).

The value proposition, the value co-creation and co-delivery system, and the value capture system are the three main components of the Value Triangle, a revolutionary business model framework proposed by Biloslavo et al. (2018). Public value, consumer value, and partner value are all included in the value proposition. Along with capital, important operational activities, consumers, partners, society, and products (i.e., goods & services), the value co-creation and co-delivery system includes all of these elements. The cost structure and the revenue model are part of the value capture system. The value capture system includes the revenue model and the cost structure.

In comparison to most other business models, the Value Triangle stands out for four main reasons: (i) it explicitly emphasizes value co-creation for society as a whole, going beyond customers and business partners; (ii) it carefully weighs the costs and benefits resulting from organizational business activities; (iii) it takes a broad definition of capital, including the environment, and (iv) its components are designed as triangles that replicate themselves to graphically represent systemic relationships among multiple actors within a business.

7. Conclusion

Social entrepreneurship is an amalgamation of the innovative and adaptive qualities inherent in conventional entrepreneurship, along with a steadfast commitment to effecting positive societal transformation. The increasingly prevalent presence of organizations that have developed effective methods for addressing fundamental human needs that have been neglected by established markets and institutions underlines the interest in the subject. Two traditionally opposed paradigms are combined in social entrepreneurship: a revenue-generating model that focuses on making a profit via commercial activity and a social welfare paradigm that is committed to societal development having the flexibility to adopt either a for-profit or a non-profit legal structure. (Battilana et al., 2012; Mair et al., 2012).

This chapter's discussion of social entrepreneurship and sustainable business models has given readers a thorough knowledge of the ways in which start-ups can support sustainable development. The research's primary conclusions concentrated on implementable sustainable business models and start-up support measures. But it has long been recognized that adopting the appropriate tactics is not the only way to successfully deploy sustainable business models; social entrepreneurs must also be dedicated to these models and make consistent efforts in this regard.

Examples of social entrepreneurship from around the world and in Türkiye demonstrate the variety and promise of sustainable company models. These instances highlighted the value of civic involvement, particularly in Türkiye, and highlighted shortcomings in the field of education. Social entrepreneurs have the ability to close these gaps, creating new avenues for sustainable growth.

Ultimately, this chapter has provided advice and strategic guidance to help social entrepreneurs during their initial stages of operation. This advice is essential for the effective use of sustainable company models and aids in overcoming obstacles that entrepreneurs may encounter. It is stressed how crucial it is to keep up with research and innovation in order to establish sustainable company models and social entrepreneurship. This study has demonstrated the vital role that entrepreneurship plays and the ongoing transformation that this area needs to undergo in order to have a sustainable future.

References

Agrawal, S., & Gugnani, R. (2014). Creating successful business model: Lessons for social entrepreneurship. *International Journal of Entrepreneurship and Innovation Management, 18*, 438–445.

Al-Qudah, A., Al-Okaily, M., & Alqudah, H. (2021). The relationship between social entrepreneurship and sustainable development from economic growth perspective: 15 "RCEP" countries. *Journal of Sustainable Finance & Investment, 12*, 44–61. https://doi.org/10.1080/20430795.2021.1880219.

Aydoğan, E., & Diallo, E. (2020). Entrepreneurship in Turkey: Present situation and sector's Strengths, Weaknesses Opportunities and Threats (SWOT). *Analysis, 4*, 31–44. https://doi.org/10.15659/ankad.v4i1.74.

Bargsted, M., Picón, M., Salazar, A., & Rojas, Y. (2013). Psychosocial characterization of social entrepreneurs: A comparative study. *Journal of Social Entrepreneurship, 4*, 331–346. https://doi.org/10.1080/19420676.2013.820780.

Bascavusoglu-Moreau, 2010. Entrepreneurship and the national system of innovation: What is missing in Turkey?, WIDER Working Paper, No. 2010/54, ISBN 978-929230-291-7, The United Nations University World Institute for Development Economics Research (UNU-WIDER), Helsinki.

Battilana, J., Lee, M., Walker, J., & Dorsey, C. (2012). In search of the hybrid ideal. *Stanford Social Innovation Review, 10*(3), 51–55.

Bedi, H. S., & Yadav, N. (2019). Social entrepreneurship: A conceptual clarity. Bedi, HS & Yadav, N., Social entrepreneurship: A conceptual clarity. *Our Heritage, 67*(10), 1006–1016.

Benzing, C. D., Chu, H. M., & Kara, O. (2009). Entrepreneurs in Turkey: A factor analysis of motivations, success factors, and problems. *Journal of Small Business Management, 47*, 58–91.

Biloslavo, R., Bagnoli, C., & Edgar, D. (2018). An eco-critical perspective on business models: The value triangle as an approach to closing the sustainability gap. *Journal of Cleaner Production, 174*, 746–762.

Bocken, N. M., Short, S. W., Rana, P., & Evans, S. (2014). A literature and practice review to develop sustainable business model archetypes. *Journal of Cleaner Production, 65*, 42–56.

Certo, S. T., & Miller, T. (2008). Social entrepreneurship: Key issues and concepts. *Business Horizons, 51*(4), 267–271.

Comin, L. C., Aguiar, C. C., Sehnem, S., Yusliza, M. Y., Cazella, C. F., & Julkovski, D. J. (2020). Sustainable business models: A literature review. *Benchmarking: An International Journal, 27*(7), 2028–2047.

Dacin, M. T., Dacin, P. A., & Tracey, P. (2011). Social entrepreneurship: A critique and future directions. *Organization Science, 22*, 1203–1213.

Davis, S. M. (2002). Social entrepreneurship: Towards an entrepreneurial culture for social and economic development. Youth Employment Summit, September 7–11, 2002.Available at SSRN 978868.

Gasparin, M., Green, W., Lilley, S., Quinn, M., Saren, M., & Schinckus, C. (2021). Business as unusual: A business model for social innovation. *Journal of Business Research, 125*, 698–709.

Geissdoerfer, M., Vladimirova, D., & Evans, S. (2018). Sustainable business model innovation: A review. *Journal of Cleaner Production, 198*, 401–416.

Glavič, P., & Lukman, R. (2007). Review of sustainability terms and their definitions. *Journal of Cleaner Production, 15*, 1875–1885. https://doi.org/10.1016/j.jclepro.2006.12.006

Goni, F. A., Gholamzadeh Chofreh, A., Estaki Orakani, Z., Klemeš, J. J., Davoudi, M., & Mardani, A. (2021). Sustainable business model: A review and framework development. *Clean Technologies and Environmental Policy, 23*, 889–897.

Haugh, H. M. (2007). New strategies for a Sustainable Society: The growing contribution of social entrepreneurship. *Business Ethics Quarterly, 17*, 743–749.

Inci, B. (2016). Social entrepreneurship in Turkey: A content analysis assessing Ashoka Fellows. *International Journal Trade, Economics and Finance, 7*, 105–112.

Jiao, H. (2011). A conceptual model for social entrepreneurship directed toward social impact on society. *Social Enterprise Journal, 7*, 130–149. https://doi.org/10.1108/17508611111156600.

Joyce, A., & Paquin, R. L. (2016). The triple layered business model canvas: A tool to design more sustainable business models. *Journal of Cleaner Production, 135*, 1474–1486.

Kannampuzha, M., & Hockerts, K. (2019). Organizational social entrepreneurship: Scale development and validation. *Social Enterprise Journal, 15*(3), 290–319.

Kubli, M., & Puranik, S. (2023). A typology of business models for energy communities: Current and emerging design options. *Renewable and Sustainable Energy Reviews, 176*, 113165.

Kulshrestha, R., Sahay, A., & Sengupta, S. (2022). Constituents and drivers of mission engagement for social enterprise sustainability: A systematic review. *The Journal of Entrepreneurship, 31*, 90–120.

Lamy, E. (2019). How to make social entrepreneurship sustainable? A diagnosis and a few elements of a response. *Journal of Business Ethics, 155*, 645–662.

Li, Y. (2014, August). Business model innovation of social entrepreneurship firm: A case study of TerraCycle. In *2014 International Conference on Management Science & Engineering 21th Annual Conference Proceedings* (pp. 507–514). IEEE.

Mair, J., Battilana, J., & Cardenas, J. (2012). Organizing for society: A typology of social entrepreneuring models. *Journal of Business Ethics, 111*(3), 353–373.

Mathur, D. A. (2011). Social entrepreneurs and the vision to build the society with ethical sustainability. *Information Management and Business Review, 2*(4), 154–161.

Mefi, N. P. (2020). Social entrepreneurship and the sustainability of small businesses at a South African Township. *Academy of Entrepreneurship Journal, 26*, 1–11.

Mintrom, M., & Thomas, M. (2018). Policy entrepreneurs and collaborative action: Pursuit of the sustainable development goals. *International Journal of Entrepreneurial Venturing, 10*, 153–171. https://doi.org/10.1504/IJEV.2018.092710.

Mort, G. S., & Hume, M. (2009). Special issue: Sustainability, social entrepreneurship and social change. *Australasian Marketing Journal, 17*, 189–191.

Mort, G. S., Weerawardena, J., & Carnegie, K. (2003). Social entrepreneurship: Towards conceptualisation. *International Journal of Nonprofit and Voluntary Sector Marketing, 8*, 76–88.

Morioka, S. N., Bolis, I., & De Carvalho, M. M. (2018). From an ideal dream towards reality analysis: Proposing Sustainable Value Exchange Matrix (SVEM) from systematic literature review on sustainable business models and face validation. *Journal of Cleaner Production, 178*, 76–88.

Muscat, E., & Whitty, M. (2009). Social entrepreneurship: Values-Based leadership to transform business education and society. *The Business Renaissance Quarterly, 4*, 31.

Noruzi, M. R., Westover, J. H., & Rahimi, G. (2010). An exploration of social entrepreneurship in the entrepreneurship era. *Asian Social Science, 6*(6).

Osyka, A. (2021). Social entrepreneurship and social services in the context of globalization. Advanced Discoveries of Modern Science: Experience, Approaches and Innovations Band 1. https://doi.org/10.36074/logos-09.04.2021.v1.04.

Ozbay, E., & Celikel, A. (2022). A case analysis on factors affecting the emergence of social innovations after Covid-19 In Turkey. *Pressacademia*. https://doi.org/10.17261/pressacademia.2022.1561.

Padhiary, S., & Patel, S. (2022). Social entrepreneurship for sustainable development: a paradigm of social work intervention during the COVID-19 crisis. *EPRA International Journal of Multidisciplinary Research (IJMR)*. https://doi.org/10.36713/epra10976.

Peric, M., Durkin, J., & Vitezic, V. (2017). The constructs of a business model redefined: A half-century journey. *Sage Open, 7*(3), 2158244017733516.

Philip, L., Emir, F., & Alola, A. (2021). The asymmetric nexus of entrepreneurship and environmental quality in a developing economy. *International Journal of Environmental Science and Technology*, 1–12. https://doi.org/10.1007/s13762-021-03670-y.

Prabhu, G. (1999). Social entrepreneurial leadership. *Career Development International, 4*, 140–145.

Santos, F. (2010). A positive theory of social entrepreneurship. *Journal of Business Ethics, 111*, 335–351. https://doi.org/10.2139/ssrn.1553072.

Seelos, C., & Mair, J. (2005). Social entrepreneurship: Creating new business models to serve the poor. *Business Horizons, 48*, 241–246.

Sparviero, S. (2019). The case for a socially oriented business model canvas: The social enterprise model canvas. *Journal of Social Entrepreneurship, 10*(2), 232–251.

Trapp, C. T., & Kanbach, D. K. (2021). Green entrepreneurship and business models: Deriving green technology business model archetypes. *Journal of Cleaner Production, 297*, 126694.

United Nations. Department of Economic and Social Affairs. (2022). The Sustainable Development Goals: Report 2022. UN.

Uslu, Y., Hancıoğlu, Y., & Demir, E. (2015). Applicability to Green Entrepreneurship in Turkey: A situation analysis. *Procedia – Social and Behavioral Sciences, 195*, 1238–1245.

Utaminingsih, A., Widowati, S. Y., & Witjaksono, E. H. (2023). Sustainable business model innovation: External and internal factors on SMEs. *International Journal of Innovation Science, 16*(1), 2024, pp. 95–113. https://doi.org/10.1108/IJIS-04-2022-0061.

Selsky, J. W., & Parker, B. (2010). Platforms for cross-sector social partnerships: Prospective sensemaking devices for social benefit. *Journal of Business Ethics, 94*, 21–37. https://doi.org/10.1007/s10551-011-0776-2.

VanSandt, C. V., Sud, M., & Marmé, C. (2009). Enabling the original intent: Catalysts for social entrepreneurship. *Journal of Business Ethics, 90*, 419–428.

WHO. (2023). Climate change: Key facts, accessed at 19.11.2023 from https://www.who.int/news-room

Zahra, S. A., Rawhouser, H., Bhawe, N., Neubaum, D. O., & Hayton, J. C. (2008). Globalization of social entrepreneurship opportunities. *Strategic Entrepreneurship Journal, 2*, 117–131.

Cagla Ozgoren
Bahcesehir University

Mine Karatas-Ozkan
Southampton University

Chapter 2 Social Entrepreneurship Education Through Freire's Philosophy: Engaging Curious and Passionate Minds by Growing Hope and Co-Developing Wisdom for Action

Abstract: Social entrepreneurship education is a global phenomenon, with various academic and non-academic institutions offering programmes to a diverse body of learners. The aim is to help develop a new generation of social entrepreneurs equipped with the values, skills, mindset, and knowledge to address social and environmental challenges innovatively and sustainably. In this chapter, we critically examine the impact of social entrepreneurship education on aspiring social entrepreneurs, emphasizing the development of competencies, life skills, and the motivation for future actions. Inspired by Paulo Freire's educational philosophy, the chapter explores social entrepreneurship education through a case study led by BRM (Bogazici University Businesspeople Alumni Association) in Istanbul, Turkey. Demonstrating SOGIP and DIBA programmes as case studies, which aim to raise awareness, provide training, mentoring, and support networking opportunities for university students interested in social entrepreneurship, we highlight the importance of applying Freire's critical pedagogy, emphasizing transformative praxis and conscientization in developing social entrepreneurship education programmes. The case studies demonstrate how education programmes contribute to developing critical thinkers and conscious individuals, essential for navigating complex societal challenges. The chapter concludes by offering insights into educational practices and policies, urging collaboration among universities, alumni associations, and multi-partner consortia.

Keywords: Social entrepreneurship education, Paulo Freire, Turkey, empowerment, co-creating wisdom

Authors have contributed equally.

Acknowledgments: We extend our heartfelt thanks to our colleagues at the BRM, Elif Bulak, Murat Ulman, Sedef Gursel and Begum Ozyer, for holding the space for us to learn the practice of inclusive business, social entrepreneurship and for the opportunity to collaborate with a diverse body of community members and stakeholders in this domain. We are also grateful to Aybuke Temel for participating in the study.

1. Introduction

Social entrepreneurship education has gained traction nationally and internationally. Several academic and non-academic institutions have developed programmes at different levels (undergraduate, postgraduate, executive education) globally (Howorth et al., 2012; Karatas-Ozkan et al., 2023). The primary motivation for social entrepreneurship education is to create a new generation of social entrepreneurs as change agents and individuals with higher levels of conscientiousness for social challenges equipped with the values, life skills, mindset, and knowledge needed to address such social and environmental issues in innovative and sustainable ways. In essence, social entrepreneurs play a fundamental role in improving the quality of our lives, as articulated by Thompson (2002), who states that an increased presence of social entrepreneurs and their inspirational stories bring about a heightened capacity to encourage and empower individuals to take proactive measures in such pursuits of social action.

Although there are different types of social entrepreneurs based on the scale and scope of the social project (Dees, 1998; Howorth et al., 2012), the main challenge for all is to manage and balance social mission and economic sustainability purposes to be more impactful (Tracey & Philips, 2007; Pache & Chowdhury, 2012). In this regard, the central role of social entrepreneurship education can be understood by bridging the interlinked levels of processes: first, raising awareness of social and environmental issues to be addressed through socially entrepreneurial ways (e.g., Howorth et al., 2012; Karatas-Özkan, 2011; Karatas-Ozkan et al., 2023); second, equipping individuals, who have this prosocial orientation and motivation to engage in social enterprise activity, with necessary competencies, skill sets, and holding space for them to connect with knowledge, expertise and networks (e.g., Karatas-Ozkan et al., 2023; Zhu et al., 2016) driven by shared values and ethos.

Universities, non-governmental organisations and international policy organisations have introduced social entrepreneurship programmes in national contexts and across the globe (Kwong et al., 2022; Zhu et al., 2016). Academic literature has also reflected on these developments, evaluating various dimensions of such programmes. Extant studies have mainly focused on the design and pedagogy of social entrepreneurship education programmes to facilitate effective learning processes (e.g., Howorth et al., 2012; Smith & Woodworth, 2012). Yet, we have limited insights into the development of competencies, life skills and the impact of the process of education on the motivation and future actions of learner social entrepreneurs. We also find that developing these competencies and skills often in constrained environments is a process with a different set of challenges, and this needs to be understood through the perspectives of social entrepreneurs and such education programme developers. Addressing this gap, we have formulated our research question: How does social entrepreneurship education facilitate the learning of aspiring social entrepreneurs to take informed action through relevant tools? In this book chapter, we focus on the impact of social entrepreneurship education to empower young and passionate individuals and influence change for the broader social entrepreneurship education ecosystem. A critical analysis of institutional strengths and gaps evident in a country context, such as Turkey, and how these could be addressed through a holistic approach to social entrepreneurship education are of paramount importance.

Drawing on Paulo Freire's educational philosophy (1970, 1985, 1994), we explore the social entrepreneurship education programmes through a specific case led by BRM (Bogazici University Businesspeople Alumni Association), which is an NGO that invites collaborations for shared value creation and social impact, based in Istanbul, Turkey. BRM has been a pioneering organisation advocating the concept of Inclusive Business in Turkey. BRM organised Turkey's first Inclusive Business Summit in 2016 in Istanbul. The summit brought together over 200 people representing academia, corporations, NGOs, social enterprises, and international institutions such as UNDP, BCtA, and IFC, sharing their know-how and vision on inclusive business models, tools and applications. Following this, the SOGIP project was won as a result of a competitive funding application process in collaboration with the local government bodies. SOGIP project refers to the Sosyal Girisimcilik Programı (Social Entrepreneurship Programme) and has aimed at raising awareness of social entrepreneurship and providing training, mentoring, project development support, and networking opportunities to university students who consider social entrepreneurship as a career path. SOGIP and DIBA (Dunyasina Iyi Bakanlar Akademisi: Academy for Those Taking Good Care of Their World) are the two demonstrative programmes we examined in this paper. As a result of a collaborative effort with the Kale Group and the Boğaziçi University Lifelong Learning Center (BŬYEM), the DIBA program is another social entrepreneurship programme with relevant stakeholders and partners. Drawing on documentary texts, a brief analysis of the interviews with the participant social entrepreneurs and programme developers, our analytical process and interpretation of data are guided by Freire's critical pedagogy, according to which the practice of education should be centred on the process of conscientization that allows for the transformative praxis of liberation of the oppressed (Misoczky, 2023). As strongly advocated by Freire (2000: 42) in the following words: "*What distinguishes the worst architect from the best of bees is that the architect builds the hive in his mind before constructing it in wax*", human beings have the capacity to contemplate the potential outcomes of their actions before embarking upon the intended course of action. Departing from this ontological standpoint, we can defer that consciousness manifests as an inherent intentionality directed towards the transformative engagement with the world (Freire, 1981 as cited in Misoczky, 2023). This is fundamentally relevant to social entrepreneurship education.

Our findings on developing competencies for social entrepreneurship extend previous studies, which focus on the growth of pedagogical tools for the design of the programs (e.g., Howorth et al., 2012; Pache & Chowdhury, 2012; Zhu et al., 2016). Except for a few notable papers (e.g., Howorth et al., 2012; Karatas-Ozkan et al., 2023, Pache & Chowdhury, 2012; Zhu et al., 2016), social entrepreneurship education has only received scant attention from management scholars, particularly through a critical lens. We contribute to the social entrepreneurship education scholarship by demonstrating the utility of Freire's critical educational methodology. It helps develop educational methods to raise students as critical thinkers and be conscious of their own "perception of realities and deal critically with it" (Freire, 1970: 32). Expanding this critical thinking, education is viewed as a social process that facilitates "the practice of freedom" that would help release individuals from their restrictions and fears by increasing their consciousness about the economic, political, social and cultural impositions and dominant forces in societies. In the context of social entrepreneurship education, we argue that this educational methodology (Freire, 1970) provides tools to develop reflexivity and criticality, connect with the real world through objectivism, develop a dialogue with the right people, and co-create actions through informed subjectivist thinking and interpretation to act upon these. Dialogical and problem-focused education are critical to Freire's philosophy, which is often used by management scholars and educators (Kociatkiewicz et al., 2022; Na Ayudhya et al., 2023; Siquera et al., 2023), and it pertains to social entrepreneurship education. We offer insights into the practice and policy for a range of institutional actors such as universities, alumni associations, and multi-partner consortia, including non-academic institutions. This will potentially allow for co-creating mentoring and education programmes and holding a space for aspiring social entrepreneurs who can get energised and motivated for prosocial action in the Turkish ecosystem.

2. Theoretical Underpinnings

2.1. Social Entrepreneurship Education

Social entrepreneurship can have multiple meanings and focuses according to different institutions, actors and scholars (Dees, 1998). In this classification, social entrepreneurs have a direct impact and generate a new and sustained equilibrium. Similarly, Zahra et al. (2009) identify three types of social entrepreneurs: Firstly, "*social bricoleurs*" usually focus on discovering and addressing small-scale local social needs; secondly, "*social constructionists*" typically exploit opportunities and market failures by filling gaps in underserved clients to introduce reforms and innovations to the broader social system, and finally, "*social engineers*" recognise systemic problems within existing social structures and address them by introducing revolutionary change. Given this diversity of approaches, the essence of social entrepreneurship is about addressing unmet needs and offering benefits to disadvantaged groups, bringing about structural change ideally. Social entrepreneurs bring considerable benefits to the economy by creating jobs, generating output or saving on public spending, and mobilising their ability to create and invest in multiple forms of capital, including social capital (Leadbetter, 1997; Karatas-Ozkan et al., 2023). Social entrepreneurs, who are a "special breed of entrepreneurs" (Dees,1998: 6) need to have various competencies for creating the optimum value of social enterprises. Accordingly, social entrepreneurship education should be inclusive, aiming to serve students, learners and aspiring social entrepreneurs by catering for their motivations, hopes and understanding and addressing their needs by connecting them to resources, networks and tools to develop competencies and life skills. Formal and informal education is crucial to improving these competencies, enabling more prosocial people to establish social ventures and organisations. In this regard, formal education in educational institutions could raise the social awareness of individuals. Configured with the right approach and tools, such education enhances learners to be more creative, think critically, approach issues more comprehensively and encourage them to be innovating more for social problems.

Social entrepreneurship is a field that blends elements of conventional commercial entrepreneurship with a strong focus on addressing social and environmental challenges underpinned by values and ethos shared by social entrepreneurs and their collaborators in the pursuit of social ventures. As the importance of social entrepreneurship grows, so does the need for education and training in this domain (Howorth et al., 2012; Pache & Chowdhury, 2012; Zhu et al., 2016; Karatas-Ozkan et al., 2023). Scholarship on social entrepreneurship education tends to focus on pedagogical tools (e.g., Smith & Woodworth, 2012), design of the social entrepreneurship education programmes that facilitate learning experiences (e.g., Howorth et al., 2012), specific frameworks to raise awareness and self-efficacy of students, unique challenges experienced by social entrepreneurs due to their social mission (Tracey & Philips, 2007), distinct set of competencies social entrepreneurs must attain to deal with complexities stemming from demands of social and business logics (Pache & Chowdhury, 2012), and multiple forms of capitals being deployed and transformed in the process of social entrepreneurship education leading to participant social entrepreneurs becoming reflexive social agents (Karatas-Ozkan et al., 2023). The authors (Karatas-Ozkan et al., 2023) argue that learners can be empowered as potential social entrepreneurs navigating complex and often uneven routes of creating social enterprises addressing social issues and inequalities. Their journey is characterised by a transformation between different forms of capital, balancing the paradoxical aspects of social impact and business reality and aligning personal values and self-interest with social good and community interests. Such alignment and critical approach underpin the success of social entrepreneurship education programmes, generating meaningful outcomes.

Social entrepreneurship education has been studied through diverse theoretical lenses, including social learning theory (Howorth et al., 2012), practice wisdom theory (Zhu et al., 2016), institutional logic (Pache & Chowdhury, 2012), and Bourdieusian theory of practice (Karatas-Ozkan et al., 2023). For instance, social learning theory sheds light on the longevity of the programmes being instrumental for reflective thinking skills since potential entrepreneurs are likely to trust others, experience familiarity and express themselves openly over time (Howorth et al., 2012). Inclusiveness of the acceptance criteria to the education program is also essential for the prospective learners and participants to develop feelings of being more open and motivated for the program, which positively impacts their skill development (ibid).

The shortcomings of the academic scholarship on social entrepreneurship education relate mainly to being unable to effectively address this alignment between social and business. We acknowledge that it is crucial to highlight the importance of developing an enterprise model and understand financial sustainability as one of the core aspects of social entrepreneurship. However, in its broadest sense, the social dimension needs to be elevated by first understanding the aspirations and motivations of prospective entrepreneurs; second, by identifying their limitations and needs; and third, by offering tools, models, networks and partnerships through an education programme to address these needs.

This group of entrepreneurs might be considered relatively more constrained and oppressed due to being at the margins and lacking relevant competencies, resources and networks. Social entrepreneurship education matters in bringing out the potential of social entrepreneurs by equipping them with relevant skills and competencies. Social entrepreneurs define problems and identify root causes underlying them; they are tasked with observing social structures such as economic, cultural, political, etc., and they can think strategically to draw the attention of society and government to these problems in various ways, such as using media for required resources, establishing connections among disadvantaged groups, volunteers and others such as influential actors. If developed and implemented effectively, social entrepreneurship education can catalyze such connections, vision, critical and authentic thinking and action. At this point, we introduce Freira's educational philosophy as it is an empowering framework to understand the instrumentality of social entrepreneurship education programmes in the current world, whereby sustainability (environmental, social and economic) challenges, resource limitations and cultural and economic and political dominations are increasingly shaping the agendas of several ecosystems and constraining several actors to lead agentic social actions and decent lives as human beings.

2.2. Paul Freire's Educational Philosophy

Paulo Freire's educational philosophy is helpful for educators in developing educational methodology, which would help students develop critical thinking, in other words being conscious of their own "perception of realities and deal critically with it" (Freire, 1970: 32) To him, education should be a social process that facilitates "the practice of freedom" that would help to release individuals from their restrictions by increasing their consciousness about the economic, political, social and cultural dominations of the society and providing tools to reflexively and critically act to overcome these limits (Freire, 1970). More specifically, the realisation of the "new awareness of the self, a new sense of dignity and a hope", they discover that "they are creators of culture, and all their work can be creative" (ibid.: 33). This realisation of self and visualisation for future through hope are critical tools for social entrepreneurship education.

2.2.1. Limit Situations and Limit Acts

Freire borrows his ideas about limit-situations from Vieria Pinto (1960). Accordingly, people are likely to overcome challenging situations as they consciously develop an understanding of these conditions as limiting situations rather than blindly submerging into the "culture of silence" and perceiving the current system as static and unchangeable. Freire encourages people to think about reality as an ongoing process with a transformative character rather than a static one. In doing so, he draws attention to the in-completed characterization of human beings, which is embedded in a historical context. Understanding concrete reality and developing a better understanding of this reality could only be achieved through the historically situated perspective of human beings and oppressor-oppressed relationships. Developing this kind of consciousness and perception of limit-situations is possible through "*separating themselves from the world, which they objectify as they separate themselves from their own action as they locate the seat of their decisions in themselves and their relations with the world and others*" (Freire, 1970: 99). The acts to confront limit situations are referred to as "limit acts" in Freire's philosophy. They imply rejecting a docile and passive acceptance of what is there and a response to a call to mobilize, "to uncover some untested feasibility" (Freire, 2014: 167; Misoczky, 2023: 7). This is a level which can be attained through a practice of liberation based on dialogical actions.

2.2.2. True Communication and Authentic Thinking

To Freire, the concept of "limit-situations" is helpful in developing a consciousness of the alterable aspects of the educational system situations. Furthermore, only through true communication and dialogue can students help ways to intervene in situations critically. To achieve this dialogue, he puts forward the importance of several conditions: comradeships, critical thinking rather than naive thinking, trust (e.g., in people, trust in faith, trust in capabilities and potentials), love and hope. Drawing on these principles, Freie makes the distinction between a banking education system, in which teachers function as "narrators" and liberal problem-posing education, in which teachers' role is to be facilitators to dialogue with a "cognitive" mindset:

> The teacher presents the material to the students for their consideration and reconsiders her earlier considerations as the students express their own to create together with the students, the conditions under which knowledge at the level of the doxa is superseded by true knowledge at the level of the logos. (Freire, 1970: 81)

Accordingly, wisdom is co-created through collaborative cultivation of knowledge, experience, and insights from various stakeholders, such as peers, mentors, and community members, to effectively address complex social challenges and innovate solutions. Specifically, this process of co-creating wisdom involves sharing perspectives, exchanging ideas, and synthesizing diverse experiences to collectively develop a deeper level of insight that surpasses what any single person could achieve alone.

2.2.3. Paulo Freire in Management Research on Education and Learning

Through the lens of Freire's contribution, critical management education is conceptualised and approached by embracing principles of thematic investigation, thematisation, and problematisation. Freire's pedagogy is a form of critical performativity with its relational, responsible and proactive nature. It can help us understand our own situations to generate relevant knowledge and insights and a catalytic force to enable change (Cavalcanti & Silva, 2024). In the Pedagogy of the Oppressed, Freire (2018) provides a three-phased framework for social action: first is investigation, which refers to acquiring knowledge on the community's current situation and struggles; second is mediation, which is to facilitate and stimulate as the community's existential and concrete situation becomes visible and it can be problematised; and third is the collaboration stage whereby through dialogue cultural actions are established that both encompass the aspirations of the oppressed and continuously problematise the meanings of such aspirations (Cavalcanti & Silva, 2024). Two key characteristics of Freire's pedagogy are problem-posing and situated, meaning it can be adapted to different scenarios, contexts and stakeholders (Shor, 2018).

Freire's insights offer clarity and perspectives to business school academics and educators to reflect on our situation and comprehend our limits in serving our communities better. In this vein, his contributions generate ways to overcome the constraints limiting our relevance and impact to effect change (Cavalcanti & Silva, 2024). Freirean contribution to management education and learning tends to be featured by our exposure to his two useful and interrelated notions: the notion of unveiling and the notion of praxis. In sustainability education, for instance, Jamil et al. (2023) put forward a call to amplify our work with our peers and students to decolonise our minds and our institutions by encouraging management learning as a praxis generating mindful conscientiousness and strengthening the encouragement of human conscience and action to serve for the love of people, planet (by considering surplus that is needed in the energy flow). The call is to test out the "untested feasibility" of our actions towards more sustainable (environmentally, socially and economically) societies with the conviction that our students' role (and our own role as educators) is to think critically about our situations, roles and place in society not only for limit situations and limit acts in Freirean terms but also to be able to move beyond these situations to find and co-create solutions for any sustainability challenges including inequalities. Social entrepreneurship education is rightly positioned in this discourse and practice as one way to mentor and raise new generations as reflexive individuals. Archer (2012: 22) defines reflexive social actors as those who continually consider how to behave in accordance with their aims, values and commitments or "ultimate concerns". Considering our individual and collective contribution to these circumstances in our professional contexts, as noted by Barros et al. (2022), is our main motivation to carry out studies of this kind, manifesting in this paper.

3. Methodology

3.1. Research Setting

The cases of social entrepreneurship education programmes we analyzed were led by BRM (Bogazici University Businesspeople Alumni Association), an NGO based in Istanbul, Turkey, that invites collaborations for shared value creation and social impact. BRM has been a pioneering organisation advocating the concept of Inclusive Business in Turkey. BRM organised Turkey's first Inclusive Business Summit in 2016 in Istanbul. The summit brought together over 200 people representing academia, corporations, NGOs, social enterprises, and international institutions such as UNDP, BCtA, and IFC, sharing their know-how and vision on inclusive business models, tools and applications. Following this, the SOGIP project was won as a result of a competitive funding application process in collaboration with the local government bodies. The SOGIP project refers to the Social Entrepreneurship Programme (Sosyal Girisimcilik Programı). It has aimed at raising awareness of social entrepreneurship and providing training, mentoring, project development support, and networking opportunities to university students who consider it a career path. Through the project, 1000 university students were reached in Istanbul; 200 students completed the capability building program, and 50 unique social impact project ideas were developed in collaboration with several corporations and local government organisations such as P&G, Interbank Credit Card Center (BKM), Besiktas Municipality, Eti Gıda and Kale Group. SOGIP and DIBA (Dunyasina Iyi Bakanlar Akademisi: Academy for Those Taking Good Care of Their World) are the two demonstrative programmes that we have examined in this paper. As a result of a collaborative effort with the Kale Group and the Boğaziçi University Lifelong Learning Center (BÜYEM), the DIBA program is a joint initiative of BRM with these stakeholders and partners. It is a social entrepreneurship program designed to support university students from all parts of Turkey who aspire to contribute positively to the world. The programme aims to facilitate these students' development, networking, and empowerment in social entrepreneurship. DIBA was envisaged as a platform that brings together university students keen to initiate goodness and take action towards caring for their world and future generations.

In an attempt to address the system's shortages and distinguish itself from others in the entrepreneurial ecosystem, DIBA positions itself as a "hope-giving mechanism to students and potential social entrepreneurs". The primary purpose of the education provided by these institutions is not only to guide students in launching their social enterprises but, more importantly, to contribute to the development of hope, self-efficacy and pertinent competencies. For instance, out of 120 applicants from diverse universities, only 2 launched their social enterprise. The rest of them increased their self-awareness, realised their potential and developed competencies in perceiving limit-situations and learning how to act.

3.2. Design, Data Collection and Analysis

We employed the "researcher as participant" approach (Gans, 1968), as advocated by social entrepreneurship education scholars (e.g., Howorth et al., 2012) since the co-author was a member of the BRM, participating in related activities since the initial Inclusive Business Summit and two founders of the programme were closely involved in generating insights and analyzing and interpreting texts and cases for this paper.

Our data sources include semi-structured interviews with the BRM members (two leaders in BRM who were actively involved in founding and running SOGIP and DIBA) and an interview with one participant social entrepreneur who attended and launched her social enterprise after completion of the program, and internal documents of DİBA. Participant social entrepreneur (graduate of the programme) is a director of the entrepreneurship student club at her university; she was not fully informed about social entrepreneurship before the programme and launched her social enterprise upon completion. The other interviewee holds a leading position in BRM and leads the case programmes described above. The other BRM colleague was the project manager of the programmes; an experienced social entrepreneur herself, and she was responsible for the design and launch of the social entrepreneurship education programmes under study.

These conversations have informed us about the lived experiences of these individuals (education designers and developers and participants), gaining insights into their reflections in terms of the economic, political and social challenges posed by the context and developing a vision and tools to transform these situations so young generations can find hope and visualize and action a future for themselves and their societies. We view this as a radical response to the context in question. BRM has demonstrated as an NGO that we should not stay in our narrow realm of practice; we have responsibility and accountability for future generations who will be motivated, inspired and educated to take their responsibility for actions accordingly. All interviews were conducted online and lasted an average of one and a half hours. They were recorded and transcribed verbatim. Additionally, we examined DIBA's internal reports including internal report from 2022 and the social impact analysis. These reports offered insights into the scale and scope of the social entrepreneurship education, as well as reflections from the participants in the social entrepreneurship program.

Drawing on interviews and documents, we sought to examine how participants and program coordinators evaluate the contribution of social entrepreneurship education to the development of competencies. We employed an iterative approach (Miles & Huberman, 1994) to ground the data in Freire's educational philosophy, which is the phase of interpretation. Freire's theoretical constructs inform our analytical orientation and interpretation but do not constrain them as such. More specifically, we begin with "initial coding", examining the content of programmes' content and the experiences of program coordinators and participant/graduate social entrepreneur. For instance, -dominance of business values in social entrepreneurial ecosystem, -importance of probing of contextual problems, -recognition of self-limit situation such as gender, and -recognition of opportunities such as being graduates of prestigious university were among the initial codes emerged from the data. As we shifted our focus to theoretical constructs of Freire, these initial codes were consolidated into "focused coding" of limit-situations. Figure 1 provides an overview of our empirical themes and conceptual categories on Freire's educational philosophy, which inform potential means and ends of social entrepreneurship education.

To enhance the "trustworthiness" of our analysis, as recommended by Lincoln and Guba (1985), the authors independently evaluated the transcripts and regularly convened to discuss the analysis. We also utilized "member-checks" by sharing our analysis with the participants to validate our interpretations.

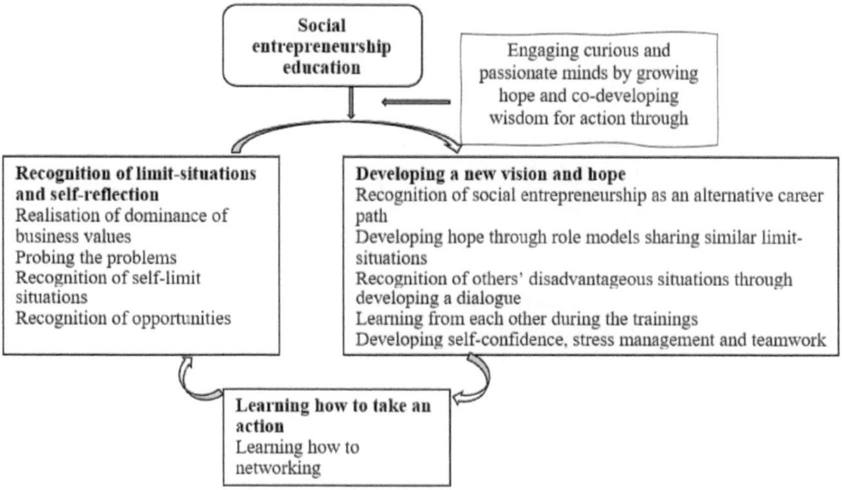

Figure 1. Data Structure

4. Findings

4.1. Salience of Social Entrepreneurship Education Context and Limit-Situations

Programme coordinators highlight the tension between commercial/business values and social impact/mission values in the social entrepreneurship sphere, which is evident in the approaches of investors and coordinators of social entrepreneurship education programs. The programme leader stresses that "*the ecosystem is centred around supporting the social entrepreneurship ideas that come with a significant profit potential; there are many competitions to fund social entrepreneurship ideas and plans. However, this conflicts with the social mission*" (Int., 1, founder of DIBA, program leader). On the other hand, considering the content of the various educational programs and courses at the universities and social media platforms, the presentation and dissemination of social entrepreneurship as an alternative career path that could be pursued easily is also criticised by participants. The following quotations illustrate this:

> Social entrepreneurship is complex, and it is much more difficult in Turkey. It is disappointing that social entrepreneurship education programs are designed and marketized with business logic, centred around how participant social entrepreneurs generate revenue. You need people who support you; you need a budget. problematic issue is

> about how social entrepreneurship has been pumped and marketized from municipalities to private companies in a way that makes it seem like a new sector with career opportunities, without articulation of challenges. (Int. 3, program coordinator, social entrepreneur)

There are significant gaps in the social entrepreneurship education ecosystem, as argued by one of the founders of the programmes:

> There are four categories of people who are interested in social entrepreneurship. On one end, some potential entrepreneurs haven't done anything about social entrepreneurship but want to do something about community benefit. On the other hand, some potential entrepreneurs are engaged with entrepreneurial processes and even have developed a prototype and are looking forward to being funded. No one is interested in the first group, while investors focus on the fourth group, whose initiatives have greater profit margin potential. Even competitions for the best social entrepreneurial ideas have been arranged. But this conflicts with the underlying logic of social entrepreneurship. (Int., 1, founder of DIBA, program leader)

Since there is a tendency to dominate business values over social mission in social entrepreneurship education, which is one of the concerns of the program coordinators, the education program is designed to inform students accordingly and raise their awareness. For instance, students are guided during the program. One of the difficulties in finding funds for their project is taking a highly business-oriented approach while engaging with investors towards social ventures. While mentoring and networking opportunities are plentiful for potential entrepreneurs, lack of financial support is a significant barrier to social entrepreneurship in Turkey. The sessions delve into the challenges of launching a social enterprise and aid students in emotional and realistic preparation, which are highly important.

Learning how to define social problems is a crucial and significant issue in social entrepreneurship education. Contrary to entrepreneurship training, social entrepreneurship education aims to enhance problem-posing, developing competencies to make connections between different situations, contexts and circumstances and find meaningful and responsible solutions by identifying concrete realities and dominations in economic, political, and cultural domains and developing critical thinking and reflexivity for limit-situations so they can transform them. Understanding the context and developing the dialogue with the right stakeholders is essential. This entails spending sufficient time and immersion in the context, developing dialogue with the community stakeholders, and identifying economic, political, and cultural dominations that create contradictions and limit situations and acts.. As elaborated by one of our participants: "*One of the shortages of our education system is an in-depth understanding of the problem. We all focus on solving the problem without pondering the problem. Our education system's main purpose should be identifying the problem and learning how to take action.*" (Int. 3, program coordinator, social entrepreneur). Further, she suggests the following to deal with this challenge in designing social entrepreneurship education programmes:

> Generally overlooked issues are problems or challenges. First, we need to deliberate problems. In our education program, participants must take at least 4–5 hours to dive into the underlying root reasons of the problems. We begin the training by reminding students of Einstein's famous quote: "If I had 5 hours to solve the problem, I would spend 4, 5 hours to think of and delve into the problem". For instance, problem tree exercises and the 5 Whys technique are utilised to define problems effectively by asking questions such as "Who will be affected by this issue? What might be the impacts of this problem?" (Int. 3, program coordinator, social entrepreneur)

Another issue raised by participants was breaking down the problem into smaller parts and segmenting the target audience, which becomes essential to understanding the underlying reasons for the main problem and making the solution achievable. In other words, identifying the root causes of the problem is a number one priority in social entrepreneurship. Once you identify these, you can generate pathways for solutions and actions, which is at the heart of social entrepreneurship education. Determining the target audience is taught in the program as the first stage of understanding the limit-situations. For instance, the program coordinator, Begum, told us: "*If social entrepreneurs are concerned with women's problems, they want to access all the women. Yet what they need to do is focus on particular people, or we tell our participants that you need to only focus on one shelter; you cannot feed all stray animals*".

Reinforcing this point, the participants reflected on their realisation of limit-situations. For instance, Aybuke, the graduant of SOGIP, was aware that she was in a patriarchal society where the role of women was sharply defined.

> I felt disadvantaged because of being a woman at the beginning of my 20s. This is a serious barrier. You can easily understand this as a barrier when meeting with investors and customers. These barriers can sometimes be quite formidable, but understandably, you recognise and understand them. The contribution of SOGIP lies in the profile of the speakers. When you see how they have done it, you think, "I can do it too." felt like I could do it after hearing from female entrepreneurs as speakers. (Int., 2, graduant SOGIP, Aybuke)

Participants acknowledge the importance of developing a dialogue with people to gain in-depth insights about the concrete reality and to develop a reflection on their limits and opportunities. Stepping into reality means talking with people, understanding their living conditions, caring about their concerns and developing accountability for their problems. This could only be fully achieved through developing "true dialogue" with "hope" and "critical thinking" in Freire's (1970) terms. Articulations of the project manager of the program about understanding contextual dynamics and actual problems illustrate this further: "*You cannot develop the project you are sitting on. To deepen and internalise the problems, you need to be with people, with disadvantaged groups.*" (Int. 3, program coordinator, social entrepreneur) because we cannot transform reality, without knowing it objectively and concretely (Freire, 1970).

Increasing awareness of reframing constraints as leverage becomes crucial in this process. Reflexive and critical elaboration of the contextual challenges and limit-situations in earlier stages of the process is a must for students in the social entrepreneurship education programmes to develop a vision with the hope that they can transform situations. According to Freire (1970), people can become self-sufficient and take action to change reality by employing a comradeship approach and developing a dialogue with others, which can only be achieved with hope and critical thinking.

4.2. Developing a New Vision, Hope and Co-creating Wisdom Through the Development of Competencies

Our findings illustrate that social entrepreneurship education aims for students to develop authentic thinking, which can only be achieved through pondering the problems, immersing into the context, and understanding concrete realities, contradictions, tensions and potential ways forward through developing a dialogue with community members (oppressed and privileged groups).

Role models are important in this process. Our data show that developing hope through role models sharing similar limit-situations and having the courage and empowering tendency to take action, rather than dealing with limit situations through denial or assimilation through the domination of the context, is essential for students' realisation of their potential. Participant social entrepreneur, Aybuke, raises this:

> Hopelessness starts at this point [as you feel limitations], and hope flourishes as you meet with women who launched their social enterprise at an early age, experienced similar challenges, and achieved something. You can only be inspired by people you can identify (attach or relate to) yourself. Otherwise, people from another world or advantageous in many aspects cannot be role models.(Int., 2, Aybuke, trainer of SOGIP)

This kind of relationality and bonding is critical in developing new vision and hope. Only social entrepreneurs concerned with a social mission who have genuinely suffered in finding capital, networking, and convincing people, among others, might be the role models to which participants could relate. Program coordinators also raise this issue:

> The individuals delivering the training should be social entrepreneurs themselves (not academics). Because when someone who has not truly experienced social entrepreneurship gives this training, it falls short. (Int. 3, program coordinator, social entrepreneur)

Self-awareness through the realisation of others' limitations is another important dimension. In the cases of SOGIP and DIBA, attachment with and developing a dialogue with role models and other participants helped students critically elaborate on their own and others' limitations and opportunities. This process of critical reflection was crucial for deepening awareness of their potential, as highlighted by the participant social entrepreneur, Aybüke: "*As I talk with other students from, for example, Anatolian universities, I recognised that they had to commute each time to attend this programme, and even getting acceptance for this programme with their university names is a challenge for them*" and she continues that "*this was important realisation for me that as a student XX I have more opportunity to achieve*" (Int., 2, trainer of SOGIP, Aybuke).

Converting problems to opportunity is a turning point for social entrepreneurship. The participant social entrepreneur, Aybuke, told us how she was guided through the process of scaling up in social entrepreneurship through the BRM training, and this process helped her to conceive the gap as an opportunity in the field to launch her social enterprise, Social Forum. She acknowledges the importance of this education: "*We noticed that the problems that had unconsciously settled in our subconscious through the training we received here. I got into this field by observing the challenges of social entrepreneurs around us. For instance, one of the problems arises from the fact that social entrepreneurs often have small teams. On one hand, they cannot allocate time to corporate marketing; eventually, they must focus more on their product or service. It both encouraged me and prompted me to look at it from that perspective*". (Int., 2, trainer of SOGIP, Aybuke).

Social learning is a valuable process in social entrepreneurship education: "*Learning from each other during the training is one of the most significant gains for the members of my project team who came from different disciplines. Students from diverse fields can challenge and enhance each other's ideas*" (Int., 2, Aybuke, trainer of SOGIP). This is also related to developing self-confidence and resilience through stress management and teamwork:

> There was a definite increase in self-confidence. Our program was intensive, and it significantly contributed to participants in terms of stress management. They gained skills related to working under stress. There were also achievements in teamwork…We

> received feedback indicating positive effects regarding teamwork and taking responsibility. It has been beneficial in terms of leadership. In the area of social responsibility, there have been more gains in problem identification and determining the root causes of the problem…Being able to speak in public and giving presentations are the most fundamental skills within a community. For example, students said, "I didn't think I could speak in front of so many people. I was very nervous, trembling, but I managed to do it." (Int. 3, Programme coordinator, social entrepreneur)
>
> They gave us a problem. It was from the P&G company, and it involved teamwork. You form a team with people you are not familiar with in an environment you are not accustomed to. (Int. 2, Aybüke, participant social entrepreneur)

Confidence building is also a part of this process, and emotional dynamics are integral to this very human nature of personal and social learning, including emotional disappointment and coping with difficult situations with stakeholders, including team dynamics:

> They will go to the municipality, to companies, of course, funding will come, but when they go to one or two companies and cannot find what they are looking for, they experience disappointment. This is because they may not have focused enough on the problem or the idea, they found is not such a fantastic solution. The second reason is that they may not have researched enough on the solution idea. What they are thinking has already been considered before. (Int.3, programme coordinator, social entrepreneur)
>
> The culture of social entrepreneurship has been transferred to us through the American system, leading to a perception that revolves more around individual leaders. There is an emphasis on a single person, a sole leader, someone featured on TED talks or receiving awards. However, social entrepreneurship is a team effort. It is essential not to forget that it is a team effort. There is always a team behind, and what is crucial is not just the social entrepreneur but a system that rewards social entrepreneurship. The impact of an individual who dedicates their time and effort is undoubtedly essential. However, the intention is to bring it to life as a group. Conflicts can arise in terms of project ownership when it comes to implementation. One person may invest more effort, but others also have their rights. In our training program, we should address this and include it in the ongoing educational process. (Int.3, program coordinator, social entrepreneur)

In summary, developing competencies instils hope, wisdom, and vision in students regarding their capabilities and what they can achieve.

4.3. Learning to Take Action with Implications for the Ecosystems

Participant social entrepreneurs and program coordinators stress that social entrepreneurship education provided them with networking, understanding and skills to help them take action. According to Freirean philosophy, learning to act against the oppressive elements of reality is imperative. Some of the components of this include which actions to take by individual social entrepreneurs and how to filter specific thoughts, observations, and realities to take the intended action that will create the intended impact.

This requires learning to take smart actions strategically and blend individual-level values and aspirations with ultimate concerns and social goals at the collective level. In other words, *what is in it for me* and *what is in it for the societies and communities that I am affiliated with* (in the context of the social problem that I am tackling) are fundamentally important questions to identify which actions to take and how to do smart-networking with all potential stakeholders including disadvantaged groups (beneficiaries), privileged groups (having resources and controlling information/knowledge, hence possessing power) and even opponent stakeholders in the ecosystem so students can understand their thought processes and contradictions in the system better so they can navigate through such situations, people and contexts through cross-fertilisation and cross-connections of ideas, resources and knowledge. This entails incorporating these key ideological aspects of Freire's philosophy, such as liberating them from fear of freedom and "discovering themselves to be the host of the oppressor" (Freire, 1970: 48) so that this can be dealt with by instilling confidence and dialogical capacity in them. This, in turn, will help to raise hope, develop understanding, and structure and critical reasoning for action. The ecosystem dimensions will be instrumental in igniting the action aspect of this by energising and moderating relevant institutional actors for the education and support of these future emerging social entrepreneurs.

Overall, our findings illustrate how Freire's educational philosophy, when applied to social entrepreneurship education, can empower students to understand limit situations, cultivate vision, hope and wisdom, and effectively take action. We have elucidated the relevance and applicability of Freire's philosophy to social entrepreneurship, offering recommendations for developers of social entrepreneurship education programs. These recommendations are detailed in the discussion section and summarised in Table 1.

5. Concluding Remarks and Recommendations for Social Entrepreneurship Program Coordinators

In this book chapter, we have focused on how social entrepreneurship education facilitates the learning of aspiring social entrepreneurs to (situationally) liberate themselves from constraining orders of societies to be able to take informed action through relevant tools. The impact of social entrepreneurship education can be immense particularly in resource-constrained and more oppressive environments. These oppressive environments are not necessarily limited to certain geographical and cultural contexts in today's world as evidently observed and revealed with the aid of social media. Resources (planetary and financial) are getting scarce all over the world and funding imperatives and arrangements tend to dictate more oppressive approaches for almost all entrepreneurial ecosystems (see The Economist, 2022 as an example to such an ecosystem). Therefore, our findings and arguments for designing and delivering social entrepreneurship education programmes, which allow for understanding the salience of social entrepreneurship education context and limit-situations, developing a new vision, hope and co-creating wisdom through the development of competencies, and learning to take informed action, transcend boundaries of countries, cultures, and contexts. This is a noble and yet heavy (in these tough times) responsibility for educators, researchers, practitioners and policymakers. Our recommendations mainly focus on educators and practitioners designing and delivering social entrepreneurship programmes in this paper. Further studies can focus on further reflections and evolution of students' perspectives in utilizing such programmes.

Table 1. Summary of specific tools and approaches for recommendation

	Data Structure	**Applicability and relevancy of Freire's philosophy**	**Recommendations for future studies and program coordinators**
Limit-situations (participants' realisation of dominance and developing vision, hope and wisdom to act)	Realisation of dominance of business values Learning how to define the social the problems Recognition of self-limit situations Recognition of self-opportunities Recognition of social entrepreneurship as an alternative career path	a-How to increase awareness of participants about dominations of economic, political and cultural spheres and help them to come to the realisation that oppressions could be transformed to the opportunity? How social entrepreneurship programs could be designed to manage social and business mission conflictions? (There are studies addressing this question and providing specific tools) b-What might be the context specific tools in addressing the social mission aspect? c-How to encourage students to frame their conditions?	Although participants told that they interrogate participants' acceptance letters and conduct several tests to understand social orientation of the participants. Yet, we suggest that program coordinators should use specific tools such articulation of scenarios discussing ethical dilemmas, challenges of the process to foster social impact mission.

Table 1. Continued

	Data Structure	Applicability and relevancy of Freire's philosophy	Recommendations for future studies and program coordinators
Developing vision, hope and wisdom	Developing hope through role models sharing similar limit-situations Recognition of others' disadvantageous situations through developing a dialogue	a-How to design education programs to become more inclusive that would encourage students from diverse universities and disciplines? b-How to choose role model speakers that participants would attach with selves and encourage them to grow their vision and reflective action?	a-We suggest that selection of collaborator firms which prioritize creating social value and see differences as richness is crucial for the programs' inclusiveness and providing equal opportunities. b-We suggest that role models should be the social entrepreneurs who are experiencing the social entrepreneurship process with all challenges and tears, rather than the academics. We also suggest that at least three social entrepreneurs who would mentoring the each team would be crucial for participants' growing their hope, vision and wisdom.

(continued on next page)

Table 1. Continued

	Data Structure	**Applicability and relevancy of Freire's philosophy**	**Recommendations for future studies and program coordinators**
Learning to take action		a-How social entrepreneurship programs could be designed to prepare student to become emotionally resilient? b-How technical competencies such as knowing artificial intelligence and data science tools could be integrated to the program? c-How social entrepreneurship could be financially supported? How to establish mechanisms to foster funding for social entrepreneurship? d-How to develop recognition programs or mechanisms that would reinforce social entrepreneurship process, rather than individual social entrepreneurs?	a-We suggest that programs should prepare students to become emotionally resilient. b-We propose that programs should at least increase awareness on and integrate the recent software application tools. c-Although students develop great projects, having huge social impact potential, finding a fund is an issue. We suggest that provision of financial support for the selected projects would encourage to take an action. d- We suggest that social entrepreneurship education programs should attach more importance on social entrepreneurship process, rather than individual social entrepreneurs.

For social entrepreneurship programme coordinators, we offer three recommendations: The first crucial starting point is *to prepare students for emotional disappointments and alert them to learn emotional regulation,* which is very difficult, particularly for younger individuals. Our study demonstrates that one of the biggest misconceptions is students falling in love with their ideas and thinking that the world will support them. The second recommendation is to create awareness that social entrepreneurship is a team effort and holding space for such collaborative work. The third recommendation includes bridging the worlds of practice and academia in designing and delivering social entrepreneurship education programmes. Specific tools and approaches for these recommendations are offered in more detail in Table.

References

Archer, M. (2012). *The reflexive imperative in Late Modernity*. Cambridge: Cambridge University Press.

Barros, C., Sani, A., & Meneses, R. F. (2022). Violência contra profissionais de saúde: dos discursos às práticas. *Configurações. Revista Ciências Sociais, 30*, 33–46.

Cavalcanti, M. F. R., & Silva, A. L. (2024). Unveiling systemic oppression in business education: Freire's contribution to our quest for social change. *Management Learning*. https://doi.org/10.1177/13505076231220121

Dees, J. G. (1998). The meaning of social entrepreneurship, Stanford University: Draft Report for the Kauffman Center for Entrepreneurial Leadership, 6 pp, available at http://www.caseatduke.org/documents/dees_sedef.pdf, (accessed 17 December 2024).

Freire, P. (1970). *Pedagogy of the oppressed* (30th-anniversary edition). Continuum International Publishing Group Inc.

Freire, P. (1981). *Ação cultura para a liberdade e outros escritos*. Rio de Janeiro: Paz e Terra.

Freire, P. (1985). *The politics of education*. Massachusetts: Bergin and Garvey.

Freire, P. (1994). *Pedagogy of hope*. New York: Continuum.

Freire, P. (2000). Cultural action for freedom. *Harvard Education Review*, 39–68.

Freire, A. M. A. (2014). Notes. In P. Freire (Ed.), *Pedagogy of hope: Reliving pedagogy of the oppressed* (pp. 167–186). London: Bloomsbury Publishing.

Freire, P. (2018). *Pedagogy of the oppressed* (50th-anniversary edition, 4th ed.). Bloomsbury Publishing.

Gans, H. J. (1968). The participant observer as a human being: Observations on the personal aspects of fieldwork. In R. G. Burgess (Ed.), *Field research: A sourcebook and field manual* (pp. 53–61). London: Allen and Unwin.

Howorth, C., Smith, S. M., & Parkinson, C. (2012). Social learning and social entrepreneurship education. *Academy of Management Learning and Education, 11*(3), 371–389.

Jamil, N., Humphries-Kil, M., & Dey, K. (2023). Infusing courageous love for universal dignity and environmental response-ability through management education and learning: Inspired By Freire's dream. *Management Learning*, 13505076231192172.

Karatas-Özkan, M. (2011). Understanding relational qualities of entrepreneurial learning: Towards a multi-layered approach. *Entrepreneurship and Regional Development, 23* (9/10), 877–906.

Karatas-Ozkan, M., Ibrahim, S., Ozbilgin, M., Fayolle, A., Manville, G., Nicolopoulou, K., & Tunalioglu, M. (2023). Challenging the assumptions of social entrepreneurship education and repositioning it for the future: Wonders of cultural, social, symbolic and economic capitals, *Social Enterprise Journal, 19*(2), 98–122.

Kociatkiewocz, J., Kostera, M., & Zueva, A. (2022). The ghost of capitalism: A guide to seeing, naming and exorcising the spectre haunting the business school. *Management Learning, 53*(2), 310–330.

Kwong, C., Cheung, C., Bhattarai, C., & Filedhouse, S. (2022). How entrepreneurial are social entrepreneurship education providers? The role of universities' entrepreneurial ecosystems in the provision of elective social entrepreneurship courses to business, *Studies in Higher Education, 47*(5), 1046–1056.

Leadbetter, C. (1997). *The rise of the social entrepreneur*. London: Demos.

Lincoln, Y. S., & Guba, E. G. (1985). *Naturalistic inquiry*. Newbury Park, CA: Sage.

Misoczky, M. C. (2023). Paulo Freire and the praxis of liberation: Education, organisation and ethics. *Management Learning*. 13505076231201734.

Miles, M. B., & Huberman, A. M. (1994). *Qualitative data analysis: An expanded sourcebook*. Beverly Hills, CA: Sage.

Na Ayudhya, U. C., Edmondson, M., Harris, A., & Littel, F. (2023). Moving from responsibility learning inaction to "responsibility learning-in-action": A student-educator collective writing on the "unnoticed" in the hidden curriculum at business schools. *Management Learning, 54*(3), 359–383.

Pache, A. C., & Chowdhury, I. (2012). "Social entrepreneurs as institutionally embedded entrepreneurs: Toward a new model of social entrepreneurship education". *Academy of Management Learning and Education, 11*(3), pp. 494–510.

Shor, I. (2018). Brazil's unintended gift to the world: Paulo Freire's pedagogy of the oppressed, fifty years later. *Programa de Pós-graduação Educação: Currículo – PUC/SP* http://revistas.pucsp.br/index.php/curriculum, OI http://dx.doi.org/10.23925/1809-3876.2018v16i4p1334-1340

Smith, I. H., & Woodworth, W. P. (2012). "Developing social entrepreneurs and social innovators: A social identity and self-efficacy approach". *Academy of Management Learning and Education, 11* (3), 390–407.

Siquera, A. C. O., Honig, B., Mariano, S., Moraes, J., & Cunha, R. M. (2023). Creating economic, social and environmental change through entrepreneurship: An entrepreneurial autonomy perspective informed by Paulo Freire. *Journal of Business Venturing Insights, 19*. https://doi.org/10.1016/j.jbvi.2023.e00386

The Economist. (2022). Chinese money is pouring into British universities: Critics claim that it comes at the cost of free speech, 12 March 2022 at https://www.economist.com/britain/2022/03/12/chinese-money-is-pouring-into-british-universities?utm_medium=cpc.adword.pd&utm_source=google&ppccampaignID=18156330227&ppcadID=&utm_campaign=a.22brand_pmax&utm_content=conversion.direct-response.anonymous&gad_source=1&gclid=CjwKCAiAkp6tBhB5EiwANTCx1BRhOY5Antx7PPJRCAK2rzyITy0-Gd-5vvSFVgcOSwJkYKVdhdC1nBoCEg0QAvD_BwE&gclsrc=aw.ds (Date of access: 23 October 2023).

Thompson, J. L. (2002). The world of the social entrepreneur, *International Journal of Public Sector Management, 15*(5), 412–431.

Tracey, P., & Philips, N. (2007). The distinctive challenge of educating social entrepreneurs: A postscript and rejoinder to the special issue on entrepreneurship education. *Academy of Management Learning and Education, 6*(2), 264–271.

Vieira Pinto, Á. (1960). *Consciência e realidade nacional: A consciência crítica.* Ministerio da Educação e Cultura, Instituto Superior de Estudos Brasileiros.

Zahra, S., Gedajlovic, E., Neubaum,, D. O., & Shulman, J. M. (2009). A typology of social entrepreneurs: Motives, search processes and ethical challenges. *Journal of Business Venturing, 24*, 519–532.

Zhu, Y., Rooney, D., & Philips, N. (2016). Practice-based wisdom Theory for integrating institutional logics: A new model for social entrepreneurship learning and education, *Academy of Management Learning and Education, 15*(3), 607–625.

Bilge Uyan-Atay
Bahçeşehir University

Hülya Denizalp
GHD Board Member

Chapter 3 Modeling the Impact of Social Enterprise in the Tourism Sector in Türkiye: Gençtur and Gönüllü Hizmetler Derneği (GHD)

Abstract: This chapter describes the characteristics, development, and institutional forces behind "Gençtur," one of the social enterprises in Türkiye, and its relationship to GHD. In which years does the evaluation of social enterprises and the basis for seeing such enterprises as social change agents in Türkiye go back to? What was the political, policy and cultural context in Türkiye in those years? What was the catalytic effect of civil society organizations on the establishment of social enterprises? What are the characteristics and institutional features of the first social enterprises? This chapter will answer the above questions and explain how the conditions of that period influenced the establishment of Gençtur, a company operating in the tourism sector. It also includes a modeling of Gençtur, a social enterprise established by GHD to raise funds. Since the establishment of the Republic of Turkey, the support provided by the government, including encouraging youth to become more involved in tourism activities, cultural exchange programs, youth empowerment, poverty alleviation, empowerment of local communities, and innovative activities created outside the mainstream tourism economy, has led to a diversification of tourism-based social projects that aim to achieve such goals. For this reason, GHD was established. Gençtur, which was established to provide funding, can be considered as one of the first social enterprises in Turkey's tourism sector to support social entrepreneurship projects with development goals such as branding, empowerment, and social change. This section presents social enterprise projects that involve community participation, a model that seeks to harness the economic power of tourism for human development, and how Turkey is better positioned through Gençtur and GHD to achieve its post-republican development goals.

Keywords: Social enterprises, tourism sector, youth empowerment, institutional theory, modeling, NGOs.

1. Introduction

Relevant literature has shown that companies interacting with society are more successful, sustainable, and resilient (Edmans, 2023; Browne et al., 2016; and Fiksel, 2003). In Türkiye, the trend of establishing enterprises based on societal needs is also gaining traction (Strzałka et al., 2021; Biroğlu, 2019; and Özlem & Çelik, 2021). A closer examination of business models, especially for-profit or non-profit, reveals that models that prioritize generating revenue and social benefits (Dart, 2004)—such as social enterprises—stand out and are valuable when it comes to creating strategies that are entwined with society to achieve sustainability (Kamaludin, et al., 2021; Voegel, L. A., Voegel, J. A., 2020; Swanson, et.al., 2020; and Zhang & Swanson, 2014). Therefore, the first thing that jumps out when examining social enterprise models is the question, "What makes it unique?" (Dacin et al., 2010). The uniqueness of social enterprises stems from their identification of a set of criteria that allow them to continuously innovate while determining if an action creates and sustains social value (Dees, 2007). If the organizational structure of social enterprises is observed, it is seen as a mirror that shows the characteristic structure of the country of origin (Rahim & Mohtar, 2015). It implies that economic structure, cultural components, lifestyle, and shortcomings are all distinct. Thus, social enterprises must be unique in order to address these shortcomings. Accordingly, each social enterprise aligns its strategic position with the social goal it seeks to accomplish.

Social enterprises aim to solve environmental or social problems (Alter, 2006, 2007). They appear due to realizing that social responsibility may need to be prioritized more in traditional business models. These enterprises seek to combine the pursuit of financial gain with a dedication to improving the environment or society. Social enterprises have their origins in non-profit and non-governmental organizations (NGOs) that engage in commerce as a means of funding their operations (Alter, 2007; Sepulveda, 2015; Teasdale, 2012). Studies in the literature have shown that when a social problem cannot be solved in the long term by nonprofit organizations, the public sector, and the private sector, social enterprises step in (Battilana & Dorado, 2010). In doing so, social enterprises disrupt the existing order, learn from mistakes, break traditions, and try to create a system through different learning and management methods. As a result, they aim to create catalytic and systemic change. (Mair et al., 2012). EADA Business School and Ashoka Spain decided to collaborate to investigate systemic change empirically and gain a better understanding of how the two organizational forms—for-profit (FP) and nonprofit (NP)—deploy their resources and capabilities to achieve systemic change. They found that cognitive shift, embeddedness, and replicability can cause this systemic change (Saluzzo et al., 2023).

Since then, different locations and situations have utilized different terminology when describing social enterprises, which can lead to terminological misunderstanding (Harding, 2004; Alter, 2007; Bacq & Janssen, 2011; Choi & Majumdar, 2014; Dacin et al., 2010). Terms such as "social entrepreneurship," "social enterprise," and "impact business" may have slightly different connotations in different societies and countries. Additionally, different standards may apply to what constitutes a social enterprise. The fact that terminology like "for-profit," "nonprofit," and "hybrid" organizations can be used synonymously or have distinct meanings depending on the location causes some confusion. These differences make it challenging to come up with a standard definition of social enterprises.

It's critical to consider the unique context, cultural particularities, and changing interpretations in various fields or locations while attempting to explain these variations. The notion of social enterprises has undergone worldwide evolution, with multiple countries spearheading and supporting this approach. For instance, the UK has put in place frameworks and laws that encourage the development of social enterprises by giving them legal status and making it easier for them to obtain capital and resources (Collavo, 2018). The Social Enterprises UK organization has been actively supporting and lobbying on behalf of the industry. In recent years, the United States has also gained popularity and recognition. The field is varied, with organizations tackling various social and environmental challenges. A different kind of legal structure, like B Corps. or certified B Corporations, Impact Investing, Venture Philanthropy, Government support, and Tech for Goods backing for policies and initiatives aims to foster an atmosphere where businesses can prosper and contribute positively to society.

On the other hand, national preferences for "social enterprises" differ throughout Europe. Nonetheless, the study in this field acknowledged that social enterprises in Europe prioritize generating social benefit through government- and EU-founded cooperatives and associations (Kerlin, 2006, 2009; Defourny & Nyssens, 2001; Defourny & Nyssens, 2010; Brouard & Larivet, 2011). More profit-oriented structures financed by the private business sector are observed in the United States. There has been a considerable increase in China's social enterprise sector lately, with operations in fields like education, poverty alleviation, and renewable energy. Nevertheless, when China or other developing nations are included in the complex structure, the legal and regulatory fields get much more complicated (Yu, 2011; Defourny & Kim, 2011). NGOs, for-profit companies, and non-profit companies all have different legal structures, which causes complexity while navigating this environment. The organizational structure and financing strategy frequently change during the process of NGOs turning into social enterprises. This study discusses the 1980s transition that Türkiye, a developing country, undertook, using "Gençtur" as a model developed by "Gönüllü Hizmetler Derneği" (GHD). These explanations help to give how a social enterprise can be unique as in its own establishment, goal, strategies. Each economic, cultural, political and sociological factor may reflect the structure.

In this study, a social enterprise in Türkiye called "Gençtur" and its relation to "GHD" is to be explained based on the objective/cause for the foundation of the association. By outlining the reasons for an association financing a social enterprise, this study addresses the origins of social enterprises in Türkiye. This research demonstrates how a social enterprise can become a part of a civil society organization and concentrate on strategic planning, revenue generation, business acumen, and developing goods and services that both meet societal needs and are feasible from an economic perspective. Analyzing Gençtur as a model will, therefore, provide a useful illustration of how social enterprise differs across countries. Examining Gençtur further illustrates how the concept of social enterprise above differs throughout countries and how it emerged in Türkiye. Gençtur is unquestionably a social enterprise and represents the introduction of social enterprise in Türkiye. Social enterprises with various forms have emerged, particularly in the past ten years in Türkiye. Since every social enterprise is idiosyncratic, it should be examined in its own context.

The organization of this study is as follows: First, it describes the current explanations of the evolution of social enterprises by examining the historical origins, definitions, and variations of social enterprises in Türkiye. The next section underlines why Türkiye is chosen as an example to explain this evolution. The model of "Gençtur" and its dimensions are introduced in the following section, which adopts the study by Boluk and Aquino (2022). The last section includes the conclusion and recommendations. The open-ended questions used in interviews are given in the Appendix section.

2. Literature Review

The concept of social enterprises has its origins in several historical movements, but they took off in the second half of the 20th century. The cooperative movement, which emerged in the 19th century and sought to address social and economic issues by establishing member-owned and operated businesses, was one significant leader. Due to several factors, including growing investor interest in impact, market demand for socially responsible goods and services, and a favorable environment for socially minded business owners, social enterprises are still expanding. Additionally, organizations combining business practices operations with a social mission began to rise in the late 20th century.

The definition of social enterprise ought to consider the reason behind its establishment. Although minimal agreement exists beyond generalization, most definitions of social enterprises highlight their capacity to use resources to address social issues (Dacin et al., 2010). Nonetheless, they might be characterized as businesses that operate in tandem with creating social value and profit. The primary goal is to develop brand-new solutions when there is a chance to create societal value (Bacq & Janssen, 2011). They also distribute the money they make from this value creation to the good of society (Barraket & Yousefpour, 2013). Although certain research admits that social enterprises are NGOs' extensions (Smith et al., 2013), they also employ market-based strategies and become profit-driven, which sets them apart from NGOs. Social enterprises may be founded to address some of the errors and misconduct resulting from private sector stakeholder management, or their aim might be to find solutions for issues in the local environments, even though their primary motivation for doing all of this is profit. Depending on the policies of the country in which they are located and the incentives they receive from institutions and governments, the extent of their profit-oriented viewpoint may differ. While some social enterprises place a higher priority on generating social benefits than on making money, others might place a higher priority on using money to solve social problems.

In Türkiye, social enterprises known as "sosyal girişim" in Turkish combine business principles with a primary focus on attaining cultural, social, or environmental goals. Social enterprises may have different conceptualizations and legal frameworks; however, they all generally aim to achieve positive effects in addition to financial stability. Certain essential features of social enterprises in Türkiye could be a wide range of industries, such as sustainability, healthcare, education, the environment, and more. Depending on their goal and area of concentration, they deal with various social concerns. Changes in the economy in Türkiye, particularly in the latter half of the 20th century, have raised public awareness of environmental and social issues (Aytekin, 2000). As society's expectations changed, businesses began investigating models that may produce profit and positive effects. The developments in social entrepreneurship around the world have an impact on Türkiye. Concepts and examples from global social enterprises have prompted the integration of social and environmental objectives in local entrepreneurs.

Nowadays, there are about nine thousand groups that fall under the category of social enterprises in Türkiye. These social enterprises include social cooperatives, businesses with a social impact goal, "new generation" businesses founded specifically as social enterprises, and economic enterprises of associations and foundations. They work in numerous industries and across all societal divisions. Of these, education is the most prevalent. Manufacturing and production, farming and agriculture, creative industries, environmental awareness and recycling, and employment and skills follow education. This demonstrates how, in Türkiye, social enterprises were viewed as serving the same purposes as civil society organizations until the past ten years. As is evident in other countries, there has been a recent rise in the number of companies that give priority to profitability as well as social benefits.

According to the report "The State of Social Enterprises in Türkiye" (2019), published in partnership with İstasyon Tedu and the British Council, it states that the majority of social enterprises in Türkiye are relatively new, with the most significant growth occurring between 2011 and 2017. The majority are found in large cities; in Istanbul, Ankara, and Izmir, there are almost 70 % of social enterprises. Despite being mostly based in the country's west, social enterprises operate across twenty-three provinces in Türkiye. The report also emphasizes that women work in social enterprises in Türkiye at a higher rate than males, both on a full- and part-time basis. In Türkiye, women constitute 55 % of managers or leaders in social enterprises, compared to 18.9 % in traditional corporations. Youthful, intelligent individuals with backgrounds in business development run some enterprises. In social enterprises, the rate of leaders under 35 is 47.28 %, while in traditional businesses, the rate is 21.4 %. Social enterprises are not given their own legal status under Turkish legislation. Other reports and research also note the absence of a clear legal framework (KOSGEB, 2014; König, 2014). However, Ersen et al. (2010) assert that social enterprises can profit from networks and support infrastructure in Türkiye. Social enterprises can receive money from the private sector to support them in achieving their objectives (Sakarya et al., 2012), and they can also access certain human and financial resources (Ersen et al., 2010; Sönmez et al., 2016).

In Türkiye, a large percentage of social enterprises (28.7 %) are registered as limited liability companies, cooperatives, and sole proprietorships (both 18.6 %). A considerable proportion (14 %) have decided to form associations, whereas a mere 3.1 % have chosen to become foundations. 13.2 % of participants are social enterprises that were established as corporations. Among the 129 respondent enterprises, 12 (or 9.3 %) have opted for a hybrid approach, utilizing a combination of legal structures (Hatipoğlu, 2021).

The idea that the formation of social enterprise is determined by the political, social, and economic conditions of a country will be explored in this study. Our goal in analyzing Gençtur and GHD is to illustrate Turkish features. Gençtur was founded in the year 1980. A detailed explanation of the rationale behind the creation of Gençtur and its connection to GHD will be provided below, along with an analysis of the sociocultural and political context of Türkiye.

The impact of Türkiye's economic and political policies on the formation of Gönüllü Hizmetler Derneği (GHD)

The first civil society regulations were implemented with the 1924 Constitution after the establishment of the Republic of Türkiye in 1923. The political, social, cultural, and economic developments that Türkiye experienced subsequently led to three amendments to the Turkish Civil Code and the Law on Societies until 1972 (Grand National Assembly of Turkey (TBMM), 2006). Three factors account for the most significant of these changes: the country's candidacy for the European Union, the democratization process, and military coups. After the Second World War, Türkiye joined the United Nations System, and the country started to democratize and experience a multi-party era (Yılmaz, 2000). The Republic of Türkiye has gone through two memorandums and two military coups. The effectiveness of civil society organizations has been called into question in a country that strives to uphold democratic norms because of military intervention in the government through coups and memorandums. NGOs were reopened in 1961 after being initially shut down after the military takeover (Ballar, 1996).

Meanwhile, the liberal atmosphere established by the 1961 Constitution and Türkiye's alliance with the European Economic Community resulted in a more diversified way of life, greater promotion of education, and amendments to the Law on Associations in 1971–1972 (Demircan, 2005). The number of NGOs adhering to EU policies surged quickly after the new law was implemented (Demircan, 2005). Since establishing the Republic of Türkiye, integration with Europe has constituted its most significant foreign policy objective. For this process to continue more successfully and in a way that serves the interests of all societal segments, the contributions of NGOs are vitally important. As is well known, the European Union views ensuring public engagement in all its decisions and actions as fundamentally required. As a result, the European Union policies have impacted the proposals and perspectives of civil society organizations. NGOs in Türkiye have also significantly benefited from EU funding. They have run their programs in collaboration with the European Voluntary Service.

Figure 1. GHD Overtime, Source: https://www.gonulluhizmetlerdernegi.org

The Association for Voluntary Service (GHD) implemented the concept of "Voluntary Service" and "Voluntary Work Camps" in 1959. These concepts were first established in the First World War, highly damaged Europe, and later expanded worldwide after the Second World War. Due to modifications in how laws are applied and the growth of its operations, GHD has changed its name over the years. GHD outlines its vision on its website as follows: "We believe that efforts to enable Turkish and foreign youth to recognize different cultures, to accept differences with understanding and respect, and to change their prejudices about other cultures will contribute to the full realization of human rights and world peace. We want a world without wars, where everyone lives together in peace within the framework of respect for differences" (https://www.gonulluhizmetlerdernegi.org). As a result, it was acknowledged that the EU effectively promotes youth exchanges.

Consequently, GHD's website states the following as its foundation purpose:

- To make sure that awareness of volunteerism and social responsibility is distributed across society,
- To act as a bridge for people to observe and acknowledge other cultures in order to contribute to global peace, with the idea that cross-cultural dialogue and understanding require respect for diverse cultures,
- To guarantee people's involvement in volunteering both domestically and abroad and to provide initiatives and opportunities that support their social, cultural, and personal development,
- To facilitate cross-cultural and cross-generational learning about one another's cultures through volunteering,

- To use funds from the Republic of Türkiye, the European Union, the United Nations, embassies, consulates, non-governmental organizations, private and public institutions, foundations, associations, schools, physical and legal persons, etc. to enable people who have limited opportunities to participate in volunteer activities due to information access, socioeconomic deprivation, physical or mental disabilities, lack of proficiency in a foreign language, etc. to take part in domestic and international training, seminars, youth exchange programs, extracurricular learning environments, and volunteer activities.

Examining the goals mentioned above, we can characterize the goal of GHD as initiatives that we may link to education in order to broaden young people's understanding of culture. Their website lists fostering an atmosphere where young people from all over the world can become closer, learn about one another's cultures and lifestyles, and alter their preconceptions as the other purposes of the foundation. The reasons behind GHD's decision to start Gençtur and why it is seen as a social enterprise will be thoroughly discussed in the next section.

History of Gençtur and its association with Gönüllü Hizmetler Derneği (Voluntary Services Association, GHD)

In 1979, Gençtur was established to carry on the GHD. Since the association law in Türkiye does not address activities that generate revenue, Gençtur was founded to support youth tourism. Thus, even though financial gain was one of its objectives, its primary goal ought to be connected to GHD's vision. A group of GHD volunteers took the initiative to establish Gençtur, which was able to continue commercial activities in the tourism sector under a legal umbrella because the laws were not supporting the economic activities of the association. These activities included organizing domestic camps, selling tickets for trains, buses, and airplanes, facilitating Turkish youth participation in camps abroad, and organizing cultural and study tours in order to generate income. Consequently, Gençtur has indicated the following as its operational area. However, in 2002, Gençtur Tourism Association was established and in 2017, its economic enterprise was established. In 2019, with the decision taken, the name was changed again as Voluntary Services Association (GHD) and the programs in numbers 5-6-7-8 were decided to continue within GHD (GHD programs, 2024)

Figure 2. Various Projects Provided by Gençtur, Source: https://genctur.com.tr

1. *Organization of International and Domestic Volunteer Work Camps:*
   These one- to three-week volunteer work programs are coordinated with local authorities and non-governmental organizations (NGOs) for the benefit of the public and have a social purpose.
2. *Sending volunteers to International Volunteer Work Camps Abroad:*
   Social content projects are arranged in 1–2–3 week cycles for the benefit of the public in 85 countries through the global networks to which Gençtur belongs.
3. *Setting up initiatives in collaboration with the European Voluntary Service (EVS-EVS):*
   Within the framework of the Erasmus+ Program, a volunteer program offers the chance to work for two to twelve months as a volunteer in non-governmental organizations in European Union member states, with all costs paid for by EU funding.
4. *Organization of the Dreams Come True Project:*
   Socially underprivileged children aged 10–14 in Türkiye are offered summer camps for personal development.
5. *East West Camp*
   Since 2008, it has been an international gathering of young volunteers in Turkey, bringing together young people from all over the world who work on volunteer projects in their local communities and are part of the solution for the place they live in.
6. *Volunteer School*
   An experiential education space created with the aim of providing an environment where young people can engage in activities in line with their own wishes and needs as a requirement of learning by doing and living.

7. *İmece*
   A social organization created by people who have dedicated their lives to volunteerism in order to provide material and moral support to primarily female students who come to Istanbul from Anatolia for university education and to mentor them by sharing their life experiences.
8. *Working with National and International Memberships and Representative Offices*
   UNESCO/ CCIVS – International Association of Voluntary Service Organizations
   ALLIANCE – European Association of Voluntary Service Organizations
   ISTC – International Student Travel Federation
   SCI – International Civil Service

Why is Gençtur regarded as one of Türkiye's pioneering social enterprises, particularly in the tourism industry?
Foundations, private, and semi-private groups founded by entrepreneurs aim to resolve social challenges in their communities (Sheldon et al., 2017). According to Sheldon et al. (2017), tourism social entrepreneurship can be defined as "process that uses tourism to create innovative solutions to immediate social, environmental and economic problems in destinations by mobilizing the ideas, capacities, resources and social agreements, from within or outside the destination, required for its sustainable social transformation." Therefore, the goal of Gençtur and GDH is the same: to have a sustainable, economic, and social influence on the tourism industry. Together, Gençtur and GHD contacted 560,000 people, provided services to 330,064 individuals, and sent 25,519 youth overseas. Over 15,522 young people from both domestic and foreign countries took part in the projects. 180,802 young people received International Student and Youth Cards. Over the course of 63 years, 1500 International Volunteer Work Camps, Youth and Children Camps, and Dreams Come True initiatives have been implemented, involving over 16,000 Turkish and international volunteers and children and young people aged 10–17.

Operating within the tourism sector, social enterprises seek to solve a range of socioeconomic concerns such as accessible tourism services, fair trade tourism, cultural preservation, training and job programs, community-based tourism, eco-tourism efforts, and educational tourism. Gençtur is a social venture in the tourism industry that provides services to those with specific needs. This can include offering activities, travel, and lodging that are accessible to people with various abilities. It also creates programs that encourage learning about sustainable agriculture techniques, local ecosystems, and wildlife protection. These activities mix tourism with education. Gençtur operates as both a tour operator focusing on particular regions by arranging guided tours centered on special interests, such as ecotourism, adventure, or culture, and a travel agency providing accommodations, flights, and packaged tours.

Gençtur is aimed at youth and frequently concentrates on meeting their particular needs, difficulties, and ambitions. It provides traveling to foster a diversity of cultural and educational viewpoints. It also emphasizes economical accommodation and travel options. Gençtur wants to collaborate with certain organizations and agencies to provide cost-effective products. They aim to allow young people to travel without exceeding their budget by providing cost-effective vacation packages incorporating transportation, accommodation, and essential activities.

Grassl (2012) in his article emphasizes that on consideration of the analysis as mentioned earlier, a viable business model for social entrepreneurship must meet these requirements (if not yet sufficient):

1. It must be motivated by a social mission (i.e., refrain from giving profits to shareholders);
2. It must create positive externalities (spillovers) for society;
3. It must acknowledge the significance of the entrepreneurial function;
4. It must become competitive in markets by implementing strategic management and planning.

Youth travelers can have a valuable and enriching experience in Türkiye and beyond through cultural exposure, cost-effective travel, freedom and flexibility, accessibility and connectivity, youth discounts, environmental sustainability, educational and social opportunities, and minimizing carbon footprint.

3. Methodology

This study is based on primary and secondary analysis, source materials and the current literature on social enterprise in Türkiye. The qualitative methodology would be valid for this study. Consultation with key actors in the social enterprise ecosystem allowed the analysis to be validated. Interviews can provide rich data with examples and experiences. This article will highlight two significant elements as it analyzes the Gençtur and GHD.

1. The influence of Türkiye's political, economic and cultural structure on developing a social enterprise model.
2. Why is Gençtur considered one of Türkiye's pioneering social enterprises, especially in the tourism industry?

In this study, the model proposed by Boluk and Aquino (2022) is used to examine Gençtur. In Boluk and Aquino's (2022) study, they propose dimensions for tourism enterprises based on Gartner's (1985) framework. Four particular dimensions were identified by Gartner (1985): (1) the individual (social entrepreneur); (2) organization (social enterprise); (3) process (individuals' actions taken to establish the social enterprise); and (4) environment (comprising the firm's attributes, strategy, and surroundings). Boluk and Aquino (2022) aim to arrange contemporary research on tourism social entrepreneurship, building on Bacq and Janssen's (2011) organization of the mainstream literature on social entrepreneurship. Here, we used their model to evaluate Gençtur's influence on the travel industry as a social enterprise. We conducted in-person interviews with Gençtur and the GHD team leader in order to identify the component. Additionally, we consulted the websites of Gençtur and GHD for secondary data. The Appendix section contains the questions. Which problems are answered, and which dimensions are clarified are as follows: Individual: Q4–5–6–7; Organization: Q1–2–3; Process: Q7–9; Environment: Q10.

Modeling the Impact of Gençtur

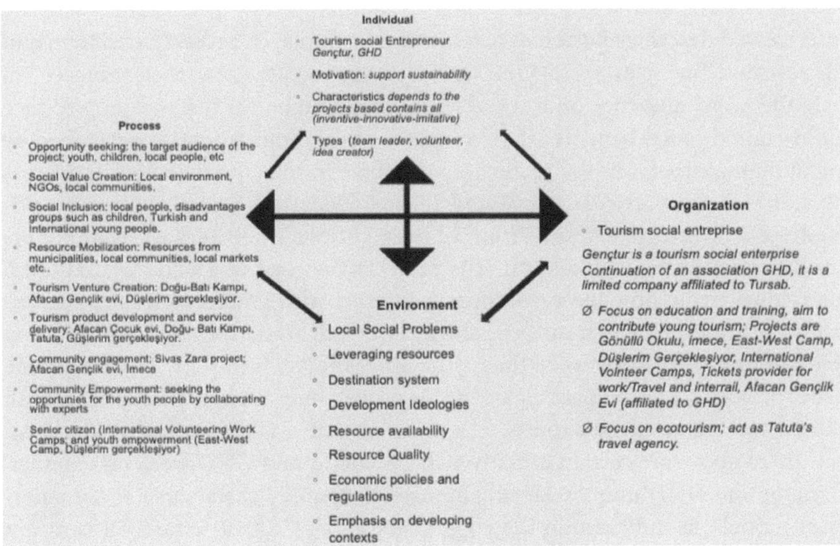

Figure 3. Dimensions in Creating Tourism Social Enterprises, Adopted from Gartner, Boluk, and Aquino's Study (2022)

**The equivalent dimension for Gençtur is indicated in italics.*

Individual

Boluk and Aquino (2022) analyzed several typologies and classifications of the literature, including inclusivity, sustainability, and cultural preservation. Sustainability is the most significant motivation of Gençtur. The primary driving force is to earn their own income. Their stated goal for establishment is to become an independent and autonomous business. In their study, Boluk and Aquino (2022) identify three essential categories of entrepreneurship: imitative, imaginative, and innovative (Koh & Hatten, 2002). This also outlines the GHD and Gençtur projects. However, every initiative ought to be assessed according to its unique merits. Therefore, it is possible to observe all three fundamental categories of tourism entrepreneurs. It is possible to characterize the Dreams come true project as entirely innovative, given that it was established by determining the community's needs. The camps, which are specifically for teenagers aged 10–14, arose out of necessity and can be described as inventive endeavors. Furthermore, children's camps overseas that are modified for Türkiye fall within the category of imitative.

According to the literature, social entrepreneurs in the tourism industry play a significant role in generating social value. Therefore, they are called ambassadors, leaders, and volunteers (Boluk & Mottiar, 2014). The entrepreneur we interviewed describes herself as a volunteer, team player, project developer, and idea creator. The managers of GHD and Gençtur consider how their projects will help the target audience on a social level. They sought, for instance, to produce child-related social benefits. The "volunteer school" initiative was developed by encouraging experts in the sector to participate in the content creation process by addressing a particular topic and raising awareness about it. They considered ways to integrate youth from all over Türkiye into the East-West Camp, another project they worked on. The project's material was also decided upon after considering how these youths will interact with youths from other countries. Furthermore, the most crucial aspect of this initiative has been fostering ties and mutual trust between them. The other project is the "My Dreams Come True" project. Children participate in this project in groups and collaborate with skilled and experienced experts. The main objective is empowering. The projects listed above are certain initiatives that Gençtur and GHD work on together. Gençtur and GHD unquestionably impose companies' sustainable social enterprise models, as indicated in the Higgins-Desbiolles' (2019) essay that is meant to be quoted here. The next section will explain each project that Gençtur and GHD have carried out. The term "organization" refers to the part below, which is Gartner's (1985) second dimension.

Organization

According to Boluk and Aquino (2022), the number of case studies pertaining to social entrepreneurs in the tourism industry has increased. These organizations are primarily motivated by social reasons and are typically non-profit. Nonetheless, social enterprises in the tourism sector seek to counterweight economic and social objectives, integrate social enterprise initiatives into local economies, and prioritize community development objectives in their operations (Aquino et al., 2018). Gençtur was founded as a social enterprise. Since civil society organizations are not considered state-owned companies, it was founded as a distinct business from GHD. Nonetheless, due to the new law enacted four years ago, GHD has again carried out all project-related activities. Gençtur has served as an organization and sold interrail and airline tickets recently. Since Türkiye lacks a legally recognized company structure for social enterprises, these organizations create their own based on the type of business they wish to operate in, such as cooperative, limited liability company, sole proprietorship, etc.

There are social enterprises related to tourism in every area of the tourism industry. The literature review goes into detail about Gençtur and GHD's areas of expertise. When deciding on the objective of the organization, Gençtur wants to support youth tourism that emphasizes training and education. It specifically targets middle-class and lower-class individuals. It gives these people a means of transportation. It sells travel tickets to the USA for business purposes. It directs youth to long- and medium-term initiatives run by European organizations. Additionally, GHD cooperates with abroad partners at international volunteer work camps across Türkiye. Its goal is to send every person who wants to go to partner organizations overseas. In addition to working as Tatuta's travel agency on the project Gençtur and GHD operated with the Buğday Derneği, they have been involved in ecotourism. They also organized the East-West camp by targeting youth over the age of 18. The young people in the "Düşlerim Gerçekleşiyor" project range in age from 10 to 14. Their goal in running the volunteer school was to increase public awareness of volunteer initiatives. By founding the "imece" group, they also hope to promote social solidarity. Afacan Youth House is run under the operation of Gençtur. They aim to offer a venue for all non-governmental organizations involved in social endeavors. As noted by Boluk and Aquino's (2022) study, when we consider all alternative projects, those initiatives are frequently recognized as niche tourism products that seek to advance sustainable tourism (Novelli, 2005) as well as provide creative tourism experiences (Boukas & Chourides, 2016).

The current literature also shows how tourism-related businesses can affect people individually, in groups, and throughout society. According to Boluk and Aquino (2022), one of them is suppliers. Examining Gençtur/GHD's suppliers, it is understood that international volunteer labor camps and the Afacan Youth House guarantee the relationship with suppliers. The Afacan Youth House only uses vendors locally. Every product is bought from local suppliers. Rather than focusing on cafes, its goal is to interact with marketplaces. The goal of the international volunteer work camps is cooperation with local NGO and small enterprises, district governorships, and municipalities. They build relationships with the companies they direct.

Process

According to Boluk and Aquino (2022), entrepreneurs identify challenges because of the trauma they have personally experienced (Roberts & Woods, 2005). Social enterprises may benefit from identifying regional issues and system shortcomings (Aquino et al., 2018; Austin et al., 2006). Boluk and Aquino (2022) have noted that social enterprises can produce substantial profits for the tourism sector when host communities drive tourism operations. These include looking for opportunities (Corner & Ho, 2010) and identity Corley and Gioia (2004) help generating social value, promoting social inclusion, mobilizing resources, creating new tourism ventures, developing and providing tourism-related products and services, empowering young people, seniors, and the community, and community engagement.

As seen in Figure 1, the project realization process encompasses all of the accomplishments listed in Boluk and Aquino's (2022) essay. Accordingly, numerous initiatives generate various benefits, including creating opportunities for empowering children and youth, carrying out community-integrated projects, and accommodating civil society organizations alongside the Afacan Youth House. Collaborating with the local community allows for the creation of value and social opportunities. An initiative to plant trees in Zara, Sivas, in 2023 went beyond its original goal, empowering local groups and allocating funding to them. Beyond its initial goal, many social events were held with locals who worked in the area and members of various associations. All youth over the age of eighteen are welcome to participate in the East-West camp procedure. The goal of this process in these camps is to facilitate communication between young people both from Türkiye and other countries. The most significant value in these camps is inclusion. It is critical that all young people are treated equally in these programs.

Environment

In their study, Boluk and Aquino (2022) noted that social entrepreneurs in the tourism sector might be influenced by political, social, cultural, and economic elements inside and outside their host communities. When these variables for GHD are examined, it is discovered that the administrators stated that it was legitimate to create the East-West camp while maintaining an equal attitude toward everybody. Local governments occasionally indicated that they didn't think it was suitable for young people from other countries, even though they did not have any particular preference in their interactions with the public. Therefore, despite GHD's managers' best efforts to treat everyone equally, it is occasionally impossible to socially align with the more traditional groups. The administrators of Gençtur desire international youth to integrate culturally into their new surroundings. This is achieved by continuing to treat them as they are treated in their current location rather than acting in their customary manner. These young people take care to display conduct that does not appear overly contradictory, even when they do not quite adjust to an environment that is different from theirs. For instance, this impacts the clothes people choose to wear.

The socioeconomic analysis of the camps and projects reveals the significance of resource allocation. The backing of the local community, municipality, association, or district governorship is required to conduct international camps. This assistance may be accommodation. Young participants can spend the night at the school or in the hotel owned by the municipality. Additionally, in some regions, the food is prepared by locals and served to them. Occasionally, an agreement is made with restaurants.

In Türkiye, young people were not always seen favorably by society. The most challenging years were particularly the 1980s. Because of their political beliefs and protests, young people were viewed as dangerous during the coup era. However, positive interactions emerged as the district governorships acknowledged GHD's good intentions. Projects were, therefore, initiated at the request of district governorships and municipalities.

GHD has had to reorganize in conjunction with the international volunteer labor camps in recent years. The main objective was to organize more activities, particularly for children under the age of 18. For this group, carrying out more relevant and social projects is significant. At this point, it is critical to comprehend the intentions of the local administration. They think that by merging the desires of the local government with the capabilities of GHD, they will be able to carry out their operations in the future through collaborative initiatives.

4. Conclusion and Discussion

This article examined Gençtur, a social enterprise founded as a branch of GHD. Gençtur was founded because of the law that took place in Türkiye during the 1970s; specifically, it stated that "associations are prohibited from establishing a money-making business within their own structure." The primary motivation for its foundation is to provide funding for the operations of the association. Selling tickets for trains, buses, and airplanes and organizing trips are services that Gençtur generates revenue. However, its main objective for establishment sets it apart from other travel companies in how it accomplishes it. This made it possible to refer to Gençtur as a social enterprise. Comparatively examining social enterprises in Türkiye and worldwide, Sönmez et al., (2016) found that social companies were primarily founded in that country to address local concerns, but they carry out certain activities internationally. It can be observed that Gençtur satisfies this criterion. Gençtur runs programs that give young people in Türkiye access to low-cost travel, opportunities for temporary employment, new experiences, and skill-building training. In line to present Türkiye to the West, which was the Republic's original intent, official policy mandates that young people broaden their horizons by engaging in Western-style education and training. Gençtur, therefore, offers a local tourism-related service to Turkish youngsters. In addition, it has ensured that young people from other countries receive services by including them in its projects. However, its primary goal was to provide local support to its country's youth. In Güravşar et al., (2001) article, social entrepreneurship is also defined as organizations that realize social innovation. Phillips and Pittman (2008) defines social innovation in his essay, defining it as "oriented towards social problems" and "the ability to produce social value." Gençtur's vision also has these characteristics. In light of the economic crisis that Türkiye experienced after World War II and the understanding that youth education relied on governmental policies, its goal was to assist youth by working with official institutions to fund and produce initiatives. As a prospective EU member, we profit from grants from European organizations and state incentives in Türkiye and use these funds for the projects East-West Camp, Afacan Çocuk Evi, My Dreams Come True, and Eco Farm Settlements. These initiatives are still being carried out, contribute to society, and present a novel viewpoint on societal issues.

Gençtur's interaction with its stakeholders shows that the following stakeholders directly influence how this initiative operates: managers, employees, collaborators, competitors, and young people. Due to the laws and modifications to the laws passed by the state at different periods, as well as its economic and political structure, changes in the administrative structure and operation of Gençtur are occasionally observed. For instance, camping and other volunteering projects were connected to Gençtur in 2017. The company's foundational goal makes it evident that young people are Gençtur's primary stakeholders and that the benefits they receive represent the company's most significant social value. Accordingly, initiatives designed to help young people develop, add value to the world, and align with the Republic of Türkiye's spirit of "being good for the country and the nation" were implemented with financial support from the European Union, the European Voluntary Service, and the European Solidarity Corps (ESC). It was founded with the spirit of social entrepreneurship, as evidenced by the fact that its managers are GHD volunteers. In light of this, the founding principles of Gençtur were to foster social innovation and voluntarism. In addition, Gençtur (2024) fits the concept of social entrepreneurship, defined as "using the money earned in products and services to create value" (Fayolle and Matlay, 2010). Examining the employee stakeholder, it is found that, unlike other social enterprises, it falls short in areas like salary payment, hiring staff, and providing opportunities for independent living. Furthermore, it is understood that the initiative benefited from free capital, and free labor (volunteers, contributions, and subsidies), which are in the definition of a social enterprise. Because of its hybrid structure, one of the most significant characteristics of social enterprise is that its workers operate voluntarily (Szmanska & Jegers, 2016). From this perspective, workers can work for free or for as little money as long as their living expenses are met. It can be said that this does not seem to have a negative impact on Gençtur and GHD workers in doing their jobs. As mentioned in the interview, there may be people who receive very high salaries and work less efficiently in the state and private sector. For this reason, "the lack of qualified and competent staff and members" as stated in Karakaş (2016) article is not included here. Therefore, it can be said that motivations such as altruism, personal growth, social connection, sense of purpose, professional development, making a difference, giving back and learning and exploration (White, 2015; Butt et al., 2017) have become more important for Gençtur and GHD workers to do their jobs efficiently.

Additionally, the absence of social media and efficient communication among certain tourism agencies operating in the sector can be the result of a professional personnel shortage. As a result, it finds it challenging to collaborate on projects with its competitors and find its bearings in the industry. It can be concluded that Gençtur's ability to generate higher financial returns through better stakeholder management is essential in terms of having a sustainable perspective. Thus, internal organizational issues like managerial concerns, as well as learning about the characteristics of social enterprises through stakeholder analysis, can be investigated. It may also be seen how the missions of the principal and agent differ based on the power dynamics between them by performing stakeholder analysis. The findings indicate that variations in the principals' and agents' individual preferences can reveal information about how they will split the profits. Therefore, if future research on social enterprise is linked to modeling stakeholder relationships, it can uncover the parameters and bargaining powers at the individual level. It is believed that stakeholder analysis will have a significant impact on theory and practice. Lastly, we would like to emphasize that Gençtur is the first social enterprise in the tourism sector in Türkiye and serves as an example for other social enterprises operating in the same industry through its projects.

References

Alter, S. K. (2006). Social enterprise models and their mission and money relationships. In A. Nicholls (Ed.), *Social entrepreneurship: New models of sustainable change* (pp. 205–232). Oxford: Oxford University Press.

Alter, S. K. (2007). *Social enterprise typology*. Washington, DC: Virtue Ventures LLC.

Aquino, R. S., Lück, M., & Schänzel, H. A. (2018). A conceptual framework of tourism social entrepreneurship for sustainable community development. *Journal of Hospitality and Tourism Management, 37*, 23–32.

Austin, J. E., Stevenson, H., & Wei-Skillern, J. (2006). Social and commercial entrepreneurship: Same, different, or both? *Entrepreneurship Theory and Practice, 30*(1), 1–22.

Aytekin, B. (Ed.), (2000). Türkiye ekonomisi üzerine kalkınma yazıları: Kuramsal ve ampirik çalışmalar (Cilt 1). İKSAD Publishing House.

Bacq, S., & Janssen, F. (2011). The multiple faces of social entrepreneurship: A review of definitional issues based on geographical and thematic criteria. *Entrepreneurship & Regional Development, 23*(5–6), 373–403.

Ballar, S. (1996). Türk Dernekler Hukuku, Beta Basım, 3. Basım, İstanbul, s:3, <http://www.tbmm.gov.tr/anayasa/anayasa24.htm> (0104.2006)

Barraket, J., & Yousefpour, N. (2013). Evaluation and social impact measurement amongst small to medium social enterprises: Process, purpose, and value. *Australian Journal of Public Administration, 72*(4), 447–458.

Battilana, J., & Dorado, S. (2010). Building sustainable hybrid organizations: The case of commercial microfinance organizations. *Academy of Management Journal, 53*, 1419–1440.

Biroğlu, M. (2019). *Co-creation of value in a social enterprise of amateur runners in Turkey: Charity run with adim adim* (Master's thesis, Middle East Technical University).

Boluk, K. A., & Mottiar, Z. (2014). Motivations of social entrepreneurs: Blurring the social contribution and profits dichotomy. *Social Enterprise Journal, 10*(1), 53–68.

Boluk, K., & Aquino, R. S. (2022). Assessing the impacts of social entrepreneurs and social enterprises in tourism. *Handbook of Tourism Impacts: Social and environmental perspectives* (pp. 117–133).

Boukas, N., & Chourides, P. (2016). Niche tourism in Cyprus: Conceptualizing the importance of social entrepreneurship for the sustainable development of islands. *International Journal of Leisure and Tourism Marketing, 5*(1), 26–43.

British Council, Turkey. (2019). "The State of Social Enterprise in Turkey". Available at: https://www.britishcouncil.org.tr/en/programmes/education/social-enterprise-research.

Brouard, F., & Larivet, S. (2011). Essay of clarifications and definitions of the related concepts of social enterprise. *Social Entrepreneur and Social Entrepreneurship*.

Browne, J., Nuttall, R., & Stadlen, T. (2016). *Connect: How companies succeed by engaging radically with society*. Hachette UK.

Butt, M. U., Hou, Y., Soomro, K. A., & Acquadro Maran, D. (2017). The ABCE model of volunteer motivation. *Journal of Social Service Research, 43*(5), 593–608.

Choi, N., & Majumdar, S. (2014). Social entrepreneurship as an essentially contested concept: Opening a new avenue for systematic future research. *Journal of Business Venturing, 29*(3), 363–376.

Collavo, T. (2018). "Unpacking social entrepreneurship: Exploring the definition chaos and its consequences in England". *Journal of Entrepreneurship, Management and Innovation, 14*(2), 49–82.

Corley, K. G., & Gioia, D. A. (2004). Identity, ambiguity and change in the wake of a corporate spin-off. *Administrative Science Quarterly, 49*(2), 173–208.

Corner, P. D., & Ho, M. (2010). How opportunities develop in social entrepreneurship. *Entrepreneurship Theory and Practice, 34*(4), 635–659.

Dacin, P. A., Dacin, M. T., & Matear, M. (2010). Social entrepreneurship: Why we don't need a new theory and how we move forward from here. *Academy of Management Perspectives, 24*(3), 37–57.

Dart, R. (2004). The legitimacy of social enterprise. *Nonprofit Management and Leadership, 14*(4), 411–424.

Dees, J. G. (2007). Taking social entrepreneurship seriously. *SOCIETY-NEW BRUNSWICK, 44*(3), 24.

Defourny, J., & Kim, S.-Y. (2011). Emerging models of social enterprise in Eastern Asia: A cross-country analysis. *Social Enterprise Journal, 7*(1), 86–111.

Defourny, J., & Nyssens, M. (2010). Conceptions of social enterprise in Europe and the United States: Convergences and divergences. *Journal of Social Entrepreneurship, 1*(1), 32–53.

Defourny, J., & Nyssens, M. (2001). Belgium: Social enterprises in community services. In C. Borzaga & J. Defourny (Eds.), *The emergence of social enterprise* (pp. 47–64). London, New York: Routledge.

Demircan, S., Avrupa Birliği ve Sivil Toplum <http://www.stgm.org/docs/1123447916AvrupaBirligi.doc> (07.03.2005).

Edmans, A. (2023). How great companies deliver both purpose and profit. *Journal of Chinese Economic and Business Studies*, 1–5.

Ersen, T. B., Kaya, D., & Meydanoğlu, Z. (2010). *Sosyal Girişimler ve Türkiye (İhtiyaç Analiz Raporu)*. İstanbul: TÜSEV Yayınları.

Fayolle, A., & Matlay, H. (2010). *Handbook of research on social entrepreneurship* (pp. 29–56). Cheltenham: Edward Elgar.

Fiksel, J. (2003). Designing resilient, sustainable systems. *Environmental Science & Technology, 37*(23), 5330–5339.

Gartner, W. B. (1985). A conceptual framework for describing the phenomenon of new venture creation. *Academy of Management Review, 10*(4), 696–706.

Gençtur, https://genctur.com.tr, 02.01.2024.

GHD programs/ about, https://gonulluhizmetlerdernegi.org/hakkimizda/, 10. 02.2024.

Grand National Assembly of Turkey, (TBMM), (2006). *Turkish Civil Code* (Law No.4721). Official Gazette: December 8, 2001, Issue:24607. https://www.mevzuat.gov.tr.

Grassl, W. (2012). Business models of social enterprise: A design approach to hybridity. *ACRN Journal of Entrepreneurship Perspectives, 1*(1), 37–60.

Güravşar, G. S., & Eliş, B. (2001). İnovasyonun Anlam Arayışı: Sosyal Inovasyon https://ankara.impacthub.net/anasayfa/inovasyonun-anlam-arayisi-sosyal-inovasyon/

Harding, R. (2004). Social enterprise: The new economic engine? *Business Strategy Review, 15*(4), 39–43.

Hatipoglu, B. K. (2021). Community-based social enterprises and social innovation: The case of women's cooperatives in Turkey. In *Social entrepreneurship* (Vol. 5, pp. 97–118). Emerald Publishing Limited.

Higgins-Desbiolles, F., Carnicelli, S., Krolikowski, C., Wijesinghe, G., & Boluk, K. (2019). Degrowing tourism: Rethinking tourism. *Journal of Sustainable Tourism.*

Kamaludin, M. F., Xavier, J. A., & Amin, M. (2021). Social entrepreneurship and sustainability: A conceptual framework. *Journal of Social Entrepreneurship*, 1–24

Karakaş, Z. (2016). Sivil Toplum Kuruluşlarında Hizmet Performansının Ölçümü, https://gcris.pau.edu.tr/bitstream/11499/1132/1/Zinnet%20Karakaş.pdf, 22 February 2024.

Kerlin, J. (2006). Social Enterprise in the United States and Europe: Understanding and learning from the differences. *Voluntas, 17*, 246–262.

Kerlin, J. A. (Ed.). (2009). *Social enterprise: A global comparison*. UPNE.

Koh, K. Y., & Hatten, T. S. (2002). The tourism entrepreneur: The overlooked player in tourism development studies. *International Journal of Hospitality & Tourism Administration*, *3*(1), 21–48.

König, A. N. (2014). Developing social impact markets in Turkey: Framework for government engagement and review of policy options. Retrieved from https://ipc.sabanciuniv.edu/Content/Images/CKeditorImages/20200327-00031375.pdf, web 08.05.2024.

KOSGEB. (2014). Türkiye Sosyal Girişimcilik ve Eylem Planı, 2015–2018. Ankara, Turkey: KOSGEB.

Mair, J., Battilana, J., & Cardenas, J. (2012). Organizing for society: A typology of social entrepreneuring models. *Journal of Business Ethics*, *111*, 353–373.

Novelli, M. (2005). *Niche Tourism: Contemporary issues, trends and cases.* Routledge, ISBN 075066133X, 978075066133.

Özlem, G. Ü. L., & Çelik, A. A. (2021). Social enterprises and the support for entrepreneurs with disabilities for an inclusive entrepreneurship ecosystem: The case of Turkey. *ICBM*, 202.

Phillips, R., & Pittman, R. (2008). *An introduction to community development.* Routledge.

Rahim, H. L., & Mohtar, S. (2015). Social entrepreneurship: A different perspective. *International Academic Research Journal of Business and Technology*, *1*(1), 9–15.

Roberts, D., & Woods, C. (2005). Changing the world on a shoestring: The concept of social entrepreneurship. *University of Auckland Business Review*, *7*(1), 45–51.

Sakarya, S., Bodur, M., Yildirim-Öktem, Ö., & Selekler-Göksen, N. (2012). Social alliances: Business and social enterprise collaboration for social transformation. *Journal of Business Research*, *65*(12), 1710–1720.

Saluzzo, M. F., Luzzini, D., & Ricucci, R. (2023). How social entrepreneurs create systemic change. In H. Peter, C. Vargas Vasserot, J. Alcalde Silva (Eds.), *The International Handbook of Social Enterprise Law*. Cham: Springer.

Sepulveda, L. (2015). Social Enterprise—A new phenomenon in the field of economic and social welfare? *Social Policy & Administration, 49*(7), 842–861.

Sheldon, P. J., Pollock, A., & Daniele, R. (2017). Social entrepreneurship and tourism: Setting the stage. In P. Sheldon & R. Daniele (Eds.), *Social entrepreneurship and tourism*. Tourism on the Verge. Springer.

Smith, W. K., Gonin, M., & Besharov, M. L. (2013). Managing social-business tensions: A review and research agenda for social enterprise. *Business Ethics Quarterly, 23*(3), 407–442.

Sönmez, A., Çağla, A., & Toksoy, A. (2016). "Dünya'da ve Türkiye'de sosyal girişimciliğin gelişimi." *Sosyal ve Beşeri Bilimler Araştırmaları Dergisi, 17*(37), 102–121.

Strzałka, A. M., Awad, D., Mironova, J., Debes, K. M. O., Er, M. M., & Tavella, E. (2021). Exploring open innovation in social enterprises in Turkey: A case study of Mikado Consulting.

Swanson, L. A., Voegel, L. A., & Voegel, J. A. (2020). Social entrepreneurship and sustainability: How social entrepreneurship can lead to Sustainable Development. *Journal of Applied Business & Economics, 22*(11).

Szmanska, A., & Jegers, M. (2016). *Annals of Public & Cooperative Economics*. Dec 2016, *87*(4), 501–527. 28p. https://doi.org/10.1111/apce.12127

Teasdale, S. (2012). What's in a name? Making sense of social enterprise discourses. *Public Policy and Administration, 27*(2), 99–119.

Voegel, L.A., & Voegel, J.A. (2020). Social Entrepreneurship and Sustainability: How Social Entrepreneurship Can Lead to Sustainable Development. *Journal of Applied Business and Economics*. 22, (11).

White, P. (2015, January). The spectrum of motivations, experiences and attitudes in technical development cooperation. In *Forum for Development Studies* (Vol. 42, No. 1, pp. 89–112). Routledge.

Yılmaz, A. (2000). *Modern Demokrasinin Gelişimi ve Sorunları, Yeni Türkiye Yayınları*, Ankara, s: 377.

Yu, X. (2011). Social enterprise in China: Driving forces, development patterns and legal framework. *Social Enterprise Journal*, 7(1), 9–32.

Zhang, D. D., & Swanson, L. A. (2014). Linking social entrepreneurship and sustainability. *Journal of Social Entrepreneurship*, *5*(2), 175–191.

Appendix: Interview Questions

(1) Could you describe the structure of Gençtur? Does Türkiye have a business model known as social enterprise?
(2) How does Gençtur support the tourism economy (travel agency, tour operations, hotel room placement, transportation, tourist attractions, activity planning, training/education, food/beverage, and retail/shopping, etc.)?
(3) Which sectors does Gençtur operate in (adventure tourism, ecotourism, community-based tourism, and volunteer tourism entrepreneurship)? Describe its activities with examples.
(4) Which of the following best characterizes you as a social entrepreneur when examining Gençtur?
a) inventive b) innovative c) imitative
(5) When you established Gençtur, what was your primary motivation? Which of the following reasons did you feel more connected to?
(a) support sustainability (b) cultural preservation (c) inclusivity
(6) Which title best sums up your personality?
Ambassador, team leader, employee, activist, volunteer, etc...
(7) What type of societal value has your work or service produced, and is it currently producing?
(8) How did your interactions with suppliers go? (For instance, was a connection made with any of the following: local companies, craftsmen and artists, souvenir vendors, restaurants, cafes, intermediary travel agencies, local tourism organizations, etc.)?
(9) How has your work benefited the local community? Describe it by giving examples.
(10) What effects have economic, social, political, and cultural issues had on Gençtur's operations, and what are their effects now? In the future, what impacts do you believe they will have?

Burçak Cebeci Perker
Bahçeşehir University

Sanem Yıldız
Askıda Ne Var

Melek Pulatkonak
Turkishwin

Chapter 4 Role of Social Entrepreneurship in Women's Empowerment: Case of TurkishWIN and Askıda Ne Var

Abstract: The importance of social entrepreneurship in addressing women's empowerment, a persistent concern across all cultures, is covered in this chapter. In addition to being essential for development, empowering women is also a matter of human rights. Governments, international organizations, and non-governmental groups might not be able to adequately address the problem, particularly in developing nation environments. In this regard, offering inclusive solutions through social entrepreneurship may be an alternative. The purpose of this chapter is to foster a deeper comprehension of the ways in which social entrepreneurship generates societal value related to women's empowerment. Successful entrepreneurial initiatives in Askıda Ne Var, Turkish Women's International Network (TurkishWIN) are investigated using the qualitative technique. Results show that Askıda Ne Var, TurkishWIN supports the economic and mental empowerment of women.

Keywords: Social Entrepreneurship, women empowerment, Askıda Ne Var, TurkishWIN

1. Introduction

As a significant research stream, the phenomenon of social entrepreneurship has garnered burgeoning interest from scholars and practitioners over the last decades (Kannampuzha & Hockerts, 2019; Rey-Martí et al., 2016). Social entrepreneurship, which has been extensively considered as a catalyst for social transition, primarily addresses the issues including poverty and human welfare (Huda et al., 2019). In this vein, social entrepreneurship as a social drive constitutes a major generator of social value that differentiates it from the traditional understanding of entrepreneurship (Bedi & Yadav, 2019). Accordingly, there is an exponential growth in the potential outcomes of social entrepreneurship to remedy societal issues (Mair & Marti, 2006). In essence, women's involvement in social entrepreneurship is viewed as a means of achieving social missions. Besides, it is widely opined that compared to men, women show better venture performance through their feminine competencies (Muntean & Ozkazanc-Pan, 2016). Therefore, women play an indisputable role in advancing socio-economic development (Kimbu & Ngoasong, 2016). Despite longstanding and mounting attention towards the role of women in social entrepreneurship, the relevance of gender still requires to be unveiled which is the mainstay of this current study. Statistics highlight a significant difference in the participation of women in different types of entrepreneurial activities in Turkey.

The rate of female entrepreneurs in Turkey is around 20 %. This suggests that one in five entrepreneurs in the country are women. While this indicates a growing presence of women in the entrepreneurial sector, it also points to a substantial gender gap, with men still constituting the majority of entrepreneurs. The rate of women social entrepreneurs is around 50 %. This means that half of the individuals involved in social entrepreneurship are women. Social entrepreneurship often focuses on addressing social issues and creating positive community impacts, which might attract more women due to its alignment with values of social change and community development.

Moreover, given that the majority of studies addressing women social entrepreneurship are contextualized in developed economies (Yadav & Unni, 2016), it lends support for the analysis of the phenomena through an emerging economy perspective.

This research aims to comprehend the significance that social enterprises play in promoting women's empowerment in Turkey.The parts that follow provide an overview of the literature on (i) social enterprises, (ii) value, and (iii) women's empowerment. The study focusing on the social entrepreneurship initiatives Askıda Ne Var and TurkishWIN provides valuable insights into how these organizations contribute to women's empowerment in Turkey. The qualitative methodology employed allows for a nuanced understanding of the impact of these initiatives on both economic and psychological dimensions of empowerment.

2. Literature Review

According to Santos (2012), social entrepreneurship contributes to the methodical identification of positive externalities that are often overlooked and offers remedies. Amplification dimensions and core (social aim & technique) aspects help to explain social enterprise. Working to maintain or improve social circumstances is a social purpose that extends beyond the purely financial gains anticipated for stakeholders. Using the social method, the organization depends on all or some of the stakeholders' goodwill. The following factors are examples of amplifying dimensions: (i) founders who accept no return or returns below market rate; (ii) workforce driven by non-financial benefits of engagement; (iii) beneficiaries or service consumers who are not expected to cover production costs, including capital costs; and (iv) board members who have a sense of stewardship for the company's social mission (Dees, 1994).

Additionally, social enterprises create goods, services, and/or institutions with the following goals in mind: (i) meeting the needs of the general public, establishing supportive structures, and giving beneficiaries as many options as possible; (ii) at the individual and community level for present or future generations; and (iii) their intention is to bring about social change that will result in sustainable development (Seelos & Mair, 2005). Providing products and services is a crucial component of social entrepreneurship, which aims to accomplish social goals and effect social change. According to Mair et al. (2012), social entrepreneurship combines economic pursuits with a social mission to improve society. Accordingly, "efforts to bring about new economic, social, institutional, and cultural environments through the actions of an individual or a group of individuals" is how Rindova et al. (2009: 477) describe entrepreneurship. The concept takes into account the local communities where the intervention is rooted, as well as the economic endeavors and aspirations for social transformation that characterize social entrepreneurship (Steyaert & Hjorth, 2006).

The concept of social entrepreneurship, which emphasizes the production of social value as the main goal through the resolution of social issues, is important. This is due to the fact that most definitions of social entrepreneurship that have been suggested share this philosophy (Dacin et al., 2011). If social entrepreneurship is viewed as the cooperation of similar and dissimilar players, then social problems can be resolved by applying commercial concepts. The evolution of social entrepreneurship theory and behavior can be understood by looking at social capital, social relationships, and cooperative behaviors that have the potential to bring about social change. More significantly, institutional arrangements form and alter as a result of (i) new resources being built, (ii) existing resources being leveraged, and (iii) institutional arrangements being reshaped. These factors all contribute to scalable initiatives that affect change. The primary collective forms are (i) social movements, cross-sectoral partnerships, and community cooperatives (Montgomery et al., 2012). Community-based businesses, social enterprises, and cooperatives are several types of organizations with the same goal of bringing about social change. The goals of a cooperative are the members' interests, which include financial gains, knowledge, instruction, and training in the activities in which the members are engaged.

Social enterprise brings about social development while also advancing the community's economic objectives. Community-based organizations and businesses also aim to accomplish one or more of several objectives (e.g., social, economic, environment, capacity building etc.). It doesn't matter what kind of organization it is; its goals are just a combination of pre-existing ones (Soviana, 2015).

Value

Value can be defined broadly as "Believe that someone or something is significant or beneficial." A social enterprise can bring together individuals who are dealing with issues that the market or government are failing to solve and work toward finding answers. The social enterprise may wish to engage in actions that benefit the public as part of this solution, such as increasing the output of five craftsmen and opening up markets for their goods. As the example shows, social entrepreneurship activities can include both value creation (such as increasing productivity) and value capture (profit-making marketing). Value is created when members' overall utility rises after taking into account the opportunity cost of the resources required for the activity.

Value is created when members' overall utility rises after taking into account the opportunity cost of the resources required for the activity. Value capture occurs when an organization or entrepreneur is able to appropriate a portion of the value generated by the activity after deducting the costs associated with mobilizing resources (Mizik & Jacobson, 2003). Value capture may be monitored at the organizational level, but the impact of value creation by a social company must be assessed at the system or society level (Santos, 2012). Value creation is the only way for a social enterprise to sustainably capture value for the good of its members or society at large. Since it places costs on society, wealth capture without value creation is unjustifiable and unsustainable.

We cannot, however, assert that value capture and creation are absolutely connected. According to Rangan et al. (2006), there may be opportunities for value capture even when some value creation activities result in value spillovers because of externalities. This is due to the possibility that, despite their willingness, some target members or beneficiaries of a social enterprise will not be able to pay for the goods and services they receive (Seelos & Mair, 2005). Organizations occasionally make choices or take actions that offer room for value capture at the expense of value creation. This is concerning because it puts the initiative's long-term viability in jeopardy. Social enterprises must balance value generation and capture while keeping this in mind.

Social enterprises encounter obstacles in their efforts to create and acquire value for the residents of their communities. The social enterprise takes care of these on its own or in partnership with appropriate organizations. The social enterprises strive to provide "accessibility, availability and quality" of (i) production inputs, (ii) investment, working capital, and insurance, and (iii) technology, equipment, business expertise, and storage, as defined by London et al. (2010) value creation limitations. This enables people to develop goods of the highest caliber that end users value. The value capture constraints are further addressed by (i) maintaining market support throughout demand variations and cyclicality, (ii) addressing information asymmetries in six transactions, ensuring transparency in transactions, protecting and enforcing rights, and (iii) making resources accessible and affordable. and the standard of transportation, infrastructure, and market understanding.

Women Entrepreneurship

When evaluated globally, it is seen that the participation of women in business life, together with cultural, social and economic developments, varies according to the country and sector (Öğüt, 2006: 57). It is becoming important to better understand the needs and motivations of women entrepreneurs and to use their full potential. On the basis of separating women's place on the basis of entrepreneurship and the formation of a separate conceptual framework as "women entrepreneur", it is due to the fact that women face much more difficulties and obstacles in business life than men, both in entrepreneurship and management (Keskin, 2014: 72). Women's entrepreneurship, which can be specified as one of the special areas of women's employment, gained importance in Turkey after the 1980s with development strategies (Kutukiz and Özden, 2018: 353). There are various differences of opinion in the literature depending on the size of the business or the person who established it as the 1st generation or the person who took over as the 2nd generation (Balaban & Özdemir, 2013: 114). Many studies have shown that the work environment is generally unsatisfactory for women, despite government support. The biggest obstacle faced by a woman entrepreneur is lack of knowledge, lack of supportive networks, lack of self-confidence, cultural barriers as well as lack of knowledge and limitations. To take advantage of new opportunities, it is necessary to start a new business or revive an existing business. The policy and institutional framework for the development of entrepreneurial skills, the provision of vocational education and training, and the economic empowerment of women have broadened the horizons of women entrepreneurs (Mathur et al., 2019: 958).

Women Empowerment

The term "women empowerment" is popular right now. Women are empowered when they "have access to and control over the means to make a living on a sustainable and long-term basis and receiving material benefits for this access and control," according to the UN Development Fund (Carr, 2000). It involves raising the women's level of awareness through education and capacity-building so they can interact with society at large and take part in decision-making by being financially independent. Women begin to exert their position and voice in family and community decisions when they gain financial empowerment. They also free their generation as a whole from the shadows. They also support other women who are similar to them, creating a powerful, never-ending chain of empowered women. Women's empowerment discourages family members from abusing and abusing these women in the future. There is proof that social entrepreneurs are dismantling the binary between "the empowered" and "the empowerer." Social entrepreneurship can empower women as clients, workers, or company owners with a real stake in the future if traditional interventions concentrate on them as recipients (British Council, 2020).

Historical Development of Women Empowerment

The idea of women's empowerment has a long history that begins with the 19th-century feminist movements. The first wave of feminism concentrated on the political rights of women, including the ability to vote. In the 1960s and 1970s, women's social and economic rights—such as access to school and equal pay for equal work—were the emphasis of the second wave of feminism. The intersections of gender, race, and class as well as the diversity of women's experiences were central to the third wave of feminism in the 1990s.

Over the past few decades, a great deal of research on women's empowerment has been done. The political, social, economic, and cultural facets of women's empowerment have all been examined in these works. Here are some of the key findings from past studies:

1. *Empowerment of women in politics:* Studies have indicated that when women are given political clout, they are more inclined to give healthcare and education policies—which benefit other women—priority. Additionally, women in leadership positions typically approach decision-making with a more inclusive and collaborative mindset.

2. *Women's economic empowerment:* Research indicates that substantial economic growth can result from giving women equal access to economic opportunities and boosting their involvement in the workforce. Enhancing women's economic status also benefits their communities and families, leading to better health and educational results.
3. The ability of women to fully engage in society, particularly in cultural and religious rituals, is referred to as women's social empowerment. According to research, women who are allowed to exercise their rights and freedoms feel more in charge of their life and are more likely to make choices that will benefit their families and themselves.
4. *Women's cultural empowerment:* The ability of women to engage in artistic and cultural pursuits, such as dance, music, and visual arts, is referred to as cultural empowerment. Research has indicated that cultural empowerment can benefit women's mental health and general wellbeing, as well as their capacity to confront prejudice and gender stereotypes.

According to the majority of research on women's empowerment, women may reach their full potential and positively impact their families and communities when they are granted equal opportunity and access to resources.

The notion of women's empowerment is complex and includes many different aspects pertaining to social justice, gender equality, and women's rights. The academic literature on women's empowerment has garnered increasing attention in recent times, leading to a multitude of research examining various facets of this issue.

Economic empowerment is a crucial component of women's empowerment. It is commonly acknowledged that increasing women's labor force participation is essential to fostering economic growth and lowering poverty. A study conducted in 2004 by Kabeer and Mahmud found that women's economic empowerment can result in higher incomes, better health and nutrition, and more authority over home decisions. Furthermore, by advancing gender equality and lowering prejudice based on gender, women's economic empowerment can benefit the larger community.

Political empowerment is a crucial component of women's empowerment. Research has demonstrated that women's involvement in political decision-making plays a crucial role in improving women's rights and gender equality. A study by Verba, Burns and Schlozman (1997) found that women's political engagement can raise the legitimacy and visibility of women's issues as well as increase the representation of women's interests in the process of formulating public policy.

Another important component of women's empowerment is education. Women who receive an education can acquire the knowledge and abilities necessary to engage more completely in social, economic, and political life. A study by Malhotra and Mather (1997) found that education can support more gender equality and social justice as well as aid to question conventional gender roles and stereotypes.

3. Case of TurkishWIN and Askıda Ne Var

TurkishWIN

Founded in 2010 by Melek Pulatkonak, the Turkish Women's International Network (TurkishWIN) is a global community of women with connections to Turkey. TurkishWIN aims to connect, inspire, and support women in their personal and professional growth, both within Turkey and around the world.

TurkishWIN provides digital platforms and resources for women to connect and collaborate, including networking events, workshops, mentoring programs, online forums, and an annual Career Fair. Through these initiatives, TurkishWIN creates opportunities for her members to share knowledge, exchange experiences, and empower the next generation of female leaders in Turkey.

One of the key goals of TurkishWIN is to challenge stereotypes and promote diversity, inclusion, and gender equality in all aspects of society. The network encourages women to pursue their passion, break barriers, and realize their full potential to build careers they love.

TurkishWIN has grown into a vibrant community with members from diverse backgrounds and professions, united by their shared commitment to supporting women's advancement and creating positive change in the world. Members can engage in various programs, share experiences, and support each other's growth. By enabling members' give-back activities, TurkishWIN also empowers her network for change system to help young women build careers they love in Turkey.

Last but not least, TurkishWIN offers corporate membership options for organizations committed to diversity and inclusion initiatives to amplify their learnings, reach, and impact. The invitation-only TurkishWIN community has over 600 members in Europe, the United States, and Turkey. BinYaprak.com is TurkishWIN's digital giveback platform and is freely accessible to everyone in the Turkish language with over 1,500 role model videos, 1,000+ blog posts with career tips, events, mentoring programs and networking opportunities serving over 25,000 members. In partnership with over 200 partners and delivering programs at BinYaprak.com, TurkishWIN members reach millions of young women in Turkey to help them build the careers they love.

TurkishWIN capitalizes on a sliding window of opportunity to flip the mind-set switch, as the future workforce dynamics make the workplace more accessible and equitable for self-learners and help us unlearn gender bias at the workplace. The bet is the belief that if the ordinary people, governments, companies, and NGOs, can collaborate to create a safe, digital trusted place—the missing middle—platforms can change the workforce composition diversely and equitably for women in Turkey.

Numerous social change initiatives exist; however, their collective efficacy remains unrealized due to inadequate overall organization. A system change targets a change in the root causes of an issue, as opposed to a surface-level change that only addresses symptoms. When we address symptoms, we add positive outcomes to existing dynamics. Instead, systems change requires a break away from the linear relationship and instead employs strategies based on scaling indirect impact and changing existing dynamics.

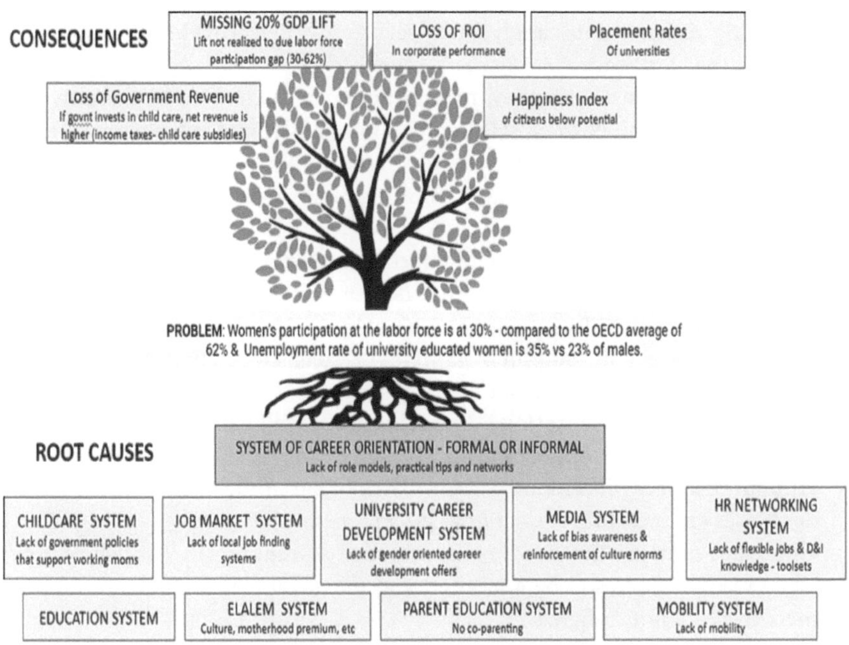

Figure 1. TurkishWIN's Systems Change Tree

TurkishWIN's give-back programs target university-educated women (18–29 years old) to help them build careers they love. In Turkey, the labor force participation for women harbors around 30 %- compared to the OECD average of 62 %. The unemployment rate of university-educated men and women have a significantly big gap of 12 % or so- 23 % vs 35 %, respectively. If the women's participation rate in the workforce is not lifted to the country's potential, the country will miss a GDP lift of 20 %, the government will lose potential revenue, the ROI of companies will not be at their potential, university placement rates will be not be lifted and the society will not be as happy and fulfilled as it could be as described in Figure 1.

The root causes of the women in the workplace problem space are varied and listed below.

Culture system: The norms and values imposed by the society that define a fulfilled and happy woman. In Turkey, a woman's status in society is mostly defined by her being a great mom and cook.

Media systems: There is a lack of awareness about the fact that we have fewer women in many fields; women get paid less than men (in different countries and fields, different rates apply); very few companies provide equal opportunities at the workplace.

Education systems: In Turkey, parents are heavily involved in the university's major selection of their children. We have a national exam where a teenager picks his/ her field of study, gets a score, and is placed based on his/her score and choices. As a result, 70 % of university graduates do not work in their field.

Mobility systems: Women are less mobile with their education and workplace options. If single, most families do not want their unwed daughters to work and stay in a different city on their own.

University career development systems: Career counseling is not gender-sensitive, and one size does not fit all.

Systems of career orientation—formal or informal: Lack of role models and informal networking opportunities.

Human resource placement systems: Lack of part-time or flexible jobs; gender biases are sectoral or functional placements.

Childcare system: There is a big motherhood premium in Turkish society; every woman aspires to be a mother; and the government childcare support incentives are not sufficient.

Parent education systems: Men do not parent or help with household chores.

Local job market system: Even if a woman graduates from a top science field from a top university, most of the time, she is expected to go back to her hometown, stay with family, and find a job. However, a smaller town may not have fulfilling or inspiring job opportunities. Even if they exist, they are hard to find.

TurkishWIN's give-back programs focus on the formal and informal career orientation systems that could be supported by readily available role models, practical career tips, and supporting networks.

TurkishWIN's proprietary network for change system has three pillars and drives her giveback strategy as shown in Figure 2.

- build an agile and social learning & sharing environment
- enable an inclusive eco-system for stakeholders and peer-to-peer networking
- create awareness time is now & we can shape the future

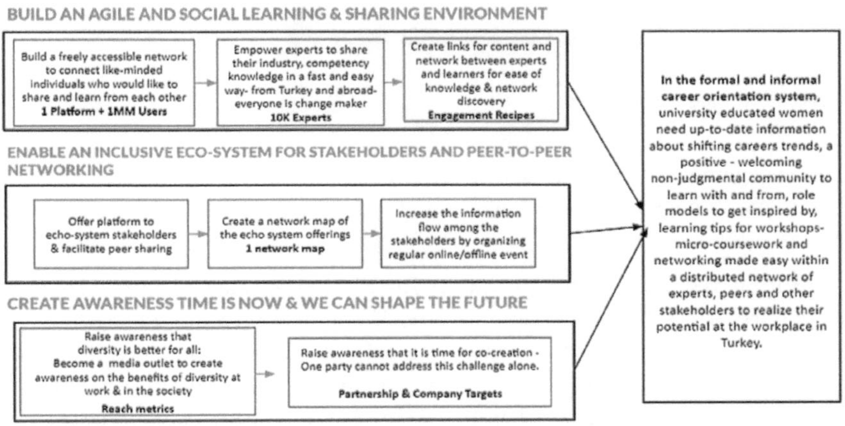

Figure 2. The Network for Change System

Pillar 1: Build an Agile and Social Learning & Sharing Environment

In 2015, TurkishWIN launched BinYaprak, a digital platform to help university-educated women and youth build the careers they love in Turkey. TurkishWIN members and partners share their intellectual, social, and giveback capital in this agile and social learning and sharing platform.

TurkishWIN's network for change experience steps is designed to start with storytelling, videos of role model women with the motto "If I did it, so can you," followed by BinYaprak membership activation and engagement. Members share their goals and needs and give the BinYaprak platform a chance to support them in their journey with social learning or mentoring programs. As members meet their goals, their digital sister, BinYaprak celebrates her success story with her and shares it to inspire others.

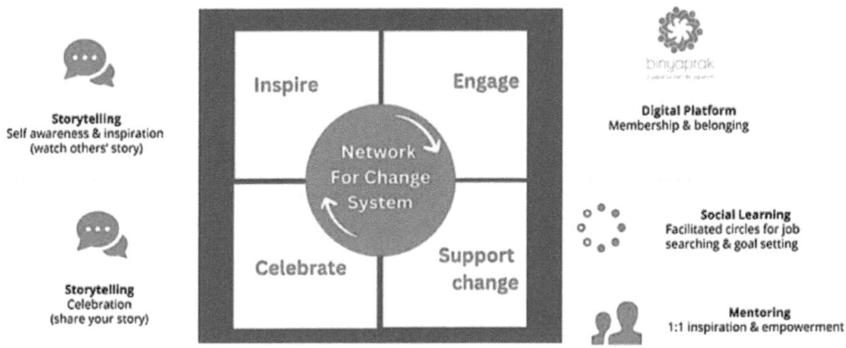

Figure 3. Engagement Steps

The engagement recipes that empower experts to share their industry, competency, and knowledge in a fast and easy way are delivered with BinYaprak programs as follows:

> **Million Women Mentor Program:** The Million Women Mentors program, dubbed Milyon Kadına Mentor in Turkish, connects private, public, and NGO sector leaders with young women (15–25 years old) for mentorship opportunities to help develop their career aspirations. The program was founded together with the U.S. Chamber's U.S.-Turkey Business Council alongside project partners TurkishWIN's BinYaprak platform, STEMconnector and TOBB.

The program convenes STEMConnector's global expertise and TurkishWIN's wide network of mentors, and mentees via BinYaprak's digital platform. Milyon Kadına Mentor program is supported by Founding Circle Partners, Akbank, Turkey, Beba Foundation, Borusan Kocabıyık Vakfı, EnerjiSA, Getir, PepsiCo Turkey, Petrol Ofisi, Unilever Türkiye and Technology Sponsor Turkcell. The program will gain strength as it grows to support women on their career journey.

Under TurkishWIN's leadership and stewardship, we built an inclusive movement where we mobilize EVERY stakeholder with the shared goal of empowering young women to build careers they love. The movement has three objectives:

Activate companies and change agents by providing an umbrella for mentorship programs for female high school, and university students, and young professionals.
Convene leading mentoring programs across Turkey to raise awareness of the amazing work of our stakeholders
Curate 1,000,000 mentoring relationships to support women and girls in their careers over the next 10 years (until 2031).

The Million Women Mentor High School program was launched in 2023 in partnership with the Informatics Association of Turkey (TBD) and is now a registered program with the Turkish Ministry of Education (MEB). The high school program enables the school administration, along with their students, to find mentors *at the newly launched program website*. The program's expansion to 15–18-year-old girls is expected to yield significant results according to studies conducted by TurkishWIN. The early pilot program consisted of nine participating high schools, 14 institutions, and 50 sessions. Anonymous results of participating students indicate survey participants who have enough knowledge to pursue STEM careers were %24 before the program and now it is %70.

Since 2021, the program has made outstanding progress with 1,150+ mentors from 180+ institutions and 2,700+ mentees in the platform, convening the ecosystem of all stakeholders supporting young girls and women in their careers. The movement mobilizes ALL stakeholders amplifying their impact and reach;

- Pledging entities are corporations, universities, and NGOs
- #BeCounted programs hail from 28 institutions that support girls in STEM that we count and promote as part of our movement
- Mentees are young girls with aspiring STEM careers (15–25)
- Network partners support the program with the announcement to target groups
- Financial supporters are our founding circle partners—10 companies—whose contributions make the program run free of charge for everyone as Turkey's largest mentoring volunteering digital system.
- Government: The Ministry of Education has made the program accessible to high schools through a group mentoring/ career counseling format.
- Knowledge partners contribute to training (intro to mentoring, mentor upskilling, mentee experience sharing, etc), events, and program development.

Pillar 2: Enable an Inclusive Eco-system for Stakeholders and Peer-to-Peer Networking

TurkishWIN thrives by co-creating with like-minded organizations with a passion for reaching gender equality at work.

In the formal and informal career orientation system, many stakeholders neither collaborate nor co-create not because they do not want to but simply because there are no simple and easy recipes to engage with one another. Managing this "missing middle" in an ecosystem involves identifying and addressing gaps between various stages of development, and resources, or supporting the ecosystem with co-creation recipes. The second pillar of the network for change strategy is enabling and including ecosystem stakeholders for co-creation and peer-to-peer networking.

TurkishWIN adds resources, the giveback of individuals in Turkey and the Diaspora, engagement recipes, and a free digital platform to the ecosystem to empower choice, connection, and progress in our community to build a gender-equal future as shown in Figure 4 below.

Figure 4. Manage the Missing Middle

The digital connection and micro-action platform, BinYaprak, provides engagement recipes and makes collaboration seamless with its programs. For every program, BinYaprak has well-defined engagement roles:

- Individuals:
  - Beneficiaries-participants: Young girls and women (18–29 years old) who seek new skills, networks, and role models.
  - Volunteers in Turkey and the Diaspora share their know-how and networks.
- Organizations: NGOs, companies, and platforms.
  - Program partners work in the design, implementation, and calibration of programs.
  - Network partners help promote the program to the right audiences.
  - Knowledge partners help design the program with their expert know-how, training, and communication.
  - Sponsors actively volunteer for the program and contribute financially to sustainability.

Pillar 3: Create Awareness Time Is Now & We Can Shape the Future

The third pillar of the network for change system emphasizes the importance of awareness-raising. It focuses on building awareness that embracing diversity benefits everyone with research partnership and by leveraging the BinYaprak digital platform to become a media outlet to create awareness on gender equity:

- In partnership with XSIGHTS Research and Consultancy, TurkishWIN has measured indicators that are important for labor force participation in Turkey since 2017, releasing research results annually.
- In partnership with Askıda Ne Var and XSIGHTS Research and Consultancy, TurkishWIN keeps the pulse of university youth with research regarding social inclusion.

Askıda Ne Var

Askıda Ne Var exists to support university students by providing them with free access to scholarships, experiences, products, and services. These include meals, clothing, theater and concert tickets, books, technological devices (laptop, phones etc), internships, mentoring opportunities and more. The social enterprise operates on a system where volunteers and brands contribute to these offerings, with individuals donating meals/scholarships and companies providing their products or services for free to support students, enabling community-support to assist students in need.

Since its inception in 2012, Askıda Ne Var has significantly impacted the lives of university students in Turkey. It has provided support to approximately

500,000 students, aiding their personal development and easing financial burdens every year. The platform not only fosters a sense of community and sharing but also helps students access resources that might otherwise be beyond their reach due to financial constraints.

The mission of "Askıda Ne Var" is to create a supportive ecosystem that enriches the lives of university students by providing them with the resources they need to succeed and thrive both during and beyond their academic years. This mission is realized through the collective efforts of individuals and organizations dedicated to the cause of educational empowerment and social change by,

- Alleviating Financial Burdens: Understanding that meals&beverages, transportation, accommodation such as dormitory can take up a significant portion of a student's budget, leaving little for other important areas like social activities/ technological devices, the initiative focuses on easing these financial burdens.
- Providing Essential Services and Products: The platform allows for the donation of meals, clothing, theater/concert/cinema tickets, books, devices and even study-abroad opportunities to students. These donations come from volunteers and various brands and organizations.
- Encouraging Personal Growth: By providing these services and opportunities and bringing them together with leaders (influencers/celebrities/writers/ entrepreneurs/ C-Levels) "Askıda Ne Var" helps students explore new interests and passions, contributing to their overall personal growth and development.
- Fostering a Sense of Community and Solidarity: The initiative brings together volunteers, corporations, and the wider community to support students. This community-based approach encourages a culture of giving, sharing, and mutual support
- Making a Broader Impact: Through its activities, "Askıda Ne Var" aims to make a significant difference not only in the lives of the students it directly helps but also in the broader community by promoting values of solidarity, sharing, and social responsibility. In summary, Askıda Ne Var creates an ecosystem.

When Askıda Ne Var was founded in 2012, its primary goal was to provide meal opportunities for university students. However, with interest from the traditional and digital media, celebrities and society at large, various brands from cultural hubs initially and later from sectors such as fashion and technology started presenting their products and services through this platform. Between 2012 and 2015, Askıda Ne Var touched the lives of hundreds of thousands of university students without any source of income. Evolving into a significant social enterprise since 2016, Askıda Ne Var has continued to ensure its sustainability through sponsorship deals with major brands. Moreover, with the support of youths, celebrities, and society, it has further expanded the ecosystem fostering social benefits.

Kampuste Ne var Social Enterprise

Kampüste Ne Var, established in 2018, is a social enterprise where university students produce blog/vlog content in 15 different categories such as "Science and Technology, Entrepreneurship, Culture-Arts," earning cash rewards, products, or gift vouchers. Collaborating with brands, Kampüste Ne Var offers students an online sustainable income model and a professional content creation experience. Additionally, it brings together youths with opportunities like internship programs, scholarship news, and workshops with artists, writers, C-levels, celebrities, and digital content creators.

Askıda Ne Var Association

The Askıda Ne Var Association was established in 2020, with a mission to cater to the fundamental and social needs of all individuals within society, prioritizing students actively engaged in educational pursuits. Its objectives include providing scholarships, offering alternative means of expression for disadvantaged groups lacking representation, facilitating visibility for their narratives, extending diverse forms of assistance, developing and implementing digital projects. Additionally, the association collaborates with various civil society organizations, initiatives, private sector entities, and universities to actualize projects beneficial to these groups, while also fostering the activation and enhancement of civil society activities in Turkey. The Askıda Ne Var Association positions itself as a bridge entity where brands, celebrities, the community, and other NGOs can provide cash scholarships to university students.

The Giveback System

The giveback marketplace has four participants: Students, individual donors, influencers/celebrities and institutions.

Students

To participate as a student in "Askıda Ne Var," students follow these steps:

Registration: Students interested in benefiting from the initiative must register on the Askıda Ne Var website. This involves providing proof of being a university student, typically through a student certificate.

Benefitting from Donations: Askıda Ne Var operates on donations from volunteers and institutions. These donors can leave scholarships, meals, tickets, other products/services for students.

Draws, Tasks, and Selections:

For Scholarships

The criteria may vary depending on the project and timeframe. However, the scholarship program consistently prioritizes students in need or facing disadvantages. Applicants who qualify for the scholarship are required to submit documentation from official institutions validating their disadvantaged or needy status, including a student certificate. Upon the successful verification of all information and documents at the conclusion of the process, scholarships are awarded to the eligible students.

For Product/Services

Brands/institutions can request students to perform marketing (traditional or digital), corporate communication, and employer-brand-related tasks. These tasks might include engaging in activities on their social media accounts, participating in research or surveys, creating video/blog content, registering on a website, downloading a mobile application, attending an event, or completing a project application form. To earn a product/service through Askıda Ne Var's website, a student verified as a university student is required to fulfill the tasks assigned by the brand. This establishes a win-win relationship between students and brands, fostering the growth of the ecosystem. In other words, rather than promoting their products through activities that don't resonate with the lives of young individuals, brands opt to both offer their products/services directly to young people—signifying “I care about you- Love you”—while also promoting their brand.

However, if a brand provides products/services to young people solely for corporate social responsibility purposes without assigning any tasks, the process progresses by distributing these to students in need or facing disadvantages.

For Mentoring/Career/Inspiring Supports:

Receiving support such as meeting celebrities (meeting backstage before/after a singer's concert, obtaining autographs, etc.), experiencing mentorship with C-level executives, participating in internship programs, gaining access to exclusive events, and similar forms of experiential rewards are progressed through the application process. Criteria might vary based on the type of campaign/program.

Brands & Institutions

They collaborate with Askıda Ne Var to achieve their marketing, corporate communication, social responsibility, and employer branding goals targeting youth, using a model of altruistic advertising, or more precisely, a socially impactful marketing approach. In conclusion, Askıda Ne Var becomes a platform that creates opportunities for institutions in "Goodvertising."

Askıda Ne Var ensures its financial sustainability not solely through partnerships or project-based collaborations with large-scale brands. In essence, it offers an opportunity for hundreds of businesses with limited marketing budgets to reach young individuals at no cost. Consequently, this enables the creation of more significant social and economic value for more young people, fostering the growth of the ecosystem.

Influencers/Celebrities

Celebrities, wielding significant influence across psychological, economic, and cultural spheres, fulfill their social leadership and drive societal awareness by endorsing Askıda Ne Var, participating in scholarship campaigns, and collaborating with brands in social responsibility projects.

Individuals

Individuals have the option to contribute cash scholarships or period/project-specific in-kind scholarships through the "Askıya Bırak" page on Askıda Ne Var's website. Each individual is positioned by Askıda Ne Var as an "ambassador of goodwill" due to their dual role in raising awareness within their circles and facilitating collaboration with familiar institutions.

In 2019, Forbes recognized Askıda Ne Var as one of the "50 Game-Changing Enterprises on the Internet—Future Billion Dollar Ventures." To date, it has participated in and received awards from over 40 national and global programs, including Effie, Felis, Stevie, Ashoka, Sabancı Vakfı Fark Yaratanlar, and ICSC Solal Marketing Awards. Maintaining sustainability for over a decade, without any investment or incentives from public or private institutions, Askıda Ne Var has consistently grown with increasing momentum each year. Supported by celebrities, it has become a milestone in social entrepreneurship in Turkey, creating social impact through youth-oriented projects and amplifying the transformative power of goodness in society.

Each year, Askıda Ne Var and Kampüste Ne Var attract over 3.5 million university students, providing benefits to more than 500,000 students through in-kind and cash rewards, educational experiences, career opportunities, and personal development prospects.

Around 60–70 % of the beneficiaries from Askıda Ne Var and Kampüste Ne Var are female students. This support aims to assist female students who encounter challenges in pursuing their education, encouraging their engagement in the workforce and facilitating their journey toward self-fulfillment.

Annually, welcoming 300–500 university students into the realm of social entrepreneurship, the initiative allows young individuals to gain experience in volunteering and awareness of social impact. This exposure serves as a career journey in the impact-oriented sector, irrespective of the industry or field, ultimately contributing significantly to the cultivation of future social leaders.

Askıda Ne Var and TurkishWIN Collaboration

Askıda Ne Var and TurkishWIN have the shared mission to empower youth and started collaborating to amplify their collective impact targeting **university clubs and female university students in programs listed below. In 2022, the partners first conducted research to** listen **to what the youth had to say on social inclusion and their needs. Next, they designed and** implemented **a new program targeting university clubs to addres**s their needs, "Let's Reach Equality-Eşitliyoruz" Program. This partnership enabled these two organizations to mobilize their ecosystem in times of a humanitarian crisis in 2023.

- **Research partnership**: In 2022, the research conducted by Xsights, TurkishWIN, and Kampüste Ne Var surveyed 3,000 university students on social inclusion perceptions. Key findings include:
    - Most associated social inclusion with equality and active participation.
    - The most excluded groups were identified as LGBT+ individuals, migrants, and women.
    - Education was seen as the most effective method to combat social exclusion.
    - Many students support gender equality programs and want universities to take more active roles in these initiatives.
- **Program partnership: "Let's Reach Equality-Eşitliyoruz" Program for university club leaders (2023-)**: After reviewing the 2022 research and the ask from students to access education to build a gender-equal campus, Askıda Ne Var and TurkishWIN designed The "Eşitliyoruz" Club Program as a leadership initiative supporting university clubs and made it available to student clubs dedicated to promoting diversity, equity and inclusion on campus. Over five weeks, participating club leaders engage in online training, peer sharing, and networking to develop inclusive cultures and deepen the impact of gender equality efforts. The program includes workshops, collaboration with NGOs, and access to gender equality resources. Upon the program completion, the

partners support student leaders to implement gender equality principles within their clubs and expand their influence in their communities.

- **Humanitarian Disaster Response Partnership (2023 Earthquake): After a devastating earthquake hit 11 cities in Turkey on February 6, 2023, the research by Askıda Ne Var revealed that impacted students' top three needs were: scholarships, technology gadgets (laptops or cellphones) and jobs to earn a living.**

The partnership: Led by Askıda Ne Var and TurkishWIN in program design and management, two strong NGOs joined as core partners (KAGIDER and PERYON) to mobilize almost all NGOs empowering youth and women to participate in the job search circle program to support young women impacted by the earthquake.

The target audience: 1100+ junior and senior female students impacted by the earthquake participated in a group mentoring program. Volunteer group facilitators, around 250 men and women, joined the program as group mentors.

The program: The BinYaprak Job Search Circle (İş Arama Kız kardeşlik Çemberi) was an 8-week program where participants joined a small group of five fellow students led by hiring managers or business leaders as facilitators. The program offers weekly online meetings to discuss career goals, receive resume and LinkedIn profile feedback, and expand job search networks.

Notable achievements:

- Quick mobilization and collaboration: After only four weeks after the earthquake, the call for participation (students and facilitators) was announced on March 8th and a fully fledged program was designed and rolled out on March 24th.
- Program results were notable:
  - Facilitators:
    Believes she/he has achieved her purpose of participation: 86 %
    Program net expectations: 92 %
    NPS score: 75 %(30–70: Great; >70 % Excellent)
  - Participants
    Feels hopeful about job search: 30 % / 62 % (before/after)
    Believes she has the knowhow she needs to reach her goals: 55 %/ 71 % (before/after)
    Felt the sisterhood support 86 %
    Found a job: 13 % & Started job search: 57 %
    NPS score: 53 % (30–70: Great; >70 % Excellent)

4. Discussion and Conclusion

Women's empowerment is the process of granting them access to political representation, healthcare, work opportunities, and education so they can take charge of their own lives and destinies. Eliminating societal and institutional obstacles that keep women from realizing their full potential is a continuous endeavor. There are many advantages to women's empowerment for individuals, groups, and society at large. Empowered women have better access to economic, healthcare, and educational possibilities, which boosts economic growth, improves health, and lowers poverty, according to studies. Additionally, more powerful women are typically represented in politics, which can result in more inclusive and equal legislation.But even in those places where progress has been made, women still have a long way to go before they are fully empowered. Major challenges still include violence, discrimination based on gender, and unequal access to resources. A complex strategy including education, community involvement, and legal and regulatory reforms is needed to address these problems.

Empowering women is crucial to building a more fair and just society. Our ability to help women reach their full potential will benefit people on an individual, community, and societal level.The role of social enterprises in women empowerment in Turkey is multifaceted. By addressing economic, social, and cultural aspects, these enterprises contribute to creating a more inclusive and equitable society where women have the opportunity to thrive and participate fully in the country's development.

As seen in the case of Askıda Ne VAR and TurkishWIN, two strong female entrepreneurs support the lives of millions of women. It reveals how big the role of social entrepreneurship is in women's empowerment. Overall, the relationship between women and social entrepreneurship is characterized by empowerment, innovation, community building, and a commitment to positive social change. Women play a vital role in driving the growth and impact of the social entrepreneurship sector, contributing their unique perspectives, talents, and leadership to create a more equitable and sustainable world.

To sum up, it can also be seen from the cases included in the study that social enterprises play a crucial role in women empowerment in Turkey, contributing to the economic, social, and cultural development of the country. Several factors influence and shape the role of social enterprises in advancing women's empowerment in Turkey:

Employment Opportunities: Social enterprises often prioritize providing employment opportunities for marginalized groups, including women. By creating jobs and income-generating activities, these enterprises contribute to

women's economic empowerment. This is particularly important in a country like Turkey, where gender disparities in the labor market have been a concern.
Skill Development: Social enterprises often engage in skill development programs that empower women by enhancing their capabilities and making them more competitive in the job market. This can include training in various fields such as entrepreneurship, technology, and vocational skills, allowing women to enter a broader range of professions.
Access to Markets: Social enterprises may act as a bridge to connect women entrepreneurs with markets. By facilitating access to markets, these enterprises help women reach a larger customer base, sell their products or services, and ultimately increase their income. This is especially significant for women in Turkey who may face challenges in accessing traditional markets.
Community Development: Social enterprises often focus on community development, addressing social issues that disproportionately affect women. This can include initiatives related to healthcare, education, and poverty alleviation. By improving overall community well-being, these enterprises indirectly contribute to women's empowerment by creating a more supportive and enabling environment.
Financial Inclusion: Social enterprises can play a role in promoting financial inclusion for women, providing them with access to credit, financial education, and resources to start and sustain their businesses. This is crucial in Turkey, where women entrepreneurs may face barriers in accessing traditional financial services.
Advocacy and Awareness: Social enterprises can advocate for women's rights and gender equality, raising awareness about issues such as domestic violence, discrimination, and unequal opportunities. By doing so, they contribute to changing societal attitudes and creating an environment that is more conducive to women's empowerment.
Collaboration with NGOs and Government: Collaboration between social enterprises, non-governmental organizations (NGOs), and government agencies can amplify the impact of initiatives aimed at women's empowerment. By working together, these entities can pool resources, share expertise, and implement more comprehensive programs.
Innovation and Technology: Social enterprises often leverage innovation and technology to address societal challenges. This can include the use of digital platforms to empower women in various aspects of their lives, from education to entrepreneurship.

References

Balaban, Ö., & Özdemir, Y. (2013). "Kadın Girişimcilerin İş-Yaşam Dengesi Algısının Belirlenmesine Yönelik Bir Araştırma: Sakarya Örneği". (İçinde) Farklı Boyutlarıyla Kadın Girişimcilik (ed. Erdoğan Kaygın, Bülent Güven), Veritas Akademi, İstanbul.

Bedi, H. S., & Yadav, M. N. (2019). Social entrepreneurship: A conceptual clarity. *Our Heritage, 67*(10), 1006–1016.

Brady, H. E., Verba, S., & Schlozman, K. L. (1995). Beyond SES: A resource model of political participation. *American Political Science Review*, 89(2), 271-294.

British Council. (2020). *The role of social enterprise in supporting women's empowerment*. British Council. https://www.britishcouncil.org

Carr, M. (2000). Women's economic empowerment: Key to development. In L. De Pauli (Ed.), *Women's empowerment and economic justice: Reflecting on experience in Latin America and the Caribbean*. New York: UNIFEM.

Dacin, M. T., Dacin, P. A., & Tracey, P. (2011). Social entrepreneurship: A critique and future directions. *Organization Science, 22*(5), 1203–1213.

Dees, J. G. (1994). *Social enterprise: Private initiatives for common good.* Harvard: Harvard Business School Press.

Huda, M., Qodriah, S. L., Rismayadi, B., Hananto, A., Kardiyati, E. N., Ruskam, A., & Nasir, B. M. (2019). Towards cooperative with competitive alliance: Insights into performance value in social entrepreneurship. In *Creating business value and competitive advantage with social entrepreneurship* (pp. 294–317). IGI Global.

Keskin, S. (2014). "Türkiye'de Kadın Girişimcilerin Durumu (Status of Women Entrepreneurs in Turkey)". *Journal of Entrepreneurship and Development, 9*(1), 72–94.

Kannampuzha, M., & Hockerts, K. (2019). Organizational social entrepreneurship: Scale development and validation. *Social Enterprise Journal, 15*(3), 290–319.

Kimbu, A. N., & Ngoasong, M. Z. (2016). "Women as Vectors of Social Entrepreneurship", Annals of Tourism Research, 60, 63-79.

Kutukız, D., & Özden, C. (2018). "Kadın Girişimciliği ve Finansal Okuryazarlığın Kadın Girişimciler Üzerindeki Etkisi". OPUS – Uluslararası Toplum Araştırmaları Dergisi, 8(Gençlik Araştırmaları Özel Sayısı), 349–365.

London, T., Anupindi, R., & Sheth, S. (2010). "Creating mutual value: Lessons from ventures serving base of the pyramid producers". *Journal of Business Research, 63*(6), 582–594.

Mair, J., & Marti, I. (2006). Social entrepreneurship research: A source of explanation, prediction, and delight. *Journal of World Business, 41*(1), 36–44.

Mair, J., Battilana, J., & Cardenas, J. (2012). Organizing for society: A typology of social entrepreneuring models. *Journal of Business Ethics, 111*(3), 353–373.

Malhotra, Anju and Mark Mather (1997), "Do Schooling and Work Empower Women in Developing Countries? Gender and Domestic Decisions in Sri Lanka", Sociological Forum 12: 599630.

Mathur, D., Jain, T. K., & Keswani, B (2019). "Impact of business incubation for women entrepreneurs". *International Journal of 360 Management Review, 7*(1), 957–962.

Mizik, N., & Jacobson, R. (2003). "Trading off between value creation and value appropriation: The financial implications of shifts in strategic emphasis". *Journal of Marketing, 67*(January), pp. 63–76.

Montgomery, A. W., Dacin, P. A., & Dacin, M. T. (2012). Collective social entrepreneurship: Collaboratively shaping social good. *Journal of Business Ethics, 111*, 375–388.

Muntean, S. C., & Ozkazanc-Pan, B. (2016). Feminist perspectives on social entrepreneurship: Critique and new directions. *International Journal of Gender and Entrepreneurship, 8*(3), 221–241

Rangan, S., Samii, R., & Van Wassenhove, L. N. (2006). "Constructive partnerships: When alliances between private firms and public actors can enable creative strategies". *Academy of Management Review, 31*(3), pp. 738.

Rey-Martí, A., Ribeiro-Soriano, D., & Sánchez-García, J. L. (2016). Giving back to society, Job creation through social entrepreneurship. *Journal of Business Research, 69*(6), 2067–2072.

Rindova, V., Barry, D., & Ketchen, D. J. (2009). Introduction to special topic forum: Entrepreneuring as emancipation. *The Academy of Management Review, 34*(3), 477–491.

Öğüt, A. (2006). Türkiye'de kadın girişimciliğin ve yöneticiliğin önündeki güçlükler: cam tavan sendromu. *Girişimcilik ve Kalkınma Dergisi, 1*(1), 56–78.

Santos, F. M. (2012). "A Positive theory of social entrepreneurship". *Journal of Business Ethics, 111*, 335–351.

Soviana, S. (2015). "Cooperative, social enterprise, and community-based enterprise: Competing, substituting, or complementing?". *Management and Organisational Studies, 2*(2), 1–14.

Seelos, C., & Mair, J. (2005). Social entrepreneurship: Creating new business models to serve the poor. *Business Horizons, 48*, 241–246.

Steyaert, C., & Hjorth, D. (2006). *Entrepreneurship as social change*. Cheltenham, UK: Edward Elgar.

Verba, S., N.E. Burns, and K.L. Schlozman (1997) . Knowing and caring about politics: Gender and political engagement. *Journal of Politics* 59 (4): 1051–1072.

Yadav, V., & Unni, J. (2016). Women entrepreneurship: Research review and future directions. *Journal of Global Entrepreneurship Research*, *6*(1), 12.

Renan Tan Tavukçuoğlu
Puduhepa and Sisters

Elif Yolbulan Okan
Bahçeşehir University

Chapter 5 Empowering Tomorrow: A Tale of Social Transformation Through Puduhepa and Her Sisters

Abstract: This chapter examines social entrepreneurship and social transformation in Türkiye, particularly emphasizing the effects of the "Puduhepa and Her Sisters" initiative, which aims to empower young girls and women. The main aim of the project is to empower girls by arousing their interest in the stories of historical female role models. Through co-creation, it effectively incorporates the community and strongly stresses collaboration. A deliberate effort must be made to destroy deeply embedded societal norms and biases in order to struggle with gender inequality. Education is crucial to this process because it challenges and modifies dominant attitudes in the society, while giving women the knowledge and skills they need to succeed. The project integrates social entrepreneurship, resilience, storytelling, and inclusion based on women's empowerment. This case emphasizes inclusion and co-created social impact, which makes a significant contribution to the understanding of social entrepreneurship in Türkiye. The chapter highlights the possibility of constructive social transformation and the importance of storytelling for empowerment. Puduhepa and Her Sisters project has shown remarkable adaptation by offering creative solutions for affected communities following the 2023 earthquake in Türkiye.

Keywords: Social Transformation, Women's Empowerment, Social Entrepreneurship, Social Impact

1. Introduction

The rise of social entrepreneurship has become an influential force for change in a world grappling with endless social problems and gender inequality. Today's world still struggles with gender inequality, which has a major impact on women's access to economic opportunities, healthcare, education, and fundamental human rights, particularly in developing nations. Well-known programs run by international organizations like UN Women, in conjunction with other public or private organizations and governmental authorities, focused on women's empowerment and gender inequality during the first two decades of the 21st century, with encouraging results. The pandemic, however, nearly undid the hard-won progress since women have been affected more severely than men in the social and economic areas. The recognition of unequal outcomes of societal events has been supported by a new term, the "shecession," which was coined to highlight the idea that "crises are gender neutral, their impacts are not" (Alon et al., 2022).

Projects aimed at empowering women are essential in addressing the specific needs of women, such as access to healthcare, safety from violence, and economic opportunities. By transferring essential knowledge and skills to the various age groups of populations including children and adults these projects break the cycle of poverty and inequality and have a long-lasting effect on promoting more just and wealthy societies. Yet, social efforts to empower women sometimes take a long time—sometimes even spanning generations. A devastating earthquake occurred in the southeast of Türkiye in February 2023, just as the COVID-19 pandemic was beginning to deteriorate the improvements made by earlier initiatives aimed at empowering women. That resulted in a downturn in women's physical and psychological safety. Horton (2012) who analyzed how Haitian women confronted numerous gender-specific challenges after the disaster emphasized that encouraging their skills is vital for gender transformation in the long term. Although improving the access to the physical needs of vulnerable populations are essential, overlooking the psycho-social aspects may result in challenges in the future. Therefore, the times of recuperation, being a vulnerable time period for the affected populations, require visionary look to enhance socio-economic outcomes. This is because women frequently find themselves trapped in the role of providing for and tending to the needs of their families, such as caring for the family members and feeding. Social programs usually concentrate on giving people's most basic needs after major calamities. This frequently leads to women being restricted to domestic responsibilities, where they are in charge of taking care of the family, which eventually worsens gender inequality (Kreutzer et al., 2023).

In summary, there is a persistent need for long-term social projects that aim to support girls' resilience and specifically empower women on the social and economic fronts. This chapter will address the importance of introducing a lasting impact on society by means of launching an innovative and highly successful program seeking a social transformation.

This study will concentrate on the "Puduhepa and Her Sisters" project, which seeks to bring about a lasting social change and has achieved notable progress in Türkiye since 2018. The main objective of the further section will be to examine the critical elements that have contributed to this notable and successful example of social entrepreneurship. Puduhepa and her Sisters' project was recognized when it earned the Women of the Earth Award from the Yves Roche Foundation in 2021 and placed second in the Garanti BBVA Momentum 2019 award.

2. Literature Review

The field of social entrepreneurship has witnessed a significant increase in academic interest, driven by the rising number of initiatives leveraging its capabilities to tackle environmental and socioeconomic issues. Social entrepreneurs are progressively being positioned as the "new humanitarians" of international development and even as change agents(Brainard et al., 2008). The background of the case "Puduhepa and Her Sisters" will be briefly summarized in the section below, along with a literature review that sets the stage for it to be regarded as an example story for the next generations.

Despite the widespread belief that substantial resources are necessary for large-scale social change, history shows instances where change agents equipped with little more than creativity, social passion, and an entrepreneurial spirit were able to trigger long-lasting transformations. These people, referred to as social entrepreneurs, have proven their capacity to make influential changes out of none to little resources. Today, social entrepreneurship has transformed into a global movement that is redefining our conception of social change and providing creative solutions to a wide range of global problems.

According to Bhardwaj et al. (2023), social entrepreneurs work with a dual goal, producing both social value for their target communities and commercial value for the long-term viability of their enterprises. Moreover, the success of these kinds of organizations hinges on their ability to strike a balance between these two goals, with a focus on their primary objective of providing increased social value to the communities they serve.

Women's Empowerment Through Storytelling for Social Transformation

Every day, women experience abuse, violence; and unfair treatment in their homes, jobs, and society due to widespread discrimination and inequality. They frequently have extremely restricted access to earning enough amount of financial resources to survive independently and get education for their professional and personal development and leadership opportunities. Compared to men; women, making up the majority of individuals living in poverty, have less power, fewer resources, and diminished influence (World bank, 2022). According to Oxfam International, less than 24 % of parliamentarians and 5 % of mayors are women, which is a shockingly low representation of women in political leadership. There are still gender wage disparities; women are paid 24 % less than men on average in all regions and industries. Approximately two-thirds of the 781 million illiterate adults worldwide are women, reflecting the disproportionate impact of illiteracy on this population. In 153 nations, policies that discriminate against women economically, such as those that cannot protect women from their husbands' opression in terms of their liberty of work, negatively impact women.

Türkiye's status in terms of gender equality is still a matter of concern, given the most recent results of the World Economic Forum's Global Gender Gap Report 2022. Türkiye's overall ranking of 124th out of 146 countries highlights the continued differences in men's and women's status across several key variables. The ranking of Türkiye as 101st in the level of education attained by women is quite alarming. The worldwide ranking indicates that obstacles remain in achieving gender parity in educational opportunities, even in light of the noted rise in women's education at the national level. Additionally, Türkiye ranks 112th for political empowerment of women, showing a need for major developments in women's representation and participation in political arenas. Even while encouraging projects are taking shape in the Turkish business community, the discouraging fact that Türkiye ranks 134th for women's economic opportunities and involvement is still a major concern. A woman in Türkiye would have to endure the discouraging possibility of having to wait 167 years for the gender gap to disappear completely, according to the gender gap calculator of the World Economic Forum (2022). The COVID-19 pandemic has worsened this current and severe problem (Gürkan, 2022). Women's overrepresentation in sectors were most affected by the pandemic; such as healthcare, education, retail, and hospitality, has led to greater job losses and economic insecurity. The closure of schools and childcare facilities has increased the burden of unpaid care work on women, limiting their participation in the workforce and affecting their career progression. Additionally, women face increased risks of poverty due to lower earnings and savings, and less access to social protections. The pandemic has also seen a rise in gender-based violence, with lockdowns trapping women with their abusers and limiting access to support services (Nordhues et. al, 2021). According to research by the Federation of the Women Associations of Türkiye, there has been a startling 78 % increase in requests for shelter homes, a 93 % increase in psychological violence, and an 80 % increase in physical violence compared to 2019 data.

All these latest statistics highlight the complex nature of gender inequality in Türkiye. The position of women in society is determined by religion and conservative understanding, social norms, educational level, culture, demographics, and economic structure in Türkiye. Accordingly, focusing on gender inequality needs a comprehensive strategy that actively engages and empowers future generations.

Türkiye, a nation bordering Europe and Asia, is well-known for its dynamic culture and rich history and for making notable advancements in social responsibility. Numerous governmental and private organizations are actively working on initiatives to promote sustainable development and enhance the well-being of communities. These social responsibility programs are essential for tackling societal problems and building a Türkiye that is more inclusive and egalitarian.

The influence of storytelling and role models can be leveraged for social transformation for women's empowerment. However, these role models are not just famous people from today's social media but also historical figures, local authorities, and everyday heroes. This expanded definition constitutes a rich tapestry of inspiration for the next generations by embracing a more inclusive and powerful perspective on gender roles. Specifically, anecdotal tales about Anatolian kingdom queens might function as compelling narratives in this transformation process. These historical figures, frequently disregarded in popular culture, can serve as potent representations of leadership, resilience, and strength. These queens and women leaders become role models for how women can succeed despite cultural norms and historical challenges by adding their stories to the broader narrative about empowering women. According to Riley (2022), who investigated the impact of cinematic role models on Ugandan secondary school students' academic performance, indicated that role models, especially when they share a similar background with their audience, can significantly empower young girls and enhance their educational outcomes.

Education is a prominent field of change and transformation in Türkiye where social enterprises are thriving. Many programs seek to guarantee that all people have access to high-quality education by focusing on marginalized communities. These businesses enable people to overcome the cycle of poverty and make significant contributions to society by constructing schools in isolated locations, awarding scholarships, and providing educational resources, including offering courses to improve skill sets of women and vocational training.

The focus on women's empowerment is another significant trend in the field of social enterprise in Türkiye. Among the initiatives, campaigns are prominent to create awareness of women's rights, mentorship opportunities, and vocational training programs. Associated institutions are committed to offering assistance, education, and resources to women who want to launch their own enterprises. These initiatives contribute to gender equality and the general advancement of society as a whole by promoting economic independence.

Women can be inspired to take up leadership roles and challenge gender stereotypes while nurturing a belief in their cultural heritage by adopting the narratives of Anatolian leading women and queens, which can help instill a feeling of pride, ambition, and resilience. These stories go beyond simple historical narratives to become potent change agents that motivate women to take charge, lead with conviction, and significantly impact the continuous social shift toward greater gender equality.

Expanding upon the current literature on the transformative capacity of social entrepreneurship, the case of Puduhepa and Her Sisters is a decisive contribution to the discourse on social impact and women's empowerment. The Puduhepa and Her Sisters project is an distinguished example of social enterpreneurship by designating many areas of change in the issue of gender inequality into a coherent project; also to be meant to inspire and motivate future generations of enterpreneurs. The importance of storytelling has already proven to be a powerful tool for social enterprise marketing, communicating values, and raising public awareness of the social impact of these businesses (Lin & Liou, 2016). The project has successfully evoked feelings, created connections, and brought about significant change by employing challenging storytelling techniques grounded in cultural heritage and authentically performed. This case provides insightful information for scholars and social entrepreneurs by highlighting the noteworthy influence that well-run social enterprises may have on the empowerment of women and broader social transformation.

Anatolian Heritage Role Models: Puduhepa and Her Sisters Project

The incredible adventure of Puduhepa and Her Sisters as a social enterprise began in 2018 with visionary social entrepreneur Renan Tan Tavukçuoğlu in the center of Istanbul. Puduhepa and Sisters are leading the way in a mission that extends beyond stories and dolls; it's about igniting social transformation for a better and more equitable future, emphasizing empowering young girls between the ages of 6–12 years of age.

The project's primary goal is to empower and invest in girls. Puduhepa and Her Sisters project uses a special toolbox that includes handmade dolls that are historical representations of real Anatolian women superheroes. These handcrafted dolls come with inspirational storybooks that were written under the guidance of child development experts.

It is true that Puduhepa existed historically and was a part of the Hittite Empire, a thriving Anatolian civilization in the second millennium BCE. Puduhepa is especially well-known for her royal queen duties and significant diplomatic achievements. She was the Hittite king Hattusili III's wife, and her title was "Tawananna," which means "Great Queen" or "Queen Mother."

Puduhepa is mainly known for her contribution to promoting peace and her involvement in diplomacy. The "Treaty of Kadesh," an agreement between the Hittites and the Egyptians in 1259 BCE, is the first recorded peace treaty in history, and she was a key negotiator in it. This extraordinary historical treaty, which describes the alliances and agreements between the two strong empires, was preserved on a clay tablet.

Puduhepa's importance in Hittite history is highlighted by her influence on state affairs and diplomatic abilities. The Puduhepa and Sisters initiative is a commendable endeavor that highlights Puduhepa's legacy, presents her as a resilient and diplomatic figure, and hopes to impress young females with her life story (Kılıç & Duymuş, 2007).

To highlight the accomplishments of Turkish women in various artistic and scientific domains, a new character has been added annually since the project's launch in 2018 with the Puduhepa dolls and storybook. The initiative has become an inspiration with Dilhan Eryurt, the first woman scientist at NASA in 2019, and Gülriz Sururi, who is a well-known actress and acts as a role model for new talents in 2020. In 2021, the project dug into science and nature, highlighting Asuman Baytop, a renowned Turkish botanist with nine plants named after her. The focus of the project switched to the literary in 2023 with the addition of famous writer Halide Edip Adıvar, whose influence throughout the War of Independence Türkiye is still felt today. These strong female role models demonstrate the project's commitment to highlighting the many achievements of women and promoting motivation in various contexts. Every story embodies resilience, strength, and the ability to succeed for a constructive change.

The project is in line with several important United Nations Sustainable Development Goals; such as Partnership (SDG17), Gender Equality (SDG5), and Quality Education (SDG4). It also provides girls with invaluable soft skills through engaging stories. Importantly, it allocates profits to fund the education of girls through the well-known and respected non-profit organization, TOÇEV (Tuvana Okuma İstekli Çocuk Eğitim Vakfı) which has a profound expertise in the resource allocation.

Responsible production, as well as the tools for empowerment, is what makes Puduhepa and Her Sisters Project a distinctively unique. Aiming to promote accountable manufacturing practices in line with SDG 12, the project employs women and enable them to work from home. Almost 100 women who are socio-economically disadvantaged from ten different regions of Türkiye have been given the opportunity to work from home through Puduhepa and Her Sisters, an organization that was founded in 2018 and supports the education of 155 girls all over Turkiye.

Resilience and Renewal: Puduhepa and Sisters' Transformative Journey After Earthquake

Some production work has been relocated to the impacted area after the devastating earthquake that struck in February 2023 in an effort to aid the local recovery. In Antakya, Hatay, Puduhepa and Sisters opened a library that was operated for at least two years following the earthquake, thereby extending its effects. The Puduhepa and her sisters' project is a dynamic endeavor that has changed to adapt to environmental shifts, such as a devastating earthquake. To aid earthquake victims, the project formed alliances with for-profit and non-profit groups; such as Shell, TEGV, TOG, and TKDFD from May 2023 to October 2023. Effective projects like the "DIY Inspiration Pillow" and "Chat Cards," (see Figures 1 and 2) which aimed to encourage communication and to offer psychological assistance to children impacted by the disaster, are the outcome of this collective effort.

Shell Türkiye established support centers in partnership with the Turkish Education Volunteers Foundation (TEGV), Community Volunteers Foundation (TOG), and Federation of Turkish Women's Associations (TKDF) to provide assistance to three non-governmental organizations operating in the earthquake-affected region. Under the direction of Shell Türkiye, TEGV, TOG, and TKDF; the project set up 20 learning centers and support units around the disaster area to assist women, children, and youth. Twelve thousands "DIY Inspiration Pillow" units were to be distributed as part of the Puduhepa and Her Sisters program, which aims to provide children with inspirational and developmental materials. This project accomplished two goals by giving job opportunities to earthquake victims—especially women—during the 2023 summer. The units came with a fabric backpack, a pillowcase, fiber to fill the pillow, a Puhudepa book; and the activity aimed at offering psychological support to the earthquake victims. Children could complete the project independently because the pre-sewn fabric came with a zipper. This symbolic and useful item within the project encouraged the children to connect with Puduhepa's inspirational story and develop virtues like hard work, patience, and goal setting. Forty seven women were employed in the production, with monthly incomes ranging from \$100 to \$300. The chance to leave their tents and interact with others in inclement weather conditions on top of catastrophic times was more valuable than any financial material. Local transportation services were used, and raw materials were acquired from suppliers in Gaziantep and Hatay.

Figure 1. DIY Inspiration Pillow—Puduhepa and Her Sisters

Note. This figure demonstrates the materials used in production of pillows to enhance psychological resilience of the earthquake victims by promoting a connection with Puduhepa known with her inspirational virtues.

In addition to the DIY pillow sets, 6,000 sets of "Puduhepa and her Sisters Chat Cards" were also given throughout the area. The cards were redesigned with the intention of improving family communication abilities. Cards about "family" and "construction" were eliminated to not to trigger any traumatic stress response regarding the earthquake, Questions in the cards prompted people to take a break from the realities of the present and foster a connection with friends that were kept. The sets, which were initially kept in boxes, were purposefully moved into fabric bags. Once again, the talented hands of women in the earthquake-affected area created these bags, which have wooden designs and fabric paint. Through their active participation in the production process, this program not only gave kids useful tools for meaningful conversations but also contributed to the revitalization and empowerment of women. Social entrepreneurs balance these objectives by integrating the logic of social welfare and commerce, which affects how they identify and grow social enterprise possibilities.

The card sets were originally packaged in boxes, but handmade fabric bags were utilized to include women in the production process actively. These were expertly made by women from the area hit by the earthquake, and they were decorated with fabric paint and wooden designs. In addition to guaranteeing that women would continue to be employed in substantive works, this tactical change was essential in rekindling their sense of purpose, keeping them engaged, and encouraging a fresh lease on life.

Figure 2. Puduhepa and Her Sisters Chat Cards

Note. The figure indicates the chat cards that have been used to foster the connection among the victims of earthquake. The cards were placed in handmade fabric bags which were produced by the women of the affected area to provide employment.

The "Chat Cards" and "DIY Inspiration Pillow" programs greatly influenced the psychological health of the children affected by the earthquake since it built hope, optimism, and self-efficacy in them under challenging circumstances. These initiatives succeeded because of Shell Corporation's kind financial support, demonstrating the benefits of collaborative endeavors during times of crisis.

One noteworthy strength that contributes to the overall impact of the Puduhepa and Her Sisters project is its inclusiveness. Inclusion may be an important element of any social entrepreneurship project; however, when an earthquake is considered, it gains even more significance. Inclusion brings the unity among the individuals while giving an opportunity of recuperation and integration within the community after a disruptive natural disaster. Top priority is given to inclusion in this initiative in several ways, starting with incorporating the women of the earthquake-affected area into the production process of pillows. By providing these women with job opportunities, the initiative not only tackles economic issues but also aim to give them a sense of purpose, meaning and involvement during difficult times. Since local vendors from Gaziantep and

Hatay are a part of the supply chain and encourage economic circulation within the region, inclusion goes beyond the direct beneficiaries to include the larger community.

3. Discussion and Conclusion

Although there has been growth in the Turkish social enterprise sector, there are still obstacles to overcome; including public awareness, regulatory frameworks, and funding. These areas need to be improved and given constant attention for further progress. However, these obstacles also offer chances for cooperation among the private sector, government, and civil society to establish a setting that supports the growth of social enterprises.

As looking to the future, social enterprises in Türkiye will be crucial in helping navigate the challenges of a world that is now changing constantly. These enterprises support economic growth and job creation while also playing a critical role in tackling urgent social and environmental challenges.

In Türkiye, the social enterprise scene is diverse and dynamic, with organizations contributing significantly to various fields. The potential for improving the society and environment in Türkiye is endless as the sector receives more and more support and attention. Social enterprises are doing more than just carrying on business; they are actively promoting change and constructing a more sustainable and inclusive future for the socioeconomical landscape of the country.

An extensive examination of the role of social entrepreneurship in social transformation in Türkiye is presented in this chapter, with particular attention to the "Puduhepa and Her Sisters" project. This creative endeavor engages young girls with historical female role models through storytelling in an effort to build a resilience. It fosters a cooperative atmosphere in the context of social transformation by embodying the ideas of community engagement and co-creation.

The program challenges and reshapes deeply ingrained social norms and prejudgments to underline gender inequality. It emphasizes the transforming value of education as an instrument, not only for empowering women with necessary skills and knowledge but also for alterating society's perception of gender roles in general. The project is an innovative example of social entrepreneurship by combining the concepts of storytelling, resilience, women's empowerment, and inclusion.

The case study mentioned here is beneficial in comprehending the dynamics of social entrepreneurship in Türkiye. It demonstrates an exemplary to showhow inclusive and co-created methods can produce significant social impacts. In the framework of social entrepreneurship, the chapter aimed at exploring the transformative power of storytelling in empowering people as individuals and as communities.

After the massive earthquake hit Türkiye in 2023, the value of social programs like Puduhepa and Her Sisters initiative became much clearer and obvious. Their quick and adaptable actions, designed to meet the needs during the crisis, showed just how crucial these kinds of efforts are when disaster strikes. It proved that a support can be remarkably beneficial and effective by staying flexible, agile, creative and responsive in tough times. Throughout this period, "Puduhepa and Her Sisters" showed incredible flexibility and resilience by providing the affected communities with creative and timely remedies. With significant contributions to the fields of social entrepreneurship and social change, this case provides an engaging illustration of how creative and co-creative storytelling can be an effective instrument in education and social reform.

"Puduhepa and Her Sisters" is steadfast in its dedication to social change. A social enterprise such as Puduhepa and Her Sisters may be a driving force behind change, as demonstrated by the initiative, which narrates a story of resiliency, community support, and empowerment. Its influence extends beyond girls' education, impacting comprehensive social change and fostering a more sustainable and equitable future.

It is important to note that the dynamics of partnerships between social entrepreneurs and outside parties needs to be investigated.. Future research ought to examine the nuances of partnerships with non-profit organizations and corporations to underline critical success elements and obstacles. It will be crucial to comprehend the means to ease collaborations among the entities for a greater social influence while ensuring mutual benefits. Moreover, given the continued significance of technology in today's global environment, it is imperative to investigate the incorporation of digital technologies into social enterprises. Studying the ways technology may improve productivity, impact, and reach—particularly in isolated or disaster-affected areas—will help social entrepreneurship in Türkiye to develop and become more effective and efficient. The combined goal of these recommendations for future research is to support positive change and social transformation and accelerate the development and sustainability of social enterprises.

It is important to recognize some limitations even though the study highlights the benefits of social enterprises in Türkiye. The area devastated by the earthquake has particular conditions, so the results might not apply to all social enterprises in all situations. Furthermore, the study is mainly concerned with the immediate results of the initiatives, which presents a constraint in our understanding if the impact of the project in affected individuals and communities is sustainable in the long-term. A comprehensive observation and empirical investigations would be required to fully evaluate the long-term impacts on the individuals and communities affected. The study also recognizes difficulties that the broad entrepreneurship sector in Türkiye faces, including access to funding, public awareness, and regulatory frameworks. To gain a more thorough grasp of the complexities of the sector, an in-depth investigation of these issues and their complex effects on the scalability and replication of social enterprises is necessary.

References

Alon, T., Coskun, S., Doepke, M., Koll, D., & Tertilt, M. (2022). From Mancession to Shecession: Women's employment in regular and pandemic recessions. In NBER Macroeconomics Annual (1 ed., pp. 83–151). (NBER Macroeconomics Annual; Vol. 36, No. 1). University of Chicago Press. https://doi.org/10.1086/718660

Bhardwaj, R., Weerawardena, J., & Srivastava, S. (2023) Advancing social entrepreneurship research: A morphological analysis and future research agenda. *Journal of Social Entrepreneurship*, pp. 1–35. https://doi.org/10.1080/19420676.2023.2199748

Brainard, L., LaFleur, V., Blum, R. C., & Talbott, S. (2008). Expanding enterprise, lifting the poor: The private sector in the fight against global poverty. Global Economy and Development, Brookings Institution.

Horton, L. (2012). After the earthquake: Gender inequality and transformation in post-disaster Haiti. *Gender & Development, 20*, 295–308. https://doi.org/10.1080/13552074.2012.693284

World Economic Forum (2022). Global Gender Gap Report. (2022). Retrieved from https://www3.weforum.org/docs/WEF_GGGR_2022.pdf

Gürkan, S. (2022). A pandemic-defying phenomenon: Gender issue during the COVID-19 outbreak in Turkey. *Filosofija. Sociologija*. https://doi.org/10.6001/fil-soc.v33i2.4714.

Kılıç, Y., & Duymuş, H. H. (2007). Hititlerde kadın ve siyaset. *Tarih Araştırmaları Dergisi, 26*(42), 85–99.

Kreutzer, W., Millerd, C., & Timbs, N. (2023). Disasters and the diminishing of women's economic empowerment. Disasters. https://doi.org/10.1111/disa.12582

Lin, W., & Liou, S. (2016). How social enterprise attract public awareness using storytelling. Research Papers in Economics. https://doi.org/10.20472/iac.2016.022.034.

Nordhues, H. C., Bhagra, A., Stroud, N. N., Vencill, J. A., & Kuhle, C. L. (2021, July). COVID-19 gender disparities and mitigation recommendations: A narrative review. In *Mayo Clinic Proceedings* (Vol. 96, No. 7, pp. 1907–1920). Elsevier. https://doi.org/10.1016/j.mayocp.2021.04.009 ·

Riley, E. (2022). Role models in movies: The impact of Queen of Katwe on students' educational attainment. *Review of Economics and Statistics*, 1–48. https://doi.org/10.1162/rest_a_01153

UNESCO. Keeping girls in the picture. UNESCO. Retrieved January 2024, from https://www.unesco.org/en/covid-19/education-response/keeping-girls-picturehttps://www.unesco.org/en/covid-19/education-response/keeping-girls-picture

World Bank. (2022). Nearly 2.4 billion women globally don't have the same economic rights as men Retrieved January 2024, from https://www.worldbank.org/en/news/press-release/2022/03/01/nearly-2-4-billion-women-globally-don-t-have-same-economic-rights-as-men

Selen Ucak
Refugee Investment Network

Chapter 6 Inclusive Social Entrepreneurship: Creating Impact in Partnership with Refugees

Abstract: Hosting nearly 4 million refugees, Türkiye has been deeply affected by forced displacement—a significant global issue cross-cutting several Sustainable Development Goals, with the number of forcibly displaced people surpassing 110 million around the world, according to UNHCR. This chapter delves into the potential of social entrepreneurship within the context of forced displacement in Turkiye, based on literature review and semi-formal interviews with social entrepreneurs and other key experts. It explores both refugee-led and refugee-supporting social entrepreneurship, highlighting the impact of innovative and sustainable ventures created by, for, and with refugees. The overarching aim is to inform and inspire stakeholders to tap into the impact potential of inclusive social entrepreneurship. The chapter synthesizes findings, spotlights social ventures that have built inclusive workforces, supported host communities, and engaged women and young refugees, and offers actionable recommendations to social entrepreneurs, support organizations, funders, policymakers, and researchers for achieving a sustainable impact on refugees and host communities in Türkiye through social entrepreneurship.

Keywords: social entrepreneurship, refugees, host communities, global forced displacement, refugee lens investing, gender, youth, inclusion, diversity, global cooperation

1. Introduction

Türkiye, as a crossroads between Europe and Asia with proximity to conflict zones, is an important destination for forcibly displaced people (Kaya, 2023). Primarily due to the war in Syria, the country has been the largest host country, with nearly 3.6 million refugees. (UNHCR, 2023).

It is important to note that "refugee" is chosen as an inclusive term for this publication, encompassing all forcibly displaced people, internally and across borders. In the Turkiye context, based on UNHCR figures as of mid-2023, Syrians Under Temporary Protection (3.3 million) and refugees and asylum seekers of other nationalities (nearly 300,000) are included in this term for practical purposes, while recognizing that nuances in legal status have implications for sense of stability and safety and economic and social integration. The author also acknowledges that the data and examples included in the chapter primarily represent Syrians in Türkiye, which also hosts forcibly displaced Afghans, Iraqis, Iranians, and other communities, whose unique experiences merit further research.

In collaboration with international partners, Türkiye has taken substantial steps to address the needs of refugees from education and healthcare to social services and livelihoods. Nonetheless, the scale of the inflows over the past decade, combined with economic pressures, recent earthquakes that caused widespread damage and displacement, and deteriorating public perceptions of refugees have exacerbated challenges.

At the same time, displaced communities in Türkiye have demonstrated remarkable resilience and entrepreneurial spirit, building more than 15,000 businesses as of 2019 (Hatipoglu, 2023). Around the world and in Türkiye, refugees are "highly active social agents, displaying considerable inventiveness in their deployment of a multitude of strategies in the face of disadvantage" (Ram, 2022). The rate of entrepreneurship among refugees tends to be higher than among native populations (American Immigration Council, 2023). Despite the challenging context, entrepreneurship offers a viable path to "refugees distinguished by perseverance, efficiency, a spirit of innovation, prior experience, adequate perceptions of barriers, and having the resources needed to implement projects" (Almohammad et al., 2021).

Refugee entrepreneurs struggle with navigating a complex regulatory environment and identifying dependable professional services, especially given language barriers. In addition, "in order to experience some of the larger gains of refugee and migrant integration, such as firm development and job creation, entrepreneurs must have access to capital" (Bahar & Dooley, 2020, p. 95). However, in Türkiye, "the inability to access finance for working capital and capital investments poses significant financial difficulty for [Syrian-owned] businesses". Türkiye's public sector organizations, NGOs, international partners, and, to a lesser degree, private sector have provided capacity building support to refugee entrepreneurs, albeit with varying degrees of sustainable impact and typically without substantial access to financing.

Social entrepreneurs from displaced communities experience similar challenges as their commercial counterparts. The local social entrepreneurship ecosystem's state of diversity and inclusion affects these challenges as well as host community social entrepreneurs' approaches to co-designing solutions with refugees. The chapter analyzes the gaps and opportunities in facilitating refugee-led and refugee-supporting social entrepreneurship. Given the intersectionality of challenges, it highlights cases through both a "refugee lens" (RIN, 2024) and a "gender lens" (2X Global, 2024) as well as recognizing the role of refugee youth as social entrepreneurs. Furthermore, the chapter explores the promise of refugee-inclusive social entrepreneurship to foster integration, social cohesion, and positive narratives and contextualizes the Turkish case within the global landscape.

Therefore, the chapter asks: what is the state of refugee-inclusive social entrepreneurship in Türkiye? To answer this core question, qualitative methodologies have captured the multifaceted narratives and experiences of social entrepreneurs and ecosystem stakeholders through semi-formal interviews. Interviews with the founders of Sector7 and Peace Therapist, among other examples, provided the information to develop brief cases for the chapter. The examples included in the chapter have been chosen for their qualities that underscore the impact of refugee inclusion; refugee women's social entrepreneurship; youth engagement; and partnerships between host and refugee social entrepreneurs, among other key topics. Literature review and insights from Turkish and global experts in social entrepreneurship, impact investing, migration, and economic development provided valuable data and real-world insights, complementing the author's active professional practice and thematic expertise in this field.

2. Social Entrepreneurship and Refugees Globally

Social entrepreneurship refers to innovative and sustainable approaches to addressing societal challenges (Dees, 2001). Social entrepreneurs are innovators and system changers (Ashoka, 2024). This chapter considers enterprises that are intentionally focused on creating social impact, specifically the inclusion and self-reliance of communities affected by forced displacement. Just as entrepreneurship is recognized as a path for economic integration, social entrepreneurship promises community impact and positive narrative change about refugees' socioeconomic contributions. Studies show that "helping to promote a culture of social entrepreneurship and a positive attitude towards the integration of refugees can be a preliminary step towards social enterprise creation and its long-term existence" (Rivna & Gress, 2023). Research has also found that, in Europe, "the relative novelty and unpreparedness of public actors have created fertile ground for the emergence of socially innovative practices both promoted from below by civil society actors and by public actors at the local level." (Campomori, Casula, & Kazepov, 2023)

Globally, there are numerous examples of refugee-led and refugee-supporting social enterprises as well as ecosystem actors that are focused on facilitating new solutions in the global displacement context. Recognized as a defining issue of our time, migration is the explicit focus of Ashoka's Hello Europe initiative and its network of social entrepreneurs (Ashoka, 2024). IKEA Social Entrepreneurship has partnered with NESsT on a refugee employment initiative to provide financing and capacity-building support to social enterprises in Poland and Romania (NEsST, 2022). In the United States, the Miller Center of Social Entrepreneurship at California's Santa Clara University ran an accelerator for solutions that support "global refugees, migrants, and human trafficking survivors" and found that "social entrepreneurial models that train and/or employ displaced people with dignified work are highly replicable," along with the scale potential of "models that utilize technology platforms to provide urgently needed services" (Miller Center for Social Entrepreneurship, 2019).

Indeed, refugee-supporting social enterprises operate in various sectors. These may include enterprises that create and market fair trade and artisan craft and culinary products, enabling refugees to leverage their skills and traditions to generate income and advocate for refugees at the same time (e.g, 734 Coffee; Peace Chocolate; NEMI Teas). E-commerce solutions expand market reach globally and satisfy consumer demand for products with social impact (e.g., Aseel.) Other tech-enabled enterprises focus on e-learning, skills development, job matching, and other intermediary functions to support refugees' inclusion in the local and digital economy while meeting a market need (e.g., Humans in the Loop; Natakallam.) Other opportunities and examples exist in access to services such as healthcare, legal, translation; housing; and improvements in humanitarian service delivery (e.g., Needs List).

International collaborations in social entrepreneurship have allowed refugee-supporting social entrepreneurs to address challenges on a broader scale and make cross-border innovation and learning possible. For example, the REInSER Project has aimed to "tap into the networking and knowledge transfer potential of the transnational as well as cross-sectional cooperation of key stakeholders" and offers cases and best practices for refugee economic integration and employment through social enterprises from six countries in the Adrion region in Europe. (Cittadini et al., 2022) In addition, some social enterprises may need help accessing larger markets due to their limited resources and capacity. There are networks and partnerships to address these challenges, such as UNHCR's Made51, a global brand of artisanal home décor and accessories, which creates livelihoods for refugee artisans by linking them to local social enterprises and providing these enterprises with capacity development market access support (UNHCR, 2024).

3. Social Entrepreneurship and Refugees in Türkiye

Refugee-focused social entrepreneurship offers potential for growth and impact in Türkiye. There have been academic studies that advocate for social entrepreneurship as a method for addressing refugee integration (Mollaogullari & Temel,

2018); provide cases "to illustrate that through social entrepreneurship there are several opportunities to create employment, sustainable income, and a viable and growing business for refugees in Türkiye" (Ates, 2020); and provide examples of Turkish social entrepreneurs that support refugees with entrepreneurial intentions (Karaboga Cici & Kodalak, 2023). Nonetheless, while "integration of refugees is a pressing issue for Türkiye, in social enterprise and wider society," "only few [social enterprises] aim to improve the quality of life through creating sustainable jobs for refugees" (British Council, 2019). Anecdotal evidence indicates that social entrepreneurs from displaced communities in Turkiye experience similar challenges as marginalized commercial entrepreneurs: lack of information about the broader ecosystem and regulations in starting and managing social enterprises; limited access to financing; and barriers that impede inclusion and collaboration with local stakeholders.

The availability of quantitative data on the social entrepreneurship activities among refugee communities in Türkiye is limited. Building Markets, an international NGO that supports local economic development and small and medium-sized enterprises in conflict-affected economies, has recently asked its network of over 2,500 Syrian-owned businesses in Türkiye about their social impact. The research has found that "generating social impact is of great importance to 76 % of the participating businesses, considering it as important as generating profits." According to preliminary findings shared by Building Markets, research has found that "generating social impact is of great importance to 76% of the participating businesses (total is 202), considering it as important as generating profits." It has also revealed opportunities to improve social impact practices of Syrian entrepreneurs: "only 29 % of the participating businesses believe that 'social impact' is of importance to investors" and "only 56 % of the entrepreneurship support organizations consider 'social impact' as an indicator for selecting their beneficiaries."

On the other hand, Gilda Borriello, a DPhil candidate at Oxford University's Centre on Migration, Policy and Society (COMPAS) and researcher in refugee entrepreneurship, has found, based on preliminary data from her research, that, of the 290 Syrian business owners she surveyed in Jordan and 587 in Türkiye, a larger share of those based in Jordan (41.7 %) identify with having a social business (defined as "a business that aims to bring about social change") as compared to those in Türkiye (28.2 %). However, when interviewed, they explained their social purpose as the founder's intention to hire other Syrians or vulnerable local communities, and did not necessarily include a social entrepreneurial business model.

Select examples of Syrian entrepreneurs in Türkiye who have also shown a commitment to impact on their communities include Mucahit Akıl, a serial technology entrepreneur who built “Ghortbtna,” a communications app to facilitate refugees’ access to information about local laws and work opportunities (ILO, 2023); and Rami Sharrack, who has been a leader in the Syrian business community since he arrived in Türkiye and has recently launched a new initiative to engage immigrant youth in networking, mentorship, and entrepreneurship (NextGen Innovation and Progress, 2024). A recent Atlantic Council documentary, entitled “Do Seagulls Migrate?,” features four Syrian woman entrepreneurs in Türkiye, including Reem, a journalist who started a radio station to increase access to information for refugees, and Khloud, an ed-tech entrepreneur with an online school to guide Syrian students and parents through the Turkish educational system. (Atlantic Council, 2021) Whether they identify as social entrepreneurs or not, these displaced Syrian entrepreneurs and many others demonstrate newcomers’ potential for social impact.

In addition to refugee entrepreneurs, local and international social entrepreneurs have also engaged in forced displacement in Turkiye. In 2016, Ashoka, the leading global social entrepreneurship network, hosted a conference entitled “Innovative Solutions for Refugees,” which showcased social entrepreneurs working in this area and created a forum for interested stakeholders. (EBRD, 2016) Another significant example was a Türkiye-led global program, the SDG Impact Accelerator, that leveraged the Sustainable Development Goals to create innovative solutions to challenges faced by forcibly displaced populations and the Least Developed Countries. (SDGia, 2019) Of the entries from Türkiye, a notable social impact start-up was Migport with a communications mobile application for refugees to help solve barriers to information and integration. (Startups Without Borders, 2019). Migport continues to serve displaced communities through social entrepreneurship programs through separate partnerships with Rutgers University, Konrad Foundation, and the U.S. Türkiye mission, with the goal to promote diversity and inclusion and create innovative, tech-based solutions. Opportunities abound for social entrepreneurs in Türkiye to impact the lives of refugees and host communities, from technology innovations for financial inclusion to impact-driven enterprises that create decent employment, especially for women. There is a significant intersection between refugee livelihoods and gender inequality given the challenges with women’s economic participation and opportunity in Turkiye, which ranks 133rd out of 146 countries (World Economic Forum (WEF), 2023). On the other hand, “the share of women with managerial roles in social enterprises is reported at 65 %, more than triple the rate in the total labor force (18 %),” demonstrating the opportunity for increasing employment for women at social enterprises (OECD, 2023). One initiative, Social Entrepreneurship Empowerment and Cohesion in Refugee and Host Communities Project (SEECO), implemented by Ministry of Industry and

Technology, administered by the World Bank, and financed by the European Union, is based on the premise that supporting solutions to mutual challenges, such as increasing women's and youth livelihoods, will advance social cohesion between refugee and host communities (SEECO, 2024).

Youth inclusion is indeed essential to the burgeoning social entrepreneurship ecosystem in Türkiye. In the case of refugees, the younger generation who has grown up and received their education in Türkiye is well positioned to integrate more fully and form a critical cultural bridge between their families and their new communities. Youth are more inclined to care about social impact, not only as entrepreneurs but also as consumers and employees, including their preference for brands supporting refugees (Erdem, Sirin, Singh, & Zhang, 2018).

Social entrepreneurship relies on key competencies such as creative problem solving, empathy, and innovation, which are also essential skills for the future of work and youth's employment prospects (Wells, 2018). One organization in Türkiye that offers this type of innovative education for Syrian youth is Karam Evi (Karam House), a partner of Karam Foundation, an organization headquartered in the U.S. with programs in Istanbul and Reyhanli. Founded by Lina Sergie Attar, a Syrian-American architect and writer from Aleppo, Karam offers creative therapy and holistic wellness for displaced families and an entrepreneurship and technology program for displaced Syrian youth. Karam's impact on Syrian youth in Türkiye, in terms of their entrepreneurial drive and potential to create social impact, is exemplified by two members interviewed for this research. Fareed Alhafez came to Türkiye in 2018 after first moving to Saudi Arabia from Syria due to the war; he is currently a 4th year engineering student at Yildiz Teknik University. Fareed and his teammates have recently won first place in Teknofest with a personal Braille printing and training product for the visually impaired community (Karam Foundation, 2023). Fareed believes that his ability to spot the opportunity for this project, develop the innovation, and diligently work it with his team came from the skills he gained as a scholar at Karam House. He is already giving back by mentoring other Karam youth and by helping to start and administer an initiative to increase the participation of refugees in Teknofest. Similarly, Youssf Abdulaziz is a young Syrian man in Türkiye, who demonstrates diligence, leadership skills, and an entrepreneurial spirit. Karam House was a transformative experience for him as well as a source of healing and hope in the aftermath of his traumatic experiences as a displaced youth. His leadership journey dates back to starting a 3D modeling and creative learning club at his high school, inspired by the Karam curriculum. Currently working as a video editor at a business incubator for migrant startups in Türkiye, Youssf has also launched an initiative that connects individuals from different backgrounds, including refugees and host community members, for language improvement and cultural exchange. Both Fareed and Youssf demonstrate the competencies and mindset necessary to become effective social entrepreneurs.

Refugee-Led Social Enterprise: Peace Therapist: A Case of Lived Experience and Community Impact

Social entrepreneur Jin Dawod has created a solution to a problem from her personal, lived experience, which fuels her passion for impact on refugee and host communities in Türkiye. Having been displaced due to the Syrian war and moved to Türkiye with her family when she was 14 years old, Jin experienced first-hand the trauma of war and ensuing mental health challenges. Common issues such as depression, anxiety, and post-traumatic stress disorder affect forcibly displaced people at higher rates, while access to services can be limited (World Health Organization, 2021). During her studies in computer engineering at Harran University, Jin got interested in entrepreneurship and started "Peace Therapist" to address this issue. Peace Therapist's ambition is to be Turkiye's leading provider of online mental health and trauma support to displaced people and survivors of natural disasters, allowing them to receive online therapy in their own language (currently offered in Turkish, Arabic, Kurdish, and English), conveniently and privately. It aims to reduce the stigma, increase awareness, and facilitate access to mental health services, especially in underserved regions such as Southeastern Türkiye and for women (who constitute 80 % of its beneficiaries.)

In addition, Peace Therapist offers flexible employment to therapists, including refugees, and creates opportunities for socialization, training, and professional development. Furthermore, through its b2b services, Peace Therapist helps NGOs and other institutions to identify qualified, multilingual counselors for their programs, increasing refugees' access to national mental health care systems, building the capacity of local healthcare staff, and supporting programs with technological infrastructure, such as AI-powered provider matching and appointment scheduling.

Following the devastating earthquakes in February 2023 and the multi-dimensional mental health needs that emerged, Peace Therapist has started offering its services to the earthquake survivors free of charge, as an important example of a refugee-led social enterprise supporting the local community (ILO, 2023). These services directly reached approximately 10,000 people in two months and indirectly impacted over 30,000 individuals. Jin says that her venture's name includes Peace because she aims to "contribute to building peace in the world and spreading inner peace in humans with the power of technology." She aspires for Peace Therapist to become a successful online platform and mobile application that can expand across the borders of Türkiye to meet similar needs in the region. Jin also has another personal mission: as the recipient of multiple local and international awards and a frequent public speaker, she has become a role model to women in technology careers, provided internships to over 60 students, and matched half of them with jobs.

Refugee-Supporting Social Enterprise: Sector7: A Case of Inclusion and Partnerships

Izabela Ersahin is an example of a social entrepreneur—an "accidental" one, in her own words—who is building a business model where sustainability, decent work, women's empowerment, and inclusion can co-exist. Sector7's "core idea is to empower artisan communities and small producers by leveraging the principles of social entrepreneurship." Izabela has already implemented this model at a successful social enterprise she founded, Bebemoss, by bringing together women from the refugee and host communities and empowering them to take part in the management of the business and become shareholders to its success. Bebemoss has been successful with international sales, became "Fair Trade Certified," and established significant collaborations, including UNHCR's Made51 brand, which connects social enterprises creating livelihoods for refugee and host community artisans with global markets.

Izabela continues to create new sources of income for women producers through similar strategies and new products, brands, and collaborations. She is currently working on a partnership that will generate sustainable work for women-led cooperatives that are made up of refugees and local women, solving a challenge such enterprises often face. On the one hand, women facing poverty in Türkiye, including disadvantaged female producers and refugee women, have a challenging time, turning their skills into a source of income. On the other hand, it is difficult for large companies that are interested in social impact through inclusive business models and fair-trade principles to establish partnerships with these underserved producers. While many cooperatives aim to create employment for women, most fail to achieve scale in the absence of sustainable private sector linkages that they can effectively manage. There is clearly a need for creative, impact-first entrepreneurs like Izabela, who can work in a principled and innovative manner both with the private sector and with women producers, NGOs, and other stakeholders.

Izabela's work draws from her professional background in design, fashion, and business, but the idea first came to her during a difficult pregnancy, when she was working on a project from home and wanted to reach women producers who needed flexible employment opportunities. While only 33 % of Turkish social enterprises operate at the international level (British Council, 2019), Izabela has ambitions to implement private sector partnerships for disadvantaged women in the region and create a cross-border impact as a model originating from Turkiye.

According to Izabela, while there may be relatively few known social entrepreneurs in Türkiye with a displacement background, she has observed firsthand that talent and passion abound among refugee women. "Among my employees, there is always that one woman who could be a successful entrepreneur if only she had the means," says Izabela, adding that social entrepreneurs in Türkiye do not always recognize the opportunities refugees present.

4. Facilitating Refugee Social Entrepreneurship Through Inclusion and Co-Creation

Greater integration between refugees and host communities, including in the social entrepreneurship field, requires building trust, intentional outreach, co-creation, and incentives such as funding and capacity development opportunities. Research from Europe suggests that social enterprises co-created with "mixed" teams of refugees and host communities "can overcome the liabilities of the foreignness of entrepreneurial refugee individuals while gaining legitimacy in both host societies and the refugee community." (Harima & Freudenberg, 2020) In Türkiye, "the economic gains to the host community as well as the prospective benefits to social cohesion between the refugees and the host community resulting from inclusion, as opposed to the sociopolitical problems that would emerge from the persistent exclusion of refugees, will need to be demonstrated effectively." (Erdogan et al., 2021) Other research recommends that local NGOs should focus their efforts on finding issues that are of common interest to both Syrian refugees and the Turkish community and design their activities in a way that will bring the two communities together around these issues (Zihnioglu & Dalkıran, 2022). The inclusion of refugee social entrepreneurs is vital for the growth and diversity ecosystem, to build bridges between different communities, and to "significantly contribute asylum seekers' social inclusion process in the host communities" (Gulerce & Okten, 2021).

Refugees bring unique talents, skills, and experiences that can drive innovation and social impact, especially for issues that affect displaced communities and their hosts. Proximity is an important factor in creating effective solutions (Larissa et al., 2023), i.e., communities with lived experience are best positioned to observe problems and devise solutions, granted they also have the entrepreneurial support, funding, and mentorship to implement them. In Turkiye, 78 %

of social entrepreneurs state that a problem they have experienced personally has been an important contributing factor for working at or establishing a social enterprise (British Council, 2019). On the other hand, interviewees for this research pointed out the concerns that refugees have about public perceptions and their political and financial vulnerability, which can hinder their ability to take risks as social entrepreneurs.

The social entrepreneurship ecosystem in Türkiye is increasingly making efforts to promote diversity and inclusion. Geographical diversity is one way to increase opportunities for refugee social entrepreneurs. While most social entrepreneurs in Türkiye tend to be young, well-educated, and based in major cities, "[this] should not lead to the conclusion that there is no potential for social enterprises outside of urban centers." (British Council, 2019) For instance, Ashoka Türkiye is expanding its nomination network and conducting outreach in underserved cities to diversify its Fellows. The Türkiye Social Entrepreneurship Network (TSEN) is ramping up its efforts to increase the inclusion of refugees in the social entrepreneurship ecosystem, including a recent conference on the topic (Enhancer, 2023). The Embark Project, a unique and innovative initiative connects diverse youth, including refugees, with local business leaders through reverse mentoring in order to foster skills enhancement, economic inclusion, and social cohesion with cross-cultural and cross-generational benefits. (Embark Project, 2024) Furthermore, in one of the most common models of social enterprise in Türkiye, economically disadvantaged Syrian and Turkish women are brought together for livelihoods opportunities at local cooperatives. One such cooperative is EKIP (Etkin Kadın İş Platformu), a female-led catering enterprise in Istanbul, which has generated important lessons learned about co-creation with refugee communities. (Blasco & Ramboux, 2023) Indeed, there are ongoing efforts to share knowledge and inform public policy about cooperatives like EKIP through the "Social Entrepreneurship Community of Practice (SECoP)," which "unites over 800 members from approximately 300 organizations co-operating to maximize the potential of social entrepreneurship in Türkiye and address the labor market gender gaps." (OECD, 2023)

A pervasive challenge is misinformation and negative narratives about refugees, affecting social integration, mental health, and livelihoods, which inclusive social entrepreneurship has the capacity to address. For example, Suha Nabhan is a Syrian social entrepreneur who, until recently, lived in Turkiye and, together with her co-founder, Amal Jibril, founded an initiative called Migration Jam that brings together migrant creative communities, such as writers and video producers, in Türkiye and abroad, to create content that reflects their unique experiences and perspectives, as well as offer cultural dialogue activities. (Migration Jam, 2024)

5. Investing in Refugee-led and Refugee-Supporting Social Entrepreneurship

Social enterprises, especially those with refugee founders, struggle with accessing mission-aligned financing. As "refugee lens investing" gains momentum worldwide, impact investors can play a pivotal role by providing seed and growth capital to social entrepreneurial solutions that intentionally support displaced communities, especially by using innovative financing vehicles. The Refugee Investment Network's (RIN) investment lens, designed to track and assess investments that further refugee self-reliance, includes refugee-owned, refugee-led and refugee-supporting companies (RIN, 2024). Furthermore, RIN's investment opportunities pipeline features several successful social enterprises that meet those criteria from around the world.

Globally, donors and impact investors are making concerted efforts to expand funding to diverse and underserved funders, such as the Adebowale Commission on Social Investment in the United Kingdom, which concluded that "social investment continues to have a serious problem with inclusion and equity particularly, although not exclusively, in relation to race" (Social Enterprise UK, 2022). In Türkiye, research shows that social enterprises rely on personal sources of finance (66–72 %, depending on the age of the ventures) and support from friends and family (34–46 %) (British Council, 2019). This reliance on personal funds and networks illustrates the disadvantages that marginalized entrepreneurs, such as refugees, face in financing their social ventures.

The following example illustrates the limitations posed by lack of financing for a promising refugee-supporting social enterprise. Founded by Rawan Hudaifa, a Syrian social entrepreneur who is no longer living in Türkiye, Tina Zita was a catering venture that aimed to create employment for refugee and migrant women. Rawan had the idea to launch this venture while volunteering for an NGO providing language classes to refugee families, as she noticed the need for a sustainable model that prioritized fair wages for women. She was able to gain traction quickly, especially thanks to connections to initial clients and resources such as social entrepreneurship training through her Turkish co-founder Duygu Vatan (also the founder of Joon, another social enterprise supporting disadvantaged populations, and a partner at Impact Hub Ankara.) Tina Zita incorporated storytelling effectively into their catering work, highlighting culinary heritage. However, transitioning to a sustainable business model presented hurdles, including understanding licensing requirements and securing financing for working capital and expansion, leading Tina Zita to close after a few years in operation. While there are numerous factors in the eventual financial sustainability and impact for a social enterprise, it is worth noting that ventures similar to Tina Zita's model and mission have been successful elsewhere with greater availability of refugee-focused impact capital, most notably Soufra, a social enterprise run by Palestinian refugees in Lebanon (Chahine, 2023) and EatOffBeat, a New York-based social enterprise powered by refugee and migrant chefs (EatOffBeat, 2024).

6. Conclusion and Recommendations

Refugee-led and refugee-supporting social enterprises hold the promise of addressing the unique challenges faced by displaced populations and fostering inclusion and social cohesion.

Insights from contributors to this research and the analysis of literature have culminated in the following recommendations to maximize the impact potential of these enterprises in Türkiye. Firstly, more needs to be known about the social entrepreneurial activities of displaced communities in Türkiye. It is also important to "map out social entrepreneurship support programs where refugees can be integrated." (Impact Hub & UNHCR, 2022) Social entrepreneurship ecosystems are encouraged "to create sustainable inclusive policies and implement programs that cater for a demographically diverse set of entrepreneurs," (Cascant, 2023), which is especially important for removing barriers for entrepreneurs with intersectional disadvantages, e.g., women and refugee entrepreneurs. An important way to achieve this is to develop on-ramps for refugees to interact with the Turkish social entrepreneurship ecosystem, e.g., internship and employment at local social enterprises and opportunities to be co-designers, nominators, and selection panel members for programs, bringing diversity of thought, organic connections to the refugee communities, and insights about challenges and opportunities. Furthermore, creating safe spaces and fostering trust for refugees to be able to discuss critical issues that affect them is a crucial support that allies in the social entrepreneurship community can offer. Developing local strategies and tools that are culturally and demographically relevant to achieve inclusion and diversity will also be helpful. In addition to being voiced in interviews for this research, similar recommendations were offered by speakers at Migration Summit, The Migration Summit (organized by the MIT Refugee Action Hub (ReACT), Na'amal and Karam Foundation), including the need to "promote and give space for diverse perspectives that can help educate the public through a more nuanced portrayal of diversity within communities." (Migration Summit, 2023).

Next, "social entrepreneurship by, for, and with refugees" requires new models that are fit for purpose, demand driven, and financially sustainable. In Turkiye, social entrepreneurship, especially in the refugee context, is practiced and recognized primarily through women's cooperatives. Expanding local examples of refugee-focused social entrepreneurship as well as adopting a sectoral approach to create new opportunities will be helpful. For instance, creative industries with a clear social mission of sustainable livelihoods for artisans, cultural heritage preservation, and community building hold potential for refugee entrepreneurs (Building Markets & Kopru, 2022). In addition, social entrepreneurs and their supporters are encouraged to create storytelling opportunities, showcase successful examples, and engage the media to demonstrate that refugee social entrepreneurs positively impact the local community.

International cooperation can further enhance the impact and sustainability of refugee-focused social entrepreneurship in Türkiye. By leveraging international networks, replicable ideas, and diverse funding sources, Turkiye is uniquely positioned to play a more active role in leading the conversation on social entrepreneurship for refugees regionally, especially in the Middle East and Eastern Europe. International convenings in Türkiye—such as Village Capital's closing summit in Istanbul for an accelerator on financial inclusion solutions for migrants (Village Capital, 2023) and the Refugee Entrepreneurship Network's annual summit in Izmir (REN, 2023)—are good opportunities for building linkages and exchanging knowledge across borders.

Developing market linkages is crucial to ensure refugee social entrepreneurs' inclusion. Partnerships with public and private sector buyers, including through the growing practice of social procurement, will provide not only sustainable revenue but also greater visibility and capacity building opportunities to these enterprises. In addition, it is important to develop stronger linkages between refugee and refugee-supporting social entrepreneurs and angel investment networks, venture funds, domestic and international philanthropies, and other funders to mobilize impact-aligned capital to seed and grow their ventures. By establishing "refugee lens investing" as a new impact vertical in the country's growing impact investing ecosystem and developing the evidence base and localized tools, local impact investors can have access to a new pipeline of investment opportunities that contribute to SDG outcomes as well as become part of an international community of practice.

Finally, there are abundant opportunities for academic and practitioner research in this space while fostering greater participation from researchers with lived experienced of forced displacement. Oxford University's Refugee-Led Research Hub offers a good model for expanding scholarship by displaced communities (Oxford University, 2024) and can build upon the existing academic work in Türkiye on social entrepreneurship and forced migration. In addition, cross-sectoral scholarship, especially with business and economics researchers, is needed to overcome the global tendency to maintain "refugee entrepreneurs as subjects of social studies rather than as agents of change in economies and entrepreneurship" (Hellbrunn & Iannone, 2020).

In conclusion, the potential of social entrepreneurship to significantly contribute to the economic and social integration of refugees in Türkiye is evident. The success of social enterprises discussed in the chapter, including Peace Therapist and Sector7, alongside numerous local and international examples, underscores the role of refugee-led and refugee-supporting social entrepreneurship in creating relevant solutions and fostering social cohesion. However, to unlock this potential fully, a concerted, multi-stakeholder effort is needed to encourage and enhance the refugee inclusive practices and resources of the local social entrepreneurship ecosystem and to address gaps in access to capital, market linkages, and visibility. By embracing "social entrepreneurship by, for, and with refugees," utilizing storytelling to highlight contributions, and leveraging international cooperation, Turkiye can lead the way in developing and scaling a robust ecosystem that not only empowers refugee social entrepreneurs and fosters partnership with refugee communities, but also amplifies their positive impact on the host communities.

Author's Note

The author would like to thank the following individuals and their institutions for their time and contributions to this research: Ahmad Sufian Bayram and Fadi Bishara, Blackbox; Berat Kjamili, Migport; Berivan Elis, Impact Hub Ankara; Bora Arican, Building Markets; Ezgi Ozkok Sefer, Ashoka Turkiye; Gilda Borriello, COMPAS; Izabela Ersahin, Sector7; Jin Dawod, Peace Therapist; Laura Batalla Adam, Hello Europe; Lina Sergie Attar, Karam Foundation; Mohammed Fareed Alhafez; Nuha Boga, Embark Project; Rami Sharrack, Tatwir Consulting; Rawan Hudaifa; Suha Nabhan, Migration Jam; Youssf Abdulaziz.

References

2X Global. (2024). What is gender lens investing? Retrieved from 2X Global: https://www.2xglobal.org/new-to-gender-lens-investing/what-is-gli

Almohammad, D., Durrah, O., Alkhalaf, T., & Rashid, M. (2021). Entrepreneurship in crisis: The determinants of Syrian Refugees' Entrepreneurial Intentions in Turkey. *Sustainability, 13*(8602).

American Immigration Council. (2023). Starting Anew the economic impact of refugees in America.

Ashoka. (2024). Retrieved from Hello Europe: https://www.hello-europe.eu/

Ashoka. (2024). Social entrepreneurship. Retrieved from https://www.ashoka.org/en-us/focus/social-entrepreneurship

Ates, O. (2020). Integration of Syrian refugees in Turkey: A social entrepreneurship case study. In S. Mosquera & P. Jardim da Palma (Eds.), *Multidisciplinary approach to entrepreneurship education for migrants*. IGI Global.

Atlantic Council. (2021). "Do Seagulls Migrate?" An Atlantic Council documentary. Retrieved from Atlantic Council: https://www.atlanticcouncil.org/programs/atlantic-council-in-turkey/do-seagulls-migrate-an-atlantic-council-documentary/

Bahar, D., & Dooley, M. (2020). No refugees and migrants left behind. In *Leave no one behind: Time for specifics on the Sustainable Development Goals* (p. 95). Brookings Institution Press.

Blasco, O., & Ramboux, S. (2023). The Journey of Ekip: A recipe for long-lasting impact.

British Council. (2019). The state of social enterprise in Turkey. British Council. Retrieved from https://www.britishcouncil.org.tr/sites/default/files/20190702_se_research_report_the_state_of_social_enterprise_in_turkey_eng_single_page.pdf

Building Markets & Kopru. (2022). *Syrian impact in the creative industries in Turkiye*. Building Markets.

Campomori, F., Casula, M., & Kazepov, Y. (2023). Understanding social innovation in refugee integration: Actors, practices, politics in Europe. *Innovation: The European Journal of Social Science Research, 36*(2), 158–170.

Cascant, E. (2023). How entrepreneurial ecosystem embeddedness reduces institutional bottlenecks faced by women refugees' social entrepreneurs in France. Diana International Research Conference 2023. Wellesley, MA: Babson College.

Chahine, T. (2023, January). The social entrepreneur's tool kit for making a difference. Retrieved from Yale Insights: https://insights.som.yale.edu/insights/the-social-entrepreneurs-tool-kit-for-making-difference?utm_source=YaleToday&utm_medium=Email&utm_campaign=YT_Y%E2%80%A6

Cittadini, S., Savoia, F., Zoppi, M., & Bolzani, D. (2022). REINSER 2022 International Conference for Sharing Best Practices: Economic and Social

Integration of Refugees and Asylum Seekers through Social Entrepreneurship. Book of abstracts (p. 45). Bologna: University of Bologna. Retrieved from https://keep.eu/projects/25271/Refugees-Economic-Integrati-EN/.

Dees, G. J. (2001). Meaning of social entrepreneurship. Duke University. Retrieved from https://centers.fuqua.duke.edu/case/wp-content/uploads/sites/7/2015/03/Article_Dees_MeaningofSocialEntrepreneurship_2001.pdf

EatOffBeat. (2024). Retrieved from https://www.eatoffbeat.com/

EBRD. (2016). Innovative solutions for refugees. Retrieved from EBRD: https://www.ebrd.com/news/events/innovative-solutions-for-refugees.html

Embark Project. (2024). Retrieved from https://www.embarkproject.com/

Enhancer. (2023). Retrieved from Enhancer – Musterek Projesi: https://musterek.sosyalgirisimcilikagi.org/

Erdem, T., Sirin, C., Singh, V., & Zhang, Q. (2018). How helping refugees helps brands. Tent Partnership for Refugees. Retrieved from https://www.tent.org/wp-content/uploads/2021/09/TENT_HowHelpingRefugeesHelpsBrands_Report_FINAL.pdf

Erdogan, M., Kirisci, K., & Uysal, G. (2021). *Improving Syrian refugee inclusion in the Turkish economy: How can the international community help?* World Refugee & Migration Council.

Gulerce, H., & Okten, S. (2021). Social entrepreneurship: Sustainable social development and social inclusion of asylum seekers. In *Migration social entrepreneurship and social inclusion*. Editoriale Scientifica.

Harima, A., & Freudenberg, J. (2020). Co-creation of social entrepreneurial opportunities with refugees. *Journal of Social Entrepreneurship, 11*(1), 40–64.

Hatipoglu, B. A. (2023). Business survival analysis of Syrian-owned enterprises in Türkiye. What works best?. Building Markets & TUYGAR.

Hellbrunn, S., & Iannone, R. (2020). From center to periphery and back again: A systematic literature review of refugee entrepreneurship. *Sustainability, 12*(18), 7858.

ILO. (2023). Entrepreneurship has no boundaries. Retrieved from ILO: https://www.ilo.org/ankara/news/WCMS_894119/lang--en/index.htm

ILO. (2023, November 10). Providing therapy to all, including traumatized refugees and earthquake survivors. Retrieved from ILO: https://www.ilo.org/global/about-the-ilo/multimedia/video/video-news-releases/WCMS_901600/lang--en/index.htm

Impact Hub & UNHCR. (2022). Global roadmap for refugee entrepreneurship.

Karaboga Cici, E. N., & Kodalak, O. (2023). Refugee entrepreneurship in the context of social entrepreneurship. In M. K. Arıcıoğlu (Ed.), *Refugee and immigrant entrepreneurship* (pp. 147–166). Cham: Palgrave McMillan.

Karam Foundation. (2023,). Karam House Scholar Fareed wins 2023 Teknofest. Retrieved from YouTube: https://www.youtube.com/watch?v=Bu10a2wWi-k

Kaya, A. (2023, November 1). The world's leading refugee host, Turkey has a complex migration history. Retrieved from Migration Policy Institute: https://www.migrationpolicy.org/article/turkey-migration-history

Larissa, M., Petrini, M., & da Silva, J. V. (2023). Understanding the motivations throughout the stages of a social enterprise's life cycle. *Brazilian Administration Review*.

Migration Jam. (2024). Retrieved from Migration Jam: https://migrationjam.com/

Migration Summit. (2023). Migration Summit 2023 Report.

Miller Center for Social Entrepreneurship. (2019). *Social Entrepreneurship at the Margins*. Miller Center for Social Entrepreneurship.

Mollaogullari, B. F., & Temel, R. (2018). Social entrepreneurship in Turkey: Social solution for refugee problem. *International Journal of Contemporary Economics and Administrative Sciences, 7*(3–4), 139–157.

NEsST. (2022, July 28). A new partnership to increase livelihood opportunities for refugees. Retrieved from NEsST: https://www.nesst.org/nesst/a-new-partnership-to-increase-livelihood-opportunities-for-refugees

NextGen Innovation and Progress. (2024). NextGen Innovation and Progress. Retrieved from https://www.linkedin.com/company/ngip-community/about/

OECD. (2023). The social and solidarity economy as a partner along the refugee journey. OECD Local Economic and Employment Development (LEED) Papers, 2023/15. Retrieved from OECD: https://www.oecd-ilibrary.org/docserver/174514e3-en.pdf?expires=1711943857&id=id&accname=guest&checksum=4772411175F4D2B6385CA603973285AE

Oxford University. (2024). Refugee-Led Research Hub. Retrieved from https://www.rsc.ox.ac.uk/research/refugee-led-research-hub

Ram, M. J.-V. (2022). What happens to refugee-origin entrepreneurs? Combining mixed embeddedness and strategy perspectives in a longitudinal study. *Ethnic and Racial Studies, 45*(16), 1–27.

REN. (2023). Retrieved from https://www.centreforentrepreneurs.org/ren

RIN. (2024). The refugee lens. Retrieved from The Refugee Investment Network: https://refugeeinvestments.org/resources/refugee-lens/

Rivna, A., & Gress, M. (2023). Social entrepreneurship as a new business model. The case of refugee integration. *Economic Research-Ekonomska Istraživanja, 36*(1).

SDGia. (2019). Turkey's first-ever international impact accelerating programme SDG impact accelerator takes off. Retrieved from SDGia: https://www.sdgia.org/turkeys-first-ever-international-impact-accelerating-programme-sdg-impact-accelerator-takes-off/

SEECO. (2024). SEECO. Retrieved from https://www.seeco.gov.tr/homepage

Social Enterprise UK. (2022). Adebowale Commission on social investment. Retrieved from Social Enterprise UK: https://www.socialenterprise.org.uk/adebowale-commission-on-social-investment%EF%BF%BC/

Startups Without Borders. (2019, July 15). The migrant entrepreneur using Big Data to disrupt Turkey's Humanitarian Sector. Retrieved from Startups Without Borders: https://blog.startupswb.com/2019/07/15/understanding-big-data-how-it-can-change-your-business-and-the-world/

UNHCR. (2023, September). Turkiye Fact Sheet. Retrieved from https://www.unhcr.org/tr/wp-content/uploads/sites/14/2023/10/bi-annual-fact-sheet-2023-09-turkiyeF.pdf.

UNHCR. (2024). About made 51. Retrieved from Made51: https://shop.made51.org/pages/about-made51

Village Capital. (2023). Financial solutions for migrants. Retrieved from Village Capital: https://vilcap.com/programs/refugeetech-and-migranttech

Wells, D. E. (2018). From social entrepreneurship to everyone a change-maker: 40 years of social innovation point to what's next. *Social Innovations Journal, 52.*

World Economic Forum (WEF). (2023). Global Gender Gap Report. Retrieved from https://www3.weforum.org/docs/WEF_GGGR_2023.pdf.

World Health Organization. (2021). Mental health and forced displacement. Retrieved from WHO: https://www.who.int/news-room/fact-sheets/detail/mental-health-and-forced-displacement.

Zihnioglu, O., & Dalkıran, M. (2022). From social capital to social cohesion: Syrian refugees in Turkey and the role of NGOs as intermediaries. *Journal of Ethnic and Migration Studies, 48*(11).

Aslı Aygüneş
İstasyon TEDÜ

Elif Muratoğlu
İstasyon TEDÜ

Sinem Güravşar Gökçe
İstasyon TEDÜ

Chapter 7 Exploring the Ripple Effect: Social Cooperatives and Their Catalyzing Role in Socioeconomic Development

1. Introduction

Socioeconomic development is commonly determined through analyzing eight main metrics: demography, employment and social security, education, health, finances, competitiveness, innovativeness, and quality of life in Türkiye (for further information; Sosyo-Ekonomik Gelişmişlik Sıralaması Araştırma Raporları). Even though these metrics offer an insight into how further along socioeconomic development is in a region, it fails to recognize the role of different metrics fostering this development. While competitiveness and innovativeness is accepted as a valid metric, solidarity and sustainability are absent from the evaluative framework. Moreover, other crucial metrics such as environmental sustainability, gender equality, democratic participation, access to social services, psychological well being, access to freedoms, and cultural diversity still remain unexplored. In addition, the role of different entities (i.e., organizations, institutions, initiatives, cooperations, public and private sector) that contribute to socioeconomic development need to be analyzed for a thorough analysis of the development of a region.

Stemming from this gap in literature, this study locates social cooperatives as agents of socioeconomic development in Türkiye and aims to articulate their social and economic contribution to the region they are operating in. Although hereby, we do not present a complete analysis of different metrics, we analyze how social cooperatives contribute to development through focusing on three main aspects; localization of impact, sustaining impact, and fostering impactful organizational culture. In doing so, we aim to show that analysis of social cooperatives through these three focus areas can present a different angle into understanding analysis of socioeconomic development in Türkiye.

2. Understanding the Social Cooperatives: Definition and Principles

According to the Statement on the Cooperative Identity (ICA, 2024) cooperatives are "*autonomous associations of persons united voluntarily to meet their common economic, social and cultural needs and aspirations through a jointly owned and democratically controlled enterprise*". In this definition, the democratic management of cooperatives is underscored, with each member having equal voting rights regardless of their capital contribution. Cooperative operations, surplus distribution, and decision-making processes are all subject to the democratic decisions made by the participation of all members. The principles of voluntary participation, democratic governance, economic participation, autonomy, capacity building, cooperation among cooperatives, and social responsibility form the foundation of cooperative functioning.

Cooperatives offer various benefits, functioning as people-centric enterprises focused on collaboration. Cooperatives as an organizational form enable the pooling of small contributions to form capital, allowing for the realization of tasks that individuals might struggle to achieve independently. This independence also increases cooperatives' resilience especially in times of crisis. Cooperative members are also the owners of the cooperative, and the financial interests of all members contribute to the success of the cooperative. Consequently, members actively provide any necessary support and assistance to strengthen the cooperative. Cooperatives also have some advantages to access to finance, especially to credits and grants, differing from traditional enterprises.

Social cooperatives came to the fore in the 1980s with the spread of the social and solidarity economy and the debate about whether cooperatives are part of a pluralistic market economy or of social and solidarity economy. It is uncontested, that cooperatives are (or should be) doing business differently from capitalist enterprises, not aiming at maximum (short-term) profit for distribution among shareholders and not focussing on capital and profit, but on people and on meeting their members' long-term needs in sustainable development. Some view them as self-help organizations serving the economic interests of members while engaging with non-members, while others see them as socioeconomic entities benefiting both members and the broader community, known as "social cooperatives" or "general interest cooperatives" (Münkner, 2016).

Social cooperatives can be defined as entities that prioritize social impact and social transformation as their missions and work towards a more equal and sustainable future. By offering goods and services for the public aligned with their missions, they are rapidly becoming an important actor in the social and solidarity economy (Guttmann, 2021; TÜSEV, 2018). As a form of community organization, social cooperatives bring different types of stakeholders together—producers, consumers and citizens. In this organizational model social cooperatives produce innovative solutions in different sectors and offer accessible and fair products/services to their beneficiaries and/or customers (CICOPA, 2004; Utting, 2016).

Social cooperatives operate in a way that is specifically committed to social good. Acting as a non-government actor, they embrace multi-stakeholderism, representation of worker-members in cooperative governance, and no/limited profit distribution to members as their organizing principles (CICOPA, 2004). Social cooperatives share commonalities with traditional cooperatives in the adoption of basic cooperative principles, but they use different methods and tools to achieve their social good mission. The importance of social cooperatives is their ability (i) to increase the representation of local and disadvantaged groups in the labor market, (ii) to offer locally relevant services and purchasing options, (iii) to focus on creative and accessible solutions compared to traditional entrepreneurship, (iv) to build local social capital, and (v) to have a capacity to transform communities they stem from (Mancino & Thomas, 2005).

Social Cooperatives in Italy: A first step towards addressing and regulating social cooperatives
In Italy, with the establishment of The Law 381/1991 on Social Cooperatives, the cooperatives that work with an explicit *"aim to pursue the general interest of the community in the human promotion and social integration of citizens"* were legally recognised as social cooperatives. Social cooperatives have emerged as significant contributors to welfare services in Italy, experiencing a steady annual growth rate ranging from 10 % to 20 % since their establishment in the late 1960s and early 1970s. This growth coincided with the emergence of welfare gaps, where specific social needs in Italy were left unaddressed by both the public and private sectors (OECD, 2022). They still contribute significantly to the socioeconomic development of the country today. Confcooperative Federsolidarietà stands as the primary Italian federation representing social cooperatives and active promoter of

The Law 381/1991, boasting over 6,200 affiliated members. These members collectively encompass approximately 229,000 individual participants and over 240,000 employees, among whom are 18,000 individuals facing various disadvantages, such as physical and mental disabilities, substance addiction, as well as individuals who are currently or were formerly incarcerated. The combined annual revenue generated by the associated members of Confcooperative Federsolidarietà totals around 8 billion EUR. Through their extensive range of services, they offer support and care to more than 4 million individuals, including 1 million individuals with disabilities (CECOP, 2021).

The Law 381/1991 marked a pioneering milestone as it is the first legislation to explicitly acknowledge social cooperatives as a legal form. Its impact has transcended national borders, serving as a catalyst for the adoption of comparable legal frameworks in Europe and beyond, including Spain, France, Portugal, South Korea, and Canada (OECD, 2022). Some countries have regulated them within other laws of broader content, such as corporate codes, laws regulating the social economy or within laws related to the activities that cooperatives can carry out. (Hernández Cáceres, 2023).

3. Emphasizing the "Social" in Cooperatives in Türkiye

First formed with government support in 1863 and first received constitutional representation in 1961, cooperative tradition became a pillar of democratic representation in Türkiye. With government support, cooperatives found an opportunity to develop operations under different pillars of social, economic, and environmental needs (Akgöz & Ercan, 2012). Today though they are mostly known in the construction and agriculture sector, traditional cooperatives also operate in the textile, tourism, service and trade sectors. In addition, as one of the actors contributing to socioeconomic development, cooperatives also enhance democratic participation and work to eliminate gender inequality and poverty in the long term through offering new inclusive and participatory organizational models (INGEV & IPM, 2021).

In Türkiye, according to INGEV & IPM's (2021) report "Resilient Cooperative for Social Solidarity Economy" there are around 60,000 cooperatives of nearly 40 different types, with a total of 6.6 million members. Union of Chambers and Commodity Exchanges of Türkiye's statistics on established and closed businesses, shows that there has been a higher rate of increase since 2018, that can be attributed to the stimulating regulations and practices implemented by the government and local authorities (Köne, 2021).

With a 150-year-long history of cooperative tradition, Türkiye offers an established ground for the formation of social cooperatives. The cooperatives, which can be defined as 'social' are the most prevalent legal form with the ratio of 37 %among other business models in Türkiye (TSEN, 2022). This fact can be explained by the long-standing historical presence of cooperatives in Türkiye and well-matched principles with social entrepreneurship such as good governance, participatory and inclusive approach, cooperation and social responsibility.

As the concept of social and solidarity economy has become more widespread around the world, social cooperatives have gained momentum in Türkiye as well. Even though economic development occurred nationally and globally, socioeconomic inequalities remain intact. Here, the social and solidarity economy, where owners, workers, consumers and citizens work in cooperation, becomes an answer to an ongoing call for battling social inequalities and disparities (INGEV & IPM, 2021). As one of the entities working in this social and solidarity economy framework, social cooperatives work alongside traditional cooperatives, charities, foundations, associations, and social enterprises to create social impact.

In Türkiye, social cooperatives endow upon the needs of populations that would otherwise remain inactive in the society. Driven from a strong community culture, social cooperatives offer employment to various groups of people and support socioeconomic development through supporting the participation of these groups in the labor force. In addition, similar to traditional cooperative structure, social cooperatives embody democratic organizing principles in decision-making and encourage partial or full member participation in cooperative business. This organizational model also offers a view into how democracy could work effectively in business settings while also prioritizing social good.

Women's cooperatives emerge as one of the most common forms of social cooperatives in Türkiye. The increase in the number of women's cooperatives could be explained by the increase in government support for women's entrepreneurship in Türkiye (Küme, 2021). Due to their non-hierarchical approach, prioritization of women's empowerment and enhancing gender equality, women's cooperatives can be analyzed as cases of social cooperatives in Türkiye. Some studies focus on the economic functions of women's cooperatives (Kızıldağ, 2019) while some analyze how women reap social and psychological benefits as well (Cinar et.al, 2021; Hatipoğlu, 2021). For instance, in their study involving twenty-three cooperatives, Cinar et.al (2021) argue that women not only find economic gains and prosperity by working in a women's cooperative, they also build stronger relations with other women in their close circle, explore collaboration opportunities with other networks, and find an opportunity to work with women from different ethnic and religious backgrounds.

In addition, social cooperatives can also be the catalyzers of system change through advocating for advancement of human rights, environmental protection, and fair production. In Türkiye, there are social cooperatives that work to strengthen the social cooperative ecosystem and increase awareness about how social cooperatives as a business model can be an alternative to traditional business structures. To exemplify, Youth Deal Cooperative's community of new generation cooperatives and the Coop Support project, as well as Needs Map's cooperatives network established under the project Centre of Excellence for Social Cooperatives are some of the examples of communities working to support the ecosystem in Türkiye.

Despite these efforts for the development of a strong social cooperative ecosystem in Türkiye, social cooperatives still face difficulties in sustaining and expanding their social impact. First, the lack of a clear definition of social cooperatives and their lack of a separate status from traditional cooperatives cause them to be regarded and taxed as enterprises (Üstün, 2024). The Directorate General of Cooperatives formed under the Ministry of Customs and Trade published the "2012–2016 Cooperative Strategy and Action Plan for Turkey" to support cooperative formation in Türkiye. This action plan aimed to create a favorable environment for cooperatives in Türkiye, foster a positive perception of cooperatives in the society, increase trust towards them, and enhance the contributions of cooperatives to economic development. This served as a guiding document for creating a supporting ecosystem for traditional cooperatives, however the plan did not address social cooperatives separately. Later, one of the most prominent efforts to promote and disseminate social cooperatives was the "Promotion, Training, Development and Implementation Project" launched by the Ministry of Trade, General Directorate of Cooperatives in 2018. As a project specifically focusing on disseminating information about social cooperatives, this project has given significant momentum to the movement. Though the project has reached an influential capacity, as a result of general elections and institutional changes, the impact soon decreased and thus the constitutional dilemma remains unsolved.

Even though there are governmental and social efforts to create an awareness about social cooperatives, these endeavors have not fully contributed to enhancing the ecosystem in Türkiye. In light of this, ongoing efforts are being made for a cooperative action plan for the years 2025–2029. Therefore, presenting studies on the definition, contributions, and principles of social cooperatives is crucial. Especially for data-driven policies to be developed, more research is needed focusing on the social good that social cooperatives create/can create in Türkiye. In order to contribute to the existing knowledge, through focusing on interviews with sixteen social cooperatives in different cities, this study aims to understand how social cooperatives contribute to the socioeconomic and sustainable development of Türkiye.

4. Crafting the Study

This study utilizes semi-structured in-depth interviews with founding or active members of social cooperatives to understand how cooperatives perceive and talk about their social and economic impact. As part of the study, we conducted online interviews with ten women and six men active/founding members of sixteen social cooperatives. In selecting social cooperatives we aimed for regional, scale, target group and sector diversity among participants to have an in-depth understanding of cooperatives' experiences. Social cooperatives are chosen according to the criteria using the social entrepreneurship ecosystem map prepared and updated by Turkish Social Entrepreneurship Network (TSEN). For specific geographical regions, we contacted Regional Development Agencies to get further information about the operational status of the cooperatives.

The social cooperatives operate in different geographical regions, including two social cooperatives from Mediterranean, Eastern Anatolia, Black Sea, Aegean and Southeast Anatolia Region each and three social cooperatives from Marmara and Central Anatolia each, parallel with the population and number of enterprises in these regions. This research focuses primarily on examining cooperatives in the late implementation and growth stages to assess the long-term impact generated by social cooperatives. Additionally, the study incorporates two cooperatives in the startup stage and two in the early implementation and growth stage to ensure a comprehensive understanding and coverage of different experiences in creating impact.

The selected cooperatives offer products and services in education, food, agriculture, culture-arts, training, design-fashion-textile and consulting. Although most of the selected cooperatives conduct activities at the local level, their impact through their products/services and supply chains is mostly at the national level. Two of the cooperatives included in the study can be characterized as system enterprises, not only seeking to expand their social impact but also aiming to address issues at the ecosystem level. Their goal is to initiate systemic change by acting as a catalyst among different entities and institutions in the ecosystem. These two cooperatives provide capacity-building services for other social cooperatives, contribute to knowledge generation in this field, conduct advocacy activities to raise awareness about social cooperatives, and unite ecosystem actors through network collaborations.

Table 1. Profile of the Interviewed Cooperatives

Coperative Pseudonyms	Region	Stage of Development	Sector	Target Group(s)	Geographical Scope
Food & Agriculture Coop1	Eastern Anatolia	Early implementation and growth stage	Food, Agriculture	Women, Rural population	Village/ Neighbourhood/ District level
Food & Agriculture Coop2	Black Sea	Late implantation and growth stage	Food	Women, Rural population	Village/ Neighbourhood/ District level
Food & Agriculture Coop3	Aegean	Late implantation and growth stage	Agriculture, Food	Rural population	Village/ Neighbourhood/ District level
Business Support & Consultancy Coop1	Aegean	Late implantation and growth stage	Business Support & Consultancy	General	National level
Sustainable Tourism & Culture-Art Coop	Mediterranean	Startup stage	Sustainable Tourism, Agriculture, Education, Culture & Art	Urban population	Village/ Neighbourhood/ District level
Business Support & Consultancy Coop2	Marmara	Late implantation and growth stage	Business Support & Consultancy, Education, Livelihood Creation, Fair Trade	General	National level
Consumer Coop	Marmara	Late implantation and growth stage	Trade and Retail, Food, Agriculture	General	Village/ Neighbourhood/ District level
Design, Fashion & Textile, Food Coop	Southeastern Anatolia	Late implantation and growth stage	Design, Fashion & Textile, Food	Woman	Multiple Cities
Food & Agriculture Coop4	Eastern Anatolia	Early implantation and growth stage	Agriculture, Food	Woman	City level
Education Coop	Central Anatolia	Late implantation and growth stage	Education	Children, Urban population	City level
Food & Agriculture Coop5	Southeastern Anatolia	Late implantation and growth stage	Food, Agriculture	Women, Rural population	City level
Culture-Art Coop	Marmara	Startup stage	Art and culture	Women	City level
Food Coop	Black Sea	Late implantation and growth stage	Food	Women	City level
Food & Agriculture Coop6	Mediterranean	Late implantation and growth stage	Food, Agriculture	Women, Rural population	Village/ Neighbourhood/ District level
Food & Culture-Art Coop	Central Anatolia	Late implantation and growth stage	Food, Culture & Art	Urban population, Rural population	City level
Textile Coop	Central Anatolia	Late implantation and growth stage	Textile	Women	City level

Semi-structured interviews lasted 50–90 minutes and in order to ensure anonymity of the interviewees and the cooperatives, pseudonyms are used. With the respondents' consent we recorded the interviews and later transcribed them. All interviews were conducted in Turkish and the segments used in this chapter are translated by us.

The transcribed segments were coded under three umbrella themes: Cooperative, Organizational Culture and Impact. Based on these themes, in order to understand how cooperatives contribute to socioeconomic and sustainable development, we analyzed the effect of local ownership, strategic ways of navigating obstacles to sustain impact and the innovative pathways for local democratic participation in business. Analyzing social cooperatives through these focal points opens a space for discussion about how social cooperatives, despite economic, organizational and social difficulties sustain their impact and hence contribute to local and national development.

5. Embracing and Rebuilding the Local

Social cooperatives, as actors stemming from and primarily operating in their locals, become entities that own, build and represent the local. Interviews suggest that, especially for food and agricultural cooperatives, contributing to the social and economic development of their local region is at the forefront of their missions.

One of the ways in which cooperatives own the local is through involving the people living in the region in the cooperative business. Some cooperatives particularly defined their contribution to the region from the lens of empowering women living in the area. This approach not just enables social development in the region but it also contributes to the economic development (Duguid et al.., 2015). For instance, Food & Culture-Art Coop described their mission to start the cooperative as getting women and students living in the neighborhood involved in the cooperative business either as members of the cooperatives or as employees. Moreover, they also articulate empowering local farmers as one of their missions. Food & Culture-Art Coop aims to strengthen locals not just economically but also socially through offering employment to farmers and women/student employees while also contributing to their knowledge building and social empowerment.

Similarly, Food & Agriculture Coop6, Food Coop and Food & Agriculture Coop1 state their mission as reaching out to women living in the area and encouraging them to be productive. Through this, they argue that cooperative members, specifically highlighting women, both gain income and as they say, continue to produce. Their motto is "A society that produces always exists. We stay strong as long as we continue production." Here, production is emphasized as key to local development and the sustainability of the impact. This focus on production stems from their aim to strengthen women in their local area. They state "We have already been producing at our houses and were selling what we produced. But we thought, if we were to do it in a cooperative, it would be easier for us to acquire production permission and it would be a good chance for us to empower other women." Another cooperative explains their mission as building a community of women and hence "battling women's poverty by increasing social awareness and fostering economic empowerment through getting them involved in commerce."

Cooperatives also contribute to local development by localizing the supply chain by purchasing materials for cooperative production from local/regional suppliers in the region. All cooperatives emphasize that they first check local distributors and ensure that their primary point of procurement is their local region. This process also aligns well with their mission to support the local production. For example, Food & Culture-Art Coop supplies all bottling equipment locally, while Education Coop ensures all products used to prepare the lunch menu comes from local suppliers to the school.

In addition, they not only incorporate local business owners, suppliers, and producers into cooperatives, but also contribute to the development of their region by ensuring the protection of resources and continuity of sustainable agriculture in the area. One of the interviewed production cooperatives is actively involved in efforts to preserve and expand the cultivation of region-specific seed diversity. They aim to preserve heirloom seeds to increase wheat cultivation in the region. They summarize their impact in this regard as follows: "If our cooperative did not exist in this region, no one would be aware of the existence of such beautiful wheat seed." Looking to create a system change, one of the cooperatives, Sustainable Tourism & Culture-Art Coop, aims to steer the interest in construction in the region towards sustainable agriculture and sustainable tourism to contribute to regional socioeconomic development. They contend that supporting local production through sustainable agriculture will bring new financial and social resources to the region. Moreover, Food & Agriculture Coop2 aims to transition to solar energy in the future and minimize the harm to the environment. These environmentally friendly practices adopted by social cooperatives contribute to the social development of the region through protecting its natural resources.

For the cooperatives active in the food and agriculture sectors, it is important to note that goods produced at the cooperative match with the local agricultural resources in the region. The fact that the cooperatives process and package products that are easily accessible and produced in the region makes it possible for regional products to be recognized in other markets and ensures the sustainability of the cooperatives' production. At the same time, since they buy raw materials from the region, cooperatives contribute to the continued production of these materials in the region. To illustrate with an example, at the early stages Food Coop started with producing wheat flour because the region is known for wheat farming. They explain that this enabled them to enter the market easily while accessing the main ingredient easily. As they gradually increased production of wheat flour, wheat farming also started to grow in the region. This direct correlation between the wheat farming and wheat flour production reflected positively on employment and economic growth in the region as well.

Cooperatives in the study strive to expand their impact by establishing ateliers with different production focuses in various geographies, and hence contribute to the empowerment of women in the entire region. Spreading their operations to different regions means using a different organizational model, which enables them to reap benefits from different regions while also ensuring financial stability. Design, Fashion & Textile, Food Coop, Textile Coop, and Food & Agriculture Coop2 can be cited as examples of this multiregional production system. Design, Fashion & Textile, Food Coop operates four workshops in different cities. Through scaling and diversifying their production according to different localities, they achieve a more widespread socioeconomic impact. Similarly, Food & Agriculture Coop2, in addition to their eleven points of sale, built three ateliers in villages, where they employ village women who cannot travel to the city center for financial reasons or because of family conflicts. The cooperative also utilizes these hives as places to keep stock and enable mass delivery of products. A slightly different model is utilized by Textile Coop working as an umbrella organization, with 4 different ateliers that operate in different fields. This enables ateliers with different production focuses to come together under the cooperative umbrella, gaining representation, and contributing to the dissemination of their impact. Taking this one-step further, as exemplified by Food & Agriculture Coop6, Design, Fashion & Textile, Food Coop and Food & Agriculture Coop2, using the skills they acquired as part of the ateliers, members start their own ventures as well.

Furthermore, in supporting socioeconomic development, cooperatives build a market bridge with other social cooperatives as well. As previously explained, social cooperatives pay attention to sourcing materials and products locally. In addition, they emphasized that they make purchases from other cooperatives to support the promotion of each other's products and contribute to the economic development of other cooperatives. For example, Food & Culture-Art Coop and Consumer Coop gather locally sourced products from diverse social cooperatives, selling them at their sales points. Essentially, these cooperatives not only provide an opportunity for social cooperatives to reach diverse markets but also serve as a vital link connecting prosumers with producers. This collaboration between cooperatives creates a circular economy, enabling sustainability of social cooperatives and their products.

Moreover, while establishing connections between different social cooperatives, cooperatives strive to form supply chains between their regions and other regions to foster a social and financial network. For instance, even though Food Coop procures the majority of needed supplies locally, for some ingredients that could not be found in the region, they collaborate with suppliers outside the region. Design, Fashion&Textile, Food Coop says, "If it's not something we can buy from the region, we pay extra attention to where we buy our raw materials. We prioritize women entrepreneurs and small family businesses. This is important for us." This approach enables different supply chains to be developed, connecting the region with different suppliers and developing inter-regional ties. Their involvement in e-commerce points also contributes to this aim by connecting them to a broader market.

As a side benefit to their production operations, cooperatives become areas for socializing and enable know-how exchange among local people. Business Support&Consultancy Coop2 stated that cooperative members have become friends, following each other's lives and supporting each other in good and hard times. They emphasized that this solidarity is a part of the cooperative culture. Some participants underlined that one of the motivations to form the cooperatives is to gather the producers living in the area to collaborate with each other. Cooperatives emphasize the significance of this experience especially for women involved in the cooperative, highlighting its role in stepping out of their homes, engaging in life, and acquiring diverse skills. Design, Fashion&Textile, Food Coop, Textile Coop, Food Coop, and Food & Agriculture Coop2 emphasize that women who previously engaged in production at home for their families and friends experience empowerment by joining the workforce and connecting with other producers in the region. Additionally, producers establish various partnerships by sharing product recipes and preparation methods with each other. In addition, Food & Agriculture Coop1 mentioned formation of a social activity committee, which plans cultural activities (touristic activities, breakfast/lunch gatherings, picnics) specifically for cooperative members to foster a warm and welcoming cooperative culture.

Similarly, in some cooperatives working for a systemic change, this coming together results in creation of alliances and communities. For the Education Coop, people with similar worries and interests about the education system came together and formed a cooperative to develop new ideas. Their collective efforts gave them an opportunity to reach out to other people in diverse settings and to develop a new approach to education. This development of a new democratic education system could be evaluated as another contribution to socio economic development. Similarly, the Business Support&Consultancy Coop1 was founded by university-graduates, who were working as white-collar workers in an institutional setting and who wished to form a business without a boss. This led them to forming a social cooperative where they could produce and gain together as shareholders. Another example is the Sustainable Tourism & Culture-Art Coop, which was formed with the motivation to bring civil society workers/volunteers under the same roof in the Mediterranean to form a cooperative and do collective work that could benefit the regional development as well. The interviewed founding member states the aim here as, "the goal was for [people living in the big cities who move to rural areas] to continue producing, especially to contribute to local development [by] offering their expertise in a specific organizational framework. Rural development, local development, social entrepreneurship, social economy, that was the idea." Here, socioeconomic development is supported by bringing in different expertise together to develop a new model that could benefit the region or the ecosystem on a different level. What the interviews suggest is that all cooperatives brought together individuals with shared interests in social cooperatives to strive for socioeconomic development.

6. Navigating Obstacles and Sustaining Impact

Cooperatives encounter many obstacles and difficulties on their journey from the initial stage to the late implementation stage. In this study, we have analyzed these challenges as milestones, focusing on how cooperatives were affected by them and how they managed to sustain their impact despite the disruptions. What we want to emphasize here is the processes and strategies that both contribute to the strengthening of cooperatives and open up new opportunities for them to sustain their effects. Disruptions mentioned in the interviews mostly stem from natural disasters or the pandemic, financial (in)stability, and difficulty of social integration into the cooperative ecosystem.

Financial stability has been raised as one of the main obstacles by the majority of social cooperatives in the study. For the Consumer Coop and Food & Agriculture Coop4, the interviewee emphasized the period following the COVID-19 period as a financially difficult time. For Consumer Coop, this financial instability demotivated the members to keep going but they got motivation from the fact that local people embraced their impact and still encouraged them to keep going. This motivation led them to seek alternative funding from international sources and hence sustain the business. Food & Agriculture Coop4, resuming production meant seeking women living in the rural areas for sewing new textile products. Here we witness that even though the cooperative experienced troubling times during the closure period, this led them to connect with new producers in the rural area and include them in the cooperative work as well. Similarly, Food & Culture-Art Coop pinpointed the pandemic period as a financially difficult time for the cooperative. When the closure period passed, Food&Culture-Art Coop created a new revenue stream by serving breakfast prepared using local products purchased from local cooperatives. Hence, financial instability encouraged them to locate new financial resources while also benefiting other social cooperatives as well. Their operations diversified and impact multiplied.

Occasionally, cooperatives acquire financial support from various national and international resources. Though these resources, big or small, assist cooperatives in pursuing their business, the issues with their realization and sustainability impede these efforts. Food & Agriculture Coop1 serves as an example to this situation. They acquired a grant from a national office to expand its operations. However, the officials withheld the national financing, leaving the cooperative with plans for the future but no source of revenue. The interviewee states;

We got funding support from a public institution but because we are a profit-making entity, they did not give us the loan in the end. We were devastated. To resume what we were doing, we got a dollar debt now. We had to take out a loan. But we still managed to build a [production] facility for roasted chickpeas. Now women [in the cooperative] are constantly working to produce roasted chickpeas to pay the debt. But it is okay, we are motivated.

In this troubling situation, the cooperative members held on to their future plans and opted in for a bank loan to sustain their impact in the region. This loan served as a catalyst to motivate them even more to continue production. Another cooperative, Food & Agriculture Coop4, relies on the space provided by the local authority. This dependency on external support creates instability, as they risk losing their production space in the event of an election or a change in government office. Similarly, Food & Agriculture Coop2 received material support from a national funding source which refused to leave the ownership of the materials to the cooperative but rather rented the equipment for free. The interviewee stated that;

We don't even use that equipment anymore because we outgrew their capacity. But they refuse to take them back, so they just sit there in the corner. We don't want to use them because they are not ours. If the equipment was ours we could sell them and invest the money into increasing production.

This situation exemplifies the lack of ownership created by the incompleteness of a promised funding. As exemplified here and as Food & Agriculture Coop2 and Food & Agriculture Coop3 further noted, government resources are not utilized effectively to build a strong cooperative ecosystem in Türkiye.

The recent earthquake is mentioned in the interviews as a disruption to the cooperatives' business. Due to its recent effect, the recent severe earthquake that occurred on 6 February 2023, was mentioned as one of the obstacles cooperatives faced. The earthquake has disrupted the production processes of some cooperatives and created a turmoil in the way financial resources and human labor is managed in the cooperative. Still, the cooperatives emphasize that despite the disruption, this obstacle paved the way for increased cooperation and motivation. For instance, Food & Agriculture Coop5 was directly affected by the earthquake, losing their equipment and offices. They had to stop their operations. However, they started looking for government earthquake relief support and managed to find a space for continuing production. They emphasize that the financial support given to the producers in the earthquake region assisted them in sustaining their operations. Additionally, although the Food & Agriculture Coop6's production offices and equipment were not damaged in the earthquake, they managed to make a quick financial recovery due to the high number of orders received from people who wish to support the local production in the earthquake region. The interviewees underline that starting production after the earthquake supported them psychologically as well. They said "We've resumed production again. Holding on tighter, standing more upright, and striving to make one into five." The orders they received not only helped them financially but it also reminded them of the impact of their business and brought their motivation back.

Pandemic and the closures have also affected cooperatives' efforts to sustain production and continue their growth. Culture-Art Coop pinpoints pandemic as a milestone for their cooperative because they faced financial difficulties. However, they found continuing production as a way forward and found motivation in focusing on doing more artworks. Food&Culture-Art Coop, although they are not located in the region, canalized their resources to lend support to the people in the region. Another cooperative, Food & Agriculture Coop3, has also contributed to the earthquake relief efforts by organizing in itself and sending in materials. These cases show that cooperatives build flexible systems to adjust troubling times and always carry collaboration and solidarity as their principles. This resulted in increased cooperation in the cooperative and creation of new strategies for effective production and easy delivery.

Another difficulty mentioned by the cooperatives is the perception of cooperatives in the society and social integration of the business. These issues become an obstacle particularly in the food and agriculture cooperatives. Multiple cooperatives underlined the difficulty they had with getting members involved in the cooperative since first, due to assumptions that cooperatives are unstable organizational models, second, due to intrinsic patriarchal gender roles. First, especially women were discouraged by their families to refrain from becoming a member of the cooperative, leading some members to opt for occasional volunteering instead of committing to full-time membership in the cooperative. Second, some women were heavily criticized for prioritizing cooperatives' needs over housework. Cooperatives had to renegotiate with families to keep members and producers coming to the cooperatives, underlining multiple times that involvement in the cooperative meant more income for the household and more social prosperity in general. Women members themselves also confronted their family members, standing firm that they enjoyed being part of a producing community. Here, even though social integration posits an obstacle on the advancement of cooperatives, it also represents another social impact created by the cooperative. Merely by existing in the region, cooperatives operate as advocates of gender equality.

Whenever the cooperative expands its operations, they encounter new obstacles and feel the need to strategize again to find financial sustainability. Building new business motivates the cooperative members to resume operations Textile Coop is an appropriate example for this as they serve as an umbrella cooperative for different ateliers. Since each atelier is a new endeavor, even though it is full of hardships opening the ateliers, the interviewee identified the opening of each was a distinct milestone. Since every atelier has a specific production focus, the cooperative was challenged to come up with solutions to overcome obstacles in order to maintain production. Here, the cooperative expanded its operations and had to improve and rebuild their plans for financial stability again. Therefore, it is crucial that cooperatives embark on future opportunities with a navigation plan in mind if they desire to multiply their social impact. This was particularly evident in cooperatives' plans for the future. When asked about their dreams and plans for the future, they mentioned growing business through buying more equipment, finding new production spaces, expanding to new regions, and employing more people or exporting their products. Moreover, Food & Agriculture Coop3, Business Support/Consultancy Coop1, and Business Support/Consultancy Coop2 mention internationalization as one of their future goals.

In the interviews, the challenges faced are described as opportunities for growth for the cooperatives. With the financial, social, or natural difficulties they face, cooperatives identified new intervention areas and took their work one-step further to address these challenges. Majority of the cooperatives find motivation to continue their work during these moments of difficulty and have developed new businesses, strategies, and partnerships to overcome these obstacles. Here, instability became a driving force, further motivating cooperatives to resume business. Thus, it is possible to say that cooperatives often emerge from these challenges with their social impact enhanced. The motivating effect of overcoming obstacles has had a positive impact on the journeys of social cooperatives participating in the study.

7. Cultivating A Democratic Organizational Culture

Creating social impact within and through an organization is deeply intertwined with its organizational culture, shaping its values, behaviors, and interactions both internally and externally. Social cooperatives, in this regard, aim to foster a nonhierarchical organizational culture, where inclusivity, openness, and democracy are the dominant principles. By essence, social cooperatives prioritize community welfare, environmental sustainability, and ethical/fair practices. Over time, they become entities that set an example for these practices and disseminate these ideals to the wider society. Thus, social cooperatives in this study emphasized the importance of becoming a democratic community while also maintaining a share of responsibility for the work being done as well as the social welfare in general. As one of the cooperatives said, "We have an ethical and conscientious community here. We stand strong with this motto. We never did background checks for anyone. Everyone feels responsibility towards each other's labor and towards the work we do. As a result, a fair and democratic community emerges. In fact, amidst this polluted world, polluted food, polluted human relationships, we see that there is another life possible."

Social cooperatives reflect their non-hierarchical organization primarily in membership and decision-making mechanisms within the organizational model. Specifically, we observed similar practices among cooperatives when we inquired about their membership acceptance and evaluation mechanisms. Most cooperatives expressed a preference for new members to be chosen from individuals who have already been involved in the cooperative's activities for several months. This approach ensures that the individual is familiar with the cooperative's purpose and its operational mechanisms. Some interviewees emphasized that new memberships are discussed at a monthly-held general assembly where all members of the cooperative participate. This enables reaching consensus among all active members and implementing collective decision-making. One of the cooperatives runs a different membership mechanism as they receive a high number of requests. Every six months, they conduct meetings with candidates for membership and two different groups evaluate these applications to ensure objectivity and fairness. On the other hand, it is crucial to note that certain cooperatives encounter challenges, or lack the inclination, in accepting new applicants because of; the complexities in establishing an equitable membership fee that adequately reflects the substantial value of the cooperative's assets, the incapacity to generate revenue for members in the current economic crisis, and struggles in managing a large number of members. However, despite these difficulties, most of the cooperatives remain committed to the open-door policy when it comes to receiving new membership applications, while also running the decision-making process transparently and collectively.

All cooperatives are eager for welcoming new members and actively engaging them in the cooperative operations. They leave the level of interaction with the cooperative to the individuals themselves, but the existing members make time to ensure swift and welcoming entry to the cooperative. As a mechanism, some cooperatives match new members with old members and create a space for know-how exchange about daily orders of the cooperative. This mentoring mechanism orients new members to the cooperative business and thus aims to integrate new members more effectively. Some interviewees emphasized that the mentoring is specifically valuable for its contribution to enhancing feelings of belonging to the community.

For effective and democratic decision-making, some social cooperatives embraced committee mechanisms. By establishing committees dedicated to specific functions or tasks, social cooperatives effectively distribute responsibilities among members, foster transparency, and promote democratic participation. This organizational approach not only enhances efficiency but also reflects the democratic ethos inherent in the cooperative movement. For example, in Consumer Coop, the cooperative operates through committees focusing on coordination, education, production, finance, and social media and communication. Similarly, Education Coop operates with four circles: project circle, finance circle, communication circle, management circle, technology circle, and transportation circle. Food & Agriculture Coop1 also operates in three committees: pricing, tasting, and social works. These three committees report to each other. Another cooperative, Business Support/Consultancy Coop1, uses a two-circle system: research circle and capacity building circle. They have a management circle that is separate from these two circles and remain solely responsible for issues regarding the cooperative's management. Whether it be circles, committees, or informal structures, social cooperatives emphasize the importance of sharing responsibilities while also maintaining transparency through reportability to all cooperative members.

Transparency emerged as an important principle for social cooperatives in the interviews. Specifically for matters concerning management and financial decisions, all cooperatives give importance to being transparent about their processes. For instance, Food & Agriculture Coop and Food & Agriculture Coop3 emphasized that they follow strict rules of reportability and transparency in their bookkeeping specifically, while Food & Agriculture Coop1 underlined being open to feedback and discussions about the cooperative's business. Embracing principles of open communication and transparency cultivates a trust-based organizational culture in which members actively engage with cooperative affairs, closely monitoring business activities. This approach not only encourages a sense of accountability but also fosters an environment where members feel secure in expressing their opinions and contributing to the cooperative's decision-making processes.

Use of technology was mentioned as a strategy for quicker decision-making rather than holding meetings every time they need to make a decision. This is particularly evident in systemic change cooperatives involved in the study. For instance, Business Support&Consultancy Coop2 stated that they prefer to use WhatsApp and Sustainable Tourism & Culture-Art Coop uses Telegram for communication among cooperative members and decision making. The pressing reason for choosing digital tools may be the fast pace of the operations in the cooperative and the necessity to arrive at a conclusive decision rather than delaying matters until the next board meeting. Here, integration of new technologies to the organizational model of social cooperatives becomes important to sustain impact by employing quick follow-up and decision-making processes.

Despite these democratic practices in management and organizational culture, occasionally, some difficulties arise in organizational culture. In line with what the literature suggests, cooperatives have organizational difficulty due to: low education level among members, especially in agricultural cooperatives, low participation of members in cooperative activities, low level of understanding of economic issues, little understanding of cooperative culture and working cooperatively, little experience in managing a business, and insufficient social capital (Duguid et al., 2015). These difficulties were also prominent in the interviewed social cooperatives. In some cooperatives, individuals decided to leave due to conflicts related to the cooperative's income mechanism or were dismissed from membership by cooperative members for contributing less to cooperative business than expected. For cooperatives that rely on volunteer labor, this becomes an imminent problem due to lack of dedication and irregularity in the number of volunteers. Although some cooperatives aim to compensate the given labor by hourly wages, participants highlighted that at times they could not prevent the conflict arising from receiving income irregularly.

Cooperatives formed with the guidance of visionary leaders, enjoy the privilege of following the leader to successfully achieve the social impact and overcome some of the organizational obstacles. Three cooperatives in the study underline the importance of leadership for the initial stages of building the business and a cooperative culture. The Food & Agriculture Coop3 was established in light of the interest in cooperatives by an influential and well-known individual in the community. Currently, when asked about the cooperative's founding story and impact, the interviewees mention the efforts made by this person and attribute the success of the cooperative to this visionary leader. Sustainable Tourism&Culture-Art Coop is founded based on the observations and dreams of an individual regarding the Mediterranean region. Cooperative's mission was defined according to this vision. This way, the principles and focus of the cooperative were clear from the beginning, and members could join with a prior understanding of this mission. The visionary leadership here, through predetermining the principles of the cooperative, fosters a belonging among new members to the mission of the cooperative.

Though having a leader can be advantageous to run cooperative business smoothly, some interviewees complained about the labor imbalance in the cooperative when other members fail to take ownership of cooperative business and fail to contribute as expected. Even though cooperatives are legally required to have seven founding members, some cooperatives in the establishment and early implementation stage place the management burden on a few active members. In these cases, leadership roles are taken up by one or two active members to ensure continuity and viability of cooperative business. For example, even though Food & Agriculture Coop5 has been active for six years, the interviewee, who is also the president of the cooperative, complained that she was left alone in the management and became the sole person responsible for cooperative activities. The interviewee describes her situation as;

I do everything here. Is this what a cooperative president does? You handle the sales. You attend the meetings. When necessary, you transport the workers to the field. If any equipment is missing in the field, you take care of it.

The reason for this is explained as lack of feeling belonging to the cooperatives' aim for creating social change. As creating belonging is a hard task, some cooperatives choose cooperative mission over member engagement and continue with the leadership model.

Despite some conflicts leading to dismissal from the cooperative, we see that cooperatives strive to resolve these processes with peaceful methods as much as possible. All cooperatives in the study prioritize open communication in conflict resolution, provide space for all conflicting parties to express their problems in disputes, and then resolve the conflict without any major rupture. To add, some cooperatives even received capacity building training on effective communication strategies to ensure fair and peaceful conflict resolution. This approach again shows that social cooperatives sustain a democratic approach in organizational culture, positing an example to the wider society. Here, it is also important to note that in the new generation of cooperatives, we see different characteristics such as a high level of education, a good knowledge of social and solidarity economy, mastery of cooperative principles and the culture of collective production, openness to collaboration and capacity building.

We contend that social cooperatives exemplify a commitment to non-hierarchical organizational structures, evident in their membership and decision-making mechanisms. Through practices such as involving existing members in selecting new members and convening regular general assemblies for collective decision-making, cooperatives ensure inclusivity and democratic participation. Additionally, the adoption of committee/circle mechanisms further enhances transparency and efficiency within cooperatives, reflecting their dedication to democratic principles. Despite these efforts, challenges such as conflicts related to income distribution and insufficient member engagement persist, highlighting the need for ongoing improvement and adaptation. By addressing these challenges and leveraging their collective strengths, social cooperatives can continue to serve as beacons of community empowerment and democratic organizing, further enhancing their impact in socioeconomic and sustainable development.

8. Reflection on the Impact of Social Cooperatives on the Socioeconomic Development

This study, in line with the existing literature, underscores that social cooperatives, as a form of organizing, offer various social and economic benefits. First of all, since social cooperatives prioritize social good as their missions, goods and services they provide are designed to meet the needs of the people in their region. Moreover, since they are people-oriented enterprises rather than profit-oriented, they aim to increase the market power of the local community by prioritizing cooperation. Their impactful work builds networks among sectors, markets, and regions. Secondly, cooperatives emphasize the participation of underrepresented or unrepresented groups into the workforce, hence, create positive socioeconomic changes. Thirdly, social cooperatives are businesses that are established by at least seven members coming together with small savings and uniting around a common purpose. Therefore, they are characterized as non-state actors and act independently in their management and decision-making. At the same time, they enable citizens to carry out impactful tasks collectively, which would be difficult for them to do individually. Finally, social cooperatives contribute to social equality and democratic life, as they adopt a structure in which each member has an equal say, both in terms of profit distribution and governance mechanisms. Drawing from the literature and the interviews with social cooperatives, the study suggests that, the social cooperatives, through the organizational model they embrace and the social impact they create, contribute to the socioeconomic development in Türkiye.

As social cooperatives embark on a journey to create social impact, they take into account the local characteristics of the region and the needs of the people living in the region to consolidate and expand their impact. In order to better understand the contribution of social cooperatives in socioeconomic and sustainable development, we conducted interviews with sixteen cooperatives operating in different regions and sectors and asked representatives of the cooperatives about the cooperative's foundation history, the encountered obstacles, the strategies implemented to sustain impact, and the cooperative's organizational model. As a result, we contend that social cooperatives remain impactful organizations, as they take social good as their primary motivation while also focusing on the social and economic development of the region they are operating in.

From the economic development aspect, cooperatives prioritize local development in all processes from production to sales. The localization of the cooperative's supply chains when purchasing raw materials and the local people working in production and sales offices are of great importance for local economic development. In this way, the cooperative not only increases its own sales and expands its impact area, but also contributes to the economic empowerment of the people—especially women—in the region. This economic impact extends to the families of people involved in the cooperative. By sending their children to school with the income they earn, members not only benefit their children's future but also contribute to the welfare of the community. They not only create avenues for social cooperatives to access different markets and regions, but also act as a bridge connecting social impact oriented consumers and local producers. We observe that the economic benefits generated also have a ripple effect across different sectors. It is possible to say that an agriculture and food cooperative not only contributes to the promotion of the local food in the region but also enhances gastronomic tourism in the area. This cross-sectoral impact becomes vital in the socioeconomic development of the region.

From the social development aspect, we see that a solidarity network is activated in the local region with the establishment of cooperatives. While this network works to promote the recognition of the region, it also acts as a catalyst to form a community of people who live in the same region but have not interacted with each other before. In some cooperatives, training activities are carried out in order to enhance the capacity of cooperative members, while others work to change the patriarchal mindset embedded in the society through including women in the workforce. In addition, cooperatives contribute to the sustainable development of the region by bringing fair trade and ethical production principles to the table. As cooperatives embrace these principles, the community gathered around them feel a responsibility towards learning them as well. Looking from a system change perspective, social cooperatives create impact in their respective sectors. One cooperative works to transform the conventional approach to education, while another cooperative strives to ignite an interest in sustainable agriculture. Hence, while cooperatives work to create socioeconomic change, they also become advocates for the social impact mission around which they were founded.

Despite the impact created by social cooperatives, the unstable support received from local authorities or funding agencies and the lack of sustainability of these resources jeopardize cooperatives' operations. The interviewees, when asked about the obstacles they faced in the cooperatives, underscored the hardships in financial regulations in Türkiye. They noted that the taxation system, which treats social cooperatives, and cooperatives in general, as traditional enterprises, places an immense financial burden on cooperatives' shoulders. Explaining this, Sustainable Tourism & Culture-Art Coop stated, "There is a need for legal regulation because the government currently views social cooperatives as profiting entities, much like a company. Therefore, you cannot receive donations without being subjected to income tax directly on the received donations. The government treats the donation as if you earned income." Thus, financial sustainability remains an ongoing problem for social cooperatives in Türkiye. In order to sustain their operations, social cooperatives need to diversify their income sources and this requires knowledge about different resources and application processes (INGEV & IPM, 2021). A change in financial regulations is necessary to accommodate the needs of social cooperatives and to support them in their efforts to contribute to socioeconomic development (for further information, see Üstün, 2024).

In addition to financial difficulties, cooperatives also tackle problems regarding member orientation, income generation, and labor equality. Though cooperatives experience organizational problems, they prioritize their social impact mission and find ways to sustain their operations. One of the ways they embrace is fostering open communication principles to remain as transparent and democratic as possible. Through openly discussing the problematic areas with all cooperative members and arriving at decisions by reaching consensus among members, cooperatives proactively engage in resolving issues at the source. We contend that social cooperatives become more resilient against crises due to their culture of solidarity and their focus on social benefits.

While this study offers new pathways for future research, it is important to recognize and discuss the inherent limitations in the research as well. Even though we paid attention to the sector, region, and size variety of the cooperatives involved in the study, this research focuses on findings of sixteen social cooperatives. This small sample size, while offering a close caption analysis of certain problems, may be limited to arrive at generalized conclusions. Thus, a bigger size study might be beneficial for offering a broader approach. On the other hand, a more focused study offering sector-specific or region-specific analysis could open a discussion into tailor-made support mechanisms or legal regulations for social cooperatives. In addition, this study encapsulates statements of founding/active members of the social cooperatives. For further analysis, a qualitative study with members, funders, volunteers, or customers would be fruitful for a thorough approach to understand the social impact of the cooperatives.

This study takes into account the variations in the development stages of the interviewed cooperatives. While the progress stages of the cooperatives were assessed using the ecosystem map published by the Turkish Social Entrepreneurship Network (ekosistem.sosyalgirisimcilikagi.org), the interviews revealed that some cooperatives were in the early implementation stage rather than the late implementation stage as indicated on the ecosystem map. Though this might alter the analysis results, variety in the stages of development offered insight into differences in created impact and experienced problems.

In Turkey, due to the absence of a specific legal definition for social cooperatives, those included in the study were selected based on their self-declarations and mission statements. Currently, the majority of the interviewed cooperatives do not generate significant income surplus. Consequently, some have not yet been able to fulfill the principle of "reinvesting profits into their mission." The classification of these cooperatives as "social cooperatives" could only be discussed when these cooperatives achieve a meaningful surplus in their operations. Here, it is important to note that this situation is expected in the developmental journey of social cooperatives, where achieving a substantial income surplus is a crucial milestone.

Cooperatives are not a new phenomenon in Turkey, but social cooperative is an organization model that has become increasingly important as social inequalities have increased. By adopting principles such as fair production, equal distribution of resources and participatory policies, social cooperatives, organizing non-hierarchically, show that a more egalitarian and participatory model is possible and moreover necessary for sustainable development.

References

Akgöz, Sedat, & Ercan, Emre (2012). Sosyal kooperatifçilik ve ülkemizdeki yeri. *Üçüncü Sektör Sosyal Ekonomi, 47* (1), 31–43.

CECOP. (2021). Lasting impact: Measuring the social impact of worker and social cooperatives in Europe: Focus on Italy and Spain. Retrieved from: https://cecop.coop/works/new-publication-lasting-impact-measuring-the-social-impact-of-worker-and-social-cooperatives-in-europe-focus-on-italy-and-spain

CICOPA. (2004). World standards of social cooperatives. Retrieved from https://www.cicopa.coop/wp-content/uploads/2017/12/World-Standards-of-Social-Cooperatives_EN-1-1.pdf

Cinar, K., Akyuz, S., Ugur-Cinar, M., & Onculer-Yayalar, E. (2021). Faces and phases of women's empowerment: The case of women's cooperatives in Turkey. *Social Politics, 28*(3), 778–805.

Duguid, F., Durutaş, G., & Wodzicki, M. (2015). The current state of women's co-operatives in Turkey. *The World Bank*. Retrieved from https://www.aile.gov.tr/KSGM/PDF/Turkiyede_Kooperatifcilik_Kadin_ENG.pdf

Guttmann, A. (2021). Commons and cooperatives: A new governance of collective action. *Ann Public Coop Economy, 92*, 33–53.

Hatipoglu, B. K. (2021). "Community-based social enterprises and social innovation: The case of women's cooperatives in Turkey". In D. M. Wasieleski & J. Weber (Eds.), *Social entrepreneurship* (Business and society 360, Vol. 5, pp. 97–118). Leeds: Emerald Publishing Limited. https://doi.org/10.1108/S2514-175920220000005005

Hernández Cáceres, D. (2023). Social enterprise in the social cooperative form. In H. Peter, C. V. Vasserot, & J. A. Silva (Eds.), In *The international handbook of social enterprise law: Benefit corporations and other purpose-driven companies* (pp. 173–192). Springer.

ICA (International Cooperative Alliance). Cooperative identity, values and principles. Accessed 25 February 2024. Retrieved from https://ica.coop/en/cooperatives/cooperative-identity

INGEV & IPM. (2021). Sosyal dayanışma ekonomisi için güçlü kooperatifçilik. Retrieved from https://ingev.org/raporlar/Sosyal_Dayanisma_Ekonomisi_icin_Guclu_Kooperatifcilik.pdf

Kızıldağ, D. (2019). "Women's cooperatives as a tool of employment policy in Turkey". In S. Grima, E. Özen, H. Boz, J. Spiteri, & E. Thalassinos (Ed.), *Contemporary issues in behavioral finance* (Contemporary Studies in Economic and Financial Analysis, Vol. 101, pp. 65–76). Leeds: Emerald Publishing Limited. https://doi.org/10.1108/S1569-375920190000101006

Köne, Aylin Çiğdem (2021). Kurulan ve kapanan kooperatif istatistikleri. Sosyal Ekonomi. Retrieved from https://sosyalekonomi.org/kurulan-ve-kapanan-kooperatif-istatistikleri/

Küme, Nilay (2021). Sosyal fayda odaklı yeni nesil kooperatifçilik: Sosyal kooperatifler. *Medium.* Retrieved from https://medium.com/gurceskop/sosyal-fayda-odakl%C4%B1-yeni-nesil-kooperatif%C3%A7ilik-sosyal-kooperatifler-d0462b1e3607

Mancino, A., & Thomas, A. (2005). An Italian pattern of social enterprise: The social cooperative. *Nonprofit Management and Leadership, 15*, 357–369. https://doi.org/10.1002/nml.73

Münkner, Hans-H. (2016). How co-operative are social co-operatives?. *Cooperativismo e Economia Social (CES), 38*, 33–75. ISSN: 1130-2682.

Needs Map. https://www.needsmap.coop/

OECD. (2022). Designing legal frameworks for social enterprises: Practical guidance for policy makers. Retrieved from https://www.oecd.org/cfe/designing-legal-frameworks-for-social-enterprises-172b60b2-en.htm

Sosyo-Ekonomik Gelişmişlik Sıralaması Araştırma Raporları. TC. Sanayi ve Teknoloji Bakanlığı. Retrieved from: https://www.sanayi.gov.tr/merkez-birimi/b94224510b7b/sege

Turkey Social Enterprise Network (TSEN). (2022). European social enterprise monitor Türkiye country report. Retrieved from https://esem.sosyalgirisimcilikagi.org/

TUSEV. (2018). Sosyal kooperatifçilik: Yasal mevzuat açısından Avrupa Birliği örnekleri ve Türkiye'deki gelişmeler. https://tusev.org.tr/wp-content/uploads/2024/06/TUSEVAtolye_SosyalKooperatfiler1.pdf

Utting, P. (2016). *Mainstreaming social and solidarity economy: Opportunities and risks for policy change. UN Task Force on SSE (TFSSE) Publication. Retrieved from http://base.socioeco.org/docs/paper-mainstreaming-sse-12-november-2016-edituntfsse.pdf*

Üstün, Yusuf (2024). Kooperatiflerin üzerindeki haksız vergi yükü. *Sosyal Ekonomi.* Retrieved from https://sosyalekonomi.org/kooperatiflerin-uzerindeki-haksiz-vergi-yuku/

Youth Deal Cooperative. https://gencisi.org/en/youth-deal-cooperative/

Senem Göl Beşer
Yeditepe University

Begüm Ötken
North Caroline University

Chapter 8 Empowering Communities: The *Good4Trust* Model for Social Entrepreneurship and Shared Economy

Abstract: Shared economy and social entrepreneurship are two prominent concepts that have gained a significant grip in recent years due to their potential to address social inequality and environmental sustainability. Walsh, B (2011) listed the shared economy as one of the ten ideas that will change the world. Without a doubt, it is causing significant upheaval intraditional industries.

While the shared economy seeks to promote the continuous circulation of materials and resources through various strategies such as recycling, reusing, and reducing, it also presents economic opportunities by fostering by innovation, job creation, and the development of new markets for recycled products. On the other hand, social entrepreneurs seek to create sustainable and innovative solutions by applying entrepreneurial principles to systemic problems such as poverty, environmental degradation, and access to health and education.

These two concepts intersect as both share common goals of sustainability, resource optimization and positive societal impact. Many social entrepreneurs embrace shared economy principles in their operations. The collaboration between these concepts represents a complementary approach towards innovative solutions in addressing environmental, economic, and socio-cultural challenges more holistically.

This chapter aims to provide a concise overview and understanding of shared economy and social entrepreneurship concepts within an emerging market in a prosumer economy. It also highlights a successful example of where circular practices and social entrepreneurship intersect via a community system named *Good4Trust*. The initiative acts as a disruptive internet technology platform whilst behaving as a utility in organizing prosumers into an economy. Within the online platform, both the producers and consumers get together to build a prosumer economy, a new shared economy formed and governed by the people participating within that system. Communicating with each other through the internet platform, producers are involved in nature-friendly production and support each other with the established system. By focusing on shared economy and social entrepreneurship and bringing *Good4Trust* initiative to attention as a best example, we aim to help policymakers, academicians, and other stakeholders advance in initiatives that contribute to a more regenerative economy while promoting social equity and well-being within the given system.

Keywords: Prosumer economy, shared economy, social entrepreneurship, Good4Trust

1. Shared Economy

The concept of the shared economy has garnered considerable attention in academic literature, encompassing various definitions and facets. This section provides an informative overview of the sharing economy, a modern concept that heavily relies on internet-based platforms to facilitate interactions between individuals.

The idea of "sharing" is not new, it has been present since ancient times. However, it got enormous attention in the last decade. Sharing can be defined as the common use of resources. Sharing economy emerged from the idea of collaborative consumption and as an economic model it aims to realize cooperative consumption through lease, exchange of goods and services, and centralized sourcing. With the developments in technology, specifically in Internet technology, the shared economy became prominently common in individuals' lives. It brought about great changes in individuals' behaviors, mindsets, and economics as well (Wang, 2022).

The basic characteristic of a shared economy is to bring demand and supply over the Internet. It is based mainly on collaboration and communication. It contributes to the increasing of society's well-being, even without producing new goods (Dirgova et al., 2018). The shared economy encompasses a diverse spectrum of terminologies, including descriptors like "asset-light lifestyle", "collaborative consumption", "collaborative economy", "peer economy", "access economy", or "sharing economy" (Böckmann, 2013). At its core, the shared economy embodies a shift from conventional commercial channels to internet-based platforms. The sharing economy enables the exchange, sharing, or temporary access to various goods, services, and resources without the involvement of traditional commercial channels, thereby promoting more efficient and cost-effective transactions (Andersson et al., 2013; Botsman, 2013; Barnes & Mattsson, 2016). Its priority lies in access over ownership, promoting optimal utilization of goods, labor, and knowledge. The shared economy encompasses diverse forms of exchange, from for-profit services to voluntary peer-to-peer sharing and gifting, all made possible by online marketplaces or platforms. In other words, it consists of various actors, initiatives, and platforms.

Key characteristics of the shared economy include the coordination of resource acquisition and distribution, often involving non-monetary compensation such as bartering, swapping, or renting, albeit excluding activities lacking compensation o involving permanent ownership transfer (Belk, 2014). This notion is echoed by Bellotti et al. (2015) highlighting the utilization of web and mobile technologies to distribute power and value among users, thereby optimizing the use of various assets including, labor, and knowledge. Another important characteristic of a shared economy lies in its ability to create two-sided consumers meaning consumers become both the providers and consumers of an experience or resource. Rather than just being only consumers or providers, individuals become prosumers and engage in collaborative consumption completing the value co-creation process.

Additionally, the shared economy embodies voluntary peer-to-peer sharing facilitated by online exchange markets and mediation platforms (Benjaafar, Kong, & Li, 2015). In 2015, the European Parliament characterized the sharing economy as an emerging socio-economic model propelled by the technological revolution, leveraging the Internet to connect individuals via online platforms for securely and transparently conducting transactions involving goods and services.

It prioritizes access and utilization over ownership, thereby maximizing underutilized resources, an aspect echoed by various scholars (Böckmann, 2013; Dervojeda et al., 2013; Cheng, 2016; Balaram, 2016).

Moreover, the shared economy is marked by a redefined market behavior through technological intervention, involving a spectrum of activities such as renting, lending, gifting, and swapping (Botsman & Rogers, 2010; Carroll & Bellotti, 2015). It also signifies a shift from fixed employment contracts to a more flexible work system, primarily observed in two-sided markets connecting service providers and consumers (Chen & Sheldon, 2016).

The integration of the sharing economy across various realms of human activity is commonly seen as a crucial foundation for advancing sustainable development. Serving as a fundamental pillar, the sharing economy enhances market efficiency, fosters price, and service quality awareness, and ensures improved market accessibility for everyone (Blazek, 2021).

The advent of online platforms has been pivotal in facilitating peer-to-peer interactions, empowering users to share and make use of underutilized goods and services (Filippas & Gramstad, 2016; Gheitasy et al., 2015). These platforms, operating as marketplaces, enable individuals to access physical resources or engage in fee-based sharing, illustrating the diverse range of activities embraced within the shared economy (Fang et al., 2016; Martin, 2015; Zervas et al., 2017).

There are a growing number of social and business companies using the shared economy business models. Car and bike sharing (*e.g.*, Zipcar and Hubway), accommodation sharing (*e.g.*, Airbnb), ride sharing (*e.g.*, Uber and Bolt), labor services (*e.g.*, Upwork and Taskrabbit), used goods (*e.g.*, eBay) are the most well-known companies (Fradkin, 2017). Especially, Uber and Airbnb were studied abundantly in the related literature as the best examples of shared economy.

Liang et al. (2018) research delved into Airbnb consumers' propensity to re-use the platform, highlighting the significance of perceived authenticity within the shared economy alongside perceived value, perceived risk, and price sensitivity; findings revealed that Airbnb users prioritize authentic local experiences, emphasizing a desire beyond mere affordability when considering repeat usage of Airbnb services.

In summary, the literature reflects the shared economy as a multifaceted phenomenon, driven by technological advancements, facilitating peer-to-peer interactions, and promoting the efficient use of resources while redefining traditional market behaviors and employment structures. In the next section, we will take a closer look at the two-sided consumer model, prosumer economy.

2. Prosumer Economy

The aforementioned sharing economy has revolutionized conventional business norms, reshaping the roles of firms and consumers alike. A pivotal aspect of this transformation is the emergence of "prosumers," individuals who seamlessly transition between the roles of providers and consumers within the marketplace. This dynamic shift underscores the importance of leveraging network effects within the sharing economy.

The advancement of technology, especially Internet technology and the rise of Web 2.0, has triggered this new approach allowing companies to collaborate with different types of consumers (i.e., prosumers) who engage in both production and consumption activities.

Today, consumers are more knowledgeable, experienced, and demanding than ever due to globalization and technology and they want to be more active in the market. They no longer want to decide whether to buy the products offered by the companies, but they want to be active in the production by informing them about their needs and expectations. The result of this new relationship is the concept of prosumption (Bartosik-Purgat & Bednarz, 2020).

Toffier was the first to put forward the prosumption concept. Although prosumption was not clearly introduced in Toffier's book called Future Shock in 1970, it was then explored and explicitly put forward by him in his The Third Wave book in the 1980s. He identified that it is gradually getting difficult to separate the producer from the consumer because of customer-centered manufacturing. During his later research, he dug deeper and found out that consumers are not just giving money for the products but also sharing important data and knowledge related to the production of those products (Bruns, 2013). Today, prosumption activity characterized by sharing is becoming a new economic and social form across the world (Tian et al., 2017).

Prosumption includes both production and consumption rather than focusing on either production or consumption. The goal is to create a balanced approach to economic activities. However, within the prosumer economy, there exists a crucial principle known as the golden rule. Traditionally, this rule advocates for treating "others" as one would like to be treated, emphasizing human interactions. Yet, from an anthropocentric perspective, it often only considers humans. To foster harmony with the planet, there's a need to expand the golden rule to encompass all living and nonliving entities. In the prosumer economy, the idea is to extend the golden rule to include all beings on Earth, not just limited to humans (Cevirme et al., 2023).

Unlike the consumer economy, the prosumer economy is characterized by Özesmi (2019) as a:

> *macro-scale circular economy with minimum negative, or even positive, ecological and social impact, an ecosystem of producers and prosumers, who have synergies and circular relationships with deepened circular supply chains, networks, where leakage of wealth out of the system is minimized (…) In a prosumer economy there is no waste, no lasting negative impacts on the ecology, and no social exploitation (…) The prosumer economy is like a laker or forest, an economic ecosystem that is productive, built-on synergistic relationships, and supportive to the planet.*

Prosumers by their two-sided activity contribute to environmental problems such as pollution, socio-economic challenges such as lowering the economic cost, poverty, and hyper-consumption (Diniz et al., 2019). Prosumption focuses on the production of goods and services, but what defines the prosumer alone is not the engagement in the production process. Instead, prosumers achieve their subjective experiences by applying personal thoughts, innovative ideas, and unique elements to production activities. It provides prosumer a subjective experience so that they can go beyond mundane economic gains (Wolf et al., 2023).

Encouraging one-sided users, whether they are consumers (such as Airbnb guests) or providers (like Airbnb hosts), to embrace both roles and engage as prosumers enhances the collective power and effectiveness of the sharing economy. For instance, individuals who participate as both Airbnb guests and hosts exemplify the versatile nature of prosumers, embodying the collaborative ethos that drives the sharing economy forward.

Thus, in this study, we diverge from the conventional shared economy perspective to explore a distinct angle, focusing on a social enterprise endeavor known as Good4Trust. This innovative initiative is dedicated to fostering a community-oriented environment that promotes equitable and environmentally sustainable production practices. As we delve into the realm of social entrepreneurship in the following section, Good4Trust serves as a prime exemplar of how businesses can integrate social and environmental objectives into their operations while concurrently generating positive impacts within their communities.

3. Social Entrepreneurship

> *Community actually cannot be achieved when it's an end in itself. Community is a result of people doing something together that they care about. Giving their gifts. Community is a matter of giving gifts. It's woven together through gifts and mutual gratitude. And mutual obligation, which isn't a bad thing, obligation. It's a knowing. Community is when you look at someone and you know that you need them. I need you. I need you.*
>
> *Charles Eisenstein, 2023*

Although the social entrepreneurship concept dates to the 1950s, it got increased attention from scholars within the broader field of entrepreneurship, in the last decade. Social entrepreneurship has been recognized for its potential to address poverty (Ghauri et al., 2014), promote women's empowerment (Datta & Gailey, 2012), instigating social transformation (Alvord et al., 2004), facilitating inclusive growth in subsistence marketplaces (Azmat et al., 2015), and instigating institutional change (Nicholls, 2008). These aspects encompass diverse and distinct phenomena within the realm of social entrepreneurship. Since it has gained attention in many diverse fields, this diversity has resulted in several definitions.

Various scholars have defined social entrepreneurship based on different aspects, including the behavioral traits of the social entrepreneur, the mission of the social enterprise, and the entrepreneurial activities that generate social value. Although there are diverse perspectives, most definitions underscore the hybrid nature of combining a social mission with entrepreneurial activities. They agree on the importance of creating social value as the primary goal of the organization. It is an important feature between social and commercial enterprises that focuses on alturism, honesty, equality and fairness (Diaz-Sarachaga & Montes, 2022). Simultaneously, the generation of economic value through commercial activities is viewed as essential but not adequate on its own (Saebi et al., 2019).

According to Austin et al. (p. 2), social entrepreneurship is described as an "innovative, social value-generating activity that can take place within or across nonprofit, business, or government sectors." It is crucial to highlight two key aspects of this definition. Firstly, the definition specifically emphasizes the importance of innovation. Social entrepreneurship inherently entails the application of novel technologies or approaches aimed at generating social value. Based on this, social entrepreneurs are like change agents in society by engaging in continuous adaptation, innovation, and learning. The second aspect emphasized by the definition is the diverse settings in which social entrepreneurship can unfold. It can encompass individual entrepreneurs, new or established entities, or governmental initiatives. In essence, there is no singular category of social entrepreneur (Certo & Miller, 2008).

Social entrepreneurship entails identifying, assessing, and capitalizing on opportunities that lead to the creation of social value—addressing fundamental and enduring societal needs—rather than solely focusing on personal or shareholder wealth (Austin et al., 2006). Social value is not primarily tied to financial gains but instead revolves around meeting essential and persistent needs, such as offering food, water, shelter, education, and medical services to those individuals in society requiring assistance.

Typically, social entrepreneurs initiate small-scale projects and they frequently address issues that may be locally specific. However, the results of their projects are significant on a global scale such as water accessibility, fostering small business development, reintegrating individuals into the workforce, and managing waste (Santos, 2012). Social entrepreneurship has substantial implications for the economic system by generating new industries, validating novel business models, and redirecting resources toward overlooked societal challenges.

There are some other concepts in the entrepreneurship literature, that are used interchangeably with social entrepreneurship or overlap with social entrepreneurship such as corporate social responsibility, non-profit organizations, or hybrid organizations. Although corporate social responsibility activities generate some social good for society beyond what is required by the law, these activities still could be seen with the company's goal of maximizing profits. Nonprofit social organizations, aim to contribute to social welfare by addressing fundamental and persistent needs like supplying food, water, shelter, education, and medical services to those in society who require them (Certo & Miller, 2008). Although these organizations may engage in income-generating activities as part of their overall budget, through fundraising and donations, the generated revenues are generally modest and tied to specific program durations. Moreover, by minimizing these income-generating activities, these organizations avoid the typical challenge of balancing conflicting institutional logic associated with social and economic value creation, which is a common characteristic in social entrepreneurship (Doherty et al., 2014). In addition to this, the income-generating activities of a nonprofit organization must last for a long time with growth and revenue to be called a social enterprise. Hybrid organizations including sustainable and development entrepreneurship may show similar characteristics as social entrepreneurship because these organizations aim to maintain economic sustainability while addressing a similar cause observed in social entrepreneurship. However, minor differences exist between these hybrid organizations and social enterprises (Saebi et al., 2019). For example, sustainable entrepreneurship involves carrying out actions that have the potential for sustainability benefits and converting these actions into products and services aligned with sustainability goals to generate shared value. It does not include sustaining current states of nature, sources of life support, and community (Shepherd & Patzelt, 2011). Development entrepreneurship can be considered a subpart of social entrepreneurship because it aims to change the existing social system to enhance social welfare. Social entrepreneurs have the same purpose, but not always. Social entrepreneurs don't need to change the existing institutions (McMullen, 2011). Keeping in mind the definition of social entrepreneurship as the initiation of a hybrid organizational structure that generates social value through market-driven approaches, creating new organizations or innovative management of existing organizations makes social entrepreneurship a different concept than any other form of entrepreneurship (Saebi et al., 2019).

While the lines between social and business realms may be blurred and interconnected, it remains crucial for social entrepreneurs to articulate a well-defined mission, outline planned outcomes, and establish measurable objectives. Securing capital, maintaining investor appeal, and leveraging resources when necessary are contingent on legitimacy, a challenge frequently encountered by social-entrepreneurial endeavors (Chandna, 2022).

4. Good4Trust.org

In 2014, a prominent social entrepreneur, Dr. Uygar Özesmi, pioneered the fusion of the prosumer economy, shared economy, and social entrepreneurship by establishing *Good4Trust,* a non-profit, community system in Turkey. The community's fundamental objective is to promote happiness/goodness by fostering a symbiotic relationship between responsible producers who create commodities that are socially and ecologically fair, and prosumers who fulfill their needs. This collaboration between these stakeholders strives to forge a world capable of addressing the adverse effects of current-day lifestyles and endure for future generations. Notably, the organization's membership-based system proposition supported by its authentic software is a global first.

One of the Council of Seven Members quoted: "*Prosumers are the ones who refuse the two polar definitions of the growth economy knowing that every producer is also a consumer and every consumer is a producer*" (cited in Özesmi, 2019). The system aims to form a global community that thrives to "*create a future where people live in peace and in harmony with nature*".

Özesmi (2019) outlines that the specific term prosumer was first defined in the 1980s by Toffier as a proactive consumer who is involved in the design and improvement of goods and services.

The term has evolved to describe an empowered consumer who consumes what they produce, and this is in multiple forms, which may or may not involve brands or the market (Paltrinieri & Esposti, 2013; cited in Özesmi, 2019). Under the private enterprise system where globalization prolifies and institutionalized production dominates the market, the prosumer economy creates a venue for local and small businesses.

When Good4Trust's platform's software structures the economy as an open source, their intention was in synch with the prosumer economy definition by Paltrinieri and Esposti (2013) as "a commons-based prosumerism arising from the use of social media to promote civic engagement and building relationships based on specific interests and mutual trust, through a process in which citizenship is activated in actions of mutual support".

Good4Trust as an online bazaar has set its foundation based on portraying civic virtues such as charity, volunteering, and bonded relationships as well as supporting ecologically and socially just production. As a non-profit social enterprise, Good4Trust upholds core values such as trust, transparency, fairness, and peace. Its ultimate goal is to act with benevolence, promote positive principles and goodness, and advocate for non-violent solutions.

Good4Trust is a legal, social enterprise that stands out for its unique mindset and terminology. It is established as a limited liability company and according to the company statement, all its shares are investment shares; as such, the company does not distribute profit as a requirement of its memorandum of association (Uygur & Franchini, 2019).

As stated on their website, there are more than 25,000 prosumers and more than 770 producers and Good4Trust gets a contribution between 3 % and 7 % for each transaction in the market to compensate for its maintenance costs. The organization has also launched a Supporter Program in 2018 to meet its financial obligations based on monthly e-bulletin subscriptions constituting 16.5 % of Good4Trust.org's operating income in 2022.

Good4Trust has adopted Endenburg and Charest (1981) sociocracy paradigm instead of a traditional hierarchical organizational structure. This approach uses a circular (team-like) design that is equidistant from the decision-making mechanism. In this particular organizational structure, a circle acts as a policy-making unit of a group of people with a common work objective (Korhonen, 2007). As of 2022, Good4Trust has a total of 11 circles, which include the Producer Relations Circle and Mycelium (Supply Networks) Circle, to promote more participatory decision-making.

The governance body under the name of the "Council of Seven" is selected among the most active prosumers of the Good4Trust community, making decisions on the acceptance and withdrawal of the producers, along with guidance to the general management policies where necessary.

As part of the inclusiveness principle, all producers can open a shop if they sign a declaration of intent and share their production process. Their application is forwarded to the Council of Seven which votes and decides whether the producer is intentional, determined, or fair.

Local producers must prioritize working in harmony with nature by avoiding toxic materials and waste, as well as adopting clean energy and fair working conditions. Prosumers, on the other hand, are encouraged to communicate their needs and preferences and participate in governance to ensure that the system is serving the community's best interests.

The council's evaluations and prosumer feedback provide valuable insight into areas where producers can improve. Progress is closely monitored through periodic assessments, and additional recommendations for improvement are issued as needed. Producers are in solidarity with each other and can solve problems together. Thus, if operated according to these principles and adhering to a goodness-based structure, this strengthens the community and transforms the economy.

Good4Trust's Grasshopper program (Good4Trust Annual Report, 2017) symbolizes the embodiment of its empowering philosophy, offering consulting and training services for social entrepreneurs who evolve into experts in generating social benefits in time. This initiative perfectly aligns with Good4Tust's mission, empowering individuals to both consume and produce goods and services collaboratively within a shared framework, thus fostering social impact.

Good4Trust embodies an innovative blend of the prosumer economy, shared economy, and social entrepreneurship, ushering in a new era of collaborative empowerment and community-driven impact. At its core, Good4Trust fosters a dynamic ecosystem where individuals seamlessly transition from mere consumers to active contributors through collaborative consumption and participatory production. This embodies the essence of the prosumer economy, wherein participants engage not only in consumption but also in the creation and sharing of goods and services.

Furthermore, Good4Trust embodies the principles of the shared economy by leveraging collective resources and assets to foster communal benefit. Through its innovative programs and initiatives, such as the Grasshopper program, Good4Trust empowers social entrepreneurs to become knowledgeable generators, driving social benefit production over time.

Dr. Özesmi's visionary initiative epitomizes the transformative potential of social entrepreneurship, demonstrating how innovative business models can effectively address societal challenges while promoting regenerative practices and widespread prosperity. By nurturing a culture of collaboration and social responsibility, Good4Trust stands as a beacon of hope for a more equitable and prosperous future.

References

Alvord, S. H., Brown, L. D., & Letts, C. W. (2004). Social entrepreneurship and societal transformation. *Journal of Applied Behavioral Science, 40*, 260–282.

Andersson, M., Hjalmarsson, A., & Avital, M. (2013). Peer-to-peer service sharing platforms: Driving share and share alike on a mass-scale. In *International Conference of Information Systems 2013, Milan, Italy*. Association for Information Systems.

Austin, J., Stevenson, H., & ei-Skillern, J. (2006). Social and commercial entrepreneurship: Same, different, or both? *Entrepreneurship Theory and Practice, 30*(1), 1–22.

Azmat, F., Ferdous A. S., & Couchman, P. (2015). Understanding the dynamics between social entrepreneurship and inclusive growth in subsistence marketplaces. *Journal of Public Policy & Marketing*, 34: 252–271.

Balaram, B. (2016). Fair share. *Reclaiming power in the sharing economy. RSA Action and Research Center*.

Barnes, S. J., & Mattsson, J. (2016). Understanding current and future issues in collaborative consumption: A four-stage Delphi study. *Technological Forecasting and Social Change, 104*, 200–211.

Bartosik-Purgat, M., & Bednarz, J. (2020). The usage of new media tools in prosumer activities—A corporate perspective. *Technology Analysis and Strategic Management*, 33(4), 453–464.

Bruns, A. (2013). *Prosumption, produsage*. In *Handbook on the digital creative economy*.

Belk, R. (2014). You are what you can access: Sharing and collaborative consumption online. *Journal of Business Research, 67*(8), 1595–1600.

Bellotti, V., Ambard, A., Turner, D., Gossmann, C., Demkova, K., & Carroll, J. M. (2015, April). A muddle of models of motivation for using peer-to-peer economy systems. In *Proceedings of the 33rd annual ACM conference on human factors in computing systems* (pp. 1085–1094).

Benjaafar, S., Kong, G., & Li, X. (2015). Modeling and analysis of collaborative consumption in peer-to-peer car sharing. *ACM SIGMETRICS Performance Evaluation Review, 43*(3), 87–90.

Blazek, L. (2021). Trends in the Development of the Sustainability of a Shared Economy. *Proceedings of the European Conference on Innovation & Entrepreneurship*, pp. 118–127. https://doi.org/10.34190/EIE.21.098

Böckmann, M. (2013). *The shared economy: It is time to start caring about sharing; value-creating factors in the shared economy*. University of Twente, Faculty of Management and Governance, 350.

Botsman, R. (2013). The sharing economy lacks a shared definition.(2013). *Online: Online:https://www.fastcompany.com/3022028/the-sharing-economy-lacks-a-shared-definition.*

Botsman, R., & Rogers, R. (2010). Beyond Zipcar: Collaborative consumption. *Harvard Business Review, 88*(10), 30.

Carroll, J. M., & Bellotti, V. (2015, February). Creating value together: The emerging design space of peer-to-peer currency and exchange. In *Proceedings of the 18th ACM Conference on Computer Supported Cooperative Work & Social Computing* (pp. 1500–1510).

Certo, S. T., & Miller, T. (2008). Social entrepreneurship: Key issues and concepts. *Business Horizonz, 51*, 267–271.

Cevirme, E. T., Satici, E. E., & Ozesmi, U. (2023). Can the Prosumer economy be the posthumanist economy? *Journal of Posthumanism, 3*(3), 287–294.

Chandna, V. (2022). Social entreprenuership and digital platforms: Crowfunding in the sharing economy era. *Business Horizons, 65*(1), 21–31.

Chen, M. K., & Sheldon, M. (2016). Dynamic pricing in a labor market: Surge pricing and flexible work on the Uber platform. *Ec, 16*, 455.

Cheng, M. (2016). Current sharing economy media discourse in tourism. *Annals of Tourism Research, 60*, 111–114.

Datta, P. B., & Gailey, R. (2012). Empowering women through social entrepreneurship: Case study of a women's cooperative in India. *Entrepreneurship: Theory & Practice, 36*, 569–587.

Dervojeda, K., Verzijl, D., Nagtegaal, F., Lengton, M., Rouwmaat, E., Monfardini, E., & Frideres, L. (2013). The sharing economy. *Accessibility-Based Business*

Models for Peer-to-Peer Markets, Business Innovation Observatory, European Commission.

Diaz-Sarachaga, J. M., & Montes, A. A. (2022). The role of social entreperenurship in the attainment of the Sustainable Development Goals. *Journal of Business Research, 152*, 242–250.

Diniz, E. H., Siqueira, E. S., & van Heck, E. (2019). Taxonomy of digital community currency platforms. *Information Technology for Development, 25*(1), 69–91. https://doi.org/10.1080/02681102.2018.1485005

Dirgova, E., Janickova, J., & Klenkova, J. (2018). New trends in the labor market in the context of shared economy. *TEM Journal, 7*(4), 791–797.

Doherty, B., Haugh, H., & Lyon, F. (2014). Social enterprises as hybrid organizations: A review and research agenda. *International Journal of Management Reviews, 16*, 417–436.

Endenburg, G., & Charest, G. (1981). La sociocratie. *Alphen aan den Rijn: Samsom.*

Ghauri, P. N., Tasavori M., & Zaefarian, R. (2014). Internationalisation of service firms through corporate social entrepreneurship and networking. *International Marketing Review, 31*, 576–600.

Fang, B., Ye, Q., & Law, R. (2016). Effect of sharing economy on tourism industry employment. *Annals of Tourism Research, 57*, 264–267.

Filippas, A., & Gramstad, A. R. (2016). A model of pricing in the sharing economy: Pricing dynamics with awareness-generating adoptions. In *Icis.*

Fradkin, A. (2017). Search, matching, and the role of digital marketplace design in enabling trade: Evidence from Airbnb. Retrieved from: https://papers.ssrn.com/sol3/papers.cfm?abstract_id=2939084.

Good4Trust. (2017) Annual Activity Report. Available at: https://good4trust.org/ reports (Last retrieved on 11 November, 2023).

https://good4trust.org (Lastly retrieved: 11.21.2023).

Korhonen, J. (2007). On the lookout for organizational effectiveness–requisite control structure in BPM governance. In *1st International Workshop on BPM Governance–WoGo* (Vol. 1).

Liang, L. J., Choi, H. C., & Joppe, M. (2018). Understanding repurchase intention of Airbnb consumers: Perceived authenticity, electronic word-of-mouth, and price sensitivity. *Journal of Travel & Tourism Marketing, 35*(1), 73–89.

Martin, C. J. (2015). "The sharing economy: A pathway to sustainability or a new nightmarish form of neoliberalism?" *Ecological Economics, 121*, 149–159.

McMullen, J. S. (2011). Delineating the domain of development entrepreneurship: A market-based approach to facilitating inclusive economic growth. *Entrepreneurship: Theory & Practice*, 35, 185–215.

Nicholls A. (2008). *Social entrepreneurship: New models of sustainable social change*. Oxford: Oxford University Press.

Özesmi, U. (2019). The prosumer economy—Being like a forest. *arXiv preprint arXiv:1903.07615.*

Paltrinieri, R., & Esposti, P. D. (2013). Processes of inclusion and exclusion in the sphere of prosumerism. *Future Internet, 5*(1), 21–33.

Saebi, T., Foss, N. J., & Linder, S. (2019). Social entrepreneurship research: Past achievement and future promises. *Journal of Management, 45*(1), 70–95.

Santos, F. M. (2012). A positive theory of social entrepreneurship. *Journal of Business Ethics, 111*(3), 335–351.

Shepherd, D. A., & Patzelt, H. (2011). The new field of social entrepreneurship: Studying entrepreneurial action linking "What is to be Sustained" With "What is to be Developed". *Entrepreneurship Theory and Practice, 35*(1), 137–163.

Tian, J., Shen, L., & Chen, Y. (2017). A study on customer prosumption concept and its impact on enterprise value co-creation. *Theoretical Economic Letters, 7*(10), 2040–2053.

Uygur, D., & Franchini, B. (2019). *Social enterprises and their ecosystems in Europe*. Luxembourg: Publications Office of the European Union.

Walsh, B. (2011, March 17). "10 Ideas that will change the world". *Time Magazine.*

Wang, S. (2022). Theoretical analysis framework of a shared economy supervision and management model using mobile information system data. *Neural Computing and Application,* https://doi.org/10.1007/s00521-022-07831-z

Wolf, M., Ritz, W., & McQitty, S. (2023). The role of affinity for prosumption experiences and values. *The Journal of Consumer Behavior, 22*, 43–55.

Zervas, G., Proserpio, D., & Byers, J. W. (2017). The rise of the sharing economy: Estimating the impact of Airbnb on the hotel industry. *Journal of marketing research, 54*(5), 687–705.

Ahmet Tuğrul Tuğer
Piri Reis University

Chapter 9 Sustainable Entrepreneurship in Circular Economy

Abstract: As an evolving subject, the Circular Economy offers new ways to combine social benefits, environmental benefits, and economic profit. Sustainable entrepreneurship combines the flow of entrepreneurship knowledge and ability with the re-used or re-gained resources. The aim of this chapter is to examine sustainable entrepreneurship in circular economy that have sustainability, closed loop resource use as their essential characteristic, in terms of value proposition. To review the sustainable entrepreneurship and social entrepreneurship in circular economy and investigate the barriers and enablers of sustainable entrepreneurship in circular economy, a systematic review of the literature is executed with an approach based on triple bottom line perspective. As a result, a synthesizing framework that reveals sustainable entrepreneurship in circular economy with the support from actual findings is offered. The chapter also underlines opportunities and challenges for researchers and entrepreneurs interested in sustainable and circular entrepreneurship.

Keywords: Sustainable Entrepreneurship, Circular Economy, Social Entrepreneurship

1. Introductıon

Following the economic growth along the heydays of industrial revolution and post-world war period, businesspeople, governments, citizens did not question their existing business models that rely on linear growth models but also increase anthropogenic carbon footprint on the planet despite the notices from ecologists (e.g., Leopold, 1949). A few decades later, the citizens acknowledged the growing ecological impact of solid waste resulting from simultaneous production and consumption (Kinnear et al., 1974). Despite the recognition of the environmental deterioration, all the stakeholders are still looking for immediate and long-term solution to alleviate the effects of global climate change (Brundtland, 1987; United Nations, 2015).

As an alternative to take, make, dispose model and end-of-life paradigm of linear economy, circular economy provides a cradle-to-cradle approach with restoration and social value via sustainable methods where waste becomes a resource of production (Bocken et al., 2016; Murray et al., 2017; Korhonen et al., 2018). Circular economy represents a paradigm shift in the ways that different stakeholders interrelate with natural resources to avoid the resource loss and increase the economic value (Suchek et al., 2022). The main principle of the circular economy is the social and sustainable responsibility of the companies to maintain the sustainable values of society and the broader approach that includes the stakeholders such as policy makers, citizens, shareholders, universities, conventional media, and social media (Lahti et al., 2018). Nevertheless, the actual habits of stakeholders require a bold renovation in the closed-loop ecosystem of circular economy. As Neumeyer et al. (2020) suggest, entrepreneurs are critical change agents that convince them to modify their perception, habits connected to linear economy model on the way to encourage consumers' and other stakeholders' involvement in the new economic activity.

Social and sustainable entrepreneurs may lead these changes in paradigms of economic and social life, offer new perspectives to exploit new sustainable opportunities and open the way for new entrepreneurial actions to contribute to economic, social, and environmental wellbeing (Crecente et al., 2021). Similarly, circular entrepreneurship, shortly described as the process of surveying and utilizing in a productive way the opportunities in circular economy, would open new social and sustainable paths that different stakeholders search for (Zucchella & Urban, 2019).

The adoption of circular economy principles requires a long-term total transformation for all stakeholders including government institutions, policy makers, companies, non-profit organizations, and citizens (e.g., consumers, entrepreneurs, managers, researchers) (Sørensen & Bærenholdt, 2020; Mehrotra & Jaladi, 2022; Costanza, 2023). In the circular economy context, entrepreneurship embodies a critical behavioral change of all stakeholders of the conventional linear economy. Yet, there are several types of business models and entrepreneurship in circular economy such as start-ups, social entrepreneurship, sustainable entrepreneurship, ecopreneurs, circular entrepreneurs (Juma et al., 2022; Suchek et al., 2022; Khan et al., 2022; Mehrotra & Jaladi, 2022; Costanza, 2023; Henry et al., 2023). Related business practices and researches offer a wide variety of new options and there is a need to review the emerging practices and findings in the circular entrepreneurship environment.

Social entrepreneurship, in line with circular economy's social value priority, is mainly determined to create social value by adopting sustainable principles (El Chaarani & Raimi, 2022). Social enterprises adopt financially sustainable strategies to pursue social aims, and address a wide a range of social problems including sustainability, poverty (e.g., cooperatives in textile and agribusiness). Likewise, sustainable entrepreneurship is the development of larger sustainability solutions that benefit society (Gupta & Matharu, 2022). Sustainable entrepreneurship contributes significantly to sustainable and social development. There are different enablers of green entrepreneurship in circular economy (such as technological, commercial, organizational, commercial, social, and environmental factors) (Mondal et al., 2023a). There is a need to interpret the cases and researches in circular economy from sustainable entrepreneurship lens with different enablers and barriers.

The aim of this chapter is to review sustainable entrepreneurship and social entrepreneurship as stimulating concepts in circular economy ecosystem. Different cases, researches in sustainable and circular entrepreneurship need a holistic view to better interpret the evolution of sustainable entrepreneurship. This chapter aims to give answers to the following research questions:

What is the current level of understanding of social entrepreneurship and sustainable entrepreneurship in circular economy?
What are the key factors, enablers, and barriers for sustainable entrepreneurship within the circular economy context?

Accordingly, this chapter aims to introduce briefly sustainable entrepreneurship, social entrepreneurship, their common points with circular entrepreneurship and to provide a literature review about the social value produced by social and sustainable entrepreneurship in circular economy. Thus, the remaining parts of this chapter are organized in the following way. After reviewing the current studies about sustainable entrepreneurship, circular economy, social entrepreneurship on Scopus database, the close link between sustainable entrepreneurship and social entrepreneurship is presented from the circular economy's closed-loop perspective. Moreover, the actual context of sustainable entrepreneurship is offered with cases and actual empirical findings from the related literature. The chapter concludes with suggestions for future studies on sustainable entrepreneurship in circular economy.

2. Methodology

With the aim of presenting the actual aspects connecting sustainable entrepreneurship and social entrepreneurship in circular economy, the data for the systematic literature review was extracted only from Scopus, since it is a wide-ranging source of indexed academic publications and data homogenization with multiple database search is avoided by relying on one source. The data extraction is executed by taking October 2023 as a deadline of publication and using the following keywords: "circular econom*" OR "circularit*" or "closed-loop*" or "sustainability" AND "entrepreneur*" within in the titles, abstracts and keywords in the case of Scopus. Based on the recommendation of Kraus et al. (2020) for entrepreneurship literature reviews, the search is limited to online databases and journal articles only. Additionally, the filter applied to article selection required only English language articles with no further filter on the research field to identify publications and capture all articles with relevance to the research. The search resulted in 245 documents.

The process of inclusion and exclusion is implemented according to the Prisma Protocol (Moher et al., 2009). The titles and abstracts of the articles are screened, included and excluded according to several exclusion criteria: (i) not written in English (n = 5), (ii) not issued in peer-reviewed conference papers or book sections (n = 65), (iii) published on topics other than social and sustainable entrepreneurship, such as labor, or technical studies (n = 60), (iv) focused on characteristics unconnected to the enablers and barriers of sustainable entrepreneurship (n = 70). After applying these criteria, 45 articles with research articles, systematic reviews, case studies and empirical studies concerning sustainable entrepreneurship, social entrepreneurship, and circular economy business models, are reviewed.

3. Findings

In the related literature, various types of sustainable entrepreneurs (e.g., ecopreneurs, grassroots entrepreneurs, circular entrepreneurs, green entrepreneurs) are described. To better interpret sustainable entrepreneurship, social entrepreneurship in circular economy context, it would be reasonable to review sustainable entrepreneurship and social entrepreneurship in the closed-loop system of circular economy without prioritizing profit purpose. Accordingly, the findings of the review of the chapter aim to provide common points between sustainable entrepreneurship and circular economy through the association of social, environmental value with the market value.

Sustainable Entrepreneurship

Sustainable entrepreneurship can be defined as "the preservation of nature, life support, and community in the pursuit of perceived opportunities to bring into existence future products, processes, and services for gain, where gain is broadly construed to include economic and non-economic gains to individuals, the economy, and society" (Shepherd & Patzelt, 2011: 142). This definition argues that businesses can have lucrative and sustainable objectives, like conserving the natural ecosystem and biodiversity, diminishing environmental degradation and climate change effects, water, air pollution, resource loss (Munoz & Cohen, 2018). Therefore, sustainable entrepreneurship is necessary to lead the business transformation among different stakeholders such as workforce, customers, policy makers, investors, and community.

Business ventures that combine sustainability with lucrative and/or social objectives support positive triple bottom line (people, profit, and planet) (Khan et al., 2022). The People deals with the responsibility of the company towards people such as human rights, gender equality, treatment of employees, and social humanitarian causes. The second dimension Planet highlights the position of the company towards the environment and the efforts to reduce the bad impact of its activities on the environment. The last dimension profit illustrates the basic objective of any business that is making profits. Sustainable entrepreneurship maintains a balance between the three dimensions.

Sustainable entrepreneurship is also connected to ecopreneurship or ecological entrepreneurship which seeks to understand how entrepreneurial action can help preserve the natural environment (Pastakia, 1998; Schaper, 2005). However, if ecopreneurship is part of sustainable entrepreneurship, it is not a synonym because it does not explicitly cover the sustainability of communities and the development of non-economic gains for individuals and societies (Shepherd & Patzelt, 2011).

Based on four case studies, Belz and Binder (2017) develop a model that describes the process of sustainable entrepreneurship including six stages: (i) distinguishing a social or ecological problem; (ii) recognizing a social or ecological opportunity; (iii) providing a double bottom line solution; (iv) progressing a triple bottom line solution; (v) funding a sustainable enterprise; (vi) producing or entering a sustainable market.

To compare sustainable entrepreneurship against regular entrepreneurs, Hoogendoorn et al. (2019) offer three arguments: market imperfections, institutional changes, and a wider knowledge source stimulate complementary challenges to the start, advance, and success of sustainable entrepreneurs. Sustainable entrepreneurs can perceive more institutional barriers concerning the lack of financial, administrative, and informational support at business start-up than regular entrepreneurs. Moreover, sustainable entrepreneurs appear to be more afraid of personal failure than regular entrepreneurs, because of the varied and challenging stakeholder relations.

In a systematic review of sustainable entrepreneurship literature, Munoz and Cohen (2018) resume several, mainly for profit and non-profit entrepreneurship definitions, motivations, objectives, barriers; and recommend that the perfect distinction among eco entrepreneurship, social entrepreneurship and sustainable entrepreneurship is offered by Schaltegger and Wagner (2011) relying on four aspects: core motivation, objectives, role of non-market objectives and organizational change. These four aspects support sustainable entrepreneurship's contribution to solve social and ecological problems via successful business ventures.

Social Entrepreneurship and Sustainable Entrepreneurship

Conventional nonprofit organizations faced the reduction of private and government funding and transformed into social enterprises integrating commercial profits to finance a social project (Ko & Liu, 2021). In this context, social entrepreneurship represents the association of social logic and the market by creating an optimum level of financial, social, and environmental value (Stubbs, 2017). As a process of taking professional and entrepreneurial perspective for value creation, social entrepreneurship provides effective mechanisms to overcome social problems such as poverty, inclusive growth, (Gupta et al., 2020; Hota et al., 2023). It can be defined as the formation of new sustainable business project that directly reacts to market requirements and offers lasting solutions to ecological and public problems of society (El Chaarani & Raimi, 2022).

Differently from classic entrepreneurship, social entrepreneurship and sustainable entrepreneurship reject the focus on profit maximization as they combine the market needs with the social sense and balance financial, social, and environmental value creation (Stubbs, 2017). Social entrepreneurs and sustainable entrepreneurs most regularly hang on low profitability and low returns on investment, nevertheless their actions provide environmental and social benefits by decreasing the consumption of new resources through reuse and recycling practices (Hultman et al., 2016). Sustainable entrepreneurship and social entrepreneurship can commonly recognize, assess, and use opportunities for social value creation through commercial, market-based activities and resource use.

Sustainable entrepreneurs look for long-term market and social solutions and perform as catalysts for sustainable development via finding, utilizing opportunities on the way to provide market-based solutions against ecological and social problems (e.g., resource waste, social injustice; Belz & Binder, 2017). With a socially market transformation perspective and social value creation perspective, Schaltegger et al. (2016: 268) define sustainable entrepreneurship as "*a sustain-ability mission-driven process of solving environmental and social problems of unsustainability by means of the exploration and exploitation of market opportunities created with innovative business models*".

With a social and ecological perspective, there are critical drivers of sustainable entrepreneurship: education for sustainable entrepreneurship, self-transcendent values, social norms, sustainability and altruism orientation, resilience, perceived desirability, self-efficacy, support from universities and other stakeholders (governments, municipalities, consumers), legislation (Gupta & Matharu, 2022). These drivers' impact on social entrepreneurship can change among generations, cultures, infrastructure, market conditions.

Sustainable Entrepreneurship in Circular Economy

Circular economy offers new paths of market innovation that provides social innovations aimed commonly by social entrepreneurship and sustainable entrepreneurship to solve ecological and social problems (El Charani & Raimi, 2022). By optimizing the ecological and social well-being dimensions, sustainablşe entrepreneurship incorporates CE practices. From the social perspective, especially in agriculture, demarginalization and motivation are crucial, rendering the ecological production of vegetable produce viable, while in ecological terms, the focus is on the gradual regeneration of the soil while maximizing production.

In the circular economy context, the open-loop format of traditional linear production and consumption is substituted with a closed-loop system where the value of products, materials and services is actively used through reducing, recycling, and reusing (Korhonen et al., 2018; Mehrotra & Jaladi, 2022). Circular economy creates opportunities for new business development, concerning resource and waste management, product design.

Circular entrepreneurship can be defined as *"the processes of formation and exploitation of opportunities, using both commercial and ecological logics to address environmental challenges with the aim of closing, slowing, and narrowing the loop of resources and regenerating/reconstituting natural capital"* (Zucchella & Urban, 2019: 195).

Circular entrepreneurship is assumed as an independent and innovative entrepreneurial activity that is embedded in a circular economy ecosystem (Henry et al., 2023).As an emerging research and management field, circular entrepreneurship has different perspectives. Foroozanfar et al. (2022) point at five factors that drive circular business models: closing loops; value formation; strategy; object matching; and circular income systems. Directly connected to these factors, sustainable entrepreneurship plays a central role in gaining value from existing circular business. Suchek et al. (2022), suggest that in circular entrepreneurship, four main topics can be assumed as critical: circular SMEs, new circular companies, and start-ups; social entrepreneurship in the circular economy; and the ecosystem for circular entrepreneurship.

Barriers and Enablers of Sustainable Entrepreneurship in Circular Economy

As circular economy represents the macro environment, it would be logical to interpret limits and challenges of its closed-loop economic system. Korhonen et al. (2018) puts 6 physical limits and challenges for the circular economy: thermodynamic limits, spatial and temporal system boundary, limits created by classical economic growth, path dependencies, managerial limits, and social, cultural limits. Moreover, they underline the importance of changing current consumption culture remain as the most critical barrier against the development of circular economy. The growth of circular economy will be directly linked to consumer behavior that will also trigger entrepreneurial motivation.

In the actual practices in CE ecosystem, there are macro and micro level barriers against sustainable entrepreneurship in circular economy. At the macro level, industry policies that still support linear growth models, complexity of regulations and laws, taxation policies harm CE business (Tura et al., 2019) and naturally discourage sustainable entrepreneurships as well.

In circular business models, Foroozanfar et al. (2022) define several drivers: economic drivers, environmental drivers, social drivers, regulatory drivers, emerging approach drivers. In an emerging economy context, El Chaarani and Raimi (2022) suggest that psychological factors, environmental factors, education, experience, leadership, and team composition are critical for successful social entrepreneurship in circular economy. Dantas et al. (2022) resume the determinants of circular entrepreneurship as entrepreneurial opportunity, family and social support, local culture, customer demand, higher profit, source of regular income, recognition as a boss, independence, personal satisfaction, self-transcendence, environmental and social concern, social objectives.

Sustainable Entrepreneurship Cases in Circular Economy

In a case study on circular economy, slow fashion, and craft-based design, Atalay Onur (2020) showed that these concepts were not separate, but they are parts of a whole, and they represent an alternative design culture. She added that designers must change their vision, and undoubtedly, reforming the educational system would support the change. A reformed education system would support sustainable entrepreneurship in circular economy. In another study that granular insights into the emerging CE practices implemented by four Italian fashion companies

In another study, Juma et al. (2022) examined the factors that motivate grassroots ecopreneurship at the base of the pyramid in Kenya. Among various factors, economic motives, necessity motives, opportunity motives, environmental motives, social-ethical motives appear as critical for grassroots ecopreneurs to initiate innovative, sustainable solutions to improve societal conditions, especially in poor contexts like the base of the pyramid in Kenya.

Costanza (2023) examines a pure non-profit organization, Al Reves, in Italy which holds the legal status of social cooperative that works in the recycling of clothes and in the social integration of immigrant workers and other weak social categories of the society. The author argues that this case shows how commercial business and social and ecological mission can increase each other within the circular economy ecosystem. Moreover, the education of all stakeholders in this case (Al Reves as sustainable entrepreneur, companies, consumers, citizens, and all community) has played a critical role to increase social and commercial value (Costanza, 2023).

Mehrotra, S., & Jaladi, S. R. (2022). How start-ups in emerging economies embrace circular business models and contribute towards a circular economy. *Journal of Entrepreneurship in Emerging Economies*, *14*(5), 727–753.

Vellesalu, A., Chkanikova, O., Hjelmgren, D., & Salomonson, N. (2023). Institutional re-configuration and value co-creation in circular product development: A service ecosystem perspective in the textile and apparel industry. *Journal of Cleaner Production*, 137682.

4. Conclusion

This chapter firstly reviews sustainable entrepreneurship and social entrepreneurship and attempts to use the common points between sustainable entrepreneurship and circular entrepreneurship. Followingly, it attempts to define the determinants, barriers, and enablers of sustainable entrepreneurship in circular economy with a triple bottom line perspective. For this objective, relevant articles published in well-known peer-review journals in the Scopus database are extracted. The articles included in the study are 45, categorized under many different taxonomies such as circular entrepreneurship, circular business models to assess sustainable entrepreneurship in circular economy.

The chapter results reveal that conceptual and empirical papers have been published more in the last decade as they are evolving. Many organizations (non-profit and/or for-profit organizations) are transitioning toward circular economy to increase sustainability and financial performances and serve multiple stakeholders associated with the business. The current chapter also brings forward the drivers and barriers of sustainable entrepreneurship in circular economy. The development of the circular economy relies on the acceptance of an entrepreneurial attitude and behavior by all the actors and stakeholders involved: for profit, non-profit organizations, policy makers, citizens, public institutions, and financial institutions.

Consequently, this study offers theoretical and practical implications deducted from separate circular economy ecosystems. Various actions and researches can be carried out by governments, high education institutions, citizens and entrepreneurs in order to adopt a good circular economy ecosystem. Furthermore, to foster collaborative actions are critical to resolving the barriers against sustainable entrepreneurship in circular economy literature.

Service ecosystem perspective with the involvement of different stakeholders

Future studies could build on the actual findings as the circular startup hubs included in this study are mostly located in developed countries and regional start-up hubs, the contextual factors that are examined in the analysis are not exhaustive. Therefore, research to investigate circular start-ups, sustainable start-ups in rural locations and in areas where circularity receives varying levels of institutional support. Further empirical research on tech infrastructure's role in circular economy diffusion is needed. Moreover, additional empirical evidence on the pandemic impacted sustainable entrepreneurship drivers and enablers in circular economy. There is a growing need for empirical studies to investigate the effects of technology acceptance as a driver of circular economy entrepreneurship.

Instructional media such as textbooks are purposefully treating sustainability as a separate area of the economy, and therefore marginalize any efforts to implement circular thinking into mainstream entrepreneurship. Secondly, while entrepreneurship (and business) students are open to the concepts of sustainability and the circular economy, they often lack exposure to foundational knowledge of waste and resource management technology and processes such as zero-waste manufacturing, recycling and recovery technologies, or eco-feedback technologies. Therefore, it is critical to refocus case study discussions on (entrepreneurial) firms adopting or developing sustainable resources and waste management technologies. Lastly, sustainable innovation also occurs on the business model and supply chain level. However, contemporary entrepreneurship education is still predominantly concerned with modeling "linear" ventures. Alternative paths exist and should be further explored.

References

Atalay Onur, D. (2020). Integrating circular economy, collaboration and craft practice in fashion design education in developing countries: A case from Turkey. *Fashion Practice*, *12*(1), 55–77.

Belz, F. M., & Binder, J. K. (2017). Sustainable entrepreneurship: A convergent process model. *Business Strategy and the Environment*, *26*(1), 1–17.

Bocken, N. M., De Pauw, I., Bakker, C., & Van Der Grinten, B. (2016). Product design and business model strategies for a circular economy. *Journal of Industrial and Production Engineering*, *33*(5), 308–320.

Costanza, F. (2023). When the business is circular and social: A dynamic grounded analysis in the clothing recycle. *Journal of Cleaner Production*, *382*, 135216.

Crecente, F., Sarabia, M., and del Val, M. T. (2021) "Sustainable Entrepreneurship in The 2030 Horizon", Sustainability, 13(2): 909-920.

Dantas, R. M., Ilyas, A., Martins, J. M., & Rita, J. X. (2022). Circular entrepreneurship in emerging markets through the lens of sustainability. *Journal of Open Innovation: Technology, Market, and Complexity*, *8*(4), 211.

El Chaarani, H., & Raimi, L. (2022). Determinant factors of successful social entrepreneurship in the emerging circular economy of Lebanon: Exploring the moderating role of NGOs. *Journal of Entrepreneurship in Emerging Economies*, *14*(5), 874–901.

Foroozanfar, M. H., Imanipour, N., & Sajadi, S. M. (2022). Integrating circular economy strategies and business models: A systematic literature review. *Journal of Entrepreneurship in Emerging Economies*, *14*(5), 678–700.

Gupta, P., Chauhan, S., Paul, J., & Jaiswal, M. P. (2020). Social entrepreneurship research: A review and future research agenda. *Journal of Business Research*, *113*, 209–229.

Gupta, N., & Matharu, M. (2022). Examining the enablers of sustainable entrepreneurship–an interpretive structural modelling technique. *Journal of Entrepreneurship in Emerging Economies*, *14*(5), 701–726.

Henry, M., Hoogenstrijd, T., & Kirchherr, J. (2023). Motivations and identities of "grassroots" circular entrepreneurs: An initial exploration. *Business Strategy and the Environment*, *32*(3), 1122–1141.

Hoogendoorn, B., Van der Zwan, P., & Thurik, R. (2019). Sustainable entrepreneurship: The role of perceived barriers and risk. *Journal of Business Ethics*, *157*, 1133–1154.

Hota, P. K. (2023). Tracing the intellectual evolution of social entrepreneurship research: Past advances, current trends, and future directions. *Journal of Business Ethics*, *182*(3), 637–659.

Hultman, M., Bonnedahl, K. J., & O'Neill, K. J. (2016). Unsustainable societies–sustainable businesses? Introduction to special issue of small enterprise research on transitional Ecopreneurs. *Small Enterprise Research*, *23*(1), 1–9.

Juma, N., Olabisi, J., & Griffin-El, E. (2022). Understanding the motivation complexity of grassroots ecopreneurs at the base of the pyramid. *Sustainability*, *14*(21), 14092.

Khan, S. A. R., Shah, A. S. A., Yu, Z., & Tanveer, M. (2022). A systematic literature review on circular economy practices: Challenges, opportunities and future trends. *Journal of Entrepreneurship in Emerging Economies*, *14*(5), 754–795.

Ko, W. W., & Liu, G. (2021). The transformation from traditional nonprofit organizations to social enterprises: An institutional entrepreneurship perspective. *Journal of Business Ethics*, *171*, 15–32.

Korhonen, J., Honkasalo, A., & Seppälä, J. (2018). Circular economy: The concept and its limitations. *Ecological Economics*, *143*, 37–46.

Kraus, S., Breier, M., & Dasí-Rodríguez, S. (2020). The art of crafting a systematic literature review in entrepreneurship research. *International Entrepreneurship and Management Journal*, *16*, 1023–1042.

Lahti, T., Wincent, J., & Parida, V. (2018). A definition and theoretical review of the circular economy, value creation, and sustainable business models: Where are we now and where should research move in the future?. *Sustainability*, *10*(8), 2799.

Leopold, A. (1970). A Sand County Almanac. 1949. New York: Ballantine.

Mehrotra, S., & Jaladi, S. R. (2022). How start-ups in emerging economies embrace circular business models and contribute towards a circular economy. *Journal of Entrepreneurship in Emerging Economies*, *14*(5), 727–753.

Moher, D., Liberati, A., Tetzlaff, J., Altman, D. G., & PRISMA Group. (2009). Preferred reporting items for systematic reviews and meta-analyses: The PRISMA Statement. *PLOS Medicine*, *6*(7), 1–6.

Mondal, S., Singh, S., & Gupta, H. (2023a). Assessing enablers of green entrepreneurship in circular economy: An integrated approach. *Journal of Cleaner Production*, 135999.

Muñoz, P., & Cohen, B. (2018). Sustainable entrepreneurship research: Taking stock and looking ahead. *Business Strategy and the Environment*, *27*(3), 300–322.

Murray, A., Skene, K., & Haynes, K. (2017). The circular economy: An interdisciplinary exploration of the concept and application in a global context. *Journal of Business Ethics*, *140*, 369–380.

Neumeyer, X., Ashton, W. S., & Dentchev, N. (2020). Addressing resource and waste management challenges imposed by COVID-19: An entrepreneurship perspective. *Resources, Conservation and Recycling*, *162*, 105058.

Pastakia A. (1998). Grassroots ecopreneurs: change agents for a sustainable society. Journal of Organizational Change anad Management 11(2):157–173

Paul, J., & Criado, A. R. (2020). The art of writing literature review: What do we know and what do we need to know?. *International Business Review, 29*(4), 101717.

Prieto-Sandoval, V., Jaca, C., & Ormazabal, M. (2018). Towards a consensus on the circular economy. *Journal of Cleaner Production, 179*, 605–615.

Schaltegger, S., & Wagner, M. (2011). Sustainable entrepreneurship and sustainability innovation: Categories and interactions. *Business Strategy and the Environment, 20*(4), 222–237.

Schaltegger, S., Lüdeke-Freund, F., & Hansen, E. G. (2016). Business models for sustainability: A co-evolutionary analysis of sustainable entrepreneurship, innovation, and transformation. *Organization & environment, 29*(3), 264–289.

Schaper, M. (2005). Making Ecopreneurs: developing sustainable entrepreneurship. Ashgate Publishing, Limited, Hampshire

Shepherd, D. A., & Patzelt, H. (2011). The new field of sustainable entrepreneurship: Studying entrepreneurial action linking "what is to be sustained" with "what is to be developed". *Entrepreneurship theory and practice, 35*(1), 137–163.

Sørensen, F., & Bærenholdt, J. O. (2020). Tourist practices in the circular economy. *Annals of Tourism Research, 85*, 103027.

Stubbs, W. (2017). Sustainable entrepreneurship and B corps. *Business Strategy and the Environment, 26*(3), 331–344.

Suchek, N., Ferreira, J. J., & Fernandes, P. O. (2022). A review of entrepreneurship and circular economy research: State of the art and future directions. *Business Strategy and the Environment, 31*(5), 2256–2283.

United Nations. (2015). Transforming our world: The 2030 agenda for Sustainable Development. https://www.un.org/ga/search/view_doc.asp?symbol=A/RES/70/1&Lang=E

Vellesalu, A., Chkanikova, O., Hjelmgren, D., & Salomonson, N. (2023). Institutional re-configuration and value co-creation in circular product development: A service ecosystem perspective in the textile and apparel industry. *Journal of Cleaner Production*, 137682.

Zucchella, A., & Urban, S. (2019). *Circular entrepreneurship*. Cham: Springer International Publishing.

Çağlar Yurtseven
Bahçeşehir University

Didem Cicerali
Bahçeşehir University

Chapter 10 The Impact of Social Enterprises to Circular Economy Transition of Turkey

Abstract: The growing urgency of sustainable development within international frameworks reveals limitations within the prevailing economic model based on unfettered consumption. The circular economy offers a viable alternative, and social enterprises play a crucial supportive role for governments during this transition. This chapter investigates how social enterprises influence this economic shift. Declarations by 80 locally active social enterprises in Turkey were categorized according to the Sustainable Development Goals (SDGs) and examined via text-based analysis (MAXQDA). Findings support the hypothesis that Turkish non-profit social enterprises focus on SDG5 (Gender Equality), SDG10 (Reduced Inequalities), SDG12 (Responsible Production and Consumption), and SDG13 (Climate Action). Analysis further indicates that social benefit generation and sustainable solutions are core objectives for these enterprises.

Keywords: Social Enterprises, Circular Economy, Sustainable Development

1. Introduction

The Industrial Revolution's acceleration of consumption patterns entrenched the linear economy as the dominant model. Abundant natural resources and labor scarcity initially fueled mass production and overconsumption in leading economies. This cycle, driven by the reckless exploitation of resources, became the prevailing definition of value creation and development (Michelini et al., 2017). The unsustainable nature of this model, where production hinges upon limitless resource disposal, poses a significant threat to present and future generations. Consequently, these risks propelled sustainable development to the forefront of the global agenda.

The sustainable development phenomenon, first defined in the World Commission of Environment and Development (WCED) report of Gro H. Brundtland (1987), is shaped around the aim of achieving intergenerational reconciliation and relatively eliminating the damages that will be inherited to future generations. The reason for this is that the world with given resources is no longer capable of sustaining the current production-consumption cycle. In this context, implementing simultaneous policies to foster sustainable development ceased to be a choice (Suchek, 2022; Kirchherr, 2017). In support of this view, the motto *"take-make-dispose"* became old-fashioned. As result, the process of rapid transition from linear economy to circular economy that prioritizes efficiency globally began.

Circular economy, recognized as new economic method that antonym of linear economy, basically aims to prevent, or at least reduce all kinds of waste and seen as the only way to make sustainable development possible (Geissdoerfer, 2017). Although phrases foundations were laid long ago, it is introduced as a holistic approach to literature by Pearce and Turner (1989). The inducing effect of climate action on the circular economy gaining importance is undeniable. The damage caused to nature, as well as the economic, ecological, and social consequences of resource consumption and waste production, are the primary reasons why the increasing trend of consumption cannot be sustained (Suchek, 2022; Sauvé et al., 2016).

The only way for this profound change in the economic structure to be possible is the reshaping of the production-consumption organizational scheme. This new structure, which demands breaking away from traditional patterns, necessitates cooperation among all actors in the economy. One of the main reasons for the necessity of synchrony is that the government cannot bear this transformation alone. Considering that transformation requires intervention with different policies in all fields of the economy, and the participation of individuals in these policies is essential. Under these conditions, it is undeniable that there is a great need for enterprises that function as a kind of social catalyst (Lacy & Rutqvist, 2015).

Social enterprises that prioritize social benefits rather than profit are fundamentally making the transition to a circular economy more feasible by providing individuals efficient alternatives of mass consumption. Therefore, the place of social enterprises is becoming more solidifies in the new economic order. Social enterprises should be supportive of the circular economy in meeting the new needs arising from disruption of traditional growth patterns (Harvey, 2011).

The aim of this chapter is to evaluate the impact of social enterprises on circular economy in Turkey. Due to the flawless legislation of regulations regarding the classification and identification of social enterprises in Turkey, the total number of active social enterprises and their operation fields cannot be officially determined. Therefore, data analysis was conducted based on social enterprises accessible through search engines and the fields of operation declared on their websites.

2. Transition to Circular Economy

The phenomenon of sustainable development, which emerged as the increasing consumption tendency threatened future generations, has accelerated the transition from linear to circular economic model. The circular economy, that is basically shaped against the concept of waste in the production process, emphasizes that both profitability and value creation should be achieved through recycling, not by the constant usage of virgin resources. It is envisaged that circularity of economy will be functioned as a tool that enables the sustainable development process. This new holistic approach to the production-consumption process (Pearce & Turner, 1989) is essentially a multi-dimensional phenomenon and has a flexible structure that can extent to almost any point that is considered problematic in the linear economic model (Sillanpaa, 2019; Sariatli, 2017).

In the most general sense, circular economy is defined as an economic model that prevents waste or at least manages it by minimizing, as antonym of linear economy (Geissdoerfer, 2017). Initially, it is assumed that product designs and production process with the principle of long-term resilience and extending the lifespan of the product will reduce resource disposal. The end-of-life product can be included as input in the production process of a different product before being disposed, thus promoting system efficiency. The last way to prevent dispose is to include the residual waste as input in the production process after going through various processes (Blomsma & Brennan, 2017; Homrich et al., 2018).

Searching for a way to prevent waste at every stage of the system will lead to more successful resource management and keeping waste within the economy. The shorter expression for this transition is the replacement of the "take-make-dispose" motto with the "rethink-reduce-reuse-recycle". With this new approach, it is aimed to end the collection of today's needs for consumption from future generations through reducing environmental damage and elimination of resource disposal (Ellen MacArthur, 2015).

Circular economy has rapidly gained global acceptance as nature began to reduce its tolerance towards resource destruction (Sillanpaa, 2019; Sariatli, 2017). The irreversible detrimental impacts of inefficient usage of resources on the climate over the years been a serious warning about the need for change in the ongoing order (Michelini et al., 2017). The sudden and severe return of the economic, ecological and social consequences of the damage caused by this triggering effect of the climate forced the supranational authorities to take rapid measures regarding the transition to circular economy.

In this context, the most comprehensive initiative was put forward by The United Nations (UN) and recognized as the only sustainable economic model.

Hence, it pioneered the start of transition in Europe with the First Circular Economy Action Plan in 2015. Subsequently, the transition was largely included in the Sustainable Development Goals (SDGs) that came into force on January 1, 2016, with the aim of increasing its impact in global arena (MacArthur & Heading, 2019; Schandl et al., 2020). Especially within the SDG-12 (Responsible Consumption and Production) and the SDG-13 (Climate Action), sustainable production-consumption cycle and protecting resources are emphasized.

The European Commission, along with the European Green Deal first shared with the public in 2019, establishes policies aimed at achieving climate neutrality by 2050 and undertakes initiatives for the transformation of the competitive economy within a fair framework (European Commission, 2023). The Green Deal, by its very nature, is a program aimed not just at taking measures against climate threats and enabling the continuity of consumption, but rather at fostering a deeper global transformation and fundamental altering the phenomenon of economy growth. This new approach, which demands intricate solutions within the context of sectors in the policies to be implemented, is shaped within a framework of consistency. It proposes the development of business and service models that minimize waste production to prevent wasteful development (TÜSİAD, 2021).

The circular economy chart published by the European Parliament Service represents the complementary nature targeted in the production-consumption cycle. It is necessary to include a large part of end-of-life product in production again and again to create further value (European Commission, 2014).

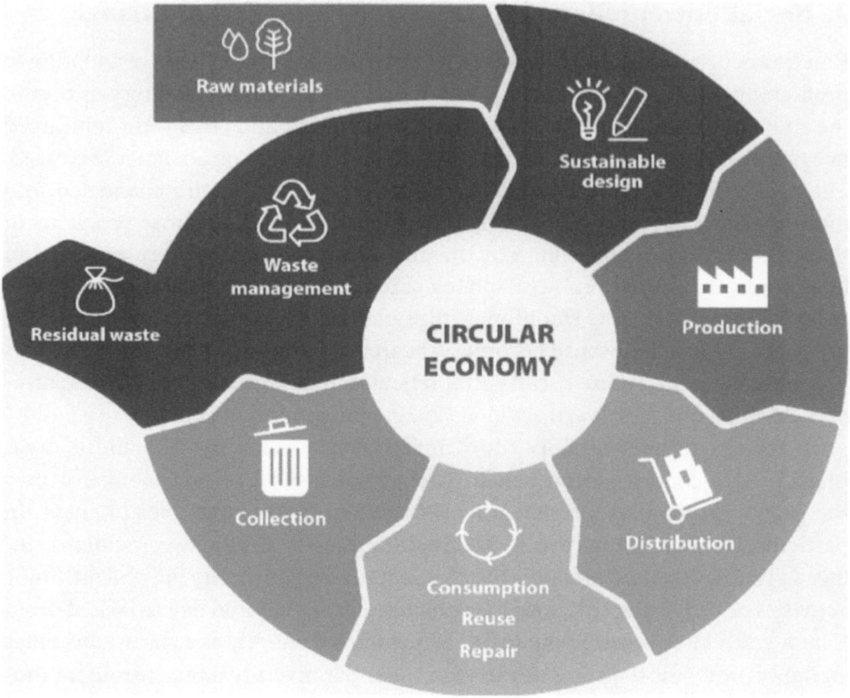

Figure 1. Circular Economy
**Source: European Parliament Research Service*

As can also be seen in Graph1, the transition to a circular economy necessitates the transformation of the government-market-producer-consumer relationship under the reshaping of the production and consumption organizational framework. This new economic model, which requires going beyond traditional patterns, requires all market actors to work synchronously. Especially in "Sustainable Design" and "Waste Management" stages of the circle, transformation is a comprehensive movement that the government cannot implement alone. At this point, the importance of social entrepreneurship becomes vital. In this sense, social enterprises act as catalyst of social change by being mutually nourished with the government (Lacy & Rutqvist, 2015).

3. Social Entrepreneurship as a Catalyst for Social Change

Entrepreneurial activities that accept uncertainty and risk by nature and pursue profitability through innovation-based opportunities are in a leading position in the transformation of societies. As these uncertainty and risks were reinforced by environmental threats, the impact of entrepreneurship on societies increased. The reason for the increased impact is that organizations who channeled into more specific fields can more easily detect, evaluate, and diagnose problems in these fields and produce solutions. In this sense, governments are expected to have relatively limited problem-solving skills due to their broader focus (Dean & McMullen, 2007). The traditional entrepreneur, who produces solutions with the profit motive, in a sense becomes a bearer of sustainable development. This is exactly the point where social entrepreneurship differs from traditional entrepreneurship (Castaño-Martínez et al., 2015; Smitskikh et al., 2020).

In social entrepreneurship, which undertakes a social mission and is organized in this context, social benefit is essential instead of profitability. It uses the profits gathered as a result of its activities to create more social benefit. In particular, it aims to improve social conditions, such as empowering disadvantaged groups, creating job opportunities, improving prosperity via philanthropic activities or proposing solutions to problems that are ignored due to lack of profit (Harvey, 2011). An entrepreneurship which started entirely as a charity, becomes an opportunity for the company to gain a comparative advantage through innovations. This is one of the reasons why companies support social benefit-based initiatives without seeking initial profit. The profits gained through comparative advantage and specialization also lead to results such as creating new job potentials or inducing innovation through new investments (Lacy & Rutqvist, 2015).

The part where social entrepreneurship overlaps with circular economy is the effort to produce solutions to problems arising from ecological factors through innovation in production process and adaptation in the consumption process. The reason why the cycle cannot be completed with only solutions in the production process is that the consumer must also participated in the solution. The new way of production with the "rethink-reduce-reuse-recycle" motto must also find a response from the consumer (El Chaarani & Raimi, 2022). Social entrepreneurship is the unit that will provide this connection, which is expressed as a catalyst for social change. In this regard, social enterprises promote the circular economy in order to propose innovative solutions to ecological or social problems and then ensure the adaptation of society to these solutions (Smitskikh et al., 2020). In this regard, it is expected that in the producer segment, resources should be revaluated through reuse or recycling before being thrown out of the economy, while in the consumer segment, the encouragement of demand for such products and support for the creation of necessary awareness are anticipated (Veleva & Bodkin, 2018).

Since the closing the cycle in the economy by making appropriate innovations in the production process and ensuring social adaptation of consumer requires sector-based concentration, social entrepreneurship acts as a bridge between government, market, and society. As mentioned, social enterprises that specialize in their fields can increase efficiency with shorter and on-site solutions, as they have greater command over limited fields. In this sense, they have the ability to produce more effective results than governments. Especially in developing countries, the government cannot drive sustainable development by itself and cannot fulfill the necessary adjustments, innovations, or adaptation of consumer (El Chaarani & Raimi, 2022).

4. Circular Economy via Social Enterprises in Turkey

In Turkey, the EU practices pioneered the formation of local strategies around sustainability, circularity and the inclusion of these strategies in the national agenda. With Turkey becoming a member of European Environment Agency (EEA) as a developing country in 2003, the importance of environment and sustainability-oriented practices began to increase. The first bureaucratic step taken was the decision to prepare the National Recycling Strategy and Action Plan (NRS-AP) in 2011, in cooperation with the Ministry of Science, Industry and Technology and the Ministry of Environment. The main purpose of NRS-AP, which was prepared and put into effect in 2014, was determined as "creating an economic base that respects the environment and people, induces effective resource use and encourages recycling" (MoEUC, 2014).

Circularity and sustainability focused practices continued in a vague and unnamed until the EU Circular Economy Action Plan (2015). It could only accelerate after 2015 with the support of Turkey being an EEA member. In this context, the Zero Waste Regulation published by the Ministry of Environment and Urbanization in 2019, and subsequently changes were imposed on the Environmental Law in 2020. The changes imposed on the Environmental Law consisted of principles regarding the dissemination and development of "zero waste" and "circular economy" practices. In addition, the obligation to reuse waste material in production process directly or after recycling is added to the Environmental Law. The climate neutrality target of the European Green Deal is emphasized as the basis of this new regulation. In the Turkey Green Deal Action Plan published in 2021. It was emphasized that the EU's Green Deal is not only a climate policy but also an economic transformation program in essence, and in this context, all stakeholders in the economies should work simultaneously (TR Green Deal Action Plan). It was also highlighted that the only way to realize high added value production in an environmentally friendly way and to make necessary innovations in this field is the synchronization of the public, private sector and universities. Additionally, a detailed calendar on this subject was announced within the same agenda (MoEUC, 2014; MoT, 2012).

In the 2023–2025 Medium Term Plan, it was stated that incentives, subsidies and guidance will be used by the government in creating environment-oriented sustainable industry areas. It was announced that the restructuring of production and consumption activities will be supported in the context of recycling and reuse principles in these newly created areas (e.g., Green Industrial Zone) (MoTF, 2024).

Ensuring more entrepreneurial activities that are environmentally friendly and consider production in the context of a circular economy through incentives and subsidies is among the goals. The fact that government cannot provide one-to-one solution in every field and every sector within the country increased the importance of private companies and social enterprises also in Turkey. Initiatives aimed at pure social benefit, which social entrepreneurship is inherently committed to, become a vital actor in accelerating and making possible the transition to the circular economy in the country (British Council, 2019; Yildirim & Esen, 2023).

Despite the great responsibility placed on social enterprises, the fact that the legal infrastructure is not fully established has a negative impact on entrepreneurial activities. In particular, the difficulty in accessing investment and financing networks is an obstacle to many entrepreneurial activities. Limited incentives and subsidies, being exposed to high taxes and not being able to benefit from grants lead to the formation of social enterprises that are largely depend on multinational companies (British Council, 2019). The lack of a legal basis also makes it difficult to determine the number of social enterprises existing in Turkey. The British Council report (2019) stated that there are nearly 9,000 social enterprises operating in different fields (British Council, 2019).

These social enterprises are mostly established with the support of incubation centers, universities, public institutions, or private companies, which often lack by financial means, by small entrepreneurs. The funds and support provided by these intermediary institutions are critically important for entrepreneurs whose primary objective is not profit-making and who utilize the acquired profits as venture capital. All social enterprises established through the support programs of these intermediary institutions play a role in assisting in the construction of social order.

In this chapter, conducted to examine the impact of social enterprises on social change within the context of the circular economy in Turkey, the methodology can be explained through the following steps. Firstly, social enterprises accessible through search engines were identified. Following this identification, classification was made based on the goals and objectives available on the enterprises' websites. Sustainable Development Goals (SDGs) were taken into account during this classification. The purpose of this classification is to determine which specific topics social enterprises active within the country are particularly focusing on and in which areas they are striving to create social benefits.

As second step, declarations found on the websites of social enterprises were utilized for text-based data analysis. The MAXQDA program was employed for this analysis. The aim of this step was to determine whether the goals used as headings by social enterprises are supported by internal discourse. Through text-based analysis, the frequencies of words used in the statements were determined. This allowed for the identification of not only the goals and objectives used as headings but also the methods employed and the underlying motivators for achieving these goals.

The classification based on the main goals and objectives stated in the declarations of 80 socially active enterprises in turkey (see Appendix for enterprises) regarding their alignment with the SDGs provided in Figure 1.

In Figure 1 SDG17 has been excluded from classification as it is universally accepted as a goal by all social enterprises and does not represent a specific area of activity. Top three of the SDGs that the enterprises primarily pursue were evaluated. When interpreted within the framework of the remaining SDGs, it is observed that most of the examined social enterprises are shaped within the goals of reducing inequalities, mitigating the impacts of climate change, reducing the threat of production and consumption chains to future generations, and facilitating the lives of disadvantaged groups such as gender inequality.

In terms of the SDGs, the prominence of goals related inequalities, climate issues, and production-consumption cycle supports the initial hypothesis. In the context of Table1, it could be argued that social enterprises in Turkey function as a kind of social catalyst in the considering the circular economy. Social enterprises aimed at instilling new habits in individuals and facilitating their access to responsible production and consumption options have taken on the task of delivering solutions to smaller units within communities.

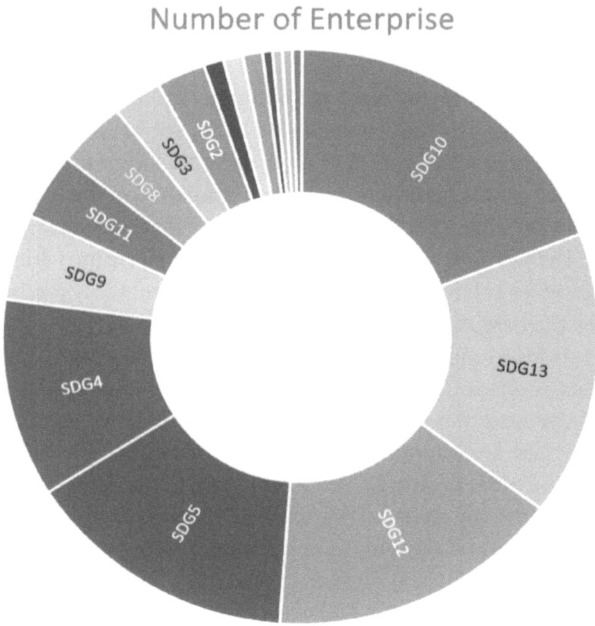

Social Development Goals
SDG1: No Poverty
SDG2: Zero Hunger
SDG3: Good Health and Well-Being
SDG4: Quality Education
SDG5: Gender Equality
SDG6: Clean Water and Sanitation
SDG7: Affordable and Clean Energy
SDG8: Decent Work and Economic Growth
SDG9: Industry, Innovation, and Infrastructure
SDG10: Reduced Inequalities
SDG11: Sustainable Cities and Communities
SDG12: Responsible Production and Consumption
SDG13: Climate Action
SDG14: Life Below Water
SDG15: Life on Land
SDG16: Peace, Justice, and Strong Institutions
SDG17: Partnership for the Goals

Figure 2. Social Enterprises with respect to SDGs

**Source: Created by authors with respect to social enterprises' declarations about SDG's*

To conduct a more in-depth analysis, the declarations of these 80 social enterprises available on their web sites were analyzed using the MAXQDA. Figure 2, created with the word frequencies obtained from the data analysis, clearly expressed the current situation, allowing for the identification of the most emphasized goal across all social enterprises' declarations.

Figure 3. Word Frequencies in Enterprises' Declarations
**Source: Created by authors with respect to word frequency in social enterprises' declarations*

As visualized in Figure 2, the emphasis is placed on social benefit, and sustainable solutions are being sought in areas that need improvement. The obtained results from text-based analysis align with the classification depicted in Figure 1. The high frequency of words such as "Food", "Climate", "Education", and "Woman" confirms that the social benefit indicator underlying the goals objectives used as headings by social enterprises is also aligned in the same direction. Additionally, secondary high-frequency words such as "Waste", "Ecological", and "Management" represents the social benefit facilitated by enterprises in the context of circular economy.

Of course, determining the amount of support generated by social enterprises in this area is a relatively more challenging task that requires deeper and more extensive analysis. Indeed, only through the establishment of legislation regarding entrepreneurship in Turkey can it be possible to determine the support received and provided by these enterprises. In terms of determining these levels of supports, making transparent declarations through government or and other higher institutions to the public will enhance the analyses in the regard.

5. Conclusion

Traditional economic development, defined by a singular focus on increasing production volume through the continuous exploitation of virgin resources, has jeopardized long-term sustainability. Resource depletion and excessive waste generation are inherent consequences of this model. Mounting environmental pressures and the inequitable burden placed on future generations have fueled a global call for a fundamental shift in economic practices. Supranational organizations, notably the United Nations, have spearheaded this transition by championing the circular economy model. Policy initiatives like the European Green Deal and the Sustainable Development Goals (SDGs) demonstrate the crucial role of supranational leadership, particularly for developing nations, in accelerating the adoption of sustainable economic strategies.

The broad resonance of policies proposed by the United Nations (UN) in Turkey began to be realized only as of 2019. With the announcement of the Zero Waste Regulation in 2019, global integration in this field accelerated, and national policies started to be developed. Subsequently, with the announcement of the Environmental Law in 2020 and the Turkey Green Deal Action Plan in 2021, national policies gained importance. The common point of almost all planned implementations to be put into effect was the assignment of supportive responsibility to social enterprises for facilitating social transformation in the transition to a circular economy.

This study investigated the influence of social enterprises on Turkey's shift towards a circular economy by analyzing the declarations of active local social enterprises. Classification of these enterprises' focal points and priorities within the UN's Sustainable Development Goals (SDGs) showed an emphasis on SDG10 (Reduced Inequalities), SDG5 (Gender Equality), SDG12 (Responsible Production and Consumption), and SDG13 (Climate Action). These findings indicate that social enterprises play a catalytic role in driving social change for the circular economy transition. They spearhead the adaptation of production and consumption processes, promote social awareness, and foster new individual habits.

Text-based analysis of the declarations highlights a focus on social benefits and sustainable solutions. The high frequency of words such as "Food", "Climate", "Education", and "Woman" indicates support for social enterprises' efforts to produce sustainable solutions. Secondary high-frequency words "Waste", "Ecological", and "Management" represents their role in the transition towards a circular economy. However, quantifying their precise impact during the transition remains difficult.

Particularly, the absence of specific regulations or legislation defining social enterprises poses challenges in their identification initially. In this regard, the ongoing legislative efforts, when completed, will not only facilitate the recognition of such entities but also contribute to an increase in their numbers. The rise in the number of social enterprises is expected to enhance the overall social benefit obtained. Therefore, in addition to governmental legislative initiatives it is crucial to increase support for initiatives actively engaged in fields aimed at social change in favor of circular economy such as adaptation of production and consumption processes, promoting social awareness, and fostering new individual habits.

Further research, as mentioned above, necessitates the establishment of legal frameworks by authorities. Additionally, full transparency in reporting all activities conducted by social enterprises in their respective fields of operation is critical, particularly for assessing the accessible volume within society. Currently, the only way to accurately measure the individuals reached by enterprises and the benefits they provide is through enterprise-specific in-depth interviews. Centralizing the activities of social enterprises in a shared database will facilitate research in the relevant field to be conducted more objectively and encompass broader areas.

References

Blomsma, F., & Brennan, G. (2017). The emergence of circular economy: A new framing around prolonging resource productivity. *Journal of Industrial Ecology, 21*(3), 603–614.

British Council. (2019). *Türkiye'de Sosyal Girişimlerin Durumu.* Retrieved from https://www.britishcouncil.org.tr/sites/default/files/20190702_se_research_report_the_state_of_social_enterprise_in_turkey_tr_double_page.pdf

Brundtland, G. H. (1987). *Our common future World Commission on environment and development.*

Castaño-Martínez, M. S., Méndez-Picazo, M. T., & Galindo-Martín, M. Á. (2015). Policies to promote entrepreneurial activity and economic performance. *Management Decision, 53*(9), 2073–2087.

Dean, T. J., & McMullen, J. S. (2007). Toward a theory of sustainable entrepreneurship: Reducing environmental degradation through entrepreneurial action. *Journal of Business Venturing, 22*(1), 50–76.

El Chaarani, H., & Raimi, L. (2022). Determinant factors of successful social entrepreneurship in the emerging circular economy of Lebanon: Exploring the moderating role of NGOs. *Journal of Entrepreneurship in Emerging Economies, 14*(5), 870–901.

Ellen MacArthur. (2015). *Towards a circular economy: Business rationale for an accelerated transition.* Ellen MacArthur Found.

European Commission. (2014). *Towards a circular economy: A zero waste programme for Europe*. United Nations.

European Commission. (2023). A Green Deal Industrial Plan for the Net-Zero Age. United Nations.

Geissdoerfer, M. S. (2017). The circular economy–A new sustainability paradigm? *Journal of Cleaner Production*, *143*, 757–768.

Harvey, C. M. (2011). Andrew Carnegie and the Foundations of Contemporary Entrepreneurial Philanthropy. *Business History, 53*(3), 425–450.

Homrich, A. S., Galvão, G., Abadia, L. G., & Carvalho, M. M. (2018). The circular economy umbrella: Trends and gaps on integrating pathways. *Journal of Cleaner Production, 175*, 525–543.

Kirchherr, J. R. (2017). Conceptualizing the circular economy: An analysis of 114 definitions. *Resources, Conservation and Recycling, 127*, 221–232.

Lacy, P., & Rutqvist, J. (2015). *Waste to wealth: The circular economy advantage* (Vol. 91). London: Palgrave Macmillan.

MacArthur, E. (2015). Towards a Circular Economy: Business Rationale for an Accelerated Transition. *Greener Management International, 20.*

MacArthur, E., & Heading, H. (2019). *How the circular economy tackles climate change*. Ellen MacArthur Found.

Michelini, G., Moraes, R. N., Cunha, R. N., Costa, J. M., & Ometto, A. R. (2017). From linear to circular economy: PSS conducting the Transition. *Procedia CIRP*, *64*, 2–6.

MoEUC. (2014). *National recycling strategy and action plan 2014–2017.* Ministry of Environment, Urbanization and Climate Change.

MoT. (2012). *Türkiye Green deal action plan.* T.C. Ministry of Trade.

MoTF. (2024). *Medium Term Program (2024–2026).* TR Ministry of Treasury and Finance.

Pearce, D. W., & Turner, R. K. (1989). *Economics of natural resources and the environment.* Johns Hopkins University Press.

Sariatli, F. (2017). Linear economy versus circular economy: A comparative and Analyzer Study for Optimization of Economy for Sustainability. *Visegrad Journal on Bioeconomy and Sustainable Development, 6*(1), 31–34.

Sauvé, S. B. (2016). Environmental sciences, sustainable development and circular economy: Alternative concepts for trans-disciplinary research. *Environmental Development, 17*, 48–56.

Schandl, H., King, S., Walton, A., Kaksonen, A. H., Tapsuwan, S., & Baynes, T. M. (2020). National Circular Economy Roadmap for Plastics, Glass, Paper and Tyres.

Sillanpaa, M. (2019). *The circular economy: Case studies about the transition from the linear economy.* Academic Press.

Smitskikh, K. V., Titova, N. Y., & Shumik, E. G. (2020). The model of social entrepreneurship dynamic development in circular economy. *Universidad y Sociedad, 12*(5), 248–253.

Suchek, N. F. (2022). A review of entrepreneurship and circular economy research: State of the art and future directions. *Business Strategy and the Environment, 31*(5), 2256–2283.

TÜSİAD. (2021). *Avrupa Yeşil Mutabakatı Döngüsel Ekonomi Eylem Planı Türk İş Dünyasına Neler Getirecek?*

Veleva, V., & Bodkin, G. (2018). Corporate-entrepreneur collaborations to advance a circular economy. *Journal of Cleaner Production, 188*, 20–37.

Yildirim, Ş. S., & Esen, Ü. B. (2023). Social entrepreneurship activities in the tourism sector: Bibliometric analysis and social network analysis. *Research Anthology on Approaches to Social and Sustainable Entrepreneurship*, 1253–1274.

Appendix

Social Enterprises		
Nivogo	Anlatan Eller	Roborel Derneği
Martı	Bilim Virüsü	Önemsiyoruz
Köstebek	Demdernek	Phoca
Fazla	Esmiyor	Composeit
Westespresso	Legal Desing Turkey	Nahil
Türkiye Materials Marketplace	Erişilebilir Her şey	Gekoo
Mumo	Kadınların elinden	Ottan
BlindLook	Gıda Kurtarma Derneği	Kokopellisehirde
Evreka	Sende Gel	Puduhepa ve Kız Kardeşleri
Otsimo	Onaranlar Kulubü	İyimserabla
Toyi	Hayata Sarıl	Kadın Emeğini Değerlendirme Vakfı

Adım Adım	Bego Jeans	Baska Bir Okul Mümkün
Fazla Gıda	Tabit	Bugday Dernegi
Givin	Tospaa	Tolkido
Kızlar Sahada	Arkerobox	Ogrenme Tasarımları
Encoding	Pulsec	Giyi
Binyaprak	Arborimpact	İhtiyac Haritası
Kodluyoruz	Dünyasına Iyi Bakanlar	Kütüpanne
Good4Trust	Inogar	Derin Yoksulluk Ağı
Beesportive	Safimera	Döngü Kooperatifi
KızCode	Genzbio	Nevruz Köyü Kadın Kooperatifi
Ucurtma Projesi	Laska	Köy Okulları Değişim Ağı Derneği
Toktut	Macerita	IDEMA
Harmoni Kadın Kooperatifi	Soyl-gel	Imece Lab
Joon World	This Is Mana	Askıda Ne Var
Turmepa	Algbio	Mikado Danışmanlık
Bego Jeans	BBOM Derneği	

Bahar Köseoğlu
Bahçeşehir University

Chapter 11 Financial Themes for Social Entrepreneurs

Abstract: This chapter focuses on the financial aspects of social entrepreneurs. Social value creation is the most studied aspect of social entrepreneurs, on the other hand financial implications for social entrepreneurs find limited space in the literature. The chapter provides a financial theme analysis in the social entrepreneurs' literature and compares findings with NAHIL, a business enterprise of The Foundation for the Support of Women's Work (FSWW), practice through an interview. Common financial themes in social entrepreneur literature are financial stability, seed capital, and alternative funding sources such as crowdfunding, impact investment and grants. Sustainable finance for social entrepreneurs is another theme studied under the umbrella of the general social entrepreneurship context. The role of innovation indirectly affects financial stability of social enterprises.

Keywords: Social Entrepreneurs, Financing Startups, Sustainable Finance

1. Introduction

Social entrepreneurship has become a buzzword during the last two decades hence the literature has been piling up. Increasing awareness in the public and business world on environment and need for economic sustainability creates an urgency on transformation of business world towards sustainable business activities. Business initiatives whose sole purpose is creating social value emerged because of this need for sustainable economic activities. A common theme in the extensive literature on social entrepreneurs and enterprises is mission-oriented businesses which are focusing on creating social value primarily rather than seeking profit. Social entrepreneurs are expected to integrate their social mission in a business model (Bygrave & Minniti, 2000; Hota et al., 2019; Lehner & Kansikas, 2012; Phillips et al., 2015; Szijarto et al., 2018).

Social entrepreneurs differ from commercial entrepreneurs not only in sense of business mission but also in sense of funding sources and distributing surplus income. (Certo & Miller, 2008) differentiates social entrepreneurs from traditional entrepreneurs in three aspects; namely mission, resource allocation and performance measures. Profitability is not always a relatable measure for social entrepreneurs. Social enterprises may measure their performance focusing on social value created by the enterprise rather than profit. Both employment decisions and funding sources may be different for social entrepreneurs than traditional ones. Long return periods for investments may pose a challenge for investors, finding eco-friendly manufacturers and suppliers may limit the production process or difficulty in attracting high quality employees may hinder the organizational structure. On the other hand, social entrepreneurs may enjoy cheaper funding, volunteer employees and brand loyalty (Berger & Udel, 2006; Irwin & Scott, 2010; Wry & Zhao, 2018).

What are the differentiating financial themes for social entrepreneurs? There are extensive literature reviews on social entrepreneurs' definition and their business model. To our best knowledge focusing on financial themes for social entrepreneurs poses a gap in the literature of social entrepreneurship. This chapter aims to mitigate that gap by focusing on financial themes in the literature on social entrepreneurs.

In this chapter a semi-systematic literature review of social entrepreneurs will be conducted to provide thematic analysis for financial themes to identify the opportunities and challenges faced by social entrepreneurs. After the systematic literature review data extraction will focus on the main objective of the research paper; financial themes and sub-themes will be identified. The following section explains the background for social entrepreneurs by reviewing literature surveys on the subject. Utilized research methodology and criteria are explained in the next section. The fourth section reports the findings, the fifth section provides an interview with a social enterprise about financial aspects of the business, and the last section concludes the research. The study aims to provide an understanding of financial challenges and opportunities for social entrepreneurs. Furthermore, the study draws attention to less explored areas for further research interest.

2. Social Entrepreneurs

Social entrepreneurship attracts increasing attention among scholars following sustainability and corporate social responsibility. Literature surveys dedicated solely to social entrepreneurship have been increasing in numbers in the last decade. This section focuses on the findings of these literature reviews to gain deeper understanding of the concept and the focus in the literature related to social entrepreneurship before carrying on to more focused scope on financial themes.

Social entrepreneurs are purpose driven while creating profit. Main themes observed in the literature are social value creation and innovation. Innovation can be understood as not only production technologies but also the utilization of resources in a new style to create social value. Social value creation is a central theme in social entrepreneurship literature. Private, government or non-profit organizations may create social value through innovative acts by overcoming market failures. Social entrepreneurs can be distinguished from traditional ones by creating new patterns to solve a social problem and contribute to social wealth. Along with the individual characteristics of an entrepreneur, institutions and social capital of an economy plays a critical role for creating an environment which is suitable for social entrepreneurs (Dionisio, 2019; Gupta et al., 2020; Lehner & Kaniskas, 2012; Phillips et al., 2015).

Gupta et al. (2020) states that approximately half of the literature they reviewed on social entrepreneurship, utilizes qualitative methods. Articles that mostly depend on qualitative methods have subjects such as social phenomenon of entrepreneurship, human resources, or innovation. Human resources themed studies mostly focus on the characteristics of social entrepreneurs, and education and training aspects of social entrepreneurship. After social aspects and human resources value creation and challenges come as most frequent themes. Financial themes are mostly observed in articles that focus on challenges of social entrepreneurs.

Findings of (Phillips et al., 2015) show that literature on social enterprises and innovation started to spike after 2010, they report no publications before 1998. Most of the articles concentrate on social innovation and social entrepreneurship. (Phillips et al., 2015) report mostly utilized methods as conceptual, theoretical, and mixed quantitative methods. According to their analysis, the role of the entrepreneur in social enterprises is the most common theme in literature. On the other hand, resources and capabilities are not a common subject in social entrepreneur literature. (Satar et al., 2023) document the change of the concept through years in the social entrepreneurship literature. Social entrepreneurship concept gains a higher portion in the literature after 2018 significantly and in the last two years it seems like the concept "social entrepreneurship" triumphs over "social enterprises".

Bibliometric analysis of (Iskandar et al., 2021) points out that social value and social innovation are popular concepts. Studies mainly focus on the concept itself by exploring the definition and motivation of social entrepreneurs. Business models of social enterprises and institutionalization are the next popular subjects in literature. Another bibliometric analysis focuses on four dimensions of social entrepreneurship, such as individual, organization, process, and environment (Dionisio, 2019). In the individual category the most popular subcategory is motivation of social entrepreneurs. In the organizational dimension funding issues comes as the third subject after strategy and dual mission. More than half of the articles focusing on the process are about management of social enterprises. The second subcategory of process is impact measurement which is observed in most of the articles as social value creation. In the last category, environment, sector specific studies are the most common ones.

3. Methodology

This chapter aims to address the question of what are the differentiating financial themes for social entrepreneurs. Semi-systematic literature review with a thematic analysis is conducted with the purpose of investigating the financial themes for social entrepreneurs. Systematic or semi-systematic literature reviews provide a subjective and structured literature analysis of the field. Semi-systematic literature review is a systematic analysis of academic papers with a flexible selection process. It enables the researcher categorizing the papers according to impact on the field and relevant themes. This approach became more common in research practices in the last decade. Semi systematic review ensures that businesses and policy makers possess balanced and transparent understanding of the subject in hand. Completing the literature search thematic review, a qualitative analysis, is utilized for data extraction for descriptive purposes for detecting financial themes in the relevant literature. Detecting financial themes is the research focus of this study. (Braun & Clarke, 2008; Kraus et al., 2020; Xiao & Watson, 2017).

The research focus is defined as financial themes such as funding sources, funding challenges, initial capital, financing options, financing restrictions, and revenue plan. Before searching the literature for financial themes review protocol developed by deciding inclusion criteria and exclusion criteria. Scopus database was utilized for semi-systematic literature review. Search terms are "Social Entrepreneurs", "Social Entrepreneurship". The Boolean operator "OR" was used. Only peer-reviewed journal articles are included in the search. The search was limited to "capital" "funding" and "financing" terms in the second step of filtration by exerting inclusion criteria. Furthermore, search is limited to the last decade. Articles after 2013 were included in the search. Implementation of the terms "funding", "capital" and "financing" limited the search to 197 articles from the beginning number, 1197 articles. Further screening was done by skimming the articles for relevancy to the financial subjects. This step reveals that most of the articles are focusing on the social capital aspect rather than the financial issues of social entrepreneurship. Creating social value is one of the main contributions of social enterprises yet this research aims to focus on the financial challenges and opportunities for social entrepreneurs. After eliminating for the subject relevancy 27 articles remain for data extraction and detailed thematic analysis. Detailed examination of articles for further relevancy or the remaining

27 articles pointed out 23 of the articles provide analysis with a financial aspect. Findings are reported in Table 2. It is carried on by analyzing financial themes.

After determination of financial themes in the literature a short empirical study was included in the fifth chapter to provide evidence from social entrepreneur practice. An interview with an employee of The Foundation for the Support of Women's Work (FSWW) was conducted about NAHIL, an enterprise of FSWW. The interview with Didem Demircan focused on the structure of NAHIL, revenue creation process, funding sources and plans for the future of NAHIL and new initiatives.

4. Financial Themes in Social Entrepreneur Literature

Financial concepts in social entrepreneur literature were searched through a semi-systematic literature review. Table 1 shows the frequency distribution among publication years and journal rankings. Research was focusing on high quality papers through screening process in the skim through reading step hence in journal rankings selection bias present. Through the end of the time frame of the research an increase in the article numbers is observed. After 2020 as it is reported in (Iskandar et al., 2021) there is a spike in the number of articles in social entrepreneurship. This shift may be due to the shift in the interest of researchers to social entrepreneurs from social enterprises along with the increase in the field combined. Also Journal of Social Entrepreneurship takes the first row with four articles.

Table 1. Frequency Distribution of Journal Ranking and Publication Year

	Rank				
Publication Year	**Q1**	**Q2**	**Q3**	**Q4**	**Totals**
2014	**1**	**1**			**2**
2016	**1**				**1**
2017	**1**				**1**
2018	**1**				**2**
2019	**1**	**1**			**2**
2020	**2**				**2**
2021	**3**			**1**	**4**
2022	**4**				**4**
2023	**4**	**2**			**6**
Totals	**18**	**4**		**1**	**23**

Source: Author's calculations

Limited access to traditional finance is mentioned in most of the literature on social entrepreneurs. Table 2 reports the articles in the search, methodology of the articles, and main findings along with the financial themes. (Gliedt & Parker, 2014) emphasize the importance of innovation in green energy services as the most effective way for overcoming financial limitations and maintaining financial sustainability in times of tight financial conditions.

Table 2. Literature Research Summary

Author/Year	Research Methodology	Main Findings	Themes
(Gliedt & Parker, 2014)	Interviews with Green community entrepreneurs.	Comparing strategies of Energy Service Organizations under sudden funding cuts with stable funding periods. Creativity in founding new services increases in funding crises periods.	Limited access to traditional finance Financial sustainability Innovation
(Siqueira et al., 2014)	Case study with three community banks in Brazil	Implementation of social currency and electronic social currency increase the welfare of low-income community by increasing the financial inclusion	Alternative financing financial inclusion
(Calic & Mosakowski, 2016)	15,075 projects data from Kickstarter website funding goal over $5000 is utilized Logistic regression	Funding project success is positively affected by the social and environmental aspects of the project; also, third party endorsements and creativity enhance the success of projects.	Crowdfunding Social value creation
(Belz & Binder, 2017)	Four case studies	Sustainable entrepreneurial processes (SEPs) are analyzed. Funding is the fifth phase of SEP. Different seed capital sources exist for all cases.	Dependence on seed capital
(Cristina et al., 2018)	Matched sample of 120 SE and traditional pairs Generalized Estimating Equations are utilized.	Young (less than 12 years old) firms are compared for their capital structure. Leverage ratios found less for social enterprises.	Low debt capital

Table 2. Continued

Author/Year	Research Methodology	Main Findings	Themes
(Cheah & Ho, 2019)	Case studies of WateRoam and Tware	WateRoam enjoys three different grants as funding sources, which indicates economic development help to raise funds in Singapore. Tware found private equity funding as seed investment.	Seed capital Grants and equity investment
(Magomedova & Bastida-Vialcanet, 2019)	Case of Carlota's House	Focusing on scaling up of a social enterprise. Growth by impact investment through Ship2B was reported.	Scaling Impact investment Innovation
(Agarwal et al., 2020)	Case study of three social businesses in healthcare industry	Balancing social mission and financial independence with pricing Managing limited personnel and in-house training Lowering cost (e.g., inhouse manufacturing of equipment) to ensure affordability	Financial sustainability
(Langley et al., 2020)	Case study of Berlin Crowdfunding	Besides enhancing social entrepreneurship, crowdfunding causing real-estate price spikes and enhance cooperative economic activity.	Crowdfunding
(Licite-Kurbe & Gintere, 2021)	Observation and descriptive analysis	Several local and national government support instruments are listed such as tax reliefs and preferential procurement contracts. Most influential one is supporting grants extended by Ministry of Welfare.	Government policies and support
(Popkova & Sergi, 2021)	Regression analysis Social entrepreneurship index (SEPR) calculated	Shortcomings in long term investments, limited R&D for public-private collaborations, investment requirements for development of future skills are risk factors for social enterprises.	Long term finance Private sector involvement

(*continued on next page*)

Table 2. Continued

Author/Year	Research Methodology	Main Findings	Themes
(Potluka, 2021)	Logistic regression and propensity score matching for 307 individuals	Supported employees of social enterprises are investigated for future employment situations. Results show that support works in favor of employment after the end of support period.	Grants and supports
(Zhao et al., 2021)	12,379 social entrepreneurs from Entrepreneurship Database Program (EDP). OLS regressions	Female led enterprises attract less equity investment. On the other hand, social value orientation affects male entrepreneurs' equity investment in a negative way, but female entrepreneurs are affected in a positive way.	Equity investment Gender Social impact
(Atahau et al., 2022)	Data was collected by questionnaires (150 samples), partial least squares-structural equation modeling is utilized.	Local wisdom enhances sustainability of Micro Finance Institutions (MFIs) and social entrepreneurship. Increased sustainability of MFI supports social entrepreneurship. Mediating effect of MFIs' sustainability on the relationship between local wisdom and social entrepreneurship is reported.	Sustainable Finance
(Chandna, 2022)	Conceptual analysis and narrative inquiry	Emphasizing the critical role of digital platforms for raising funds. Sharing economy paradigm allows interaction in the community and enhance connectivity.	Crowdfunding Digitalization
(Gigauri & Bogacz-Wojtanowska, 2022)	Semi-structured interviews, 17 case studies	Challenges and opportunities due to Pandemic for social entrepreneurs in Georgia are analyzed. Drop in sales, rising taxes, lack of government support, disruptions in supply chain, and additional finance requirements force entrepreneurs to be more innovative. Improvements in legislation and the support system are required.	Financial sustainability

Table 2. Continued

Author/Year	Research Methodology	Main Findings	Themes
(Lall & Park, 2022)	panel data set of 3,401 social OLS regression	Receiving grant affects social ventures positively in employment and receiving debt finance, yet no effect is observed on equity finance and revenues.	Grants and Supports Scaling
(Bacuilima et al., 2023)	15 in-depth interviews with Ecuadorian SEs, interpretative research methodology	Most of the SE are aware of the impact of investment but they are not enjoying it due to lack of information for application process or unavailability of proper guidance.	Impact Investment
(Chen, 2023)	Crowdfunding data from Indigogo platform (2011 -2017) Textual analysis and Logistic regression	Evaluating the crowdfunding performance of SE shows that frequent communication with social platforms and strong social ties with partners are indicators for success in fund raising.	Crowdfunding Social connectivity
(Fernandes et al., 2023)	Data of 601 SE is analyzed. Regression analysis is conducted.	Determinants for access to finance for SEs are examined. Technology use and incubation process positively affect success for financial access. Also, green tech industry and B2B2C models have higher financial access in impact investing.	Impact investment
(Hussain et al., 2023)	Systematic literature review on crowdfunding for SE	Benefits of crowdfunding such as low implementation cost or legitimacy; and determinants of crowdfunding such as social value creation are reported.	Crowdfunding Social value creation
(Kaushik & Tewari, 2023)	A Hybrid Delphi and Best-Worst Approach with 24 experts	17 opportunity indicators for SEs are determined (10 subjective and 7 objective indicators).	Impact investment Tax benefits
(Schin et al., 2023)	Survey of 145 NGOs Descriptive statistical analysis	High involvement of public administration attracts both European funds and private sector financing.	Grants and Supports Private sector partnership

Source: Author's compilation

Financial sustainability is crucial for social enterprises considering the limited access to traditional financing. Financial sustainability may focus on different sub-themes such as stable funding, pricing strategies and financial independence.

Alternative funding is an important focus for social entrepreneurs. Crowdfunding has become a crucial way of alternative funding according to the 3rd European Alternative Funding Report with a volume about 260 billion euros at the end of 2015 (Ziegler et al., 2018). Success of crowdfunding depends on the social connections and social value created by the business. Also crowdfunding itself creates a cooperative economic environment (Calic & Mosakowski, 2016; Chen, 2023; Langley et al., 2020). Crowdfunding can be a way of raising seed capital along with other practices such as loans, private funding, founders' own capital and public funding (Belz & Binder, 2017). Impact investment and grants from global institutions or governments are other financial sub-themes come up under the alternative funding theme. Lack of information may pose a problem for social entrepreneurs to access funding (Bacuilima et al., 2023). (Schin et al., 2023) show that involvement of the public sector in projects not only attracts more global funds but also increases the interest of the private sector.

Financial sustainability is important for any business entity and a sustainable financial environment is crucial for long term success of businesses in any sector. Sustainable finance depends on the financial institutions' strategies for social entrepreneurs. Financial institutions may enhance the relation between social entrepreneurs and institutional investors. Also, financial institutions may create an environment to increase financial literacy of managers of SEs and provide more hybrid funding models for social businesses (Atahau et al., 2022; Siqueira et al., 2014).

The link of innovation with financial stability of social enterprises in long term is indirectly studied in literature. Carlota's House is an example of the effect of innovative business practices on the financial aspects. (Magomedova & Bastida-Vialcanet, 2019) quote José María, founder of Carlota's House, "our idea was not to create a social enterprise that integrated people with disabilities into the workplace; we simply wanted to hire talented people, with a singular way of perceiving reality, who would contribute genuinely new ideas." In this case social value creation by hiring people with Down syndrome and autism leads to profits. Innovative business approach in human resources provides an edge in design business.

5. NAHIL: A Market Platform for Women's Productions

NAHIL is a business enterprise of The Foundation for the Support of Women's Work (FSWW). The aim of this social enterprise is providing a marketplace for authentic local production of women. NAHIL was founded in 2002 by FSWW in the building of the foundation. The foundation's board is the executive body of NAHIL. Seed capital of NAHIL came from the foundation as the place and workforce. FSWW accepts second hand donations, these donations are sold through NAHIL shop. NAHIL continued its activities as product development consultant to women. Products that are suitable for development and marketing through NAHIL determined mostly by collaborations with women cooperatives. International funds are utilized through projects born from these collaborations. Also, women-child centers of FSWW contributes to find eligible products to sell in NAHIL, such as wooden toys and child sleepwear. The product development process is conducted professionally including design and feasibility steps.

NAHIL focuses on the local products which are produced by women. Several different project funds are utilized for the development of these products and facilities required for production. Selection of the products is determined by a collective effort of FSWW and local authorities such as the chamber of commerce of the town or agriculture department of the town. Communicating with local women and institutions ensure to determine a sustainable local product such as local Bıttım soap or leather handbags. The aim is creating sustainable income for women by providing business know-how, technical support, and funding.

NAHIL as a business enterprise is paying taxes and employee salaries. Revenue of NAHIL depends on the commissions from the sales. Remaining revenue goes to producers individually or to cooperatives. Individual sales are part of the revenues. Also, private sector demand for the products of NAHIL collaborators is one of the main revenue generators. NAHIL provides support at every step of the business; starting with the design and creation of the product, the production, and logistic processes, continuing with the sales via e-trade and accounting processes. It acts as a bridge between market and producer. Besides the direct effect of NAHIL, it also inspires women cooperatives to represent themselves more actively and take initiatives for business.

KPIs of NAHIL are the number of new collaborations, new products, new institutional customers, revenue creation for new individuals, total revenue, and profitability. Profit of NAHIL is used for new product development. Pricing is based on the requirements of the producer and administrative costs. NAHIL's production is not limited to physical products, it started to focus on services by initiating guest houses as a new business model. Creation of these business models are inspired from the local opportunities. Dairy farm in Çanakkale or guest house in Mardin, Gaziantep, Şanlıurfa and İstanbul are examples of different business initiatives of NAHIL. Turkish bath, Namazgah is another upcoming project for 2024. NAHIL also provides inspiration by an upcycle park in Kasımpaşa, İstanbul. Part of the facility consists of ateliers for upcycling waste such as textile waste as cloth.

6. Concluding Remarks

This chapter focuses on the financial aspect of social entrepreneurship by studying the financial themes in social entrepreneur literature. Main themes are financial sustainability, alternative funding, sustainable finance, and innovation. Sub themes appear as role of governmental bodies through grants and supports, importance of digitalization such as crowdfunding, impact investment as alternative funding. Furthermore, findings are focusing on social value creation effect on financing, gender effect on access to funding, low debt capital in comparison to equity capital, and public involvement effect on access to finance.

Alternative funding finds a large place in literature, on the other hand sustainable finance rather has a small part. Indirect results of several studies point out that the ecosystem creates positive externalities for social entrepreneurs. Social entrepreneurial culture in financial systems would enhance the funding opportunities for social enterprises. The role of financial institutions for social entrepreneurs poses research opportunities for the future. Crowdfunding and impact investment are hot topics and have several aspects to exploit.

NAHIL case presents an effect of positive externality: creation of a network and culture of women production cause women cooperatives take initiative for new business ideas on their own and represent themselves more actively. NAHIL's mission is creating sustainable revenue for women through different business initiatives by focusing on local characteristics and products. NAHIL creates access to funding via international grants. Also, NAHIL creates a network for producers and customers who prefer social value creating businesses.

References

Agarwal, N., Chakrabarti, R., Prabhu, J. C., & Brem, A. (2020). Managing dilemmas of resource mobilization through jugaad: A multi-method study of social enterprises in Indian healthcare. *Strategic Entrepreneurship Journal*, *14*(3), 419–443. https://doi.org/10.1002/sej.1362

Atahau, A. D. R., Lee, C. W., Kesa, D. D., & Huruta, A. D. (2022). Developing social entrepreneurship in rural areas: A path mediation framework. *International Sociology, 37*(4), 475–495. https://doi.org/10.1177/02685809221095912

Bacuilima, E., Morocho, J., Aguirre, J., Coronel-Pangol, K., & Mora, P. (2023). Financing Ecuadorian social enterprises: What is the role of impact investment? *Sustainability (Switzerland), 15*(14), 29–40. https://doi.org/10.3390/su151411210.

Belz, F. M., & Binder, J. K. (2017). Sustainable entrepreneurship: A convergent process model. *Business Strategy and the Environment, 26*(1), 1–17. https://doi.org/10.1002/bse.1887

Berger, A. N., & Udell, G. F. (2006). A more complete conceptual framework for SME finance. *Journal of Banking & Finance, 30*(11), 2945–2966.

Braun, V., & Clarke, V. (2008). Using thematic analysis in psychology, qualitative research in psychology. *Journal of Chemical Information and Modeling, 3*(2).

Bygrave, W., & Minniti, M. (2000). The social dynamics of entrepreneurship. *Entrepreneurship Theory and Practice, 24*(3),

Calic, G., & Mosakowski, E. (2016). Kicking off social entrepreneurship: How a sustainability orientation influences crowdfunding success. *Journal of Management Studies, 53*(5), 738–767. https://doi.org/10.1111/joms.12201

Certo, S. T., & Miller, T. (2008). Social entrepreneurship: Key issues and concepts. In *Business Horizons* (Vol. 51, Issue 4, pp. 267–271). Elsevier Ltd. https://doi.org/10.1016/j.bushor.2008.02.009

Chandna, V. (2022). Social entrepreneurship and digital platforms: Crowdfunding in the sharing-economy era. *Business Horizons, 65*(1), 21–31. https://doi.org/10.1016/j.bushor.2021.09.005

Cheah, S., & Ho, Y. P. (2019). Building the ecosystem for social entrepreneurship: University social enterprise cases in Singapore. *Science, Technology and Society, 24*(3), 507–526. https://doi.org/10.1177/0971721819873190

Chen, W. D. (2023). Crowdfunding for social ventures. *Social Enterprise Journal, 19*(3), 256–276. https://doi.org/10.1108/SEJ-05-2022-0051

Cristina, A., Siqueira, O., Donahue, P., Guenster, N., & Vanacker, T. (2018). *A longitudinal comparison of capital structure between young for-profit social and commercial enterprises.*

Dionisio, M. (2019). The evolution of social entrepreneurship research: A bibliometric analysis. *Social Enterprise Journal, 15*(1), 22–45. https://doi.org/10.1108/SEJ-05-2018-0042

Fernandes, E. da S., Grochau, I. H., & Ten Caten, C. S. (2023). Impact investing: Determinants of external financing of social enterprises in Brazil. *Sustainability (Switzerland), 15*(15). https://doi.org/10.3390/su151511935

Gigauri, I., & Bogacz-Wojtanowska, E. (2022). Effects of the pandemic crisis on social enterprise: A case study from Georgia. *& Sociology*, *15*(2), 312–334. DOI:10.14254/2071-789X.2022/15-2/19

Gliedt, T., & Parker, P. (2014). Collective response or individual adaptation strategy to funding cuts in Canada (2006–2012). In *International Journal of Social Economics* (Vol. 41, Issue 7, pp. 609–625). Emerald Group Holdings Ltd. https://doi.org/10.1108/IJSE-05-2013-0125

Gupta, P., Chauhan, S., Paul, J., & Jaiswal, M. P. (2020). Social entrepreneurship research: A review and future research agenda. *Journal of Business Research*, *113*, 209–229. https://doi.org/10.1016/J.JBUSRES.2020.03.032

Hota, P. K., Subramanian, B., & Narayanamurthy, G. (2019). Mapping the intellectual structure of social entrepreneurship research: A citation/co-citation analysis. *Journal of Business Ethics*, https://doi.org/10.1007/s10551-019-04129-4.

Hussain, N., Di Pietro, F., & Rosati, P. (2023). Crowdfunding for social entrepreneurship: A systematic review of the literature. In *Journal of Social Entrepreneurship*. Routledge. https://doi.org/10.1080/19420676.2023.2236637

Irwin, D., & Scott, J. M. (2010). Barriers faced by SMEs in raising bank finance. *International Journal of Entrepreneurial Behaviour and Research, 16*(3), 245–259.

Iskandar, Y., Joeliaty, J., Kaltum, U., & Hilmiana, H. (2021). Bibliometric analysis on social entrepreneurship specialized journals. *WSEAS Transactions on Environment and Development*, *17*, 941–951. https://doi.org/10.37394/232015.2021.17.87

Kaushik, V., & Tewari, S. (2023). Modeling opportunity indicators fostering social entrepreneurship: A hybrid Delphi and best-worst approach. *Social Indicators Research*, *168*(1–3), 667–698. https://doi.org/10.1007/s11205-023-03139-0

Kraus, S., Breier, M., & Dasí-Rodríguez, S. (2020). The art of crafting a systematic literature review in entrepreneurship research. *International Entrepreneurship and Management Journal*, *16*(3), 1023–1042. https://doi.org/10.1007/s11365-020-00635-4

Lall, S. A., & Park, J. (2022). How social ventures grow: Understanding the role of philanthropic grants in scaling social entrepreneurship. *Business and Society*, *61*(1), 3–44. https://doi.org/10.1177/0007650320973434

Langley, P., Lewis, S., McFarlane, C., Painter, J., & Vradis, A. (2020). Crowdfunding cities: Social entrepreneurship, speculation and solidarity in Berlin. *Geoforum*, *115*, 11–20. https://doi.org/10.1016/j.geoforum.2020.06.014

Lehner, O. M., & Kaniskas, J. (2012). Opportunity recognition in social entrepreneurship: A thematic meta analysis. *Journal of Entrepreneurship*, *21*(1), 25–58. https://doi.org/10.1177/097135571102100102

Licite-Kurbe, L., & Gintere, D. (2021). Analysis of financial support instruments for social enterprises in Latvia. *Rural Sustainability Research*, *45*(340), 76–84. https://doi.org/10.2478/plua-2021-0009

Magomedova, N., & Bastida-Vialcanet, R. (2019). La Casa de Carlota: A studio where the diversity wins. *Entrepreneurship Education and Pedagogy*, *2*(4), 350–362. https://doi.org/10.1177/2515127419835699

Phillips, W., Lee, H., Ghobadian, A., O'Regan, N., & James, P. (2015). Social innovation and social entrepreneurship: A systematic review. *Group and Organization Management*, *40*(3), 428–461. https://doi.org/10.1177/1059601114560063

Popkova, E. G., & Sergi, B. S. (2021). Dataset modelling of the financial risk management of social entrepreneurship in emerging economies. *Risks*, *9*(12). https://doi.org/10.3390/risks9120211

Potluka, O. (2021). How effective is European Public Support granted to social enterprises for employment in the Czech Republic? *Journal of Social Entrepreneurship*. https://doi.org/10.1080/19420676.2021.1961287

Satar, M. S., Aggarwal, D., Bansal, R., & Alarifi, G. (2023). Mapping the knowledge structure and unveiling the research trends in social entrepreneurship and inclusive development: A bibliometric analysis. In *Sustainability (Switzerland)* (Vol. 15, Issue 7). MDPI. https://doi.org/10.3390/su15075626

Schin, G. C., Cristache, N., & Matis, C. (2023). Fostering social entrepreneurship through public administration support. *International Entrepreneurship and Management Journal*, *19*(2), 481–500. https://doi.org/10.1007/s11365-023-00831-y

Siqueira, A. C. O., Mariano, S. R. H., & Moraes, J. (2014). Supporting innovation ecosystems with microfinance: Evidence from Brazil and implications for social entrepreneurship. *Journal of Social Entrepreneurship*, *5*(3), 318–338. https://doi.org/10.1080/19420676.2014.927388

Szijarto, B., Milley, P., Svensson, K., & Cousins, J. B. (2018). On the evaluation of social innovations and social enterprises: Recognizing and integrating two solitudes in the empirical knowledge base. *Evaluation and Program Planning*, *66*, 20–32.

Wry, T., & Zhao, E. Y. (2018). Taking trade-offs seriously: Examining the contextually contingent relationship between social outreach intensity and financial sustainability in global microfinance. *Organization Science*, *29*(3), 507–528.

Xiao, Y., & Watson, M. (2017). Guidance on conducting a systematic literature review. *Journal of Planning Education and Research*, *39*(1), 93–112. https://doi.org/10.1177/0739456X17723971

Zhao, Y., Lee, J., & Ellenwood, C. (2021). The persistent influence of gender stereotypes in social entrepreneurial financing. *Journal of Social Entrepreneurship*. https://doi.org/10.1080/19420676.2021.2004206

Ziegler, T., Shneor, R., Garvey, K., Wenzlaff, K., Yerolemou, N., Hao, R., & Zhang, B. (2018). *Expanding Horizons: The 3rd European Alternative Finance Industry Report With the support of.* https://ssrn.com/abstract=3106911https://ssrn.com/abstract=3106911Electroniccopyavailableat:https://ssrn.com/abstract=3106911Electroniccopyavailableat:https://ssrn.com/abstract=3106911

Ayşe Aslı Bozdağ
Bahçeşehir University

Chapter 12 Buzzing into the Future: AI-Driven Social Entrepreneurship in Turkish Agriculture the Case of BeePlant

Abstract: This chapter explores the transformative role of Artificial Intelligence (AI) within the social entrepreneurship landscape of Türkiye, particularly emphasizing its impact in the agriculture sector, with a special focus on apiculture. This sector serves as a crucial case study, illustrating the power of disruptive innovations to address urgent, interconnected challenges and how social entrepreneurship can leverage these advancements to meet specific sector needs. In this context, the chapter zeroes in on BeePlant, a pioneering tech startup that exemplifies the integration of AI to redefine beekeeping and apiculture. BeePlant's initiatives underscore the significant transformation underway in Türkiye's social entrepreneurship, setting new standards for efficiency, inclusivity, and environmental sustainability. The case tackles previously overlooked challenges and enhances manual labor efficiency, social well-being, and the quality of bee products with AI. This attempts to create a sustainable, inclusive, and economically viable agricultural ecosystem in Türkiye. The narrative showcases the synergy between technological innovation and social entrepreneurship, underscoring the role of innovation and technology democratization in creating an inclusive industry ecosystem. In Türkiye's vibrant setting, the case study stresses the significance of multidisciplinary teams and widespread technology access, which is critical for social entrepreneurs aiming for comprehensive benefits.

Keywords: BeePlant, Social Entrepreneurship, AgriTech, Disruptive Entrepreneurship, Artificial Intelligence, Creative Destruction

1. Disruptive Entrepreneurship

In today's rapidly evolving landscape, ecological and agricultural systems are at a critical juncture. Challenges such as climate change, population growth, and resource depletion are not isolated issues; they are interconnected, affecting environmental, social, and economic structures. Traditional methods are increasingly falling short in addressing these multifaceted challenges. It is within this context that the role of innovative solutions and social entrepreneurship becomes indispensable for innovations.

To understand the transformative power of disruptive innovations, it's instructive to consider theoretical frameworks that elucidate the dynamics of change. Joseph Schumpeter's (1942) concept of *creative destruction* provides a foundational understanding. He posited that innovation leads to dismantling established structures, thereby catalyzing the emergence of new, more efficient systems. This idea sets the stage for Clayton Christensen's (1997) construct of *disruptive innovation*, which offers a more granular look at how such changes can displace existing market leaders and practices. While Schumpeter (1942) focuses on the cyclical nature of economic change driven by innovation, Christensen (1997) delves into the mechanics of how these changes occur. Together, these theories offer a comprehensive view of how ventures can disrupt existing frameworks to pave the way for more equitable and effective solutions. In essence, it is creative destruction in action, which is about breaking down the old to make way for the new. It's a transformative and cyclical process, which serves as a theoretical backdrop against which specific instances of disruptive innovations can be understood. In this context, *social entrepreneurs are seen as change agents*, using technology to drive societal progress, embodying the essence of Schumpeter's and Christensen's theories in practical, impactful ways.

For instance, *Grameen Bank* did not merely refine existing banking models as social entrepreneurship; it revolutionized the financial landscape by offering small loans without collateral, thus enabling financial inclusion for impoverished communities previously considered unbankable (Akbulaev et al., 2017). This is disruptive because it democratizes financial access, challenging the conventional wisdom that financial services are only for those with existing assets or stable income. Similarly, companies like *M-KOPA Solar* have disrupted traditional energy provision models in Africa by offering affordable, pay-as-you-go solar energy systems (Rastogi, 2018). Rather than making incremental improvements to existing energy infrastructures, it has introduced a new model that makes sustainable energy accessible and affordable, even in remote areas. This is not just an enhancement but a paradigm shift that addresses economic and environmental sustainability.

Telemedicine platforms like *Teladoc* have democratized access to healthcare services, particularly in remote areas where medical facilities are scarce. Unlike traditional healthcare models that rely on physical infrastructure and proximity, it leveraged digital technology to provide medical consultations regardless of geographical limitations (Chakraborty, Edirippulige & Ilavarasan, 2023). *One Acre Fund* has revolutionized traditional agriculture by providing smallholder farmers with asset-based financing and agriculture training. Instead of making incremental changes to existing agricultural lending models, it has created a new framework that combines financial services with education, thereby addressing the root causes of food insecurity (Jones & Augustine, 2017). These disruptive innovations often begin as localized experiments but have the potential for broader acceptance and scalability. For instance, *M-Pesa*, a mobile money transfer service initiated in Kenya, has expanded its operations across multiple countries, revolutionizing financial inclusion and contributing to economic development (Ngugi et al., 2010) Such instances underscore the inherent potential of disruptive innovations to transform global systems, often displacing established market leaders and overturning traditional business models in the process.

Through disruptive innovations like the above, social entrepreneurship redefines socio-economic frameworks, embodying creative destruction to serve underserved communities, dismantle barriers to essential services, and foster equitable, sustainable systems. These instances demonstrate *the essence of social entrepreneurship—leveraging technology for economic resilience and emphasizing environmental and social well-being—and transform theoretical disruptive innovation into tangible outcomes that drive societal progress. Disruptive entrepreneurs* redefine socio-economic frameworks, embodying creative destruction to serve underserved communities, dismantle barriers to essential services, and foster equitable, sustainable systems. Offering a holistic approach to global challenges, they pave the way for an in-depth exploration of the sector's impact, particularly in agritech and Artificial Intelligence (AI). The chapter thus transitions from discussing the broader implications of social entrepreneurship to focusing on AI's transformative role in Social Techpreneurship and AgriTech, with BeePlant serves as a pivotal case study to illustrate these dynamics in action.

AgriTech

Agricultural technology, commonly known as *agritech*, is a burgeoning field that leverages technological advancements to solve complex challenges in agriculture. Emerging from the confluence of traditional farming practices and modern technological innovation, *agritech* has evolved significantly over the years. It now encompasses various technologies—from precision farming and automation to data analytics and AI. It serves as a focal point where disruptive innovation meets traditional farming practices, offering transformative solutions that go beyond incremental changes. Its role in the broader tech ecosystem is increasingly significant as it intersects with advancements in data science, machine learning, and the Internet of Things (IoT).

For example, traditional methods for diagnosing plant diseases often rely on manual inspection and may require expert consultation, making the process both time-consuming and expensive. To address these limitations, academic research and social entrepreneurship are making significant contributions to agritech, albeit in different capacities. On the academic front, for instance, a study by Yağ and Altan (2022) proposed a robust hybrid classification model that employs swarm optimization and deep learning algorithms for real-time detection of diseases in apple, grape, and tomato plants. Their model, embedded in *Unmanned Aerial Vehicles (UAVs),* demonstrated high accuracy and low computational cost, contributing to increased agricultural efficiency. Similarly, a study conducted in Morocco by Orchi et al. (2023) presented an innovative method using *YOLOv8*, an object identification approach, for real-time diagnosis of plant diseases. Their system analyzes leaf images at a rate of 70 FPS and has shown exceptional efficiency in speed and accuracy, further solidifying the role of advanced algorithms in agricultural innovation. However, it is imperative to note that the efficacy of these academic advancements hinges on their practical application and scalability. In this context, social entrepreneurs serve as the conduits for translating these academic innovations into actionable solutions, thereby playing a pivotal role in transforming agriculture. Companies like Cropin, Prospera, and Cognitive Pilot exemplify this trend within the realm of social entrepreneurship.

Cropin, based in India, provides farm management software and mobile apps that enable data-driven farming, offering features like remote sensing and weather advisory, embodying the social entrepreneurship ethos by enhancing agricultural practices. Prospera, an Israeli firm, employs computer vision technologies to monitor plant health and development continuously. Their technology not only captures climate and visual data from the field but also translates these into practical recommendations, thereby enhancing the accessibility of sustainable farming (Zhai et al., 2020). Cognitive Pilot from Russia specializes in developing and using software for agricultural digital economy projects, leveraging computer vision and artificial intelligence, operating under a social entrepreneurship model that prioritizes technological innovation for sustainability. These companies embrace business models that marry profit with social impact. For instance, Cropin uses data analytics for crop advisories, generating revenue while serving a social mission, illustrating their role as social entrepreneurs by blending profit with purpose. Similarly, Cognitive Pilot employs AI and computer vision to boost agricultural efficiency, aligning tech innovation with sustainability and reinforcing their social entrepreneurship identity.

Nonetheless, the transformative potential of agritech is not without its complexities. Integrating diverse disciplines into this field presents challenges and opportunities for social entrepreneurs. While it allows for a more nuanced understanding of the intricate systems, it necessitates a multidisciplinary approach to ensure sustainable and equitable solutions. Collectively, advancements in academic research, social entrepreneurship, and interdisciplinary methodologies are doing more than just enhancing efficiency. They are synergistically contributing to the creation of economic, social, and environmental value in a manner that is both sustainable and impactful (Satishkumar et al., 2023).

AI for Good

It's worth noting that a common thread tying these innovations together is the increased application of AI, which is revolutionizing various aspects of agriculture. Traditional agricultural practices often suffer from inefficiencies, requiring substantial human resources and lacking precise data on critical factors like weather, soil conditions, and fertilizer use. To address these challenges, various computational methods have been introduced. One such method is *Fuzzy Logic*, which handles uncertainty and vagueness, providing a foundation for decision-making systems in irrigation and crop management (Zadeh, 1965). Unlike traditional binary logic systems that deal in absolutes (true or false), Fuzzy Logic allows for degrees of truth, making it more adaptable to the complexities of agricultural environments. In recent years, its application has evolved to incorporate advanced sensors and IoT devices, enabling real-time data collection and analysis for precision agriculture.

This has led to the exploration of other machine learning techniques, such as *Artificial Neural Networks (ANNs)*, which offer a different approach. ANNs emulate the human brain's interconnected neuron structure to learn from data and have found applications in diverse agricultural contexts. For example, Wakchaure et al. (2023) applied ANNs in soil nutrient analysis and crop yield prediction. Similarly, Elizondo et al. (1994) used ANNs to predict the flowering and maturity of soybeans, considering variables such as air temperature and photoperiod. These machine learning methods, including ANNs, are part of ongoing efforts to enhance agricultural efficiency and sustainability. They offer solutions to farmers who face challenges in yield prediction due to insufficient or imprecise data on various crop parameters. However, ANNs require significant computational power and extensive data sets for training, which can be a barrier in resource-limited settings. This limitation has led researchers to explore alternative optimization techniques that are less resource-intensive.

One alternative is *Genetic Algorithms (GA)*, introduced by John Holland in 1992. Inspired by genetic principles and the steps of natural selection, GAs provide optimal solutions for complex problems and have been widely adopted in agriculture due to their effectiveness and accuracy. These algorithms iterate through multiple generations of solutions to find the most effective farming strategies, such as planting schedules or pesticide applications. While powerful, they can sometimes converge on local rather than global optima, meaning they find good but not necessarily the best solutions. These computational techniques have been increasingly applied across various agricultural processes. For example, UAVs equipped with advanced navigation systems are used for aerial imaging, providing real-time data that can inform decisions about irrigation and harvest timing, thereby contributing to sustainability by optimizing resource use. Robotic crop harvesting, on the other hand, reduces the need for manual labor and allows for more precise and timely harvesting, which can significantly reduce waste and improve yield quality. These innovations represent more than mere technological advancements; they are transformative shifts that enhance agricultural practices' sustainability and efficiency (Wakchaure et al., 2023).

This shift is a methodological reflection of social entrepreneurship's philosophical commitment to *embracing complexity, not as an obstacle but as a space for innovation.* In this light, the application of numerous techniques can be seen as a metaphor for the social entrepreneurship process itself—leveraging sophisticated, adaptable tools to make sense of and effectively respond to the dynamic, uncertain conditions that define pressing global challenges.

Social Techpreneurship in AgriTech with AI

While these computational techniques have made significant strides, there remains a quest for even more advanced and specialized algorithms capable of handling the increasing complexity and variability in agricultural data. This leads us to *deep learning*, a specialized subset of AI, which has shown particular promise in this context. These algorithms are trained on extensive datasets, such as thousands of images of plant leaves, to recognize patterns and anomalies. Once trained, they can offer timely and accurate diagnoses of diseases or pest infestations, representing a leap in efficiency and a potential for broader systemic change. However, the rapid integration of AI also calls for a nuanced understanding of its associated risks and externalities.

As Tzachor et al. (2022) suggest, mitigating these risks requires a multidisciplinary approach. This could involve rural anthropologists and applied ecologists in the technology design process, adopting responsible and human-centered innovation frameworks, and establishing data cooperatives for improved transparency. Interestingly, the multi-disciplinary nature of these strategies aligns well with the ethos of social entrepreneurship, which often thrives on cross-disciplinary innovation to address complex societal challenges (Mair & Marti, 2006). Social entrepreneurs, operating at the nexus of technology, business, and social impact, are uniquely positioned to integrate these diverse perspectives into actionable solutions. For example, piloting in controlled environments, known as *digital sandboxes,* is recommended to refine these technologies further and assess their impact (Tzachor et al., 2022). These sandboxes allow real-time evaluation and adjustment, ensuring the AI's sustainable and equitable deployment. Such comprehensive strategies can bridge information and financial gaps in rural agricultural landscapes, fostering economic, social, and environmental value (Sharma et al., 2023). This multi-faceted approach is crucial for managing sustainably, contributing to a country's GDP, and addressing the broader issues of food security.

Advancements in AI and sustainable practices in agriculture and beekeeping are not just technological feats but also ripe opportunities for social entrepreneurship. A recent study highlights how AI technologies, including robots and drones, are employed to optimize irrigation, automate weeding, and enhance the application of pesticides and herbicides, thereby contributing to productivity and sustainability in agriculture (Talaviya et al., 2020). These innovations yield a unique opportunity to turn this crisis into a catalyst for sustainable innovation, creating business models that are both profitable and environmentally responsible. It is crucial to distinguish social entrepreneurs from their traditional counterparts.

According to Dees (1998), what sets social entrepreneurs apart is their primary focus on creating social value instead of merely accumulating financial wealth. This focus manifests in various ways, including pursuing missions that serve marginalized or underserved communities, employing innovative solutions to social problems, and reinvesting profits to amplify social impact. One of the challenges social entrepreneurs often face is measuring intangible outcomes such as community empowerment and social equity. Traditional metrics like Return on Investment (ROI) often fall short of capturing the full impact of social entrepreneurship, which aims to address complex issues like community empowerment. This gap is filled by methodologies like Social Return on Investment (SROI), which quantifies social and environmental outcomes by assigning them monetary values. In doing so, SROI provides a more nuanced understanding of impact, making it a valuable tool for tackling intricate social challenges.

Türkiye's Social Agripreneurs

Social entrepreneurship is particularly well-suited to address complex social issues that defy simple solutions. For example, they may tackle systemic issues like food insecurity, unequal access to healthcare, or the digital divide, often employing multi-disciplinary approaches that integrate technology, community engagement, and policy advocacy. Despite these complexities and challenges, social entrepreneurs drive meaningful change across sectors and geographies by leveraging community engagement, technological advancements, and innovative funding models. Social businesses, despite facing unique challenges, have the potential to be as innovative as traditional for-profit enterprises, especially in addressing complex social issues (Yunus, 2009b). Through these concerted efforts, they contribute to solving urgent global issues and set a precedent for how businesses can simultaneously thrive economically while fostering social and environmental well-being.

In Türkiye, a nation steeped in a rich agricultural and beekeeping heritage, the current ecological crisis serves as a catalyst for transformative change. Situated at the crossroads of civilizations, Türkiye's Anatolian heartland has been an epicenter of agricultural innovation for millennia. The ancient Hittites, for example, were among the first to utilize iron tools for farming, a technological leap that influenced modern agricultural practices. Similarly, the Ottomans developed sophisticated irrigation systems that have informed contemporary water management techniques. Agriculture has thus been a cornerstone of societal development, making Türkiye a natural birthplace for pioneering solutions in modern AgriTech. Building on this legacy, a new wave of social entrepreneurs is rising to meet the challenges posed by ecological crises and the evolving need for sustainable agriculture in Türkiye.

For instance, in Türkiye, *FruxTR* is pioneering the use of AI and the Internet of Things(IoT) in vertical hydroponic farming. This innovation aims to address the challenges of land scarcity and water usage by offering predictive algorithms that ensure optimal growing conditions. *MOVE ON AI* is making strides in AgriTech by developing autonomous software for tractors and farm management, targeting the inefficiencies and labor-intensive aspects of traditional farming. *Orbiba Robotics* is taking organic farming to the next level by offering affordable, AI-driven robot platforms prioritizing clean agriculture and sustainability. They all aim to reduce the use of harmful pesticides and increase crop yields through precision farming. These entrepreneurs are not solely driven by economic gains; they are also deeply committed to creating social and environmental value. This dual focus aligns them with the broader movement of social entrepreneurship, which aims to balance social responsibility with economic viability (Mair & Martí, 2006).

Among these groundbreaking initiatives is Beeplant, a Turkish startup founded in 2021, which has developed an automatic beekeeping system housed in a mobile hive. BeePlant leverages AI and image processing technology to address the complexities of royal jelly production, a process that traditionally involves meticulous manual labor for tasks such as larva transfer and harvesting. By automating these tasks, Beeplant's mobile hive significantly reduces the workload and enhances the quality of the royal jelly produced. Beyond streamlining operations, Beeplant's system offers innovative solutions to the pressing challenges facing bee populations. Advanced image processing capabilities enable early detection of disease or parasite infestation, facilitating timely interventions that can be crucial for colony survival. The automation also minimizes human error in hive management, reducing stress factors that make bees more susceptible to disease. Moreover, the mobile hive's controlled environment offers a layer of protection against adverse weather conditions and potentially harmful pesticides. In this multifaceted approach, Beeplant serves a dual purpose: it optimizes beekeeping operations while also contributing to the well-being of both human and bee populations.

The decline in bee populations is not just an ecological concern but a critical issue with far-reaching implications for global agriculture and human food security. Bees are indispensable for pollinating a wide variety of plants, including essential food crops like fruits, vegetables, and nuts. For example, bumble bees are responsible for sustaining about one-third of our food supply and 80 % of flowering plants (Cameron & Sadd, 2020). This aligns with broader environmental theories such as ecosystem services, which emphasize the multifaceted roles that species like bees play in maintaining ecological balance and overall biodiversity. Amidst this crisis, the role of beekeepers, or practitioners of *apiculture*, has become increasingly important. The term *apiculture* refers to the science and art of beekeeping, a practice that has been around for thousands of years but has gained scientific recognition more recently. *It is a living reminder that humans are not isolated entities but integral components of a larger ecosystem.*

Recent research has shown evidence of divergent selection in bee communities related to factors like thermoregulation and stress (Samad-zada et al., 2023). This highlights the importance of continuously monitoring genetic diversity and adaptive processes, especially as bees confront challenges like anthropogenic disturbances and global warming. Given these, the limitations of traditional apicultural methods have become increasingly apparent. The situation has reached a point where international guidelines and standards for pesticide use and commercial bee trade are urgently called for (Cameron & Sadd, 2020). In light of these urgent challenges, Beeplant emerges as a game-changing force in the realm of apiculture. By leveraging automation to simplify intricate tasks, the startup alleviates the labor-intensive nature of traditional beekeeping and elevates the quality of royal jelly production. This disruptive innovation is a compelling example of social entrepreneurship, as defined by Dees (1998), by striking a balance between technological advancement and social responsibility. In effect, Beeplant is redefining the benchmarks for sustainable and efficient apiculture, offering a blueprint for how innovation can address both ecological and social imperatives.

2. Methodology

The primary aim of this chapter is to explore the transformative potential of AI in the realm of social entrepreneurship, with a specific focus on its application within the agricultural sector in Türkiye. This research follows a qualitative paradigm to provide an in-depth understanding of the phenomena under study. The chapter draws on two key theories to understand AI's transformative role in social entrepreneurship. First, it cites Schumpeter's (1942) creative destruction, which argues that innovation disrupts existing economic structures. Second, it uses Christensen's (1997) disruptive innovation, focusing on how new technologies change existing markets and practices. These frameworks elucidate how AI is not just incremental but fundamentally disruptive in social entrepreneurship. Utilizing BeePlant as a case study, the chapter aims to uncover the dual mission of social enterprises in achieving both economic viability and broader social and environmental objectives, as conceptualized by Mair and Martí (2006). Inspired by Dees (1998), who highlights social entrepreneurs as change agents, and Yunus (2009a), who focuses on innovation in solving social issues, this chapter aims to enrich existing literature. It explores how BeePlant's AI innovations in beekeeping democratize technology, reduce labor, and enhance sustainability, aligning with social entrepreneurship principles.

This case study incorporates insights from stakeholder interviews to understand the role of AI in social entrepreneurship, specifically within BeePlant. An interview was conducted with Jibran Qadri, Co-Founder of BeePlant, who specializes in developing crowdfunding and investment strategies, B2B potential client relations, and team development. Qadri also shared insights from his co-founder, Hakan Aktan, to explore the challenges, solutions, and impacts of integrating AI into their beekeeping operations. The study aims to enrich the academic discourse on the role of technology in fostering social impact and provide valuable insights for industry stakeholders in social entrepreneurship.

Data Collection Method

n alignment with the qualitative research paradigm, stakeholder interviews from BeePlant were conducted to deepen the empirical understanding of AI's role in social entrepreneurship. The main research question is, "How is the application of AI transforming social entrepreneurship within the agricultural sector in Türkiye, particularly in terms of achieving economic viability while fulfilling broader social and environmental objectives?"

To address the research question, the following interview questions aim to explore the use of AI in demonstrating social entrepreneurship's innovative potential:

1. Can you describe how AI technologies have been integrated into BeePlant's operations to fulfill its social entrepreneurship goals?
2. What were the most significant challenges BeePlant faced when integrating AI into its beekeeping operations, and how were these challenges mitigated?
3. Could you elaborate on the AI-driven solutions BeePlant has developed to address unmet needs in traditional beekeeping?
4. How do BeePlant's AI-driven methods compare to traditional beekeeping techniques regarding efficiency, inclusivity, and environmental impact? Do you have any examples, statistics, or quantifiable data to support these observed impacts?
5. What has been the observed impact of BeePlant's AI-driven approaches on various stakeholders in the beekeeping industry?
6. Can you elaborate on BeePlant's B2B revenue model?

These questions were designed to delve into the challenges, solutions, and impacts of integrating AI into beekeeping, providing a comparative analysis with traditional methods within the framework of social entrepreneurship.

3. BeePlant as Social Entrepreneurship

Nectar of Innovation in Apiculture

In the interview, BeePlant's Co-founder, Mr. Qadri, elucidated the company's foundational ethos, aligning with Dees' (1998) characterization of social entrepreneurs as change agents. He explained that the inception of BeePlant was driven by an urgent need to rejuvenate the largely traditional and unchanging beekeeping sector. Fully aware of the industry's susceptibility to the adverse effects of climate change and a declining interest in beekeeping, the company saw an opportunity for transformation through artificial intelligence. To this end, BeePlant has developed a specialized robot designed for royal jelly production. This robot utilizes advanced image processing and larva transfer technologies, which are further optimized by machine learning algorithms for ongoing refinement. In addition, BeePlant has pioneered early-warning systems to detect bee diseases promptly. These technological breakthroughs serve dual purposes: they simplify the beekeeping process and significantly increase yield—by as much as fivefold. Looking ahead, BeePlant aims to integrate these various technologies into a single, automated system that will revolutionize beehive management. This multi-faceted approach aligns well with the Triple Bottom Line framework, which advocates for a balanced focus on environmental, social, and economic sustainability (Elkington, 1994). Moreover, by using resources more efficiently and sustainably, BeePlant's strategy resonates with the principles of Natural Capitalism, emphasizing the critical interdependency between human-made and natural capital (Hawken et al., 1999).

From Code to Comb: The Multidisciplinary Challenge

The primary obstacle in BeePlant's journey was not the availability of technology but rather assembling a team with the requisite expertise to operationalize their innovative ideas. Only Mr. Aktan had a computer science background among the co-founders, underscoring the team's need to acquire a foundational understanding of AI. Guided by Mr. Aktan's expertise, the team undertook a self-directed learning process to equip themselves with the knowledge needed to select additional team members capable of implementing their AI-driven solutions judiciously. This scenario resonates with Dees' (1998) concept of social entrepreneurs as change agents, posing that social entrepreneurs often face hurdles regarding financial resources and human capital. The need for a multidisciplinary team, especially in a tech-driven social enterprise like BeePlant, is a testament to the complex nature of social entrepreneurship.

A technical constraint they encountered was the Royal Jelly machine field test seasonality; spring emerged as the sole viable season for such evaluations. The team executed an exhaustive series of tests under diverse conditions to mitigate this limitation, thereby amassing a comprehensive dataset. Another pivotal challenge was the task of sensitizing traditional beekeepers to the advantages offered by this technological paradigm shift. The team's self-directed learning and adaptation to overcome these technical constraints align with resilience and adaptive capacity principles, key tenets in sustainability theories (Folke, 2006). Adapting and learning is crucial for any venture's long-term sustainability, especially one that seeks to balance social, economic, and environmental objectives.

Transforming Apiculture with AI

BeePlant's robotic technology showcases the venture's role in social entrepreneurship through its innovative use of image processing, larva transfer, and machine learning for enhanced apiculture. The robot's capabilities in monitoring bee health, optimizing royal jelly production through precise larva placement, and learning from its performance to increase effectiveness highlight a significant advancement. Additionally, its early-warning systems for detecting threats like the Varroa Destructor mite are vital for protecting bee populations and human health. This integration of technology not only streamlines beekeeping operations and boosts yield but also exemplifies disruptive innovation, underlining BeePlant's commitment to ecological balance and public health.

The integration of these technologies serves dual purposes: it significantly streamlines the beekeeping process and amplifies the yield by as much as fivefold. The robot can perform multiple functions, including producing honey and royal jelly and the intricate task of transferring bee larvae. It employs analytics to determine the number and location of honeycomb cells most conducive to healthy royal jelly production. Moreover, it keeps track of the ages of bee larvae, which is vital for effective hive management. This comprehensive approach not only saves time for beekeepers but also enhances the overall health and productivity of the bee colonies, which is a form of disruptive innovation and creative destruction.

The case exemplifies innovative resilience in combating apicultural challenges and redefines social entrepreneurship, illustrating a nuanced approach where technology's role extends beyond efficiency to embody a guardian of ecological balance and public health.

AI-Driven Sustainability in Beekeeping

Under the leadership of co-founder Mr. Qadri, BeePlant has made significant strides in beekeeping technology, enabling beekeepers to manage up to 100 hives, a substantial increase from the traditional limit of 20. This fivefold enhancement in operational efficiency is attributed to the innovative AI tools, which not only streamline hive management but also play a pivotal role in environmental conservation by minimizing bee mortality rates through real-time monitoring of temperature, humidity, and colony health.

Such efficient use of technology aligns with and advances the principles of the circular economy, emphasizing waste reduction and resource optimization (MacArthur, 2013). BeePlant's approach reflects a deep dedication to sustainable practices at the heart of social entrepreneurship. The system's ability to precisely regulate honey harvesting, ensuring colonies are robust enough to thrive through winter, embodies the concept of shared value, creating a symbiotic relationship between economic efficiency and societal well-being (Porter & Kramer, 2011).

This balance is crucial in demonstrating BeePlant's role in addressing societal and environmental challenges through innovative solutions. This startup epitomizes the raison d'être of social entrepreneurship: tackling critical issues with sustainable, value-driven practices that benefit the economy and society by fostering resilience, sustainability, and shared prosperity. In doing so, BeePlant contributes to environmental well-being and sets a standard for integrating technology into natural conservation efforts, reinforcing the importance of a harmonious relationship between nature and commerce.

Code v.s Culture

Mr. Qadri emphasized the intricate challenge of persuading traditional beekeepers to recognize the merits of AI technologies. Many of these beekeepers are deeply rooted in time-honored methods and show a marked reluctance to transition to newer, technological solutions. This hesitancy serves as a significant barrier to the broader adoption of AI in the beekeeping sector. Such resistance can be interpreted through the lens of creative destruction. The reluctance of traditional beekeepers acts as a form of inertia against the destructive aspect of creative destruction, thereby slowing down the pace of technological advancement and the realization of its potential benefits (Schumpeter, 1942).

Schein's (1985) organizational culture model offers valuable insights to understand this resistance further. According to him, organizational culture operates at three levels: artifacts, espoused beliefs and values, and underlying assumptions. The reluctance to adopt AI technologies may not only be about the visible practices (artifacts) but could also be tied to deeply held beliefs about the sanctity and effectiveness of traditional methods (espoused beliefs and values). These, in turn, could be underpinned by fundamental, often unconscious, assumptions about the right way of doing things that have been internalized over years or even generations (Schein, 1985). This complex cultural landscape underscores the multifaceted role of social entrepreneurs like Mr. Qadri. They find themselves at the intersection of innovation and tradition, tasked with introducing disruptive technologies and engaging with these deeper cultural elements. This requires a nuanced approach that goes beyond mere technological innovation; it demands a deep understanding of the community's values, fears, and aspirations (Dees, 1998). Therefore, the role of a social entrepreneur extends to being a change agent, a mediator, and an educator, all while driving forward the technological advancements that could benefit the community and the industry at large

Democratizing the Hive

BeePlant is committed to revitalizing the beekeeping industry through technological innovation and public engagement. To fulfill this mission, they provide educational courses using a variety of platforms, including a state-of-the-art Virtual Reality BeeTraining system. On the business side, BeePlant adopts a B2B revenue model that allows beekeeping companies and associations to rent their specialized machines at no initial cost. These machines come equipped with integrated hardware and software that accurately measure the amount of royal jelly produced. BeePlant then charges a commission fee, capped at 10 % of the royal jelly yield, providing a cost-effective solution for their business partners. This dual focus on social impact and financial sustainability aligns closely with the concept of social businesses that aim to solve social issues through innovative business models (Yunus, 2009a). BeePlant's business model can be interpreted as a form of technology democratization. By offering their specialized beekeeping machines to companies and associations without an initial cost, BeePlant effectively lowers the financial barriers to entry for adopting advanced technological solutions in the beekeeping sector.

This resonates with Winner's (1986) advocacy for making technology more democratic. Democratization is not just about access but also about participation; it's about enabling people to have a say in the technological changes that will affect their lives. BeePlant's approach provides more than just tools; it empowers beekeepers to engage with and benefit from technological advancements, thereby leveling the playing field. This fosters a more inclusive industry and facilitates the spread of innovative solutions aimed at tackling pressing environmental and social issues. This embodiment of technological democratization aligns closely with the core principles of social entrepreneurship, which *prioritize innovation, inclusivity, and empowerment, ensuring that the benefits of new technologies extend to all stakeholders, particularly those previously marginalized.*

4. Findings & Future Recommendations

The case study emphasizes the significance of multidisciplinary teams and technology democratization for inclusivity, marking them as key for social entrepreneurs to deliver extensive benefits. It illuminates the difficulties in gauging social impact and the success of financial models that further social goals, advocating leveraging change for favorable results. Additionally, it underscores the necessity of such teams and democratization as pivotal strategies for social innovators to achieve broad advantages, detailing the complexities of measuring social impact and presenting financial strategies that support social objectives, all while encouraging change adoption for positive outcomes.

This narrative illustrates the essence of social entrepreneurship through sustainable, value-driven practices that offer societal and economic advantages, embodying Clayton Christensen's (1997) concept of disruptive innovation by challenging the beekeeping industry's norms. For BeePlant to evolve into a catalyst of creative destruction, as Joseph Schumpeter (1942) envisioned, it needs to revolutionize industry standards, necessitating not only innovation but a commitment to inclusivity in transforming practices. Achieving this transformative potential depends on a combination of factors, including industry standardization, economic restructuring, and regulatory influence, which together facilitate the broader acceptance and integration of new solutions.

Central to this process is ensuring advancements transcend economic and environmental gains and promote adaptation and transition among stakeholders, overcoming resistance to change. Social entrepreneurs are crucial in pioneering accessible and beneficial innovations, potentially requiring educational initiatives, collaboration with traditional practitioners, and creating pathways to mitigate adverse impacts. Such efforts prioritize community well-being, embodying social entrepreneurship's inclusive, sustainable, and equitable principles.

The shared value generated by Beeplant exemplifies a model for policy synergy, drawing governmental interest in sustainable agriculture and potentially fast-tracking Beeplant's technology as the industry standard, a manifestation of creative destruction. Beeplant's scalability enhances its disruptive capacity, suggesting that locally generated shared value could extend globally, amplifying societal benefits and market reach, thus contributing to the industry's economic restructuring.

At this juncture, it's essential to recognize that social entrepreneurs aim not just to sustain but to revolutionize traditional practices in their industries, embodying a transformative concept of sustainability focused on innovation and systemic change rather than mere preservation. This approach enhances industry resilience against future challenges, paving the way for inherently more sustainable systems. By ensuring their technologies are accessible and affordable and by building a comprehensive ecosystem—including supply chains and educational frameworks—around their innovations, social entrepreneurs set the stage to supplant traditional methods. Such achievements embody Schumpeter's (1942) vision of innovation as a force that disrupts and renews industries, creating more efficient systems in place of established structures.

5. Closing Remarks

In a world increasingly shaped by technological advancements and environmental challenges, BeePlant stands as a beacon of innovative social entrepreneurship, which navigated a labyrinth of technical, social, and environmental complexities to bring forth a new approach to beekeeping. Their journey, marked by challenges that span from team formation to technological constraints, provides a compelling narrative that exemplifies the resilience, adaptability, and ingenuity commonly exhibited by social entrepreneurs. Their multifaceted AI-driven solutions promise to redefine the beekeeping industry and serve as a testament to the transformative power of technology when wielded responsibly and creatively. The business model, a harmonious blend of social impact and financial sustainability, echoes the principles of Circular Economy and Shared Value, thereby setting a new standard for future social enterprises (Yunus, 2009a; MacArthur, 2013; Porter & Kramer, 2011). Moreover, their efforts to democratize technology resonate with the broader discourse on inclusivity and social equity, making them not just business innovators but also change agents committed to a more sustainable and equitable future. *This illustrates that the road to innovation is not a solitary endeavor but a collective journey that requires a balance of technological prowess, social awareness, and an unyielding commitment to sustainable development.* In the end, BeePlant's tale is not just about the bees or the honey but about a sweeter future for us all.

References

Akbulaev, N., Ahmedov, T., & Aliyev, Y. (2017). Yoksulların Bankası: Grameen Bank. *Uluslararası Türk Kültür Coğrafyasında Sosyal Bilimler Dergisi, 2*(1), 56–70.

Cameron, S. A., & Sadd, B. M. (2020). Global trends in Bumble Bee Health. *Annual Review of Entomology, 65*, 209–232. https://doi.org/10.1146/annurev-ento-011118-111847

Chakraborty, I., Edirippulige, S., & Ilavarasan, P. V. (2023). The role of telehealth startups in healthcare service delivery: A systematic review. *International Journal of Medical Informatics, 174*, 105048. https://doi.org/10.1016/j.ijmedinf.2023.105048.

Christensen, C. M. (1997). *The innovator's dilemma: When new technologies cause great firms to fail.* Harvard Business Review Press.

Dees, J. G. (1998). *The meaning of social entrepreneurship*. Stanford University.

Elizondo, D. A., McClendon, R. W., Hoogenboom, G. (1994). Neural network models for predicting flowering and physiological maturity of soybean. *Trans ASAE, 37*(3), 981–988.

Elkington, J. (1994). Towards the sustainable corporation: Win-win-win business strategies for sustainable development. *California Management Review, 36*(2), 90--100.

Folke, C. (2006). Resilience: The emergence of a perspective for social–ecological systems analyses. *Global Environmental Change, 16*(3), 253–267.

Holland, J. H. (1992). *Adaptation in natural and artificial systems: An introductory analysis with applications to biology, control, and artificial intelligence*. The MIT Press.

Hawken, P., Lovins, A., & Lovins, L. H. (1999). *Natural capitalism: Creating the next industrial revolution*. Little, Brown and Company.

Jones, J., & Augustine, G. (2017). "Innovation at one acre fund: Seeing the forest for the trees". https://doi.org/10.1108/case.kellogg.2016.000158

MacArthur, E. (2013). Towards the circular economy. *Journal of Industrial Ecology, 2*(1), 23–44.

Mair, J., & Martí, I. (2006). Social entrepreneurship research: A source of explanation, prediction, and delight. *Journal of World Business, 41*(1), 36–44.

Ngugi, B., Pelowski, M., & Ogembo, J. G. (2010). M-pesa: A case study of the critical early adopters' role in the rapid adoption of mobile money banking in Kenya. *The Electronic Journal of Information Systems in Developing Countries, 43*, 1–16. https://doi.org/10.1002/j.1681-4835.2010.tb00307.x

Orchi, H., Sadik, M., Khaldoun, M., & Sabir, E. (2023). Real-time detection of crop leaf diseases using enhanced YOLOv8 algorithm. In 2023 International Wireless Communications and Mobile Computing (IWCMC), Marrakesh, Morocco (pp. 1690–1696). https://doi.org/10.1109/IWCMC58020.2023.10182573

Porter, M. E., & Kramer, M. R. (2011). Creating shared value. *Harvard Business Review, 89*(1/2), 62–77.

Rastogi, C. (2018). M-Kopa solar: Lighting up the dark continent. *South Asian Journal of Business and Management Cases, 7*(2), 93–103. https://doi.org/10.1177/2277977918774648

Samad-zada, F., Kelemen, E. P., & Rehan, S. M. (2023). The impact of geography and climate on the population structure and local adaptation in a wild bee. *Evolutionary Applications, 16*, 1154–1168. https://doi.org/10.1111/eva.13558

Tzachor, A., Devare, M., King, B., et al. (2022). Responsible artificial intelligence in agriculture requires systemic understanding of risks and externalities. *Nature Machine Intelligence, 4*, 104–109. https://doi.org/10.1038/s42256-022-00440-4

Schumpeter, J. A. (1942). *Capitalism, socialism, and democracy*. Harper & Brothers.

Wakchaure, M., Patle, B. K., & Mahindrakar, A. K. (2023). Application of AI techniques and robotics in agriculture: A review. *Artificial Intelligence in the Life Sciences, 3*, 100057. https://doi.org/10.1016/j.ailsci.2023.100057

Satishkumar, D., Joshua Daniel Raj, J., Anoopkumar, H. S., Chethan, D. R., Deekshith More, B., & Kushal, A. Y. (2023). Herbs ailment diagnosis using AI techniques for sustainable innovation in agriculture. In *2023 4th International Conference on Innovative Trends in Information Technology (ICITIIT)* (pp. 1–4). Kottayam, India. https://doi.org/10.1109/ICITIIT57246.2023.10068575

Sauvé, S., S. Bernard and P. Sloan (2016), "Environmental sciences, sustainable development and circular economy: Alternative concepts for trans-disciplinary research", Environmental Development, Vol. 17, pp. 48-56.

Schein, E. H. (2004). *Organizational culture and leadership* (3rd ed.). San Francisco: Jossey-Bass.

Sharma, R., Kamble, S., Gupta, S., Belhadi, A., Rana, N. P., & Kumar, K. (2023). Interlinkages Between Digital-Social Entrepreneurship and Technological Capabilities for Sustainable Value Creation. Journal of Global Information Management (JGIM), 31(1), 1-26. https://doi.org/10.4018/JGIM.328515

Talaviya, T., Shah, D., Patel, N., Yagnik, H., & Shah, M. (2020). Implementation of artificial intelligence in agriculture for optimisation of irrigation and application of pesticides and herbicides. *Artificial Intelligence in Agriculture, 4*, 58–73. https://doi.org/10.1016/j.aiia.2020.04.002

Winner, L. (1986). *The whale and the reactor: A search for limits in an age of high technology*. University of Chicago Press.

Yağ, İ., & Altan, A. (2022). Artificial Intelligence-based robust hybrid algorithm design and implementation for real-time detection of plant diseases in agricultural environments. *Biology, 11*(12), 1732. MDPI AG. Retrieved from http://dx.doi.org/10.3390/biology11121732

Yunus, M. (2009a). *Creating a world without poverty: Social business and the future of capitalism*. PublicAffairs.

Yunus, M. (2009b). *Building social business: The new kind of capitalism that serves humanity's most pressing needs*. PublicAffairs.

Zadeh, L. A. (1965). Fuzzy sets. *Information and Control, 8*(3), 338–353.

Zhai, Z., Martínez, J. F., Beltran, V., & Martínez, N. L. (2020). Decision support systems for agriculture 4.0: Survey and challenges. *Computers and Electronics in Agriculture, 170*, 105256. https://doi.org/10.1016/j.compag.2020.105256

Neşe Saruhan
İstanbul Gedik Üniversitesi

Chapter 13 How to Build an Effective Neuro-Leadership in Social Enterprises with Neuro-Divergent Team Members

Abstract: The definition of entrepreneurship is the drive to launch and manage a new business to generate employment opportunities and favorable conditions for both clients and staff. When organizations are devoted to social development and transformation, these organizations are known as social enterprises. Prioritizing social aims, social values, and solutions to social issues are the core focuses of social entrepreneurship. Since social entrepreneurial organizations have quite different objectives and purposes from one another, current theories of leadership cannot adequately describe the leadership functions involved in the formation, expansion, and sustainability of these companies. Organizations need to establish new human resource strategies in order to be more inclusive of neurodiversity. The main purpose of this paper is to analyze the relationship between neuro leadership and social entrepreneurship while leading neurodiverse teams and how neuro leadership builds and maintains social enterprises with neurodiversity in mind.

Keywords: Neurodiversity in leadership, Social Entrepreneurship, Inclusive human resource management

1. Introduction

Due to globalization, there are several major technological, economic, political, and environmental changes have occurred within the last few decades. These changes have resulted in several different new perspectives on entrepreneurship that are essential for the economic development of societies. Entrepreneurship itself has been defined as a curiosity to start a new enterprise and to run this enterprise to generate new jobs and create new opportunities for employees and customers (Kawharu et al., 2017; Vita et al., 2012). However, Social enterprises are organizations that have the mission of social change and development. Social entrepreneurship mainly prioritizes social contribution and social value (Brieger & DeClerq, 2019), social goals (Doherty et al., 2006), and solutions for social problems (Mair, 2019). Leading upcoming social organizations has become another research subject for researchers due to the unique leadership needs of social enterprises. Social entrepreneurial leaders establish and manage innovative entrepreneurial organizations. Since the purpose and mission of these social entrepreneurial enterprises are quite different from each other, the current leadership theories will be not adequate to explain leadership functions on establishment, growth, and sustainability levels of social entrepreneurial organizations. So, the field of neuroscience will assist in explaining the human decision-making process and show us how to change the milestones of leadership theories. At this point, neuro leadership is a new arena to explain how to lead employees based on neuroscience principles. On the other hand, there have been changes to the workforce's composition. There is a greater variety of workers, including both talented and neurodiverse ones, make up the human resource pool today. Neurodiversity refers to the diversity of people mainly with neurological or developmental conditions such as ADHD or learning disabilities, and bipolar. Organizations must develop new human resource strategies to be more inclusive of neurodiversity. Neuro leadership will be more compressive in managing people in social enterprises. Therefore, this research explores a simple question: "How neuro leadership perspective assist in managing social enterprises with neuro-divergent teams?"

This paper aims to bridge the gap between neuro leadership and social entrepreneurship while leading neurodiverse teams. Neuroscience is the newly developed way of understanding human behavior through the latest neuroscientific tools. Then neuro leadership field will be explained in social enterprises and how neuro leadership assists in the management and development of organizations. How neuro leadership includes neurodiversity while developing and sustaining social enterprises.

2. Social Entrepreneurship

Social entrepreneurship refers to establishing businesses or funds for different social issues (Saebi et al., 2019). Social entrepreneurship is the practice of using the ideas and strategies employed by entrepreneurs to a business that directly social issues or brings about social change. As Monir and Geberemeskel (2023) stated social entrepreneurship is different from other start-up businesses in solving social problems mainly related to economic situations, environment, and societies. The main driving force behind a social entrepreneur is the desire to address a universal social or cultural issue. These issues have been regarded as valid ways to reduce poverty (Tobias et al., 2013), accessible health care and education, better financial conditions (Azmat et al., 2015), and improving better on overall living conditions of societies such as empowering women (Haugh & Talwar, 2016). Researchers found that social enterprises bring positive social change to the social communities (Lumpkin et al., 2018). As it was stated by

Avelino et al. (2019), social innovation would be another important subject for further research to develop new practices while solving fundamental social problems.

Social entrepreneurial organizations may be financed outside of their activities. Conversely, these organizations may be sufficient to fund these activities by themselves in line with their core mission. These economic activities may have social missions. In addition, they can be for-profit organizations that attempt social changes. Generally speaking, social entrepreneurship advances general social, cultural, and environmental objectives that are frequently connected to fields like community development, healthcare solutions, and poverty lessening. (Thompson, 2002). A unique behavioral pattern of social entrepreneurs is their desire to do something good for society (Tiwari et al., 2020).

There are several different research studies on the main drives or motivation factors behind social entrepreneurship (Maalaoui et al., 2020; Tiwari et al., 2020). They indicated that social enterprise is motivated by personal enjoyment (Dey & Lehner, 2017), fame and recognition (Tucker et al., 2019), strong influence from childhood experiences even indirect experiences (Dickel et al., 2020), solving social problems (Yitshaki & Kropp, 2016). However, there is a limited number research on how to lead these social enterprises to be successful. Social entrepreneurs motivate others to handle greater social responsibilities and contribute toward the development of the economy or social problems. Neuro-leadership will assist in establishing new ideas for social problems.

3. Social Entrepreneurship in Turkey

The goal of social entrepreneurship is to create a business model, service, or product that addresses societal issues. In order to accomplish their social objectives, social enterprises are profitable; however, unlike commercial businesses, they reinvest their earnings. Instead of focusing on rivalry, social enterprises prioritize sustainability, solidarity, and long-term social impact. In Turkey, social entrepreneurship has expanded dramatically, especially over the past 20 years. There is no separate legal status for social enterprises in Turkey. Social enterprises may choose one or more legal statuses according to their needs. The British Council (2019) prepared a report on social entrepreneurship in Turkey. This report defines social enterprises as "social or environmental impact determines creation as its primary goal, more than half of its revenues are commercial business and spend their profits primarily for social purposes" (The Situation of Social Enterprises in Turkey, 2019: 22). Cooperatives are most common legal status of enterprises followed by associations, foundations, and joint stock companies. Esen (2023) focused on social entrepreneurship activities in Türkiye and she indicated that the main goal of social entrepreneurship initiatives is to improve the welfare of societies. She suggested standardizing the legal status of social enterprises in Turkey. In addition, there will be a national organization to connect with the networking and social entrepreneurship ecosystem in Turkey. Social entrepreneurs mainly pay attention to basic human needs such as food, shelter, etc., and education in terms of social development. Esen (2023) stated that there would be more social enterprises to improve environmental quality.

Similar to most developing nations, Turkey has a relatively low number of civil organizations per 10,000 citizens. By 2020, Turkey will have 84 million people living there. Even then, 121,720 associations, 5,775 foundations, and 84,232 cooperatives will exist, for a total of 211,727, according to official government statistics (Işık, 2022). Also Işık (2022) stated that social entrepreneurship has a significant potential for the younger population in Turkey, as evidenced by the country's young population density and interest in social enterprises.

4. Social Entrepreneurial Leadership and Neurodiversity

Social entrepreneurial leaders are those who develop and run innovative entrepreneurial companies that aim to address social problems (Prabhu, 1999). Leadership studies do not clearly explain the role that social entrepreneurial leaders play in the establishment, development, operation, efficacy, collapse, and dissolution of social entrepreneurial organizations.

Common characteristics of small social entrepreneurial organizations are providing innovative products or services and having strongly committed leaders with loosely organized communities. So, social entrepreneur leaders have to provide considerable discretion, rapid response to get action, and flexibility to their supporters. For small entrepreneurs, it is more important to get notice of shared values and ideologies for a specific common purpose. But, moving to a larger organizational structure, these non-hierarchical organizations will have some management problems in their organizations. There would be a high diversity of members coming from different cultural and educational backgrounds. It should also be taken into account that these members would include a number of neurodivergent individuals.

The term "neurodiversity" is widely used to characterize variations in the functioning of individual brains. Also, this term refers to brain processes, learning styles, and/or behavioral patterns that deviate from "typical." The premise is that there isn't a single "right" way for the brain to function. Rather, people view and react to the world in a variety of ways, and it is important to celebrate and value these differences. Neurodiversity is the term used to describe a wide range of behavioral characteristics and brain functions, such as social communication, attention spans, emotional recognition and expression skills, and several cognitive functions. (Dawson et al., 2022). Neurodiversity is no longer viewed by practitioners as a disease in and of itself. Rather, they see them as distinct ways of acquiring and analyzing data.

Neurodiversity commonly refers to a variety of conditions including autism spectrum conditions, attention deficit hyperactive disorder (ADHD), dyslexia, dyspraxia, dyscalculia and other unspecified conditions. The idea of Neurodiversity asserts neurological development outside of the atypical "normal" human thinking is a biological variation, deserving both understanding and support. The term Neurodiversity was established in 1998 by Judy Singer, an Australian social scientist, who coined the term neurodiversity to promote equality and inclusion of "neurological minorities." The goal of the neurodiversity movement, which was established in the 1990s, is to embrace neurological differences and promote greater acceptance and inclusion of all individuals.

When faced with various challenges and interpersonal difficulties, people with varying cognitive abilities can benefit from their intelligence and dedication, which can lead to a variety of advantageous traits (Hutson & Hutson, 2023). Saleh et al. (2022) indicated that neurodiverse employees are more likely detail-oriented such as autistic employees. They are viewed as reliable, disciplined, focused, and extremely passionate about what they do. Several researches showed that ADHD employees with hyperfocus and energetic characteristics (Fabritius, 2022), and individuals with dyslexia tend to have strong spatial intelligence and entrepreneurial tendencies (Smith-Spark & Gordon, 2022). The neurodiverse population can contribute unique skills such as creative storytelling, coding, and empathy to workplace offices (Hutson & Hutson, 2023). Even though neurodiverse people have different talented functions to generate creative solutions to problems, there is a need for different leadership aspects for successful management. Entrepreneurial leadership is a distinct leadership approach that concentrates on enabling diverse talents to function more imaginatively and creatively within an organization while adapting to an unpredictable business environment (Fontana & Musa, 2017). So, organizational neuroscience has been applied to the process of making entrepreneurial decisions and managing emotions in a number of studies conducted in recent decades (Cucino et al., 2023). In the past ten years, there has been a growing interest in neuroscientific theory and the subsequent investigation of how the human brain shapes behavior (Kuhlmann & Kadgien, 2018). Social scientists have long studied how people behave in groups. So, the neuro-leadership approach has become a very popular leadership theory in recent years due to the need for effective and profitable organizations.

5. Neuro-leadership

Rock & Schwartz (2007) stated that neuro-leadership integrates leadership, management, organizational development, and neuroscientific knowledge. The Neuro-leadership approach also broadens the definition of leadership characteristics, directs efficient organizational procedures, and results in the creation of "brain-based coaching". Finding new ways to improve leadership skills and implement organizational change is one of neuro-leadership's most valuable goals. It's challenging to break a habit, and it can be especially challenging to break the habits of a big group of people in an organization (Kuhlmann & Kadgien, 2018). According to Rock and Schwartz (2007), by providing a deeper comprehension of the circuitry underlying learning and habit formation, neuro-leadership can assist us in developing more effective strategies to bring about change while indicating the role of focus, attention, and expectation in learning.

The purpose of neuro-leadership field is to improve leaders' effectiveness and efficiency in organizations and help them to succeed through understanding how the brain works (Ringleb et al., 2013). Neuro-leadership examines individuals in their social organizational environment, looking at how they make decisions, solve problems, regulate their emotions, collaborate, influence others, and facilitate change (Rock & Schwartz, 2007). As Saruhan (2023) pointed out that neuro-leadership takes its roots from the psychological theory of self-determination theory. Self-determination theory consists of people's psychological needs of competence, autonomy, and relatedness. These psychological needs are universal for all cultures. Without satisfying these needs in the organization, there would be no way to be successful in the business environment.

6. How to integrate neuro-leadership approach into neurodiverse teams

Social entrepreneurship organizations consist of members from different educational backgrounds, ethnic origins, and neurodiverse skills. So, leaders should consider all aspects of a team while leading them. The neuro-leadership approach will assist social entrepreneurs in leading their teams effectively. Neurodiverse members will be very useful on different tasks at different functions of the social entrepreneur organizations, but there should be several issues to take care of while leading and managing the team. Neuro-leadership makes points to individual differences of the team while leading them. To manage the neurodiverse team, leaders should pay attention to several issues.

While it is primarily a social justice movement, neurodiversity research and awareness in the business environment are increasingly important in how human resources and organizational psychologists view and address certain disabilities and neurological conditions in the workplace. Neuro-leadership mentions the importance of differences of each individual in a way of their perception of the environment. Similar to the common employee impression, a neurodiverse person would like to perceive that he/she has value and status in the workplace. For example, Ringleb et al. (2013) indicated the FMRI study looked at brain activity in the ventral striatum, which is responsible for processing values and rewards. Different information was shown to experiment participants with varying social statuses compared to those with a relatively higher or lower status. This study demonstrated that people are more receptive to and respectful of information from higher-status individuals. Therefore, one could say that a person wants to get better and maintain their social standing in society. So, neuro leaders should develop a working environment where all employees including neurodiverse employees feel valued. The status of neurodiverse employees should as the same as of the other team members.

The human brain looks for certainty when the situation is ambiguous as well as future positions. The person starts to feel anxiety and fear due to the uncertainty of the environment. For example, Peters, McEven, and Fristen(2017) indicated that people become uncertain when believe that something will not work out as they had anticipated. A crucial limitation on the amount of cerebral energy required would arise when cognitive systems work to lessen uncertainty about future events. When there is a high need for cerebral energy, this may lead to brain malfunctions such as impaired memory, diabetes, and several cardio events. Neuro-leader should pay more attention to communication activities among employees to provide enough information about all the relevant subjects of their jobs. Therefore, employees do not feel any uncertainty about the future. This condition is also very important for neurodiverse employees who need a little bit more consideration about their perception of uncertainty. When neurodiverse employees have enough and relevant information about their requirements, deadlines, and future concerns, they may feel more secure and safe in their workplace. These positive feelings will assist them to work more effectively. Employees who are neurodivergent have distinct ways of interacting with the outside world and processing information. This suggests that they will approach issues and problems from a unique perspective, which could affect the development of creative and thorough solutions. A neuroscience experiment conducted by Leotti and Delgado (2011) indicated that autonomy activates the ventral striatum, which is key to the brain's reward system. Autonomy allows a person to respond with choice to situations. So, people who have more autonomy feel less stressed and more confident. Neuro-leaders should focus on providing autonomy to neurodiverse team members. Neuro-leaders can empower their neurodivergent team members just like they can any other employee. When someone's skills are trusted and they are given the opportunity and autonomy to solve problems, make decisions, and oversee the completion of tasks, they become empowered.

Relatedness boosts team members' motivation and strengthens their sense of community. Moreover, relatedness amongst team members facilitates the sharing of knowledge within the group and fosters mutual trust, which in turn helps the group grow into a more cohesive social organization. Neurodivergent, inclusive, and empowered teams can be developed by leaders who are committed to recognizing the values that each member of the team brings to the group, who set clear expectations and procedures that are easy for all members to understand, and who offer continuous feedback. So, neuro-leaders should provide a climate that holds all members to be valued and part of this team. Since social entrepreneur enterprises usually have no profit mission while helping other people, relatedness of the same social mission is crucial to keep team members motivated and effective on their mission.

How fair a group is depends on how each individual perceives the other members of the group to have divided the available sources. Employees act aggressively and lack cooperation when they feel unfairly treated. The transparency of information is essential to developing a perception of fairness and certainty. So, neuro leaders should promote open and clear communication in order to establish psychological safety among team members. This is also very important for neurodivergent people. They would like to get clear-cut performance metrics and regular feedback about their performances. Effective communication among employees improves the perception of fairness in social enterprises. Team members of social enterprises, who typically labor for very little pay, are more motivated in this positive work environment.

7. Implications for neurodiverse team members in social entrepreneurial organizations

The neuro-leadership approach mainly emphasizes understanding individual differences among team members while adapting leadership functions. Since neurodiversity is a broad spectrum, each person's needs and skills will be unique. It's critical to keep in mind that dyslexia, dyspraxia, dyscalculia, and ADHD are all considered forms of neurodiversity. Although neurodivergent workers occasionally take a different approach to their work, this does not imply that they are any less productive or effective than their neurotypical colleagues. In order to protect these workers' well-being and promote neurodiversity and inclusivity in the workplace, managers and employers must become less dogmatic and give up trying to apply one solution that works for everyone. Flexible work environments are essential for fostering new ideas and perspectives on the workplace. Neuro-leaders should pay more attention to including all team members with flexible working conditions in social entrepreneurial organizations. Social enterprise team members typically receive little or no compensation for their work. So, there should be small arrangements for team member's work environment such as sound sensitivity of a quiet break space, and noise-cancelling headphones. Neuro-leaders should provide a clear communication style in the organization with the avoidance of sarcasm, and implied messages. They should provide more written instructions with clear task descriptions.

Teams that can focus on goals and utilize each member's strength will be more productive and high-performing than those that are built on inflexible procedures and authoritarian work environments. When there are clear performance standards, well-organized and transparent procedures, acceptance of individual differences, a search for innovative solutions, and management that encourages employee differentiation, everyone performs better. So neurodivergent workforce has an opportunity to be a part of social organizations. A rise in neurodiversity will promote a more equal and collaborative workplace. This will increase creative solutions for problems in the workplace.

8. How to integrate neurodiverse people on social enterprises in Turkey

In Turkey, studies on social entrepreneurship have received a lot of attention in recent decades. These studies mainly composed of several construction concepts such as the theoretical framework of social entrepreneurship (Özdevecioğlu & Cingöz, 2009), poverty and social entrepreneurship (Kümbül Güler, 2011), conceptual analysis of social entrepreneurship in Tourism (Günlü, 2015), social entrepreneurship as a social change catalyst (Katı & Toker, 2021). However, there is few research mainly focused on leadership in social enterprises such as social entrepreneurs' ethical and servant leadership behavior and gender (Bahçekapı & Yıldız, 2021). In addition, Türkeş & Özgeldi (2023) mentioned that social entrepreneurs are people who make an effort to solve social problems, seek social and economic advancement, sustainably resolve environmental problems, and generate social value. According to Gencer & Aydınoğlu (2020), task leadership, social value creation, inventiveness, dreaming, leadership competency, dedication, and accountability are the salient traits of social entrepreneurs.

However, a social entrepreneurial leader should have other characteristics like ethical service, empowerment of others, communitarian sense, and participative decision-making (Adjibolosoo,2000). As it was indicated, neuro-leadership is the newly emerged leadership approach to understanding human beings while leading people. Neuro-leadership will be a more effective leadership style while managing diverse teams.

Social enterprises in Turkey should pay more attention to hiring more neurodiverse people to increase diversity in their organization which will assist in developing more creative solutions. Yaşbay Kobal (2021) found that the goals of social entrepreneurship are to serve society and provide ecological balance based on her research on social entrepreneurship in Turkey and the regions in which it operates. Social enterprises primarily focus on four areas: preserving the environment, assisting the disabled person, advancing civil society, and advancing sustainable agriculture. She emphasized the importance of effective communication, conflict resolution, and leader trust as social entrepreneurs' leadership attributes to carry out these processes. It seems that the competencies foreseen in terms of leadership also have a place in neuro-leadership. For example, neuro-leadership indicates the fairness as main element of the trust within the organization and employees act aggressively and lack cooperation when they feel unfairly treated. So, the transparency of information is essential to developing a perception of fairness and certainty. If neuro-leaders want to foster a psychologically safe atmosphere for their team members, they should promote open and honest communication. This is also very important to neurodivergent people. Also, Neuro-leaders in social entrepreneurial firms should put more of an emphasis on giving each team member flexible working conditions in Turkey. When the neurodivergent worker in Turkey has the chance to interact with social groups, there will be an increase in neurodiversity. This will encourage a workplace that is more equitable and cooperative. This will lead to more innovative solutions to issues at social enterprises in Turkey.

References

Adjibolosoo, S. B. K. (Ed.). (2000). *The human factor in shaping the course of history and development*. Lanham, MD: University Press of America.

Avelino, F., Wittmayer, J. M., Pel, B., Weaver, P., Dumitru, A. Haxeltine, A., Kemp, R., Jorgersen, M. S., Bauler, T., Ruijsink, S., & O'Riordan, T. (2019). Transformative social innovation and (dis) empowerment. *Technology Forecasting and Social Change, 145*, 195–206.

Azmat, F., Ferdous, A. S., & Couchman, P. (2015). Understanding the dynamics between social entrepreneurship and inclusive growth in subsistence marketplaces. *Journal of Public Policy & Marketing, 34*(2), 252–271.

Bahçebaşı, H., & Yıldız, M. L. (2021). Sosyal girişimcilerin etik ve hizmetkâr liderlik davranışlarının cinsiyet bağlamında karşılaştırmalı analizi. *Marmara Üniversitesi İktisadi ve İdari Bilimler Dergisi, 42*(2), 329–347.

Brieger, S. A., & De Clerq, D. (2019). "Entrepreneurs' individual-level resources and social value creation goals: The moderating role of the cultural context". *International journal of Entrepreneurial Behavior and Research, 25*(2), 193–216.

British Council. (2019). The state of social enterprise in Turkey. Retrieved from https://www.britishcouncil.org.tr/sites/default/files/20190702_se_research_report_the_state_of_social_enterprise_in_turkey_eng_single_page.pdf

Cucino, V., Marullo, C., Annunziata, E., & Piccaluga, A. (2023). The human side of entrepreneurship: an empirical investigation of relationally embedded ties with stakeholders. Management Research Review. 10.1108/MRR-08-2022-0593.

Dawson, G., Franz, L., & Brandsen, S. (2022). At a crossroads—Reconsidering the goals of Autism early behavioral intervention from a neurodiversity perspective. *JAMA Pediatrics, 176*(9), 839–840.

Dey, P., & Lehner, O. (2017). "Registering ideology in the creation of social entrepreneurs: Intermediary organizations 'ideal subject' and the promise of enjoyment". *Journal of Business Ethics, 142*(4), 753–767.

Dickel, P., Sienknecht, M., & Horisch, J. (2020). "The early bird catches the worm: An empirical analysis of imprinting in social entrepreneurship". *Journal of Business Economics*, Published online, 25 February 2020.

Doherty, B., Thompson, J., & Spear, R. (2006). "Social entrepreneurship: A different model?". *International Journal of Social Economics, 33* (5/6), 399–410.

Esen, D. (2023). Türkiye'deki sosyal girişimcilik faaliyetlerinin Sosyal Gelişme Endeksi bağlamında içerik analizi ile incelenmesi. *KOCATEPE, İİBFD, 25*(1), 92–109.

Fabritius, F. (2022). *The brain-friendly workplace: Why talented people quit and how to get them to stay*. Rowman & Littlefield Publishers.

Fontana, A., & Musa, S. (2017). The impact of entrepreneurial leadership on innovation management and its measurement validation. *International Journal of Innovation Science, 9*(1), 2–19.

Gencer, Z. T., & Aydınoğlu, Ö. (2020). Sosyal sorumlu mu? Sosyal girişimci mi? Kavramsal boyutuyla sosyal girişimciliğin dönüşümü. *Gümüşhane Üniversitesi İletişim Fakültesi Elektronik Dergisi, 8*(2), 1057–1080.

Günlü, E. (2015). Sosyal Girişimcilik Olgusunun Kavramsal Analizi ve Turizmde Sosyal Girişimcilik. *Sosyal Ve Beşeri Bilimler Araştırmaları Dergisi, 35*, 23–42.

Haugh, H. M., & Talwar, A. (2016). Linking social entrepreneurship and social change: The mediating role of empowerment. *Journal of Business Ethics, 133*(4), 643–658.

Hutson, P., & Hutson, J. (2023). Neurodiversity and inclusivity in the workplace: Biopsychosocial interventions for promoting competitive advantage. *Journal of Organizational Psychology, 23*(2), 1–17.

Işık, V.(2022). Recommendation of active employment policy based on entrepreneurship and social innovation: Social entrepreneurship support model for youth in Turkey. *Istanbul Business research, 51*(2), 517–533.

Katı, B. K., & Toker, K. (2021). Bir sosyal değişim katalizörü olarak sosyal girişimcilik. *İstanbul Ticaret Üniversitesi Girişimcilik Dergisi, 5* (10), 145–164.

Kawharu, M., Tapsell, P., & Woods, C. (2017). "Indigenous entrepreneurship in Aotearoa New Zealand: The Takarangi framework of resilience and innovation." *Journal Enterprising Communities: People and Places in the Global Economy, 11*(1), 20–38.

Kuhlmann, N., & Kadgien, C. A. (2018). Neuroleadership: Themes and limitations of an emerging interdisciplinary field. *Healthcare Management Forum, 31*(3), 103–107.

Kümbül Güler, B. (2011). Yoksullukla mücadelede sosyal girişimcilik: Ashoka üyelerinden sosyal yenilikçi örnek uygulamalar. *Dokuz Eylül Üniversitesi Sosyal Bilimler Enstitüsü Dergisi,* 13(3), 79–111.

Leotti, L. A., & Delgado, M. R. (2011). The inherent reward of choice. *Psychological Science, 22*(10), 1310–1318.

Lumpkin, G. T., Bacq, S., & Pidduck, R. J. (2018). Where change happens: Community-level phenomena in social entrepreneurship research. *Journal of Small Business Management, 56*(1), 24–50.

Maalaoui, A., Tornikoski, E., Partouche-Sebban, J., & Safraou, I. (2020). "Why some third age individuals develop entrepreneurial intentions: Exploring the psychological effects of posterity". *Journal of Small Business Management, 58*(3), 447–473.

Mair, J. (2019). "Prospects for the study of market-based activity and social change." In *The Oxford handbook of Corporate Social Responsibility: Psychological and organizational perspectives*, edited by A. McWilliams, D. E. Rupp, D. S. Siegel, G. K. Stahl, & D. A. Waldman, 359. Oxford: Oxford University Press.

Monir, M. M. S., & Geberemeskel, A. N. (2023). Social entrepreneurship and social innovation in the entrepreneurial ecosystem. *Proceedings of the 17th. International Conference on Business Excellence*, pp. 822–838.

Özdevecioğlu, M., & Cingöz, A. (2009). Sosyal girişimcilik ve sosyal girişimciler: teorik çerçeve. *Erciyes Üniversitesi İktisadi ve İdari Bilimler Fakültesi Dergisi, 32*, 81–95.

Peters, A., McEven, B. S., & Friston, K. (2017). Uncertainty and stress: Why it causes diseases and how it is mastered by the brain. *Progress in Neurobiology, 156*, 164–188.

Prabhu, G. H. (1999). Social entrepreneurial leadership. *Career Development International, 4*(3), 140–145.

Ringleb, A. H., Rock, D., & Ancona, C. H. (2013). *Neuroleadership in 2011 and 2012.*

Rock, D., & Schwartz, J. (2007). The neuroscience of leadership. *Reclaiming Children & Youth, 16*(3), 10–17.

Saebi, T., Fass, N. J., & Linder, S. (2019). "Social Entrepreneurship" research: Past achievements and future promises. *Journal of Management, 45*(1), 70–95.

Saleh, M. C., Chang, H. Y., Bruyère, S. M., & Vogus, T. J. (2022). Neurodiverse applicant screening, interviewing, and selection. In *Neurodiversity in the Workplace* (pp. 98–123). Routledge.

Saruhan, N. (2023). The impact of organizational neuroscience and self-determination theory on Neuro-Leadership Theory. *Istanbul Management Journal, 94*, 65–72.

Smith-Spark, J. H., & Gordon, R. (2022). Automaticity and executive abilities in developmental dyslexia: A theoretical review. *Brain Sciences, 12*(4), 446.

Tiwari, P., Bhat, A. K., & Tikoria, J. (2020). "Mediating role of prosocial motivation in predicting social entrepreneurial intentions". *Journal of Social Entrepreneurship, 1*(24), 118–141.

Thompson, J. L. (2002). "The world of the social entrepreneur". *The International Journal of Public Sector Management, 15* (4/5), 413.

Tobias, J. M., Mair, J., & Barbosa-Leiker, C. (2013). Toward a theory of transformative entrepreneurial: Poverty reduction and conflict resolution in Rwand's entrepreneurial coffee sector. *Journal of Business Venturing, 28*(6), 728–742.

Tucker, R., Croom, R. M., & Bacq, S. (2019). "Feeling your pain, pursuing my gain: Assessing status striving, empathy, and social entrepreneurship intent". *Journal of Business Venturing*, 12, 100–142.

Türkeş, N., & Özgeldi, M. (2023). "Sosyal Girişimcilerin Motivasyon Faktörleri Nelerdir? Farklı Ülkelerde Yapılan Çalışmaların İncelenmesi." *Doğuş Üniversitesi Dergisi*, 24(2), 435-456. https://doi.org/10.31671/doujournal.1229786

Vita, Z., Iveta, S., Kaspars, F., & Eriks L. (2012). "The understanding of resilience and the role of entrepreneurship in its implementation." *International Journal of Social Science and Humanity Studies, 4*(2), 479–488.

Yaşbay Kobal, H. (2021). Türkiye'de sosyal girişimcilerin özellikleri ve sosyal girişimcilerin paradoksal liderlik becerileri. *Pamukkale Üniversitesi, Sosyal Bilimler Enstitüsü Dergisi, 42*, 97–111.

Yitshaki, R., & Kropp, F. (2016). "Motivations and opportunity recognition of social entrepreneurs". *Journal of Small Business Management, 54*(2), 546–565.

www.ingramcontent.com/pod-product-compliance
Ingram Content Group UK Ltd.
Pitfield, Milton Keynes, MK11 3LW, UK
UKHW041827100926
8556IPUK00002B/54

9 783631 915110